# PLANNING AND
# COMMUNITY DEVELOPMENT

D1597249

# PLANNING AND COMMUNITY DEVELOPMENT

## A Guide for the 21st Century

NORMAN TYLER AND ROBERT M. WARD

W. W. Norton & Company

New York • London

Copyright © 2011 by Norman Tyler and Robert M. Ward

For information about permission to reproduce selections from this book, write to
Permissions, W. W. Norton & Company, Inc., 500 Fifth Avenue, New York, NY 10110

For information about special discounts for bulk purchases, please contact W. W. Norton
Special Sales at specialsales@wwnorton.com or 800-233-4830

Manufacturing by QuadGraphics, Taunton, Connecticut
Book design by Jonathan D. Lippincott
Production manager: Leeann Graham
Electronic production: J. Lops

Library of Congress Cataloging-in-Publication Data

Tyler, Norman.
    Planning and community development : a guide for the 21st century / Norman Tyler, Robert M. Ward. — 1st ed.
       p. cm.
    Includes bibliographical references and index.
    ISBN 978-0-393-73292-4 (pbk.)
1. City planning—United States. 2. Regional planning—United States. I. Ward, Robert Madison, 1936– II. Title.
    NA9031.T95 2010
    307.10973—dc22

                                                                                                    2010029408

ISBN: 978-0-393-73292-4 (pbk.)

W. W. Norton & Company, Inc., 500 Fifth Avenue, New York, N.Y. 10110
www.wwnorton.com
W. W. Norton & Company Ltd., Castle House, 75/76 Wells Street, London W1T 3QT

0   9   8   7   6   5   4   3   2   1

# CONTENTS

Acknowledgments 7
Introduction 8

## SECTION 1: OVERVIEW OF PLANNING

**1. The Practice of Planning 13**
*The Profession of Planning / What Is Planning? / Skills for Success / The Certification of Planners / Compensation and Specializations / Planners in the Private Sector / The Education of Planners / Birth of Planning as a Profession / Summary*

**2. Conceptual Approaches to Planning 21**
*Significant Conceptual Approaches to Planning / Other Planning Concepts / Traditional and Tactical Approaches to Planning / Summary*

**3. The Scope of Planning at the Federal, State, Regional, and Local Levels 34**
*Planning at the Federal Level / State and Regional Planning / Local Planning / The Politics of Local Planning / The Role of the Public in the Planning Process / Summary*

## SECTION 2: ELEMENTS OF THE COMPREHENSIVE PLAN

**4. The Comprehensive Plan 53**
*Overview of the Comprehensive Plan / Creating the Comprehensive Plan / Components of a Comprehensive Plan / Review and Amendments / Subarea Plans / Limitations of Planning / Summary*

**5. Planners and the Design Process 69**
*The Importance of Urban Design to Planners / Historical Perspective / Key Principles of Urban Design / The Design Process / Envisioning a Community's Future / Summary*

**6. Urban Planning and Downtown Revitalization 86**
*Understanding the Urban Fabric / Qualitative Considerations in Urban Development / The Role of Downtown Retail / Downtown Revitalization / Engines of Revitalization / Smart Growth / Urban Growth Boundaries / Summary*

**7. Housing 101**
*The Importance of Housing to Planners / Demographics of Housing / The Government's Role in Housing / Other Housing Issues / Alternative Types of Housing / Inclusionary Housing / Code Enforcement / Housing and the Private Sector / Summary*

**8. Historic Preservation and Planning 114**
*A Brief History of the Preservation Movement / The Value of Historic Preservation / Historic Preservation and the Comprehensive Plan / Financial Incentives for Historic Structures / Establishing a Historic District Ordinance / Preservation and Sustainability / Summary*

**9. Local Economic Development 124**
*Creating a Successful Economic Development Plan / Evaluating an Economic Development Plan / Other Economic Development Strategies / Organizations for Promoting Economic Development / Economic Development Programs / State and Local Programs / Evaluating Information and Generating Incentives / Summary*

**10. Transportation Planning** 140
*Historical Development / Impacts of Transportation / Role of the Department of Transportation / Designing Infrastructure / Transportation Modeling / The Role of Public Transit / Individual Transportation Alternatives / Designing for Life / Summary*

**11. Environmental Planning** 155
*The Environmental System / Environmental Policies and Programs at the Federal and State Level / Environmental Planning at the Local Level / The Environment as Resource and Hazard / Sustainability and Planning / Summary*

**12. Rural and Transitional Land Use Planning** 165
*Rural Land Use in the United States / Planning in Rural and Transitional Areas / Mapping Rural and Transitional Areas / Geographic Information Systems (GIS) / Summary*

SECTION 3: IMPLEMENTATION OF
THE COMPREHENSIVE PLAN

**13. Evolution of Land Use Controls** 181
*The Basis for Land Use Law in the United States / Early Land Use Patterns in North America / Zoning as an Evolving Tool / Summary*

**14. Zoning and Other Land Use Regulations** 188
*Conventional Zoning / Eminent Domain / Takings /*

*Zoning and the Comprehensive Plan / Negotiated Alternatives to Conventional Zoning / Performance Zoning / Form-based Codes / Religious Land Use and Institutionalized Persons Act / Rural Zoning / Summary*

**15. Subdivisions, Site Plans, and Site Plan Review** 203
*Subdivisions / Site Plans / Site Plan Review / Summary*

**16. Capital Improvements Program and Local Government Financing** 210
*The Capital Improvements Program and Budget / CIP and the Community Planning Process / Local Government Financing / Summary*

**Appendix A: The Rivertown Simulation** 221
**Appendix B: Rivertown Comprehensive Plan (Abridged)** 226
**Appendix C: Rivertown Zoning Ordinance (Abridged)** 230
**Appendix D: Maps** 241

**Notes** 245
**Glossary** 252
**Abbreviations and Acronyms** 256
**List of Exercises** 257
**Selected Readings** 258
**Credits** 260
**Index** 262

Throughout the text, planning exercises are presented using the fictional city of Rivertown.
These exercises are complemented by the Rivertown Simulation, found online at cityhallcommons.com.

# ACKNOWLEDGMENTS

We wish to thank a number of people who made important contributions to this manuscript, beginning with the following individuals who provided content and guidance in their particular area of expertise: Devany Donigan (Private Sector Planning), John Enos AICP (Site Plan Review), Eugene Jaworski (Environmental Planning), Richard Norton (Zoning), Angela Peecher (Navy Pier), Denise Pike (Baltimore's Inner Harbor), Jeffrey Purdy (Form-Based Zoning), James Schafer AICP (Politics of Local Planning), and David Schneider (Capital Improvements Program). However, the authors recognize that responsibility for errors in information are entirely their own.

Many sets of educated eyes reviewed drafts of the manuscript, helping us to polish our approach as well as make astute revisions to the specific content of the book. Thanks go to the following individuals who gave their precious time to our endeavor: Adam Cook, Michael Davidson, Susan Lackey, Tracy Mullins, and James Murray.

We extend special thanks to three individuals who provided invaluable editing for the entire text. Anne Sullivan, a graduate student in the planning program at Eastern Michigan University, gave input from a user's perspective and helped to clarify topics. Karen Levine, a professional editor, gave a thorough review of the formatting of the book's contents and offered valuable suggestions. Nancy Green at W. W. Norton carefully assessed the final manuscript and made it smoother and more easily readable. We owe her special gratitude for her guidance to bring the project to fruition.

Class after class of undergraduate and graduate planning students at Eastern Michigan University have helped us rethink, reshape, and refine the content of this book and its companion, the online Rivertown simulation. Their use of these materials indicated what worked and what did not work for them. Many of them have become planning professionals in large cities and small communities throughout the United States and abroad. Others are practitioners in the allied fields of municipal government, land law and investment, engineering, and resource management.

And first in importance, we want to acknowledge and thank our wives, Ilene Tyler and Judy Ward, for their unflagging support and encouragement. Each day they listened to ideas and responded with fresh input, enormous patience, and an extraordinary appreciation for the magnitude of work involved in bringing this book to fruition. We are profoundly grateful to them both.

# INTRODUCTION

With the understanding that those who fail to plan, plan to fail, *Planning and Community Development: A Guide for the 21st Century* describes how American communities are, or should be, planned. The book focuses on planning at the community level, presenting practical planning applications to address local issues. Professional and lay planners, planning students, local officials, and individuals interested in better understanding how their communities currently are being planned and how they have evolved over time will benefit from what the book offers. Planning is a broad field with many perspectives and numerous areas of specialization. While this text is introductory in scope, an ideal "first book on planning," it also offers enough depth to serve as a continuing reference for those who already have planning experience and expertise.

Throughout, the book links planning issues with planning practice. It takes readers from a general discussion of a topic through related policies and programs to an examination of techniques, which finally are coupled

*0.1. The planner's hand*

with practical case studies and exercises. For example, a discussion of the impact of zoning leads to a detailed description of the components and administration of a zoning ordinance, followed by an exercise in which the reader utilizes a sample zoning ordinance. In this way, topics go from the general to the specific to the applied—from the conceptual to the pragmatic.

*Planning and Community Development* examines a wide range of planning topics. The book is divided into three sections. The first contains a general introduction to the field of community planning. The second section describes the comprehensive plan, the primary tool used for good community planning. The third section describes tools for implementing the comprehensive plan. The following paragraphs give an overview of each chapter.

The first three chapters describe the practice of planning in American communities. Chapter 1 gives a general introduction to the profession of planning. It describes the education of planners, their activities as practitioners, their certification and professional standards, and the role of the private sector planner. Chapter 2 offers insights into various conceptual approaches to planning. It reviews significant contributions of master planners throughout history, in the United States and elsewhere. It also explores differences in "traditional" versus "tactical" approaches to planning. Chapter 3 describes the scope of planning at the federal, state, regional, and local levels, with emphasis on the role of the public in the process of community planning.

Chapter 4 looks in detail at the comprehensive plan as a document that guides community growth, describing the plan's significance as well as its various elements. Chapter 5 explores the process of design, an increasingly important aspect of planning. A historical perspective precedes a description of contemporary approaches, along with principles and examples of good design. An exercise challenges readers to design an ideal town plan. Chapter 6 discusses the importance of planning in urbanized areas, emphasizing redevelopment and revitalization. The chapter highlights the evolution of American downtowns and describes programs and techniques for downtown planning. Chapter 7 focuses on housing and community development and reviews government programs during the twentieth century which had a large impact on housing availability. The chapter also examines the current private sector housing industry, including a section looking at the economics of housing affordability. Chapter 8 discusses the governments' role in historic preservation, the establishment of regulatory historic districts, and the economics of preservation. Chapter 9 includes perspectives on the important role of planners in local economic development, one of the most overlooked, but important, areas of expertise for planners. Chapter 10 covers issues of transportation planning, an area that has had a huge impact on the development of both cities and exurban areas. A historical overview precedes the presentation of current issues of transportation planning. Also included is an introduction to the transportation modeling system used by most transportation agencies. Chapter 11 considers environmental issues, programs, and policies at all levels of government, including the important issue of sustainability. It includes descriptions of the process of environmental assessment and brownfield redevelopment. Chapter 12 explores the unique aspects of planning in rural and transitional areas and addresses critical concerns pertaining to these areas, particularly growth management and the protection of agricultural land and open space.

Chapter 13 contains the history of land use controls and regulations and provides an overview of how the current system of planning and zoning evolved. Chapter 14 looks in detail at planning's most significant implementation tool, the zoning ordinance. A discussion of conventional zoning precedes descriptions of alternative types of zoning and regulation. Chapter 15 reviews the importance of site planning, and examines the site plan review process as an important responsibility of public sector planners. Chapter 16, the closing chapter,

explores the close relationship between capital improvements budgeting and community planning.

This book is written in a manner that recognizes the commonalities in planning among the local, state, and federal levels. Although it has a community focus, the information presented has a national scope. Some aspects of planning as they are practiced in one local area, region, or state may differ from another, and readers should understand that details regarding various topics may differ from community to community. Large cities have different needs from rural or transitional areas. Established East Coast communities may have perspectives and priorities that vary from those of western cities. For this reason, the book offers examples from across the United States.

We have selected certain terms from the varied vocabularies used by planners. Specifically, the phrase "community planning" is used to represent planning done in cities, towns, villages, townships, boroughs, parishes, and other such jurisdictional units. Similarly, the term "municipal council" represents various forms of elective bodies, including city councils, town councils, village councils, township and county boards, and others. The term "comprehensive plan" is used to represent what some communities refer to as the master plan or general plan. They should be considered equivalent in meaning and purpose.

To encourage readers to interact with information as it is presented, we have woven a continuing case study of the fictitious midwestern community of Rivertown throughout the chapters of the book. It is used to simulate a typical small city found throughout the United States. (A color map of the City of Rivertown is provided in Appendix D.)

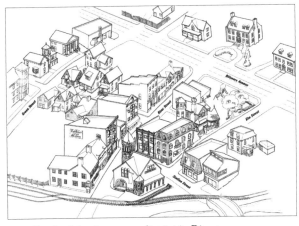

*0.2. Sketch of the downtown district in Rivertown*

In simplified form, the Rivertown exercises simulate processes local decisionmakers use when deciding on various strategies to deal with issues in their community. To this end, the reader should assume the role of an entry-level planner who is given tasks relating to community planning activities. The exercises represent what one confronts when deciding, for example, how to revise a capital budget, review a proposed site plan, or best cope with the problems of a new adult bookstore. By working through these issues, readers practice solving the kinds of problems they will face professionally and develop insights from first-hand active involvement.

Background information on Rivertown, its people, and its environs, appears in Appendix A, which contains a brief "history" of the community and describes some of its people, districts, and current issues. This and other appendices include useful maps, drawings, and the city's comprehensive plan and zoning ordinance. Additional information appears strategically throughout the book where it is most relevant to each of the exercises.

Section 1

# OVERVIEW OF PLANNING

# 1
# THE PRACTICE OF PLANNING

## The Profession of Planning

The work of planning practitioners is more than a job or a way to earn a living. It is a career that means accepting responsibility for improving communities and the quality of place for all citizens. Surveys have shown that planning is one of the most satisfying careers for an individual. Part of that satisfaction comes from the sense that a person's daily activities make a difference in a community and improve the life of its residents over time. *U.S. News and World Report* has referred to planning as a "multi-faceted job for a multi-talented person."[1] *Money* magazine selected planning as "one of the best jobs," based primarily on compensation, growth, and overall job satisfaction.[2] The U.S. Bureau of Labor Statistics indicates urban and regional planning will have faster than average employment growth over the next 10 years, especially in the private sector in technical services.[3] The online magazine *Fast Company* lists urban planning as one of the "Ten Best Green Jobs for the Next Decade," and referred to it as "a linchpin of the quest to lower America's carbon footprint."[4] The *Green Careers Guide* indicates that an increasing number of governments are turning to urban planning to make their communities green: "the career outlook for an urban planner is very good."[5]

At its best, planning incorporates what are sometimes referred to as the three Cs: it is comprehensive; it is coordinating; and it is continuing. Planning is comprehensive because the role of the planner is to examine development issues in their totality. Planning is coordinating because a planning department's role is to facilitate the process of development to the advantage of all parties, that is, the community and the developer. Finally, planning is continuing because professional planners are trained to see local decision-making from a long-range perspective. No other municipal agency fulfills all these functions for a community in the same way. The comprehensive plan is the planner's primary tool. This plan identifies a community's resources and goals and objectives for growth in the short term and, more importantly, in the long term. Through maps and text, it establishes in detail the many facets of developing a plan to give a vision of a community's future and to bring it growth, a sense of purpose, direction, sustainability, and a broader positive image.

*1.1. Planners reviewing map from comprehensive plan*

## What Is Planning?

### Defining the Term

The term "planning" as it applies to urban and regional areas is difficult to define. Planning educator John

Friedmann suggested, "Planning attempts to link scientific and technical knowledge to actions in the public domain." Architect-planners Andres Duany and Elizabeth Plater-Zyberk referred to it as "the conceptualizing of the built environment in response to human needs and desires."[6] The *Encyclopedia Britannica* gives a more complete description for urban planning, defining it as "the design and regulation of the uses of space that focus on the physical form, economic functions, and social impacts of the urban environment and on the location of different activities within it."[7]

Economist Ann Markusen suggests activities of a planning practitioner should have four primary characteristics.[8] First, planners should include the exercise of forethought and be able to anticipate the future, focusing on sustainability for future generations. Second, they should embrace the notion of the commons, that is, the development of the public realm, including spaces that cannot be provided by market means. Third, a planner's philosophy should recognize the importance of collective action and encourage participation and representation of the general public to ensure greater equity. Finally, there should be a focus on the quality of place and the multifaceted sense of the "good life." This includes material and environmental amenities. Ultimately, each planning practitioner must rely on his or her perspective, experiences, and value system to derive a personal approach to planning and actions in the public domain.

Because there are many types of planners—financial planners, military planners, schedule planners, even wedding planners—we need an appropriate modifier to describe planning as it is used throughout this text. What should it be? The term "urban planner" is too limited in scope, as is "city planner" or "town planner," for planning extends well beyond the limits of the city. The term "land use planner" focuses on physical planning, but does not incorporate social, economic, and political aspects that should be included. Specializations can define roles within the profession—transportation planner, environmental planner, or community development planner—but such terms represent only a single aspect of what is a broad discipline. Job descriptions often take a generic approach and describe positions simply as Planner I, Planner II, Senior Planner, or some variation based on the level of experience and responsibility associated with a position. The most commonly used general term may be "urban and regional planner," since it recognizes the relationship of the city to the surrounding rural areas.

In spite of all those possibilities, we have chosen "community planner" as the most appropriate term to use because it represents the function of public and private sector planners at the local level. It is the local level of government that is the primary focus of this book. Planning at the regional, state, and federal levels is more policy-oriented and less directly involved with individual residents. In contrast, planning at the "community" level is project-oriented and touches citizens most directly. Because this is a book about planning communities, the term "community planner" fits best.

### Distinguishing "Good Planning"

Communities can grow and evolve without planning. However, they will grow and evolve better with good planning. They will be more functional and more beautiful. Planners and others use the phrase "good planning" routinely, but often without giving meaning to what they are saying. It is relevant to consider the question, what is good planning?

Many people consider good planning to be based primarily on physical form and layout. This is a reasonable starting point since a physical plan should optimize the needs of clients and the community. However, planning should extend beyond physical design to two other significant elements. The social needs of the community should be accommodated because planning directly impacts individuals and families. Similarly, planning should address issues pertaining to local economic development. The physical, social, and economic perspectives are all important to a good plan. For example, assume a proposal is presented for a new medical facility serving a community's elderly population. The proposed plan needs to satisfy location and land use requirements, such as property availability, zoning, utilities, transportation services, and other physical factors. The proposed plan should recognize the social impacts of such a facility, including existing or needed programs, policies, and other agencies. In addition, economic considerations should be part of the plan, that is, the financial feasibility of the project, the economic influence it will have on the surrounding area, and the role of the private and public sectors to provide potential funding and support. A good plan encompasses projects from all of these perspectives and brings balance to the areas of concern.

Good planning involves good leadership. Planners are in a unique situation because they have a central role and access to information through which they can influence decisionmakers. Communities face many problems and planners can see such situations as problems or opportunities. Too many planners stay in the background when a community faces challenges. They are concerned about appearing to take sides on an issue and whether expressing an opinion would impact their job security. As Paul Farmer, executive director and CEO of the American Planning Association (APA), stated, "Let's say you're the planning director. You should step forward and accept key responsibilities." He continued, "A planning director recently told me that his strategy was to hunker down and try to ride out this crisis. He feared that the slightest misstep might lead to his dismissal. My reaction was a straightforward one: Get out of the way and let someone take over who will provide the leadership our communities deserve."[9]

## Skills for Success

A person considering planning as a profession must feel comfortable working with people. The daily life of a planner requires interaction with the public, officials, and other professionals and the ability to acquire diverse information from an array of sources. Planners need to develop strong communication skills as speakers, listeners, and writers because much of their time is spent using these to serve their communities effectively.

Poise and polish are essential. Planners need public speaking skills because they are often called upon to make presentations in professional settings and at public gatherings where clarity is critical and conciseness appreciated. It is agonizing to watch a planner who is awkwardly relying on note cards stumble along in a public session. The stress increases if, during a question-and-answer session, the planner is unable to respond extemporaneously to challenges from a sometimes hostile audience. Speaking is an art form that seems natural for some people, but must be developed by others through experience. Effectiveness requires both knowledge of a topic and self-confidence to discuss it publicly.

Another important character trait for planners is to listen with complete attention. Planners need to be able to understand and quickly assess what someone is asking or trying to say. The temptation to antici-

1.2. *Planning presentation at public meeting, Danbury, Connecticut*

pate and then interrupt must be stifled; hearing out a speaker is more courteous and ensures better understanding. Critical listening, combined with reflective thinking, keeps the planning process moving in a successful direction. Planners can learn more by listening than by speaking.

Planning professionals must possess strong writing and graphic skills because reports are constantly used to communicate. In the past, maps, charts, and diagrams were prepared using hand drafting techniques. Today, planners should be adept at using computer graphics software like PowerPoint to create presentations and Geographic Information System (GIS) to generate maps. These are two of the many graphics programs planners find useful to have in their skill set. Their aptitude should extend beyond creating graphics to integrating them into meetings and written materials.

Creative problem solving should be high on a planning practitioner's list of attributes. A community's desires and decisions to change and grow frequently require innovative solutions. Planners must be equal to that task because dexterity in thinking can be critical to weighing arguments and evaluating alternatives. Solutions may not always come directly from coldly rational analysis; sometimes, a creative perspective that synthesizes information and takes a new direction is needed. The planner who can innovate can make meaningful positive contributions with significant impact to his or her community.

Planners should continue to grow professionally through lifelong learning. Once they complete their formal education they should participate in professional activities that include conferences and special training sessions. Planners need to understand, analyze, and sometimes even debate new concepts and legislation before they can apply these successfully.

## The Certification of Planners

The American Institute of Certified Planners (AICP), administered by the American Planning Association (APA), established a Code of Ethics and Professional Conduct for planning practitioners who achieve AICP certification. The Code provides certified planners with "aspirational principles" to guide them in their work. It creates rules of conduct for planners to govern themselves and procedures for the AICP Ethics Committee to investigate claims of violations of the Code. The Code states that the planner's primary obligation is to serve the public interest. The public good as a higher gradient is useful to planners who must navigate the sometimes tenuous waters of competing interests from public officials, developers, special interests, neighborhood advocates, and even the institutional politics of their employers. Potential conflicts of interest should be carefully considered. The Code is a guide that helps planners exercise good judgment and discretion on the job. This applies equally to certified professionals across the public, private, and nonprofit sectors.

Many organizations prefer hiring planners with AICP certification, and the initials after one's name provide evidence that a planner meets professional levels of knowledge and skills. Some employers even make certification a prerequisite to hiring. However, AICP certification is not legally required to work as a planner in the way that passing a state bar exam is required to practice law or state boards to practice medicine. Nevertheless, planners without certification should be equally committed to the principles espoused by the Code.

Planners interested in becoming AICP certified must be APA members, possess a minimum number of years of experience (e.g., two years' experience and a graduate planning degree from an accredited program, three years' experience with an accredited undergraduate program, or other levels for unaccredited programs) and pass an exam showing knowledge of techniques, theory, history, and ethics of planning. The benefits of professional certification are many, including financial. A 2008 survey by the APA indicated that certified planners earned $18,000 more annually on average than noncertified planners.

Certified or not, planners also have a responsibility to their profession and should regularly give back to it through volunteer work, educational programs, or in other ways to build stronger communities. Finally, planners have a responsibility to themselves, to practice with high integrity and to keep developing knowledge and expertise in the field.

## Compensation and Specializations

The APA regularly conducts a salary survey of professional planners across the country. The collected data are the best representation of the likely compensation for someone in the field. The APA's 2008 survey includes responses from almost 13,000 full-time professionals.[10] It found that the median annual salary is $70,000, an amount that has risen in the previous years at a rate above the core rate of inflation. Some states and the District of Columbia have median salaries considerably above the national average: D.C., $95,500; California, $86,400; and New Jersey, $83,000. According to the survey, the typical (median) planner is 43 years old and has been in the planning field for 14 years. Most planners surveyed indicated they specialized; the two most common areas are community development/redevelopment (51 percent) and land use or code enforcement (44 percent). Other common specializations are transportation planning, environmental and natural resources planning, urban design, and economic planning and development. The survey found that 67 percent of the planners work in public agencies and 25 percent in private consulting firms. The others have more diverse roles.

## Planners in the Private Sector

Planning practitioners work in the public sector or the private sector. Both require a similar technical background, but often this expertise is applied to different tasks. Public sector planners typically work in community agencies where their focus is representing public concerns. Because the focus of this book is community planning, most of the topics addressed pertain to planning from a public sector point of view.

In contrast, private sector planners often work closely with developers who have a vested interest in the use of land they control and a financial motive. It is natural for them to ask planning consultants to create site plans that maximize development potential, income, and desired profitability.

Private sector planning consultants can be specialists or generalists. A specialist planner develops a name and reputation for specific services in a key area of planning, such as transportation planning, residential planning, or urban design. In contrast, generalist consultants are more flexible with broader overall skills. They can work on a greater variety of planning projects, but often rely on specialists to assist in certain areas.

Private sector planners often have client communities (cities, townships, villages) who hire them to prepare comprehensive plans and/or advise them on important planning issues such as the community's zoning ordinance and its amendments. While they interact with officials and the general public in a more limited way than public sector planners, private consultants frequently have contact with stakeholders during public meetings or scheduled conferences. For that reason, certain personal attributes are important to the effectiveness of all planners. These traits include political savvy and the ability to build relationships quickly, ask relevant questions, correctly interpret comments and concerns, and think and respond quickly.

When a municipal government recognizes that it has a project requiring an outside consultant, a competitive bid process called the Request for Qualifications or Proposals (RFQ/P) process is employed. The RFQ process addresses the consultant's qualifications to do the work required by the municipality. This often does not require the consultant to include a proposed fee for the delineated services. RFPs are more detailed. The proposal submitted requires the consultant's qualifications, and typically a detailed scope of work, fees, and information that describes how and when the work will be completed. As an alternative, consultants (individuals or firms) may provide a work schedule based on a weekly, monthly, or annual retainer fee for specific services required by the municipality.

Many private sector planners are also practitioners in the fields of architecture, landscape architecture, engineering, or construction. Land development requires knowledge and expertise from each of these disciplines, so professionals with different backgrounds often work together. Planners must be familiar with the skills and

contributions of each discipline to communicate effectively as partners in planning efforts.

## The Education of Planners

Most planners enter the profession after completing a university degree program in planning. Others come to the profession from public administration, environmental studies, economic development, or allied disciplines. There are few professions that are as interdisciplinary as planning, since it takes a working knowledge of both physical and socioeconomic factors for a planner to shepherd plans successfully through implementation.

*1.3. Planning students discussing their project with a local official at the site*

Many degree and nondegree planning programs exist across the country. Those that meet rigorous standards can seek accreditation by the national Planning Accreditation Board (PAB). This is a review committee sponsored jointly by three organizations: the AICP, the Association of Collegiate Schools of Planning (ACSP), and the APA. Accreditation ensures that programs have a broad range of courses and meet minimum guidelines for academic autonomy, resources, and community outreach. Approximately 70 accredited programs exist in the United States; the majority of these are at the graduate level. The ACSP maintains lists of schools offering accredited degree programs in planning.[11] In addition, many programs are available that are not accredited but that provide important education and training in planning skills.

Accredited curricula cover a broad range of topics, grouped under four categories: professional practice, comprehensive and land use planning, planning and urban theory, and planning technology. Each category provides important background, knowledge, and skills essential to becoming a well-rounded professional, regardless of an individual's interest in developing a particular area of specialization. Students are encouraged to undertake internships as a means to bring practical experience to their academic studies. Some degree programs require that students satisfactorily complete an internship as part of the curriculum; others encourage it as an option. Surveys of students have shown that many feel their internship was a highlight of their academic years. These experiences frequently lead to a job offer from the firm or agency in which the student interned, or from another organization that appreciates the hands-on knowledge the graduate gained during a work opportunity.

---

## Personal Advice from a Planner to Planning Students[12]

As a private planning practitioner who went through a university planning program, I would like to offer some "words of wisdom" to incoming planning students.

*Seek a variety of internship opportunities.* Working as an intern in a planning office can be a great experience. Consider working for a real estate developer, or short-term positions with villages, rural townships, or small cities. If necessary, create a position for yourself by attending local planning commission meetings and city council/township board meetings. The purposes of your attendance are to learn and to listen for opportunities to assist public officials with special projects. Arrange for an appointment with the mayor, city manager, supervisor, or others to discuss their needs and how you can help.

*Make use of your alumni network.* There may be dozens, if not hundreds, of planning graduates working in a wide variety of public and private sector organizations that would be willing to help you get your first career opportunity. Each "real world" experience on your resume makes you much more employable after graduation.

*Write a research paper.* The ability to communicate in writing is vital to your future success as a community planner. Research and prepare a paper of publishable quality on a planning-related topic, whether it is required for your degree or not. A concise and well-written paper (with an even more concise executive summary) can become a valuable part of your portfolio of materials to present to prospective employers. If you are weak in a particular area (zoning, environmental analysis, economic development, historic preservation), researching, writing, and consulting with a faculty adviser on that particular topic is one way to become more knowledgeable.

*Experience life.* If you have the means, take a month, a semester, a summer, or a year away from academics to tour Italy, or assist with a community improvement project in Ghana, or a historic preservation project in Gettysburg, Pennsylvania. In other words, expand your understanding of the world (people, places, markets, cultures, the environment) wherever you can. Your experience will look good on a resume and may influence the direction of your life and career for years to come.

*Involvement.* Attend and volunteer at your state's annual planning conference. If possible, attend the American Planning Association's national conference. Many of your program's professional planners attend these conferences. Determine who they are, learn about their interests, and seek opportunities to talk with them.

---

## Birth of Planning as a Profession

Many planning historians target 1909 as the year in which city planning in the United States became a profession. That year the first National Conference on City Planning, sponsored by the Committee on Congestion of Population, was held in New York City. Architects, landscape architects, engineers, and others attended, although none, at that time, could claim to be a full-time planning practitioner. The conference became an annual event for planners and continues today as the annual conference of the APA.

The initial 1909 conference was a seminal event, but its timing correlated with other significant planning activities. For example, the Chicago Merchants Association commissioned Daniel Burnham to develop a plan for their city. On July 4 Burnham presented the *Plan of Chicago*, one of the most notable documents in the history of American city planning.

In 1909 the first planning commissions were established. One, in Chicago, was associated with Burnham's plan. Another was the Civic Plan and Improvement Commission in Detroit. Wisconsin became the first state to pass an enabling law that permitted its cities to plan. (Enabling legislation permits communities to take certain actions not otherwise allowed.) Los Angeles stipulated uses for land, which essentially created zoning for large areas of undeveloped land. The first course in city planning was taught in the Harvard College Landscape Architecture Department. Even overseas, 1909 was significant. Britain passed its Town Planning Act, which authorized local governments to create plans for future development. Based on these many milestones, it can be argued that planning as a profession began in 1909.

Planning continued to play a pivotal role in guiding the growth of cities across the country during the ensuing decades. Planners took responsibility for creating designs for many grand public places. They developed innovative and forward-looking plans for transportation systems, parks and recreation areas, public amenities, and orderly, human-oriented communities. It was an era of planning visionaries.

The Great Depression of 1929 brought another reality to urban planning. Local governments could no longer afford to build the grand public spaces associated with the City Beautiful movement. City planners needed to focus on critical urban problems such as the need for affordable housing, good educational facilities, properly functioning utility systems, and similar practical needs. A new approach to planning, the City Efficient or City Practical movement, resulted. (See Chapter 14 on Zoning for more on the City Efficient movement and the history of land use regulation.) The zoning ordinance was the primary tool developed during this period, but the movement also focused on efficient transportation, utilities, public facilities, and other practical and economic considerations. It represented "the beginning of an idea that the American City might be disciplined by the progressive develop-ment of human knowledge, state regulatory mechanisms, and public welfare provisions."[13]

The Depression changed the country's perspectives in various ways. President Franklin D. Roosevelt used planners to help the country's economy recover and a number of important federal planning programs emerged. The Tennessee Valley Authority (TVA) was an early example of a federal government regional planning agency. The TVA provided electricity to many rural areas and served as an important economic development agency. The federal government created innovative policies and programs to give work to the unemployed, which resulted in many civic improvement projects. The National Planning Board, established in 1933, coordinated these efforts. Typical projects included the construction of highways and streets, water and sewer systems, and recreational facilities. Planner Rexford Guy Tugwell was put in charge of Roosevelt's Resettlement Administration, which sponsored the planning and development of a series of "greenbelt" cities. These were designed to allow poor residents who lived in central city slum areas to move to new towns with gardens, parks, and other wholesome amenities.

American cities were largely neglected throughout the Depression and during the years of World War II. After the war, however, the planning profession had increased visibility and growth. Programs and funds emerged to regenerate urban areas and build new exurban developments. Planners played a central role during the 1950s and 1960s, and especially in the 1970s, when federal funding for development was tied with a requirement for communities to have a comprehensive plan. During those decades, the number of university planning programs more than quadrupled and the number of newly graduated and qualified planners increased from approximately 100 per year to 1,500 per year. It was a period of great activity for the profession and urban redevelopment programs, which culminated with the multitude of Great Society programs under President Lyndon Johnson. One of these initiatives was the establishment in 1965 of the Department of Housing and Urban Development to coordinate federal urban policies. Planning had a key role in the development of communities across the country.

The election of Ronald Reagan as president in 1980 saw a shift in federal policy. "Reaganomics" was a political philosophy based on reliance on the free markets. Its foundation was to remove government as much as possible from peoples' lives. During this period, a series of initiatives limited federal planning efforts. The U.S. Department of Housing and Urban Development was stripped of most of its urban redevelopment functions and basically became a housing administration department. Under Secretary of the Interior James Watt, federal lands and properties were sold in great numbers as a means to cover budget shortfalls. During this period, planning assumed a minor position among other priorities. As a result, planners slipped into a bureaucratic mode and were responsible primarily for reviewing and approving plans created by the private development community. Seldom did planners initiate ideas or create visionary plans.

The current status of planning is a reflection of these previous decades. Its role remains pivotal in establishing and promoting an orderly physical environment in which to live in cities and the countryside. However, as other segments of society have taken an increasingly active role in planning our communities, many planners have stepped back from their traditional leadership positions and become functionaries, rather than the visionaries they were a century earlier. As planner Leonardo Vazquez wrote, "One of the biggest challenges to strengthening the profession will be overcoming the 'comfort of powerlessness.' Many people complain about their supposed lack of power to change situations, but in fact it makes life easier. When you are powerless, you do not have to take responsibility." He continued, "The answer: Planners are unique among other professionals in their range of knowledge and their ability to be balancing points for urban growth. Planners have the power to shape perceptions and expectations of urban growth and development. The greatest strength a planner has is not in doing demographic projections or cost-benefit analyses, but in influencing the hearts and minds of all actors in urban growth."[14]

## Summary

Planning is a career that focuses on improving communities and the quality of place for residents. It includes improvement of the physical, social, and economic aspects of community life. The field is interdisciplinary in scope; good planning requires partnering with a broad range of individuals and groups.

Planners need proficiencies that include good communication skills in listening, speaking, and writing. Professional training is largely through university degree programs and internship experience. The American Planning Association provides professional support and resources to planners. The American Institute of Certified Planners encourages practitioners to uphold the discipline's professional standards and offers a certification program for planners meeting professional levels of knowledge and skills. Compensation varies based on geographic location, professional specialization, and whether one works in the public or private sector.

The majority of practitioners work in public sector jobs. These individuals interact directly with other community leaders and officials. The activities and involvement of practitioners in the private sector differ from those of public sector planners. Although private consultants also work with municipalities, they extend their functions to work on projects initiated by land developers.

The history of the planning profession is only a century old. In 1909, a number of significant events formed the basis for the new discipline. The City Beautiful movement of the early 1900s emphasized physical urban form. It was supplanted after the Great Depression by City Efficient principles. These pertained directly to the functional aspects of planning, with the primary implementation tool the zoning ordinance. After World War II, the growth in planning activities focused largely on the redevelopment of older cities and development of new cities and suburbs. It became more limited in scope in the 1980s as a result of new federal economic policies. During the first decade of the twenty-first century, policies were formulated to deal with an economic recession and planning for recovery from its effects. Throughout these periods of change, planning has remained focused on its role of influencing positive change in our communities.

## 2
# CONCEPTUAL APPROACHES TO PLANNING

## Significant Conceptual Approaches to Planning

Throughout history, individuals have approached the planning of cities and communities in ways that are conceptually diverse. We survey a number of noteworthy individuals and the concepts underlying their ideas related to urban and regional planning in this chapter.

The historical figures featured were seldom planners in the way we think of planning today. They were not members of a well-defined professional discipline, since many lived centuries ago and planning as a profession did not exist before the twentieth century. What these individuals have in common is their efforts to strive for beauty, function, and viability for cities. Each emphasized those qualities from a different perspective. Several concentrated on physical design in their plans; others incorporated more social aspects. All made important contributions to planning through their perceptiveness, innovation, and understanding. Understanding that this diversity exists helps planners develop an intellectual framework for decisionmaking they can apply to their professional practice.

*Pope Sixtus V: The Use of Obelisks in Rebuilding Rome*
Once the capital of a great empire, Rome was attacked and pillaged in the fifth century. Several tribes reduced much of the city to rubble. Its population declined from more than a million at the height of the empire to 15,000 to 20,000 people. By the time of the reign of Pope Sixtus V in the sixteenth century, what had been a vibrant crowded city during the classical period became a largely empty city whose buildings were in scattered locations within the city's walls. A number of remaining Roman Catholic churches were the basis of what limited cultural life remained in this once legendary city.

During the five years of his pontificate (1585–90) Pope Sixtus V was determined to reestablish Rome as the center of the Catholic Church. He recognized the need to rebuild the city and knew that this process would require more than his lifetime to achieve. Instead of creating a detailed master plan for rebuilding the city, the Pope developed a simpler concept. He used the city's existing churches as a means to bring order to the city's layout. He directed the strategic placement of obelisks (free-standing columns) as focal points at key locations throughout the city. This directed the movement of religious pilgrims from one church to another and provided visual order to better connect public spaces.

An excellent example of the use of an obelisk is the Porta del Popolo, the city's main gate. An obelisk erected as the centerpiece of this plaza provided a visual focus and orientation for arriving travelers and became a centerpiece for surrounding buildings and streets. Similarly, an obelisk in front of St. Peter's Basilica in Rome was the

*2.1. Piazza del Popolo, Rome*

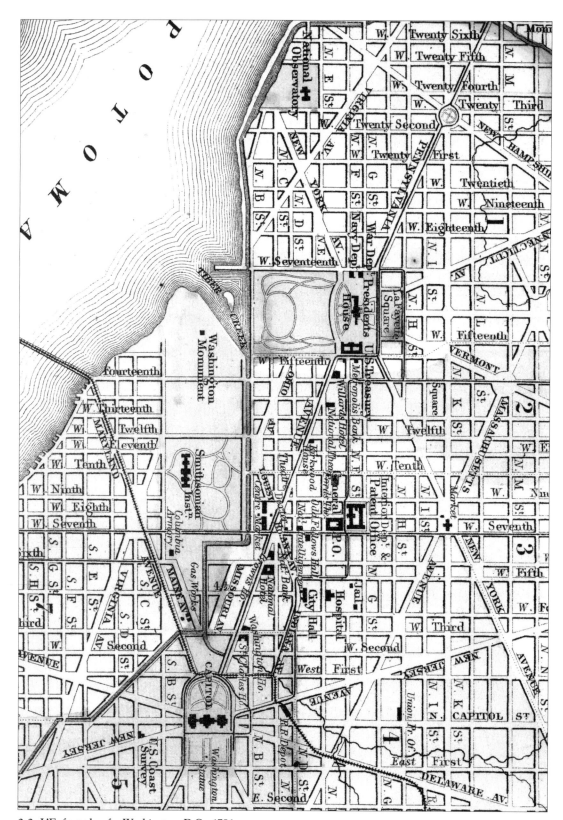

*2.2. L'Enfant plan for Washington, D.C., 1791*

first step in the evolution of that church's grand piazza. Completed over the course of centuries, St. Peter's Square evolved into one of the greatest urban open spaces anywhere in the world.

The long-term impact of a powerful initial idea should not be underestimated. Sixtus V utilized a planning concept that has remained a guide to Rome's city planners as the city was constantly being rebuilt over the centuries. As planner Edmund Bacon put it, "Any really great work has within it seminal forces capable of influencing subsequent development around it, and often in ways not conceived of by its creator. It is the second man who determines whether the creation of the first man will be carried forward or destroyed."[1]

### Pierre L'Enfant: The Symbolic Value of the Mall in Washington, D.C.

When a national capital was being conceived for the new District of Columbia in the late 1700s, a number of individuals, George Washington and Thomas Jefferson among them, proposed city plans. However, in 1791 the plan of a young French-born American, Pierre Charles L'Enfant, a friend of President Washington's, was selected.

L'Enfant's plan, bold in scope and beautiful in design, was based on planning principles of broad avenues, large squares, intersecting diagonal street patterns, and monumental sculpture, all characteristic of the European baroque period. The plan's most prominent feature was a mall extending from the Capitol to a cross-axis with the lawn of what was then called the President's House (now the White House). This feature symbolically represented the sharing of power between Congress and the President. The crossing eventually was accentuated with the construction of the Washington Monument, a tall obelisk similar to those used by Pope Sixtus V in Rome.

Politics surrounding land sales caused L'Enfant's plan to be sidelined by the District of Columbia's commissioners, who dismissed him and commissioned a more mundane approach based on property speculation. It was not until more than a century later, in 1902, that L'Enfant's plan (as part of a report from the McMillan Commission, a senate committee) became the cornerstone for rebuilding the city. The original plan was reinforced through construction of the Lincoln Memorial, which serves as a visual terminus at the west end of the mall,

and the Jefferson Memorial, which provides a focal point to the south of the Washington Monument. L'Enfant's original concept was reinforced by these additions and modifications, The original plan finally received the recognition it deserved, with its grand scale worthy of America's capital city.

### Haussmann: Avenues and the Redesign of Paris

Paris has always represented the heart of French culture, but by the early nineteenth century it had become a dirty, polluted, and depressing city. In 1853, Napoleon III appointed Baron Georges-Eugène Haussmann as the city's prefect, commissioning him to produce a series of planning initiatives to beautify the city and correct its many deficiencies. A man with a strong sense of purpose, Haussmann took the city's existing medieval plan with its narrow, crowded, and confusing streets, and through sheer force of will sliced through existing block upon block to create broad avenues to connect major urban nodes. Some of these places already existed, but some were created by Haussmann to serve as terminuses for various avenues. For example, his Avenue de l'Opéra was a new avenue carved from the city's old fabric, creating a beautiful boulevard that extended from the Louvre, the city's most important museum, to the front of the new Paris Opera House.

Haussmann's authoritarian urban planning and iron-fisted control were essential to overcoming the interests

*2.3. Avenue de l'Opéra, Paris*

of politicians and landlords that controlled Paris at the time. He was responsible for many improvements to the city, including a new water supply, a new sewer system, new bridges, and a series of public buildings. His changes were aesthetic and utilitarian. However, his most significant and enduring change to the plan of the city occurred with the construction of Paris's now legendary broad avenues, which serve as connectors and provide an efficient movement system between different parts of the city. They also provide better orientation by tying together important public plazas, monuments, and buildings.

### Daniel Burnham: Urban Planning through Architecture
Daniel Burnham is arguably the most important and influential urban planner in U.S. history. His powerful personality captured the imagination of many political leaders and caused them to see urban planning as an essential ingredient of a successful city. Trained by, and apprenticed under, the Chicago architect William LeBaron Jenney, Burnham achieved prominence as the leader of the distinguished team of architects, planners, and landscape architects who planned Chicago's World's Columbian Exposition of 1893 and who designed many of its buildings.

The plan for the Exposition grouped its primary buildings together around a Grand Basin, which included primary entrances at either end, one from the fair's railroad stations, and the other through a waterfront colonnade to serve fairgoers arriving by Lake Michigan ferries.

What brought this magnificent plan to life, however, was Burnham's use of classical architecture to provide a consistent monumental style to the grand-scale buildings that surrounded the Grand Basin and focused on the fair's principal structure, its Administration Building. Through the architecture and planning of Burnham's team of designers, the Columbian Exposition initiated the City Beautiful movement, which set in motion cities across the country to initiate public improvements on major public buildings, parks, avenues, and related infrastructure projects.

### Frederick Law Olmsted: Open Space Planning and Central Park
Frederick Law Olmsted created plans for many major city parks. He is probably best remembered, along with Calvert Vaux, for conceiving the plan for Central Park in New York City. At the time the street pattern for Manhattan formulated in 1811 by its city commissioners was a relentless grid. The arrangement was established because "a city is to be composed principally of the habitations of men, and that strait sided [sic], and right angled houses are the most cheap to build, and the most convenient to live in."[2] Olmsted and Vaux's park design brought into the center of Manhattan's grid a grand urban amenity on a scale never before seen. The plan provided a beautiful physical landscape. More than 2.5 miles long, the park's layout was akin to an English garden, with open fields, wooded areas, ponds, carefully landscaped roads and walkways, a zoo and conservatory, and large public and intimate spaces. Many of the city's residents were living in overcrowded tenement buildings that provided minimal sunlight or fresh air. Olmsted's

*2.4. Administration Building on the Grand Basin, Columbian Exposition, Chicago, 1893*

*2.5. Central Park, New York City*

social consciousness and egalitarian idealism led him to devise a plan that was one of the first to recognize the need to create and preserve open space for all citizens— what now are called public parks. Olmsted continued to design beautiful public spaces across the country, among them his 1869 plan for the new town of Riverside, Illinois (discussed in Chapter 5), the landscape of the World's Columbian Exposition in Chicago previously mentioned, and plans for many other communities throughout the United States.

## Walter Burley Griffin: Canberra, A New Town Planned for Growth

Walter Burley Griffin (1876–1937) designed over 350 buildings in the United States, but his plan for Canberra, Australia, is his most renowned work. In 1912, when Griffin was still essentially unknown, he entered an international competition to design a new capital city for Australia. In his research as a student, Griffin had found that virtually nothing had been written or published on the topic of contemporary town planning. In the absence of published information, Griffin drew inspiration from earlier examples. He based his design for Canberra on his study of Christopher Wren's seventeenth-century plan for London and L'Enfant's eighteenth-century plan for Washington, D.C. Ultimately, Griffin's design was selected winner from the 137 entries submitted.

His distinctive drawing for the competition illustrates a layout that connects the Capitol and Government Group district with the Civic Centre and Market Centre nodes across a newly created lake. Distant Mt. Ainslie commands a view of the plan's central axis and the surrounding countryside. The influence of Baroque

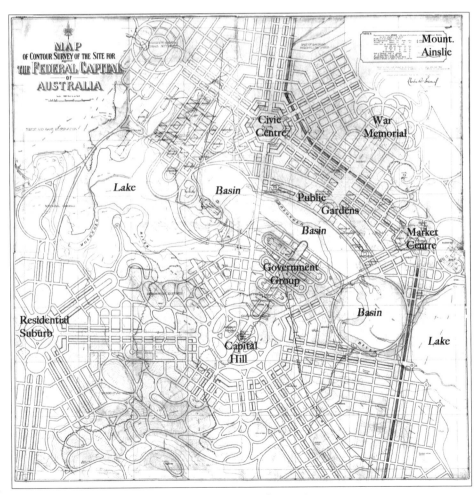

*2.6. Walter Burley Griffin's plan for Canberra, Australia, 1912*

planning patterns on Griffin's plan with its wide boulevards, prominent axes, and dominant nodes is obvious; the plan utilized a successful concept that works at small and large urban scales.

The genius of Griffin's plan lies in its conception of a city that can function as a complete urban environment at every stage of growth. Each district had its center, and although designed to be self-sufficient, the districts were designed so they blended well into the larger composition as the city expanded. The first phase consisted of the capitol and commercial and residential areas. As the city grew, connections were established to new neighborhood nodes. The pattern of boulevards and streets connected the parts.

Griffin's plan originally was criticized for being too large, with its primary elements distant from one another. He explained that it was a plan created for the long term. But public pressure to downsize under the economic burdens of the World War I period prevailed. The validity of his concept did not become apparent until the 1960s, when central elements of his plan were implemented, including creation of the lake and the design and construction of a new capitol building on Capitol Hill.

### Ebenezer Howard: Metropolitan Growth and Garden Cities

The history of planning contains moments when important planning concepts come unexpectedly from individuals whose backgrounds are unrelated to the practice of planning. Ebenezer Howard's new town concept is one such moment. In London, in the late nineteenth century, Howard was employed as a clerk when he developed an idea that was to be one of the most influential in the history of planning. One can almost imagine him sitting at his office window in the center of what could well be considered the most crowded, polluted, and ill-planned city that had yet existed and wondering if there were a better way for civilized English citizens to live.

The basic concept was simple: marry the best parts of city life—good jobs, abundant services, social opportunities, flow of capital—with the best parts of country life—

clean environment, ease of movement, low rents, and abundant land. As described in his 1898 book, *Tomorrow: A Peaceful Path to Real Reform*,[3] Howard envisioned this happening through the development of what he called "garden cities." His concept was to build satellite towns outside of London's urban area. They would be limited to 40,000 people, have a mix of economic and social classes, be governed by their residents, and contain green open space at their core and be surrounded by a green belt. Growth would come from replication in new locations.

Howard's concept of building garden cities on the perimeter of metropolitan areas was unique in its time. The British government had an urgent need to solve London's urban problems and adopted his approach. Two garden cities, Letchworth and Welwyn, were constructed during Howard's lifetime. The concept proved strong enough to continue, and more satellite towns were built in England after World War II. In the United States similar satellite towns were constructed, notably Radburn, New Jersey; Greenbelt, Maryland; and Chatham Village

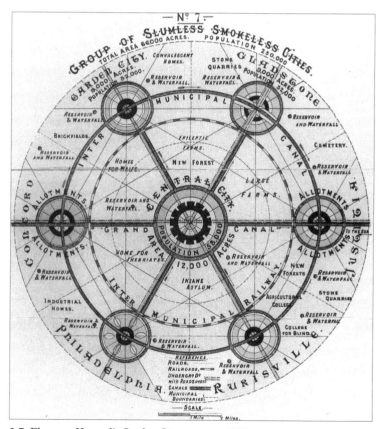

2.7. *Ebenezer Howard's Garden City concept, 1898*

in Pittsburgh, Pennsylvania. Howard's ideas were so well conceived that they now seem obvious. Many American suburbs have been built in imitation of the original garden cities. Sadly, many of these are poor imitations; however, the ideas presented by this clerk in his original book remain an important milestone in the history of city planning.

### Le Corbusier: The Contemporary City Concept and the Value of Density

Charles-Edouard Jeanneret-Gris, who chose to be known as Le Corbusier, was a Swiss-French architect, sculptor, and planner. His plan for a "Contemporary City" represents an early-twentieth-century European concept of an ideal urban lifestyle based on the social, environmental, and economic values of increased population density. Le Corbusier was dedicated to improving the living conditions of residents in large industrial cities. He saw the dawning of the modern age embracing the idea of the city as a "machine for living," its citizens as members of a vast urban society housed according to their status and usefulness.[4]

Le Corbusier described his ideal city this way: "The air is clear and pure; there is hardly any noise. What, you cannot see where the buildings are? Look through the charmingly dispersed arabesques of branches out into the sky towards those widely-spaced crystal towers which soar higher than any pinnacle on earth. These translucent prisms that seem to float in the air without anchorage to the ground—flashing in the summer sunshine, softly gleaming under grey winter skies, magically glittering at nightfall."[5]

Le Corbusier's ideas were influential in the design of large urban projects in cities throughout the world. In many instances, older low-rise buildings were demolished and replaced with tall glass towers, creating controlled spaces high above city streets. His Plan Voisin for the redevelopment of Paris called for demolishing much of the city's historic core to build high-rise glass structures that would tower above an untouched green landscape. Such projects recognized the potential of new construction techniques and technologies, including steel framing, high-rise elevators, and glass-walled exteriors, but they completely ignored the intrinsic value of the existing cityscape.

### Frank Lloyd Wright: Broadacre City and Decentralization

During the Depression of the 1930s, when even successful architects like Frank Lloyd Wright had little work, professionals needed to find other outlets for their abilities. Wright decided to utilize his time and energy on development of a new and unique approach to city planning, incorporating his ideas of Jeffersonian democracy and its emphasis on the worth of the individual. No more striking counterpoint to Le Corbusier's Contemporary City can be found than Wright's Broadacre City proposal. It is difficult to call it a city plan since its emphasis on decentralization largely denied the idea of urban life.

The primary tenet of Wright's concept was that each resident family should own at least a 1-acre parcel of land and have adequate space for a home garden and small, domesticated animals. This close tie to the land was intended to create citizens who were largely self-sufficient and not dependent on a central government for support to function effectively. Broadacre City would rely on new transportation systems, including high-speed roads and personal flying machines. Government

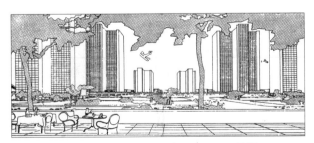

*2.8. Le Corbusier, Contemporary City concept, 1922*

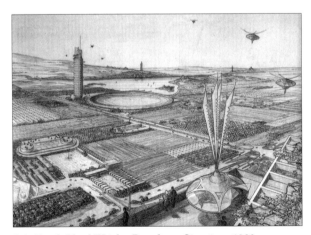

*2.9. Frank Lloyd Wright, Broadacre City view, 1932*

business would be conducted by telephone and through efficient transportation and communication systems. Working at home would be common.

Although seen as impractical and unfeasible at the time, suburban areas have become largely unplanned versions of Wright's concept. Suburbs represent sprawling low-density land use, with residents relying on interstate highways for daily commuting; they are increasingly dependent on electronic communication. Perhaps Wright saw this trend to accommodate antiurban sentiments more clearly than later planners. However, his relatively sophisticated concept of controlled decentralization remained largely ignored for the rest of the century.

### Robert Moses: Rebuilding New York City through Administrative Control and Financing

One of the most ambitious builder/planners in American history was Robert Moses. His career in New York City spanned the decades from the 1920s to the 1960s. The extent of his planning projects is legendary; they include development of Jones Beach on Long Island, construction of the regional parkway system, two of the largest bridges ever built, development of a large number of city parks and housing projects, construction of Lincoln Center for the Performing Arts, the World's Fair of 1964, and many other projects. Although not trained as a planner, Moses personally controlled more of the planning of the nation's largest city than anyone before or since.

Moses's successes were largely a result of the power and financing he brought to his role, primarily as Parks Commissioner, but also in a variety of other appointed positions. He developed great resources, had 80,000 people working under him, and at one time controlled all federal development money coming into the city. Although Moses never held elected office, he had money, power, and expertise to build the public realm throughout New York City, largely derived through control of tolls collected from the bridges built under his supervision. In his 40 years as a city government appointee under numerous mayors and administrations, he changed New York from a crowded, dirty city of tenements and immigrants to a modern, business-oriented metropolis.

The lessons learned from a study of Moses's career are many.[6] Moses was not a corrupt official, but he held such power that he had no patience for those who opposed his plans or projects. He did not recognize that what was good for the city overall could be disastrous for residents who were directly impacted. For example, his Cross Bronx Expressway project relieved much of the traffic congestion in that part of the city, but required the demolition of many apartment buildings and the destruction of entire well-established neighborhoods. As one critic noted, he hurt thousands, but helped millions. Commenting on his own planning strategies, Moses said, "You can't make an omelet without breaking some eggs."[7] More than anyone since Haussmann, Moses represented the view that success in planning is achieved through the use of power. According to his philosophy, planners with no ability to build or implement their plans cannot be effective or successful.

### Edmund Bacon: Learning from History

Planner Edmund Bacon's book *Design of Cities* remains one of the most influential books in the history of urban planning. Written during Bacon's tenure as executive director of the Philadelphia City Planning Commission, the book was prepared originally to educate the city's planning commissioners on elements of good planning and gain support for the plan his department had created for the city's downtown area. Only after describing in the book the strengths of many historic plans over time and around the world, from the Acropolis in Athens to ancient and baroque Rome, Haussmann's Paris, London and other European cities, the Forbidden City in Beijing, and Brasília, the modern capital of Brazil, does Bacon turn his attention to Philadelphia. He illustrates how similar planning concepts can be utilized in the contemporary plan for his own city.

What is significant about Bacon's contribution is the recognition that key city planning concepts developed over the centuries can still provide essential design tools for contemporary planners. Good planning is not the product of any specific era; it has been evidenced in many cultures at key times throughout history. *Time* magazine recognized his importance in a cover article in 1964, and a decade later architecture critic Suzanne Stevens wrote: "Bacon left an indelible imprint on Philadelphia in the postwar decades. As the executive director of Philadelphia's City Planning Commission from 1949 to 1970, he revitalized a decaying center city with a group of strategies akin to those of Sixtus V of Rome in their scope of design vision."[8]

## EXERCISE 1
### REDEVELOPMENT OF THE BILTMORE FARMSTEAD SITE

*The city of Rivertown recently purchased Biltmore Farmstead, a property just to the rear of three historic houses located along Biltmore Avenue, including the Biltmore Mansion. (See Appendix A for more information about Rivertown.) Burnham Daniel, the city's planning director, has determined potential exists for a significant development project at this location. He anticipates that this site can become a centerpiece and focus of the community's revitalization efforts. You are his assistant planner, and he has asked you to develop a concept for the site to give it a strong image for the city.*

*For inspiration you should draw on the conceptual approaches described in this chapter. The previous sections have presented a variety of approaches that could be emulated. For example, Pope Sixtus V used a prominent vertical element as a focus. L'Enfant saw the value of a well-defined formal mall, while Olmsted designed country garden–like parks for passive recreation. Haussmann used boulevards with plazas to connect areas. Burnham emphasized elegant architecture to create a special place. Howard and Griffin plans focused on future growth. Le Corbusier argued that more density was desirable, while Wright advocated low-density development. Robert Moses was concerned about practical solutions and functional efficiency. If none of these seems appropriate, develop an alternative concept.*

*Your specific task is to write a memorandum to Mr. Daniel describing in narrative a concept for use of this site. Explain why you feel this is an appropriate approach. Keep in mind that several important questions may arise when your plan is considered.*

*1. What criteria have you used to evaluate various alternatives? (The development of alternatives is an important part of the planning process. See Chapter 4 for further discussion.)*

*2. What are the pros and cons of the city's purchasing*

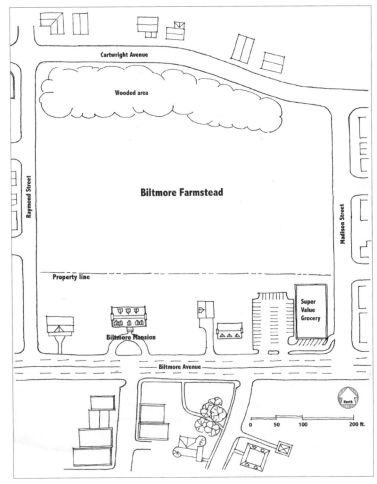

2.10. Biltmore Farmstead site, Biltmore Avenue, Rivertown

*this property versus making it available to a private owner? (The value of private sector ownership of land is discussed in Chapter 9.)*

*3. What relative costs is the city likely to incur as a result of each of the proposed concepts? (The funding of public projects is described in Chapter 16.)*

## Other Planning Concepts

The ideas developed by the individuals described in the previous section may be considered classic examples of physical planning concepts. They also represent the evolution of the planning profession over the centuries. In recent decades, others have expanded perspectives on planning by incorporating more social aspects into the physical planning process. A brief review of some of these contributions illustrates significant ideas and planning-related concerns of influential individuals.

## Alice Constance Austin: A Woman's Perspective

Some people have criticized planning and resulting land-use decisions as aimed too much at serving the business community and not sufficiently oriented toward what are often considered women's issues, such as directly serving the needs of individuals and families, and promoting community vitality. Certainly there were few women of influence during the early development of the planning profession. Alice Constance Austin, however, was an early-twentieth-century architect and city planner who focused on issues of low-cost housing; gender equity in wages, social security, and welfare; and universal health care. Many of these ideas were incorporated in her most noteworthy project developed in 1916 for Llano del Rio, an ideal socialist community located in Palmdale, California. The community was planned for a population of more than 10,000 people. Austin described the plan as a circular city with six sections, all linked by a Grand Avenue with housing grouped around a Civic Center.

The city was planned as a complete community, with housing, schools, churches, markets, and restaurants. A significant innovation was the development of kitchenless houses. To free housewives from the responsibilities of daily cooking, meals were prepared in a large, centralized, community kitchen and delivered to each housing unit via a small railroad in underground tunnels. This railroad also transported people, supplies, and laundry, largely eliminating the need for individual household shopping, washing, and ironing. Nine hundred resi-

dences were eventually built at Llano del Rio; however, due to a lack of capital and a shortage of water, the community ultimately moved to a new location in Louisiana. In her 1935 book, *The Next Step: How to Plan for Beauty, Comfort, and Peace with Great Savings Effected by the Reduction of Waste*, Austin reviewed her concept, its potential, and its problems.

## Jane Jacobs: Planning for Neighborhoods

In the 1960s, planners and city officials who had supported new development through their policies often met strong opposition from groups of residents who felt that older but intact neighborhoods were being overrun by big urban projects. The Cross Bronx Expressway in New York, conceptualized and built under the direction of Robert Moses, was one such subject of contention. When Moses later proposed a plan for an expressway to cross lower Manhattan that would destroy intact residential neighborhoods, Jane Jacobs, a housewife and writer who lived in the area, became a community activist. Her landmark book, *The Death and Life of Great American Cities*,[9] criticized planners like Moses for ignoring people when approving such massive development projects. She opened her argument; "This book is an attack on current city planning and rebuilding. . . . It is also, and mostly, an attempt to introduce new principles of city planning and rebuilding, different and even opposite from those now taught in everything from schools of architecture and planning and the Sunday supplements and women's magazines."[10]

Jacobs argued convincingly that city planners used statistics and maps to make their plans and ignored the reality of what was happening on the streets. She held that many urban neighborhoods seen by city officials as needing redevelopment actually had a strong community vitality that could not be recognized by only reviewing planning documents and reports. Jacobs wrote of "eyes on the street"—monitoring what was happening on their streets and understanding the dynamics better than planners or policemen or other officials ever could. She recognized that city planning needed to be more than physical planning; it also needed to accommodate social and cultural aspects. Following publication of her book the concept of "advocacy planning"

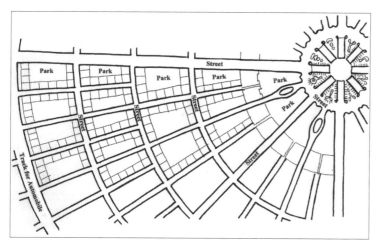

*2.11. Alice Constance Austin's plan for Llano del Rio, 1916*

emerged, recognizing and advocating for citizens and residents to be integral members of the planning process.

### Norman Krumholz: Equity Planning in Cleveland

Thanks to Jane Jacobs and others, it was recognized that planning decisions were being made by people in power and a large proportion of the population was not represented in the decisionmaking. Norman Krumholz, director of the City Planning Department in Cleveland, Ohio, in the 1970s, made great strides in correcting these inequities through an approach referred to as equity planning. He consciously tried to counter traditional policies and programs by redressing the inequitable distribution of costs and benefits while assisting the city's poorest citizens. Krumholz saw this not as creating conflict between the haves and have-nots, but as an expression of his belief "that equity in the social, economic, and political relationships among people is a requisite condition for a just and lasting society."[11] He wrote: "Conventional planners basically view themselves as giving their bosses choices—or finding the most efficient means to an end chosen by their bosses, whom they assume represent the people through the democratic process."[12] Equity planners, in contrast, view existing democratic institutions as biased against the interests of those at the bottom of the social system; consequently, they seek to create a system of better downward redistribution. Despite the political risks, Krumholz outlined four reasons he felt this was needed and appropriate: "(1) the urgent reality of conditions in Cleveland, (2) the inherent unfairness and exploitative nature of our urban development process, (3) the inability of local politics to address these problems, and (4) our conception of the ethics of professional planning practice."[13] Krumholz brought a new perspective to the role of planning in a diverse society, and his Cleveland Policy Plan was declared a "Planning Landmark" by the American Institute of Certified Planners.

### James Rouse: Planning to "Grow Better People"

James Rouse was a successful shopping center developer in the 1960s when he decided to expand his range of activities to create an entire new town. He quietly bought 140 parcels of farmland totaling 14,000 acres in Howard County, Maryland, located strategically between Washington, D.C., and Baltimore, and in 1964 announced his intention to build a new town named Columbia, Maryland.

Rouse brought a special perspective to this project. He wanted it to go beyond physical planning, to be people-oriented. "The only legitimate purpose of a city is to provide for the life and growth of its people. . . the task of making the American city a fit place to grow our people is the No. 1 priority of our civilization."[14] He put together an unusual team of 14 individuals from diverse backgrounds who became known as the Work Group. They spent two days, twice a month, for six months discussing a wide range of issues pertinent to planning a new city. The group included planners, architects, and engineers as well as teachers, ministers, psychiatrists, and sociologists.

The planning group for Columbia eventually agreed that the focus of the new city's plan should not be its downtown, or industries, or businesses, or public spaces. They acknowledged that all of these are important considerations in a city plan, but found the true core of a community to be its elementary schools. As a result, the plan for Columbia began with the location and planning of its elementary schools and grew from there.

Columbia's downtown, built as another of Rouse's numerous shopping centers, seemed almost an afterthought in the original plan. The plan for a new town center was developed recently in a community charrette, a forum for individuals to contribute to the design process. Over 1,000 participants redefined the downtown they wanted as a dense, diverse, and walkable town center.

By 2009, Columbia had a population of over 100,000 residents and 5,500 businesses employing 63,000 people. In 2006, *Money* magazine ranked Columbia as the fourth best city to live in in the United States.

## Traditional and Tactical Approaches to Planning

The individuals described above represent differing approaches to the practice of planning communities. Whether or not they were planners, and most were not, their viewpoints illustrate how planning has evolved historically. As their stories show, planning is a broad discipline with numerous paths to guide its practice. Today, however, it can be argued that there are two general underlying approaches to planning: traditional and tactical.

The traditional approach, also referred to as rationalist or normative, takes an objective, long-term look at a district, community, or region, and develops plans and policies for it based on reliable research, analysis, and decisions. This approach is well represented by Daniel Burnham and his 1909 Plan for Chicago. The traditional view makes assumptions that the world is objectively knowable, more-or-less static, and exists with certain universal principles. As a result, we can understand our communities and reasonably predict their futures.[15]

Traditional planners generally utilize the following step-by-step process: (1) identify problems, (2) recognize assets and constraints, (3) determine goals and objectives, (4) propose alternative solutions, (5) evaluate alternatives and select an appropriate alternative, (6) implement the plan, and (7) evaluate and update it on a regular basis (see chapter 4). The rationality of this approach tends to foster confidence regarding its validity.

However, the traditional approach does not fully recognize that a community's decisionmaking is not so clearcut and is often messy. In the 1960s a new movement arose out of a period of social unrest, when some planners saw that the traditional approach to planning could not fully serve an American society beset by racial strife, social disenfranchisement, antiwar sentiment, the impact of new technologies, and concerns about the environment and preserving heritage. Leaders of this movement argued that good planning needed to better recognize the political system and social issues to remain relevant.

Tactical planners are more involved with the public in the day-to-day process of decisionmaking, represented by the work of planning director Norman Krumholz in Cleveland. Tactical planning is less comprehensive in its scope than traditional planning and more oriented toward immediate short-term issues. Where traditional planning focuses on guiding decisions, tactical planning focuses on implementing decisions. This alternative approach has been described by many names, each with its own specific meaning—action-oriented planning, negotiated planning, collaborative planning, and transactive planning, among others. With respect to potential planning decisions, tactical planners ask who, what, why, where, when, and how much does it cost. One critic has suggested it is an approach based on "Ready! Fire! Aim!" because of the tendency among local decisionmakers to send up trial balloon policies to see if they will be accepted in the court of public opinion.[16]

Questions inherent in tactical planning ask whether planners should remain completely objective in their role, or follow their own judgment. Planner Tore Sager suggested that "the modern role of the planner is by no means only technical and analytical. The role includes various forms of conflict management, like facilitation, negotiation, and mediation."[17] John Forester explained, "Planners not only give information on fact, but also on how to evaluate fact; they not only inform, but educate imaginations; they not only report, but cultivate appreciation and good judgment; they not only exercise power, but also empower."[18]

The issues facing communities are complex. All of them cannot be determined at the development stage of a plan; some must be resolved through communication and compromise. As Krumholz recognized, "A great many students enter the profession believing that public policy decisions are made within an orderly, rational context that hinges heavily on planners' recommendations. Nothing could be further from the truth. The public decision-making process is generally irrational and chaotic and always highly politicized."[19] Tactical planning relies on building coalitions in city hall and within communities, winning over key leaders and developing participatory planning processes.

|  | Traditional Approach | Tactical Approach |
|---|---|---|
| Primary tool | Comprehensive plan | Communication and political persuasion |
| Timeframe | Long range | Short-term (e.g., political campaigns) |
| Process | Step-by-step process | Accomplishment of the possible |
| Goal | Rational master vision | Democratic, representative process |
| Criticism | Too idealistic | Too pragmatic |

2.12. Traditional versus tactical approach to planning

## Summary

Significant planning concepts can be found throughout history and throughout the world. Knowledge in the field of planning advances best when contemporary planners understand the historical basis of their discipline and the legacy created over centuries by seminal figures in the creation, practice, and advancement of planning. Many important concepts were developed by individuals who were not planning professionals, but who understood the need to improve the quality and function of their cities and communities. Their ideas extended from site-specific projects to the creation of entirely new communities.

Although planning is frequently seen through the limited perspective of physical development, it also extends into social and economic areas. Planners must recognize how decisions are made and affect communities. The concern for minorities and underrepresented citizens, groups of people who had often been ignored in the planning process, has added a sense of inclusiveness.

Planners should be aware of two basic approaches to planning: traditional and tactical. Traditional planning uses a rational process of objective decisionmaking. Its primary tool is the comprehensive plan, which guides a community's future growth and change. Although the tactical approach should occur within the context of a community's comprehensive plan, it focuses more on short-term political agendas and immediate concerns of interest groups as integral parts of the planning process. Well-rounded planners strive to integrate both approaches in the course of their professional practice.

3

# THE SCOPE OF PLANNING AT THE FEDERAL, STATE, REGIONAL, AND LOCAL LEVELS

Planning takes different forms at the federal, state, regional, and local levels. Historically, in the United States the power to govern was provided through a confederation of states, and under this principle of federalism, powers not granted to the national government nor prohibited to the states by the U.S. Constitution are reserved to the states or the people. The following section reviews how this constitutional basis of governing relates to planning our communities and indicates the powers and activities at each level.

## Planning at the Federal Level

A person might reasonably ask, is there such a thing as national planning? The answer is yes, but not in the same sense that planning occurs at the state and local levels. The federal government has never been particularly comfortable dealing directly with community planning. Federal officials have remained detached from interfering in the local-level planning process. Significant planning policies and programs at the national level impact local-level government, but in a general way rather than being directed at planning individual communities.

As an example, the interstate highway system resulted from post–World War II federal planning initiatives. Although the national highway acts of 1954 and 1956 were not targeted to specific cities, the resulting interstate highways have had tremendous impact on the growth of local communities. Similarly, national housing programs have determined how and where new housing gets built in a general way, but those programs have created many incentives for suburban sprawl that directly affect the growth of existing communities.

Other programs illustrate how the federal government, through funding and its relationship with local government, influences project selection, development, and implementation in a secondary way. The Community Development Block Grant program, for example, provides federal funds for community improvements, but decisions on how to allocate the funds are made by local officials. The National Park Service establishes historic preservation policies at the federal level, but it leaves the administration and decisionmaking for historic districts to local commissions. These and other examples show the significant, but indirect, involvement of the federal government in planning communities.

Federal government decisions have other types of impacts on communities. For example, the federal government controls the location of post offices. In the past, they were located in central city or downtown areas and served as a focus for residents who not only came to collect or send mail but to meet their neighbors informally. In recent years, however, the government has located larger post offices outside the central city. One result is that customers typically find it inconvenient to walk to post offices, shifting an important community activity away from the central core and, as a result, decreasing downtown activity.

Deferring control to the local level is a distinctly American phenomenon. In many other countries, the national government plays an active role in planning at all levels, through both national planning agencies and more direct involvement with local municipal activities. For example, Canadian planning directors have more power over development planning and, in general, have a high profile within government and the community. Canadian planners lead and developers follow. In contrast, American planning departments tend not to define development projects, but to respond to petitions for developer-initiated proposals. While American society stresses individual decisionmaking—"life, liberty, and the pursuit of happiness"—Canadians emphasize a stronger role for government with their motto, "peace, order, and good government."

In 1970 Senator Henry Jackson, Democrat from the State of Washington, proposed federal legislation entitled the Land and Water Resources Planning Act, which contained provisions for the 50 states to conduct inventories of their resources including water, soil, and coasts/rivers; key facilities such as airports and power plants; utilities such as sewer/water lines, power lines, roads, and other infrastructure; archaeological sites and historical features; and other specified items. The legislation called for each of the states to send its inventories to Washington, D.C., where the information would serve as the foundation for a national plan. The bill failed in the House of Representatives. Similar attempts in the 1970s and 1980s to create resources for federal planning were also unsuccessful.

There are several primary ways, however, in which the federal government has a significant and somewhat more direct impact on planning: as a landowner, through various grants-in-aid programs, and through federal mandates. We discuss each of these briefly below.

### The Federal Government as Landowner
According to the U.S. Department of Agriculture's Economic Research Service, more than one-quarter of all land in the United States is owned by the federal government and its agencies. This makes it the country's largest landowner.[1] Consequently, it would be difficult to overestimate the significance of the federal government's role in American land use.

More than one-eighth of the land area in the United States is controlled by either the Bureau of Land Management (BLM) or the U.S. Forest Service. The BLM, an agency within the Department of Interior, manages 264 million acres comprising surface lands primarily located in 12 western states. These lands encompass vast stretches of desert and high desert shrub, but also snow-capped mountains, coastal territories, and other areas suited to human outdoor activities; even larger in scope is the BLM's management of subsurface mineral deposits

throughout the country. The value of these resources is substantial, yet currently these lands are rapidly gaining recognition for their recreational use. Consequently, the BLM's mission is beginning to shift from its traditional emphasis on the leasing of grazing, mining, and logging rights to one that is broader in its perspective.

3.1. *Denali National Park, Alaska*

In administering these lands, the agency's decisions are guided by many laws, the most important of which is the Federal Land Policy and Management Act of 1976. This law establishes guidelines for the sale of public land. Additional acreage is administered by the National Park Service, the National Forest Service, and the Bureau of Sport Fishing and Wildlife. Federal holdings of various types can significantly impact planning of a community where the properties are located, including properties held by the U.S. Forest Service, National Park Service, federal office buildings, military facilities, and others. For most of these land uses, local governments have little or no meaningful input over their development, redevelopment, or resource removal. Although local communities typically have little involvement in planning these facilities, they can engage in regular communication with the federal government's General Services Administration, the agency responsible for the procurement and sale of office space and other federal properties.

### Federal Grants-in-Aid
One of the greatest impacts the federal government has on local communities is through its grant-in-aid programs. Some programs provided funding directly to support local planning efforts and pay for expertise needed by local agencies. The Section 701 program (1950s through 1970s) provided over $1 billion in direct aid to

pay for local planning. A great number of planning studies resulted from this act but drew criticism. Communities created plans not because they were needed but simply to qualify for funding from available programs. This led to Section 701's termination in 1981. Since then, there has been little direct federal support for local community planning efforts, although federal money has continued to be available for hundreds of grants for specific programs, such as housing, transportation, redevelopment, and pollution abatement. Perhaps the most significant of these is the Community Development Block Grant (CDBG) program established in 1974 and administered by the U.S. Department of Housing and Urban Development. This program provides over $4.5 billion annually in disbursements to 1,200 local communities and states to spend at their discretion. The funds target low- and moderate-income families. (See Chapter 7 for more information on the CDBG program.)

### Federal Mandates

The federal government often establishes legislative mandates that must be followed by state and local governments, but many include no funding for implementation. Increasingly this policy shifts the burden of paying for federal programs to state and local governments. An example of an unfunded mandate is the Americans with Disabilities Act of 1991, which established that it is a civil rights violation to fail to give persons with disabilities ready and convenient access to all public spaces. This means that buildings must provide ramps, elevators, larger rest rooms, and other facilities for individuals who are in wheelchairs, or alternative resources or facilities for those who are hearing or visually impaired, or who have other disabilities. The law has resulted in increased costs for new construction and sometimes considerable expense to renovate older buildings. Although the act was an appropriate legislative mandate, essentially no federal funds were allocated to assist property owners to accomplish the changes and no money was provided for local agencies to establish a program for review and inspection. The Unfunded Mandates Reform Act of 1995 tried to stem the tide of unfunded mandates, but it has not been effective. The U.S. Supreme Court has ruled such unfunded mandates illegal, but the process continues, largely because of the federal government's control over states through its power to tax and disburse revenues to the states. Thus, state and local governments fear losing favor with federal authorities.

## State and Regional Planning

As noted in the introduction to this chapter, states are the primary source of authority to engage in planning. States have authority to plan land use but can cede this through enabling legislation. Most have delegated much of that authority to local governments, and follow the federal model of a more hands-off approach, but what the states have delegated, the states can take back.

State-level planning can take different forms. In Delaware, for example, the Office of State Planning Coordination has responsibilities that involve effective coordination of state, county, and local planning efforts. The Office coordinates state agency review of major land use change proposals prior to submission to local governments; conducts research and analysis; disseminates information concerning land use planning; and helps meet informational needs of state agencies and local governments, especially spatial data and Geographic Information Systems (GIS) analyses.[2]

Maine's State Planning Office (SPO) is part of the Executive Department. It provides planning assistance, policy development, program management, and technical assistance to Maine communities, businesses, and residents. Furthermore, it advises the governor on developing and implementing policy, assists the legislature with information and analyses, and provides local and regional financial and technical assistance. The SPO's areas of responsibility include land use planning, land protection, code enforcement training and certification, economics and demographics, energy, flood plain management, coastal programs, a community service commission, waste management, and recycling.

Some states have limited planning responsibilities and rely on plans targeting a particular issue or need—for example, Oklahoma's Statewide Intermodal Transportation Plan. Many states in the Great Plains are moving rapidly to plan for future water needs. Some states have economic development plans or natural resource plans.

Some states, like Michigan, have no official state planning office or agency, but rely on legislation alone to achieve and regulate land uses, economic development, environmental policies, and other such activities. The Michigan Association of Planning, a membership organization composed of lay and professional planners and the largest such planning organization in any state, provides much of the state's needed planning coordination through its activities in policy analysis, coordination, and lobbying.

Other states share administrative responsibilities with regional agencies. The construction of the Erie Canal across New York State or the designation and development of the Appalachian Trail, which extends from Maine to Georgia, are examples of regional planning. Other regional programs include the Tennessee Valley Authority, a public corporation established in 1933 that had sufficient flexibility in its operation to provide for a variety of redevelopment activities in the Tennessee Valley watershed. A similar regional program, the Columbia Basin Project, involved construction of the Grand Coulee Dam, which was completed in 1941 and harnessed the Columbia River to provide irrigation, electric power generation, and flood control in the Pacific Northwest. But one of the best examples of regional planning was an association with no official role in government: the Regional Planning Association. Formed in 1922 and focused on New York City's metropolitan area and parts of New Jersey and Connecticut, the association published a landmark plan in 1929 that continues to guide the region. Follow-up plans in the 1960s and in 1996 contained proposals on land-use, transportation, open-space preservation, economic development, and social issues. The Regional Planning Association remains influential as a planning agency as a result of the proven efficacy of its ideas.

Some organizations have adopted regional planning focused on particular issues. The Great Lakes Basin Commission comprises eight states bordering the Great Lakes. The purpose of the Commission is to protect the valuable fresh water resources available in the five Great Lakes and to promote their orderly, integrated, and comprehensive development. This activity is enhanced through participation in the International Joint Commission (IJC), a U.S./Canadian organization focused on protecting the Great Lakes and the St. Lawrence Seaway. The IJC is an outgrowth of the International Boundary Waters Treaty of 1909 between the United States and Canada. It was initiated to resolve disagreements pertaining to water usage. The Commission takes proactive positions on contentious issues involving the stability of lake levels, since they have a direct effect on

economic activities from commercial shipping to local marinas and recreation. For example, the IJC is concerned with a proposal to divert water from the Great Lakes to drought-prone lands in the Great Plains.

Although many regional agencies focus on the environment, some address other planning issues. In 1965, the Appalachian Regional Planning Commission (now the Appalachian Regional Commission) was established to confront poverty and promote economic development in West Virginia and parts of 12 other states. The organization was threatened with elimination in the 1980s but developed a new strategic policy in 1994. This initiative focused on attracting and retaining businesses in the Appalachian region, job skill training, and the development and improvement of roads, water, and sewer services. It has continued to serve as a successful model for federal-state-local planning and partnership.

Regional planning is a means to resolve inequities in the tax structure. In many older urban areas, the disadvantaged population that remains in the central city has the lowest income, the highest tax rate, and the greatest need for services. Although regional governance is an obvious way to mitigate these inequities, wealthier exurban areas are reluctant to commit their resources to problems they do not see as their own, so regional tax programs usually are not successful. Tax-base sharing requires governments in a metropolitan region to share a certain percentage of their revenues from tax-base growth. Its purpose is to minimize competition for tax revenues and encourage a more balanced program of growth across municipalities. Tax-base sharing reduces the need for local governments to outbid each other to offer public subsidies such as tax abatements to attract development. Even though the overall gains in a region may be minimal, the redistribution effect can reduce the inequities between poorer cities saddled with many social needs and their richer suburbs.

## Spotlight on Minnesota's Regional Tax-Base Sharing Program

Minnesota has a history of regional planning. In 1967, the State Legislature established the Metropolitan Council to coordinate planning and development in Minneapolis, St. Paul, and seven adjacent counties. Over the years, the Council incorporated other agencies and its scope of activities expanded to include transportation, transit systems, and waste control. The Council's four primary goals are coordination of planning and infrastructure investments, working collaboratively on land use and housing, enhancing the regional transportation system, and preserving vital natural areas and resources. Its funding comes from state and federal funds and user fees.

One of the most interesting tools of regional planning in the Minneapolis–St. Paul area is the creation and continued use of the Minnesota Fiscal Disparities Act of 1971. In many metropolitan areas, there is a sizeable difference in revenues available through taxes for different municipalities. The reasons for a fiscal imbalance are not necessarily the fault of the individual jurisdictions, but rather the result of larger development patterns. Minnesota's Fiscal Disparity Plan has successfully implemented a regional tax-base sharing scheme. The plan encom-

passes 186 cities, 48 school districts, and 60 other taxing authorities. As described by the Commission of Behavioral and Social Sciences and Education, "each year local governments in a seven-county area calculate changes in the assessed value of industrial-commercial property and contribute 40 percent of the growth to an area-wide pool. Each government receives funds from this pool, according to a formula that takes into consideration the community's population and is inversely related to its fiscal capacity, defined as per capita market value of all real property (i.e., larger cities with lower fiscal capacity receive more funds)."[3] The plan has been successful at narrowing the regional business tax rate disparities. In 2000, 28 percent of the region's commercial-industrial tax base was shared among jurisdictions.[4]

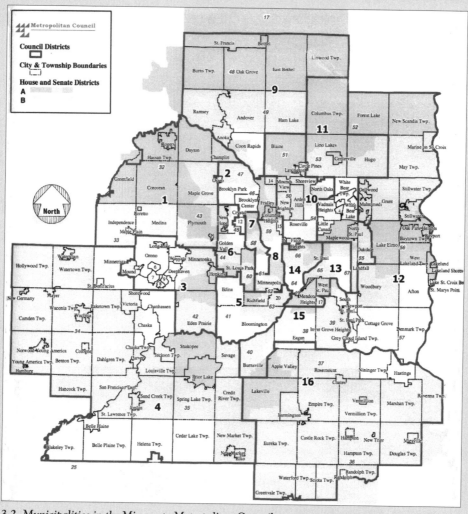

3.2. Municipalities in the Minnesota Metropolitan Council

Regional planning within states may be unpopular in many parts of the country because local communities identify strongly with their area and relish the autonomy of controlling their own governance. Officials and residents in local jurisdictions are reluctant to concede any of their powers or share them with adjacent municipalities. They are concerned about the larger scale of government that is more distant from them. Elected officials fear that shared governance will reduce their role and political power base. As a result, planning at the regional level is usually less effective than it could be, and is largely advisory. However, the need for greater regional planning continues to increase throughout the nation as a way to contain unlimited sprawl. Also, a regional approach to economic development allows adjacent municipalities to present a stronger image to potential investors and developers.

### Councils of Governments (COGs)

A regional Council of Governments (COG) is an agency providing many regional planning services to its member governments. Of the 39,000 local communities in the United States, more than 35,000 are served by regional councils.[5] Members include counties, cities, villages, townships, parishes, boroughs, intermediate school districts, community colleges, and public universities. Funding for the agencies comes from federal and state grants, contracts, and membership fees. Membership is voluntary, but requires that dues be paid to receive COG benefits.

A COG can support local government planning that emphasizes activities crossing jurisdictional boundaries, for example, transportation, environmental, community and economic development, education, and law enforcement. First conceived in the 1960s, regional councils are broad-based organizations that rely on consensus building to create partnerships, while providing a variety of services and fiscal management to their client communities. Regional councils often use a roundtable forum to resolve neighboring community conflicts. They mediate and facilitate, but do not adjudicate, and regardless of the interests and concerns of member communities, the authority to make policy decisions remains with local officials.

The Top of Alabama Regional Council of Governments (TARCOG) is an example of a COG. Established in 1968 in northern Alabama, its membership

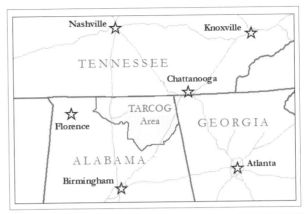

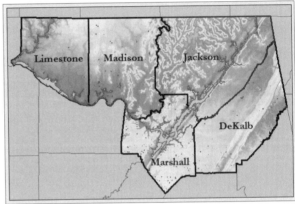

3.3. The Top of Alabama Regional Council of Governments

comprises local officials from a five-county region. TARCOG's Planning Department helps communities to develop their comprehensive plans. It conducts visioning and strategic planning studies pertaining to matters of regional interest. The organization's "Your Town Alabama" program provides an intensive training program for local officials, with case studies and interactive group problem-solving to help individuals become better prepared for decisionmaking in their communities.

### Metropolitan Planning Organizations (MPOs)

In 1962, Congress passed legislation mandating the formation of Metropolitan Planning Organizations (MPOs) to give local authorities more control over how federal transportation funds are spent in their jurisdictions. The legislation required that a designated MPO be established for any urbanized area with a population greater than 50,000. Congress created MPOs to ensure that transportation expenditures were based on a continuing, cooperative, and comprehensive ("3 C") planning process. Currently there are almost 400 MPOs in the United States.

Often, a region's COG agency serves as its MPO, since a COG usually is heavily involved in transportation planning. Statewide transportation offices sometimes have been reluctant to fully support the MPO structure because MPOs assume many of the responsibilities and funding formerly housed in the state agencies. However, as part of various federal transportation acts, beginning with the Intermodal Surface Transportation Efficiency Act (ISTEA) of 1991, transportation fund allocations were given to MPOs to administer, so state transportation departments, which now must consult with MPOs on many aspects of their work, lost autonomy.

### Consolidated Metro Governments

A number of regions have tried consolidated metro governments in which cities, counties, and townships function beneath one administrative umbrella. Examples of communities that established consolidated government structures include Miami–Dade County, Florida; Louisville–Jefferson County, Kentucky; Grand Rapids–Kent County, Michigan; Jacksonville–Duval County, Florida; Portland, Oregon's Metro Government; and Indianapolis–Marion County, Indiana.

### Spotlight on "Unigov" in Indianapolis

The city of Indianapolis and surrounding Marion County, Indiana, established a form of federated regional governance in 1970. Known as "Unigov," it is one of the most successful consolidated governments in the United States and its joint City–County Council has attracted significant economic growth and development in the Indianapolis metropolitan area.

Indiana Senator and former Indianapolis mayor Richard Lugar led the effort to bring community leaders and officials together to create this innovative approach to public sector management. Under the agreement, the city of Indianapolis expanded its boundaries to encompass all of Marion County, making it the twelfth largest city in the nation. Public offices and services that had been under many different agencies were combined for greater efficiency and easier public access. The restructuring into one municipal unit allowed the city to keep federal funding that would have been lost because of depopulation within the city at the time of

3.4. Downtown Indianapolis

Unigov's formation. (A few communities chose not to participate and retained their own mayors, councils, and boards, but are obligated to pay county taxes.)

Under Unigov, the mayor is the chief executive officer of both the city and the county. Five departments, Capital Asset Management (physical infrastructure), Metropolitan Development (code enforcement, planning and zoning, redevelopment and historic preservation), Public Works, Public Safety (police and fire departments, emergency management, animal control), and Parks and Recreation have their own directors. School districts remain independent, as do the airport authority and county library.

In addition to Unigov, the Indy Partnership, composed of government and business leaders from Indianapolis and its surrounding counties, provides coordination of economic development efforts in the region. The partnership promotes the central geographic position of the metro area, which contains about 75 percent of the U.S. and Canadian populations within a one-day (24-hour) drive. Indianapolis is the only U.S. city with four interstate highways coming to or through it, and it is one of the most affordable housing markets in the country.

## Local Planning

In most communities, the roles and responsibilities of planning are distributed among the municipal council, planning commission and planning department. An overview of each entity's involvement in the planning process is necessary to understand its function.

### The Municipal Council

Virtually all public policy within a community eventually passes through the hands of its municipal council. It provides leadership through its legislative, administrative, and financial power over city functions.

The council makes policy; other city agencies follow policy. In addition it administers local taxes, enacts ordinances and resolutions, exercises executive oversight regarding budget, and administers public services. It also engages in ceremonial duties.

**3.5. *City Council meeting, Sammamish, Washington***

A municipal council comprises elected representatives of the community. In small- and medium-sized cities and townships, councils typically include five to nine individuals. Council members usually are not trained for the job, although some may have occupied local government positions where they gained relevant experience. Because they are responsible directly to their constituency through the elective process, their actions may be based less on consistent policy than on political expediency.

Council members can be elected by ward (district) or at-large. The method of election influences how the board functions as a group and how individuals react as council members. Typically, ward-elected council members have a narrower view of their role in municipal government. In contrast, at-large council members represent the city as a whole and thus recognize a larger constituency. Certain communities have a combined board, with some members elected from districts and some elected at-large.

Typically, the head of the council (e.g., mayor, township supervisor, or county director) presides over council meetings and is elected either through the general election or by the council members. Alternatively, a chairperson may be elected from within the council. City governments may have a "strong mayor" or "weak

mayor" form of governance. A strong mayor plays a prominent administrative role as chief executive and often has a city manager and staff to serve the executive functions. Also, a strong mayor has the power to make appointments and dismissals without council approval and to veto legislation passed by the council. With a weak-mayor form of governance, the mayor has a largely ceremonial role, with the council possessing both legislative and executive authority. A weak mayor does not have veto power and needs council approval for appointments. Weak-mayor governance is more common in small towns.

### The Planning Commission

During the late nineteenth and early twentieth century, in many communities the development process had become unduly subject to pressures by political officials. Political bosses regularly awarded contracts as favors to private individuals to enhance their own re-election chances. Planning commissions were a response to these problems; they would reduce graft because they exist outside of the political structure.

During the 1930s, planning commissions assumed considerable power related to budgeting and planning of roads. By the 1950s, they had become integral to many housing programs. As Riverdale, Utah, stated in the description of its planning commission, "The major reason for establishing a Planning Commission of local citizens is because planning is too important to be left entirely to City staff. The Planning Commission represents the values and aspirations of citizens it serves."[6]

Planning commissioners are usually appointed by elected municipal officials. State enabling legislation often specifies the number of commissioners and their term. Most commissions comprise individuals from a variety of backgrounds, for example, attorneys, real estate agents, mechanics, architects, contractors, sales clerks, community leaders, retirees, and other local residents. Ideally, they should come from different geographical areas in the community and represent diverse groups. Planning commissioners, through their meetings, provide a forum for the public as part of the legally required development review process. The commission serves as the watchdog on the planning process and directly reflects the public's interests.

However, in recent decades the effectiveness of planning commissions has been questioned; commissioners can be subject to the same political pressures as council members. In some instances, commissions have been dissolved when their determinations conflicted with a council's preferences. Also, some critics argue that this extra layer of bureaucracy between the planning department staff and city council is unnecessary. However, many communities continue to rely on a local planning commission as part of their approval process for development proposals, and the planning commission remains an integral part of decisionmaking.

In some communities the planning commission is empowered to make final planning-related decisions; elsewhere they make recommendations to the governing council or board. Commissioners are most effective when they guide and review the direction and priorities of the planning department, but do not micromanage work. Commissioners may be "accommodators," who feel their role is to expedite the process of land use change and see that it operates as smoothly as possible, but ensure that technical qualities have been satisfied. Conversely the commissioners may be "reformists" who use their position to guide the city by supporting projects that they feel contribute to achieving ideal goals and impeding those which do not.[7]

A planning commission has five major functions:

*1. Satisfying the development review process required by law.* Many states and municipalities require commissioners to review all developments of a certain minimum size or scale. The commission must provide this official review and either approval or recommendation as part of the mandated process.

*2. Reviewing technical criteria determinations made by planning staff.* The planning department staff provides information related to codes, ordinances, and adopted plans, but planning commissioners give them definition and interpretation in light of community interests.

*3. Acting as an arbiter for planning staff, applicants, and citizens.* Sometimes a developer submits a development proposal that satisfies local criteria but concerned citizens oppose the project for a variety of reasons. The planning department may be obligated to recommend approval, since there is no basis for not doing so. Planning commissioners, however, are conscious of citizen concerns and arbitrate among these conflicting interests. Commissioners must realize they may be legally liable if they deny a project that meets all applicable requirements. However, they may choose to discuss the project with the applicant and try to mitigate the problem by encouraging at least some accommodation to the citizens' concerns. This process of mitigation is an important part of the commission's overall role.

*4. Adjusting the review process to local political realities.* Commissioners also should recognize that, to a significant extent, planning is tied to the local political process. Being actively involved in community life, commissioners sometimes can provide methods for resolving conflicting interests through personal persuasion.

*5. Evaluating the planning director.* The director of the planning department is responsible for the work of the staff planners, but the commission's responsibility may include review and evaluation of the planning director.

### The Planning Department

The planning department provides technical advice to elected officials, appointed commissioners, city departments, and residents to help them better understand their community's comprehensive plan, zoning ordinance, and other documents that pertain to community development. Cities with a population over 25,000 generally are large enough to have a planning staff. Smaller communities may have only one or two planners. When there is no planning department, planning-related activities may be contracted to a private planning consultant. Consultants may also be used in larger departments if the governing body needs special expertise or legal input.

A planning director oversees planning department employees. The director coordinates in-house work and must possess a broad knowledge of planning, be able to delegate work to staff, and communicate effectively. Planning staff members may be generalists or specialize in a particular area, such as site plan review, economic development, mapping and graphics, grant preparation, data management and projections, or other needs. Staff planners interact with community leaders and citizens by gathering and providing information, answering questions, and making presentations. These responsibilities result in written reports and recommendations.

Depending on the priorities of a community, the work of the planning department can cover a wide range of activities. Some planning units may be part of a larger management department that includes environmental specialists, building inspectors, code enforcement personnel, and possibly civil engineers. In these cases, the department may have a more all-encompassing name, such as the Department of Community Development and Planning or the Department of Planning and Environment.

Five key responsibilities are allocated to the planning staff; these activities often require interaction with other city departments:

1. *Maintain/update the comprehensive plan and coordinate city planning efforts.* The comprehensive plan guides growth and development of the community. It is a constantly evolving document and should be maintained and updated on a regular basis. If used properly, it can steer the disparate interests of a community in a common direction.

2. *Provide planning recommendations to the planning commission.* Planning commissioners need good information to make informed judgments on planning and development proposals that are presented to them for review, recommendation, and possibly for approval. The planning department staff is in the best position to provide this information, which may consist of a review of codes, regulations, policies, and goals from the comprehensive plan, and other information useful to guide new development.

3. *Supply information to the community's elected officials and the public.* Planning staff members provide information to planning commissioners, council members, other city agencies, and the general public. The department's files, archives, and resources should include planning documents and policies, pertinent legislation, demographics, maps, geographic information system (GIS) files and databases, current and previous development proposals, and other materials related to the community's patterns of growth and development.

4. *Prepare the capital improvements program and budget.* One of a community's most important documents is the capital improvements program because it allocates financial resources for future development. The five- to seven-year span of the budget establishes priorities for spending public funds, and private investment in a community is closely linked to public expenditures. Community budget allocations can potentially leverage significant amounts of private investment as part of a public–private partnership.

5. *Facilitate interdepartmental cooperation.* The planning department coordinates development activities in municipal government. This oversight function can give a broader, long-range perspective to decisions than may be seen by elected officials, who commonly base decisions on the two- to four-year time frame inherent in the election cycle. The planning department facilitates interdepartmental cooperation and coordinates information needed for decisions on development in the community.

## The Politics of Local Planning

Planners need to recognize that understanding local politics and functioning within a political environment is a necessary part of their job. Planner Melvin Webber once said of the profession, "there are no scientifically or technically correct answers, only politically appropriate ones."[8] For many, "politics" is a dirty word spoken

*3.6. Information counter at Placer County Planning Department, Tahoe City, California*

*3.7. Village Politics, engraving by Paul-Leon Jazet, 1820*

with disdain. Definitions of the term range widely, but it may be defined as the art of consensus building to gain and maintain power. Politics is inescapable in the way we make collective decisions, including planning decisions, in the United States. For purposes of this discussion, it is essential to establish three simple ground rules. First, in the interplay between planning and politics, all actions must be legal. Second, politics is neither positive nor negative; it is simply the process used to build consensus and gain power. *How* individuals exercise their individual political power may be positive or negative, but that does not make politics in itself either positive or negative. Finally, it is okay to say the words "planning," "politics," and "power" in the same sentence. All are important to the planning process and it is important to define them and explore their connotations.

### A Balanced Approach to Planning

One of the foundations of American society is an abiding distrust in how government works. That distrust is part of the essence of the Constitution and was a guiding principle in the Declaration of Independence. The ownership, transfer, and use of land are equally important issues in the founding of the United States. It is in this context that a planning system evolved that seeks to balance protection of individual liberties with those of the collective whole. Planning is done for several reasons, but fundamentally it serves to balance continued economic growth and development (jobs, tax base, economic vitality) with social and natural environmental concerns (quality of life, the preservation and protection of natural resources). The goal is to optimize this balance through the planning process.

Citizens want to protect their interests regarding land ownership and use while constraining or minimizing the public interest in limiting those individual rights. In this context, planning can be understood as a check on the perceived and real excesses of the political process and a balance to the short-term focus

of political decisions. For this reason, it is important to observe how the planning and political processes relate, differ, and conflict. The business of both planning and politics is conducted by participants who typically include:

| | |
|---|---|
| planners | banks/financial policymakers |
| planning commissions | public administrators |
| elected officials | attorneys/legal professionals |
| zoning boards of appeal | the press |
| realtors | developers/builders |
| special interest groups | designers |
| other communities | autonomous boards |
| other governments | the general public |

These participants are independent and largely self-serving and they work to ensure that the political and planning processes benefit them, or at least do not harm them. They possess varying degrees of power, which they may or may not use to influence the planning and political processes. Planners are important in this process, but they are only one of many interest groups.

When considering the interplay between politics and planning, three significant, divergent perspectives point to why planning is conflict-laden: timeframe, compromise, and public interest. Given the usual two- or four-year election cycle, elected officials in the United States need to show that their decisions have produced results in a short time, typically within a one- to three-year period if they wish to be re-elected. This short time frame does not coincide with the need for long-term evaluation of the impact that short-term decisions have on the development of a community.

In contrast to the short-term political calendar, traditional planning is a decidedly long-term endeavor. Planners create plans for 10, 15, or 20 years into the future. They are concerned with the implications of current

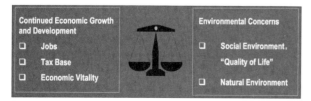

3.8. *The balance of planning*

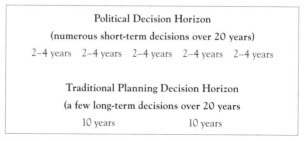

3.9. *Comparison of planning and political decision horizons*

decisions on the long-range development of communities and on constituents who range from those not yet born to the dying. This means there is a significant disconnect between the short-term decision making world of elected officials and the evaluation of the impact of those decisions over a longer time period. This becomes the basis for conflict between planners and elected officials, and a justification for a community to engage in planning.

Elected officials need to compromise. An urban planning legend illustrates this: A wise old politician once chastised a young planner after a particularly ugly public hearing on a controversial planning decision. After a night of discord and negative public comment, the elected official was overheard to say, "Never, never, never put a politician in a corner." Elected officials need to be flexible in their responses to community decisionmaking, since they represent their constituents' differing perspectives. They seldom have the luxury of working with issues that are black and white; they struggle to find a reasonable middle ground.

Planners and elected officials both wish to serve the public interest. The questions are: What is in the public interest and how is that determined? As we have noted, elected officials tend to use constituent responses as the basis to define public interest and seek immediate public feedback to gauge what people want. Planners, however, use a number of methods to engage and solicit public input: public hearings, focus groups, surveys, committees, and planning programs. As a result, planners and elected officials often irritate each other and, in short, generate conflict.

What is to be done? The key for elected officials is to use the planning process to gain an expanded perspective on their decisions, one that includes constituents and an appreciation of the impacts of current decisions on the fabric of a community. Conversely, planners should realize the need to provide local officials with a range of planning strategies and give them the flexibility they want while trying to move them toward long-range planning objectives. There is no single way to achieve planning goals; it is only through the political process that those goals ultimately can be accomplished.

*Influence Makers*
In many communities, the truly influential people are not always the apparent, designated decisionmakers.

Sometimes individuals with the most influence have no official title, but exert considerable control. The question of the true power of community decisionmaking was described by sociologist Floyd Hunter. Hunter studied social dynamics in Atlanta, Georgia, and found a small, stable group at the top of the city's social structure. Although this group's decisionmaking role was not known to the public, the individuals, singly or collectively, were responsible for much of what was done or not done in their community. This influential group consisted primarily of major business owners, executives, and corporate lawyers. They lived in the same neighborhoods, belonged to the same clubs, sat on each other's boards, and knew each other well. A follow-up study of Atlanta by Clarence Stone showed that the political structure worked to aid this alliance of business interests while discouraging and fragmenting neighborhood groups: "What makes governance in Atlanta effective is not the formal machinery of government, but rather the informal partnership between city hall and the downtown business elite. This informal partnership and the way it operates constitute the city's regime; it is the means through which major policy decisions are made."[9] Later studies by others supported and generalized this finding. Informal alliances behind the scenes tend to be most concerned about issues of growth and development.

Although their influence can be broad, large cities may have more than one pyramid of influence makers. Each group may be oriented toward different issues, but each nonetheless comprises a select and largely inbred group of powerbrokers.

## The Role of the Public in the Planning Process

Public input is a mandated part of the decisionmaking process of local government, and a public hearing provides officials with the information they need to make fair and informed decisions. A public hearing should not be conducted to persuade the public or to justify an action. This would mean a decision had been made before the public had a chance to express opinions on the issue. As Supreme Court Justice Louis Brandeis once said about deliberations on public law, "Since government is not an exact science, prevailing public opinion concerning the evils and the remedy is among the important facts deserving consideration."[10]

# Public Meeting

**Your opinion is requested...**
**on the reuse of the Navy Marine Center,**
**located in the 600 block of Kenhorst Blvd**
*(across from the State Police Barracks)*
**Thursday, June 11th**
**7 p.m.**
**7th Day Adventist Church**
*Fellowship Room in the lower level*
*Parking is available in the lot behind the church*

The City of Reading Local Redevelopment Authority (LRA) is holding a public meeting on Thursday, June 11th at 7 p.m. for presentations on the proposed reuse of the Navy Marine Center by the Reading School District, Reading Hospital and Berks Women in Crisis-Mary's Shelter. The LRA will also be presenting the first draft of the proposed reuse plan.

The Navy Marine Center was decommissioned in 2005 and the Navy will be moving out by the end of 2010. The Reading LRA needs to learn what type of new use you would favor and what type of new use would support the best interests of your family and your neighborhood.

For more information contact the
City Council Office at (610) 655-6204
or council@readingpa.org

3.10. Notice of public hearing for Local Redevelopment Authority in Reading, Pennsylvania, 2010

Public hearings must be advertised well in advance and are intended to allow the community an opportunity to speak to local officials before final action is taken. "Open meetings" law refers to the body of legislation mandating that the public be able to observe the workings of the government and prevent the deliberate exclusion of the public from this process. This means that decisions should not be made behind closed doors. For these purposes, a meeting is defined as any occasion when there is a convening of a public body for the purpose of conducting public business. There are some exceptions, such as the meeting of charity organizations. Also, public bodies may go into a closed executive session to discuss and act on certain issues, such as threats to public safety, imperiling the investigation or prosecution of a criminal process, matters relating to individual employees and their records, the buying or selling of real property, and other topics as specifically allowed. Legally, decisions made by a local government that do not follow procedures of the applicable open meetings act may be

challenged and possibly overturned in court, so prudent planners read their state's Open Meetings Act. Public input traditionally has been gained by conducting meetings in an accessible venue, but new technologies such as e-mail and the Internet offer citizens alternative ways to be heard.

Like the Open Meetings Act, the Freedom of Information Act (FOIA) promotes transparency in government by allowing citizens access to government records and information. Although government agencies generally are more comfortable if their actions are not fully exposed to the public, assurances of open government have existed in common law since the colonial period and access has increased in recent decades. All agencies of the federal government now are required to disclose records upon written request unless exempted for reasons of national security. States have similar provisions through their open records laws. Each state has a list of appropriate exemptions.

## Community Activism

Community residents are primarily concerned about quality-of-life issues, especially the impact changes may have on residential areas. Although residents have no direct day-to-day role in the decisionmaking process, their input can be effective in two ways: by expressing their opinions at the public hearings required for most large development projects and by electing local government officials who respect their opinions and respond to their concerns. Through sheer numbers, residents have an important role to play in community development decisions. As Jane Jacobs wrote, "Meaningful change doesn't come about through lots of clout and lots of money. It comes about through lots of little changes everywhere."[11]

Barbara Roelofs, a long-time community activist in Grand Rapids, Michigan, has suggested how residents can be effective in presenting their viewpoint and be successful in the political environment of local government.[12] When addressing the community, she says, first be absolutely convinced you are right, since this conviction influences your actions and instills confidence in yourself and the person with whom you are talking. Second, do your homework; become informed so you know more than the opposition. Third, be present when policy decisions are being made. Make clear that you are recording the discussion, either through use of a recorder or note taking. Fourth, learn to count votes and know whom to approach to solicit support. Fifth, develop personal skills of persuasion and never be intimidated by the responses, or even threats, of others. Finally, be willing to make friends with local officials and compromise when it is appropriate. Other tactics include learning to use publicity to your advantage and loading your organization's board with attorneys, since they best understand how to maneuver through the difficult currents that are part of governmental decision-making. She emphasizes honesty in these strategies; dishonesty will catch up with you.

### Community Surveys

One of the most common and best methods for local planners to gain useful public input is to conduct a survey. Surveys can be administered to residents, merchants, local officials, or others (all included in the term "respondents") to gain important perspectives. Surveys can elicit useful information on public attitudes and opinions, typically providing original (raw) information and data not available from any other source. These will help to establish effective policies.

*Survey Types.* Mail surveys have certain advantages. They tend to be less expensive than other types because they do not require person-to-person contact to administer. Mail surveys allow respondents to take as long to complete as they wish. A mailed package can include background material useful in educating respondents before they complete the survey. The wording of questions is important to gain accurate information. On the downside, mail surveys generally get a lower rate of response than other kinds of survey, which subjects them to nonrespondent bias.

Telephone surveys traditionally have been effective for polling a cross-section of the population. Telephone surveys usually are conducted by trained interviewers who read questions according to a script. The script can target certain types of respondents and the interviewer can probe deeper if respondents fit a prescribed profile. Companies with large banks of phones specifically for this purpose conduct computerized interviewing service on a contract basis to groups and organizations. However, as cell phones supplant land lines, reaching residents at their home phones is not as reliable a sur-

*3.11. Conducting a telephone survey*

vey method as it once was, and caller IDs can hinder contact.

The most effective and informative surveys occur with in-person contact. Although such surveys tend to be expensive and time-consuming, skillful face-to-face interviewers can elicit information in much greater depth and with more flexibility than mail or phone surveys. In-person interviews can be conducted with focus groups if a group response is desired.

Online surveys are becoming more in vogue but suffer bias as well. Both e-mail surveys and Internet surveys can be efficient ways to obtain information, but they require hardware and software and, of course, can be conducted only with respondents who have access to computers. If you have e-mail addresses for the survey group, e-mail surveys are quick to prepare, inexpensive to administer, and require little setup. However, they must be written in a format that can be read by different e-mail servers. E-mail surveys typically work well with cohort groups (e.g., interoffice staff members) who are accustomed to responding to e-mail. Although they take more knowledge and experience to create, Internet surveys allow more flexibility in formatting and may include graphics and even sound. They are easy to update or modify as needed and can be revised by the surveyor quickly. Research indicates that people not only give more honest answers to an electronic survey than to a mail survey, but that Internet surveys also yield higher response rates.[13]

*Basic Principles of Good Surveys.* A survey questionnaire should begin with a brief introduction indicating who is sponsoring and conducting the survey, explaining how the information will be used, and informing respondents that their views will be kept confidential. The first question is one of the most critical because it establishes whether a person is likely to continue and complete the survey. A good first question for a recreation survey might be: "Do you feel that the community provides enough recreational facilities for your family's needs? Indicate your level of satisfaction: __Very satisfied; __Somewhat satisfied; __Somewhat unsatisfied; __Very unsatisfied."

A good survey should have the following characteristics:

*Clarity.* Avoid questions with double meanings. For example, if the recreation survey could ask, "Do you find bikes in the neighborhood objectionable? __Yes; __No," this could be confusing since the term "bikes" may indicate either bicycles or motorcycles. A pretest of the survey should indicate whether questions are ambiguous. Do not rely on hypothetical questions, such as, "If such and such, then would you . . . ?" These require assumptions that may be inappropriate for the respondent. Do not combine two questions in one. For example, the question "Do you use city facilities or go elsewhere for recreation?" does not allow a simple yes/no answer and the respondent may utilize both places or neither. Avoid technical jargon and define uncommon terms. Avoid leading questions, loaded words, and authoritative statements and questions that can be answered "I don't know." Formulate questions that ask for the respondent's opinion, rather than fact. Instead of asking, "Is the downtown park a dangerous place at night?" ask, "Do you think the downtown park is a dangerous place at night?"

*Brevity.* Survey questions should be as concise as possible. For example, the question: "Many people in the city have recreational vehicles. It would be helpful for the city to know how many are owned and used by its residents. How many recreational vehicles are owned by individuals in the household where you live?" would be phrased better as: "How many recreational vehicles are owned by individuals in your household?"

*Completeness.* Multiple-choice answers can be confusing if they do not include all possibilities, as in this example: "When do you make most use of the community's recreation facilities? __Spring; __Summer; __Warm months; __Cold months." A better question would be: "Indicate the seasons when you most often use the community's parks and recreation facilities (check as many as appropriate): __Spring; __Summer; __Fall; __Winter."

### EXERCISE 2
### PREPARE A SURVEY OF DOWNTOWN SHOPPERS FOR RIVERTOWN

*Rivertown's merchants are concerned that downtown does not attract enough shoppers for the economic vitality of its businesses. The Rivertown Merchants Association has asked the city to survey residents about downtown shopping. You have been given the task of preparing the survey.*

*Compose an effective downtown shopping survey to distribute to a random sample of city residents. It should consist of no more than eight questions; pretest it by administering it on a trial basis to eight individuals who assume the role of Rivertown residents and answer the questions from their point of view. The answers will be fictional, but can indicate important information on whether the survey would be effective in an actual situation. After the survey, ask the pretest respondents: Were the questions clear or confusing? Did you have any concern about giving the type of information requested?*

*Based on the feedback, revise the survey and prepare a brief report on the relative effectiveness of the survey questions.*

### Planning and Communication via the Internet

Information is a valuable commodity in our society. The input of a huge volume of incoming information in hard-copy format is a critical bottleneck for cities. In an average city, thousands of objects (land parcels, persons, buildings, pipes, trees, fire hydrants, etc.) must be described in millions of terms (factual information, shape, position, temporal change, etc.). Many data are collected on paper forms, which are expensive to process, time-consuming, and hard to locate.

With the transition from paper-based analog information systems to digital information systems, the ability of planners to evaluate information will gain in speed and efficiency. Planners who collect, analyze, synthesize, and evaluate information in a timely fashion are likely to have an advantage in problem solving. A digital environment makes these tasks much easier. However, it must satisfy some important criteria to be useful for planning and city governance. The hardware, software, and connectivity must be readily accessible and affordable. Online information technology must be standardized for use by all computers and operating systems to serve the public effectively. Procedures and protocols for management are vital so users searching for information, even residents with a minimum of computer experience, can find it easily.

As a result of the increasing use of the Internet, it is important, even critical, for communities to become more reliant on online resources for local government functions. Many such resources are available, and most communities now have web sites with descriptive information. However, there are many resources available in the online environment not being utilized by local officials and residents. Part of the reluctance to rely on the Internet for local government functions is the fact there are many disparate formats, sometimes requiring a lengthy learning curve. There is a great need to create a network for providing applications with interfaces that are more standardized, interactive, linked, and user-friendly.

The Internet can serve as an important means to create greater participation in the decisionmaking process and may bring more accountability into public discussion. Online communication increases the circle of participation and understanding. A public system should include a means to provide imagery, including a wide variety of images that illustrate the effects of the various choices. Digital photos and three-dimensional models can show before-and-after effects, provide historic annotation of past events, and create three-dimensional representations of future events. Programs to promote user education and increased information literacy should be provided throughout the community.

## Summary

All levels of government are involved with community planning, either directly or indirectly. Historically, the power to govern was given first to state governments, which over time have given certain powers and responsibilities to both the federal and local levels. State governments are major landowners and have the legal authority to control land use. However, they are usually considered too large to manage local planning, and have deferred to local governments many of these responsibilities.

The federal government has a role in planning because it is a major landowner and it is responsible for broad policies and programs on natural resources, economic development funding, and physical infrastructure (such as interstate highways). Attempts in the past to develop significant national planning often have been thwarted by people who question the political motives underlying such efforts.

Regional governments, such as Councils of Governments and others, comprise groups of counties and municipalities within counties, and frequently function as educational, advisory, and coordinating bodies. They typically have less regulatory authority.

Most community planning is done at the level of local government. The responsibility for local planning and its regulation (e.g., zoning) is transferred from states to local officials through enabling legislation. Actions taken by elected and appointed local officials are noticed readily by their constituents and provide a check against improper activities and policies.

At the local level, planning responsibilities are distributed between the municipal council, planning commission, and planning department or staff. The municipal council establishes public policy and provides leadership, administrative, and financial authority. A

*3.12. Using the Internet for city functions*

community's planning commission represents the public perspective in the planning process. Its planning staff or planning consultant is responsible for its comprehensive plan and coordination of planning activities at the local level.

Politics plays an important role in planning, and planners need to recognize the impact of influence makers on decisions. The public also has an important role in the planning process. Planners make an important contribution toa furthering this understanding by the ways they interact with the residents of their community.

The public needs to be fully involved in the planning process. Important input can be gained through community surveys. Internet technology provides new and innovative methods to communicate with constituents.

Section 2

# ELEMENTS OF
# THE COMPREHENSIVE PLAN

# 4

# THE COMPREHENSIVE PLAN

## Overview of the Comprehensive Plan

Planning and creating a great, even a good, community is a process that involves many people and institutions over a long period of time. Communities are not created whole, and some of our best cities were previously some of the worst. They have benefited from a long process of continuous planning as well as simple trial and error. Bad areas have been removed or replaced, good areas reinforced, and gradually cities emerged, functioning well at the physical, social, and economic levels. As law professor and real estate authority Charles Haar put it, the comprehensive plan is a form of "impermanent constitution," indicating it is a document that should undergo revision continually as the community changes. It can be viewed as both a process and a product.[1] With this perspective its usefulness is properly realized.

The plan primarily guides land uses but its scope can extend to other aspects of community life. A properly prepared and executed comprehensive plan should be internally consistent, with each of its sections complementing and reinforcing the others. The plan serves a number of purposes. It gives direction for positive change and indicates how much and what kind of development is appropriate. It provides local officials with day-to-day guidance in the development process and examines the impact of changes over time. For example, a transportation department can plan a community's circulation system based on expected future growth, or developers and builders can propose projects compatible with the goals of the plan. The plan should also serve as a guide for related actions, such as zoning ordinances, subdivision regulations, and the community's capital improvements program. Finally, the plan

helps local citizens understand proposed changes and put them in the proper context. The planning department and planning commission, the mayor or supervisor, and the municipal council should refer to the comprehensive plan regularly; even the best plan is of no use if left on the shelf.

After a comprehensive plan has been prepared, the municipal council may adopt it or accept it. Adoption means the plan and its policies are recognized as an official program for action. Acceptance, in contrast, is not legally binding and indicates simply that the council acknowledges the plan and must decide whether its provisions should be supported through other documents and policies. In many states, the plan is a legal prerequisite for regulatory statutes, including adoption of a zoning ordinance, a historic district ordinance, a capital improvements program, or a growth management program. Although a community's comprehensive plan is not a land use regulation or ordinance, courts of law may consider it in deciding a case, so its provisions can have legal implications.

Comprehensive plans can be created in various forms. Many communities prepare their comprehensive plan as a single document composed of a series of sections describing various elements. Other communities develop a comprehensive plan that consists of a series of documents, each considering in depth one particular issue, such as housing or transportation. This series-of-documents approach means the entire plan does not need to be written and accepted as a whole, but can be approved incrementally whenever a particular aspect of it is timely. The comprehensive plan may further include subarea (or small-area) plans that pertain to areas or districts within the community and address the specific needs of that geographic district. Subarea plans are most useful in large jurisdictions where districts are subject to considerable change.

## Creating the Comprehensive Plan

Comprehensive plans typically are developed using the traditional or rational planning process, a step-by-step procedure illustrated in the diagram below. It begins with the decision to plan and ends with implementation and review.

The decision to create or revise a plan involves the support of the community's elected officials and its planners. Although a comprehensive plan may have a 20-year horizon, budgetary allocation should be made to update it on a regular basis, generally every 5 to 10 years. The creation of a comprehensive plan, as well as the updating and amending of it, is typically the responsibility of a community's planning department or planning board. The community's legislative body should support the process and allow staff or consultant time for its preparation.

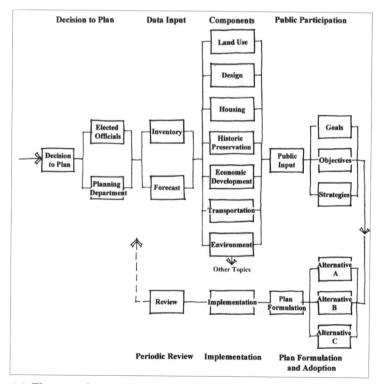

*4.1. The comprehensive plan process*

### Inventory of Existing Conditions

Before a community can map a route to its future, it must identify its current situation. To make intelligent decisions, officials need to have a firm grasp of both their community's assets and its weaknesses; this is sometimes referred to as "asset mapping." Planners have the responsibility to collect and document an inventory of existing resources and facilities to serve as a base for the plan. They create maps to show the geographic distribution of resources and possible areas for future growth. Some of the data, such as soil types and land contours, remain constant over time, but much important data—for example, demographics, traffic statistics, or land uses—can change significantly, especially during periods of rapid community growth.

Needed information can be collected from a variety of sources. The first step is to determine what data are needed to avoid wasting time. Facts gathered from any available source without determining their usefulness (data fishing) not only wastes staff time but can also result in establishing improper priorities based on data that are available, rather than those that are germane. Establish beforehand what data are needed, and if not available directly, use proxy information as a substitute.

The data most commonly needed by communities include demographic information; employment; housing (type and number) and residential districts; land use and growth; transportation systems; water, sewer, and storm water facilities; parks, open space, and recreation; schools and libraries (even though they may be autonomous authorities); historic districts; and police, fire, hospital, and emergency medical services.

How are such data used? As an example, assume you wish to compare home sales in your community with national trends. You could begin by accessing the U.S. Census Bureau's information on new home sales and inventory nationally. Then you could collect data for local home sales by reviewing recent reports and studies prepared by the city and outside consultants. Additionally, you could consult local and state libraries, state agencies, and universities. Bear in mind that not all information sources are reliable, so you'll need to verify their validity. A good rule of thumb is to accept data if they appear in two distinct sources, that is, as long as one source is not the basis for the other. Once you are confident that your numbers are valid, you can compare national information with state or local information to determine whether your community is faring better or worse than the national average. Then you can take appropriate action.

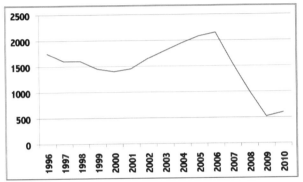

4.2. *New home construction based on permits and starts (in 1000s)*

A final word: When preparing data to present, use a consistent format that is easy for the general public to understand. It is helpful to convert numerical data to graphs and charts. Remember to compare apples to apples: if timelines from one source present data on a two-year basis, then ensure that other data appear in two-year increments as well.

### Demographics

Demographics is defined as the characteristics and statistics of human population. It is important to planners because it denotes a community's population growth or decline, densities, distributions, mobility, residents' ages, gender, and other useful information. Demographic analyses can show how populations have changed in the past and allow planners to project what they are likely to be in the future. Demographic data are important in creating comprehensive plans, developing relevant policies, conducting opinion research, and other planning-related activities. Although demographic analysis relies on many types of data, it relies on four basic rules.

*Rule 1: If you weren't born, you don't count.* Demographers look at fertility statistics to understand the relative growth in population. Thus, if a certain number of babies are born in a given year, it can reliably be predicted that

an estimated number of children will be entering kindergarten in five years (setting aside other factors, such as families moving). The fertility rates of women relate directly to other statistical categories.

*Rule 2: Some people have more children than others.* There has been a long-term trend in the United States toward smaller families. The number of women in the 20- to 35-year-old group is the best indicator of population growth. In the post–World War II period of the 1950s, the average fertility rate was 3.8 children per woman, raising serious concerns about providing resources and services for young families. In 2009, the fertility rate averaged 2.0 (this varies depending on ethnic and racial groups), meaning the demand for services for each household is significantly less. To interpret this in terms of planning policies, if a community has a growing population, coupled with smaller family size, a significant increase in the demand for housing units and services can be anticipated and should be considered in any planning effort.

*Rule 3: Some people live longer than others.* A significant demographic trend is the increase in elderly population in the United States. The number of persons aged 65 and older is expected to increase from 1 in 8 in 2000 to 1 in 5 in 2030. As the baby-boomer generation reaches retirement age, planning and policies need to shift to accommodate needs and concerns of this large cohort group. Many of them will seek a warm place to spend the winter, and they will need ready access to medical services. The oldest segment of our population, those who are 85 years and older, is the fastest growing. The aging of America has been called "the most important trend of our time."[2]

*Rule 4: Some people move more often than others.* The

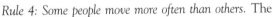
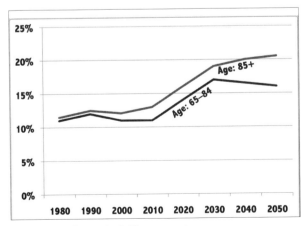

4.3. *Projected growth of older generation*

United States has a mobile population. Ties of citizens to their place of birth are not as strong as they were in the past. Migration patterns, and how they shift from decade to decade based on economics, climate, social patterns, and transportation changes, must be part of a relevant comprehensive plan. Issues include not only how many people are moving in or out of a community, but what types of groups, and in what ages and socioeconomic categories. For example, individuals in the 20 to 35 age group are the most likely to move, while those over 55 move much less frequently.

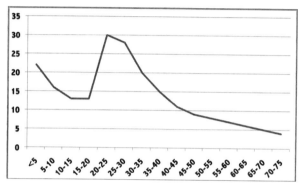

*4.4. Annual migration rates by age, 2004–2005*

One of the most distinctive population shifts over the past two centuries is migration from rural to urban areas. The greatest population growth in the U.S. in the twentieth century occurred in the suburbs. Central cities stayed largely the same in size (although this varied greatly from city to city). Nonmetropolitan areas decreased in population for most of the century and more markedly beginning around 1960.

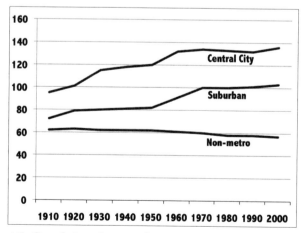

*4.5. Growth in urban population in the United States (in millions)*

The combined urban-suburban population in the U.S. has grown from under 10 percent of the total population in 1800 to over 80 percent in 2009. This rural to urban migration has been largely the result of a push-pull effect. Families have been pushed off the farms by agricultural industrialization and the replacement of human labor by large tractors, combines, and other equipment that can do the work of numerous traditional farmers. The pull is represented by economic opportunities available in urban areas, where there are more types of jobs for workers at all levels and where educational opportunities, medical care, and varied cultural resources are available.

### Using Census Data

The Bureau of the Census in the U.S. Department of Commerce has a constitutional responsibility to enumerate the population and housing of the United States every 10 years. On census day the Bureau conducts the census, counting all people and recording where they are living, with information about housing and economics. It asks every citizen the same core questions at the same time, making comparisons in data relatively easy and productive. Survey questions may change from census to census. For example, specific groups may press to add questions based on their special interests, and sometimes questions are dropped when they are no longer deemed relevant, for example, the number of telephones per household.

The Census Bureau has an annual budget of over $800 million used to gather and disseminate a huge quantity of information. Local planners seldom examine data that are much beyond their community, although data on Standard Metropolitan Areas provide information that places the local community in a regional context; this information is especially useful for planners working in COG offices.

The Census Bureau also makes available other data useful to planners—business trade and services, agriculture, construction and housing, economics, manufacturing and mineral industries, transportation, and others. The wealth of raw data can be interpreted to discern local, regional, and national trends, and provides a way to plan more effectively for the future.

The decennial census is the primary tool used to redraw political boundaries for voting. Based on population information, states or bipartisan commissions redistrict their electoral and constituent boundaries to rebalance congressional districts. Planners work within the political environment, so such changes can have significant impacts on community decisionmaking. Sometimes this process becomes highly politicized, with the party in power manipulating boundaries to gain political advantage, a process known as gerrymandering.

*Census tracts.* Census tracts are bounded areas created to include populations of approximately 3,000 to 6,000 people who generally possess homogeneous characteristics. Each tract is given a number to identify it within a city or rural area. Arterial roads or significant geographic features, for example, a river or major street, often border tracts. Tracts typically are the most valuable level of quantitative information for urban and rural planners.

Planners can extract from census tracts population data by gender and age cohort groups. If planners determine that a new local industry will cause the population to exceed 9,000 citizens, for example, it may prompt local government officials to recommend splitting the affected census tract into two separate divisions to achieve the preferred population size. Tract number xx would be renumbered xx.01 and xx.02. Retaining the original census boundary in some form makes it possible to compare subsequent data to those from previous decades. In rural areas a census tract may coincide with a township boundary, but if adjoining townships are sparsely populated, two or three of them may be combined to create one census tract.

Public sector officials and staff are not the only users of census tract data. Major business owners or marketing companies use these data, combined with transportation maps and locations of competitive businesses, to determine the best location for a large grocery store or shopping mall, for example.

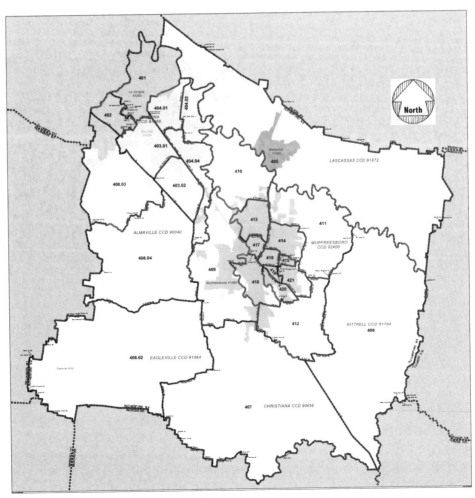

4.6. *Census tracts, Rutherford County, Tennessee*

**4.7. Sample TIGER/Line file comparing the Census Bureau TIGER road file and parcel-level data for Richland County, South Carolina**

*TIGER/Line files.* TIGER/Line files were developed by the Census Bureau as a way of providing a digitized database for geographic features such as roads, rivers, lakes, and legal and statistical boundaries. TIGER (Topologically Integrated Geographic Encoding and Referencing) files are available for the entire U.S. and provide a consistent format for many uses. A TIGER database includes information such as latitude and longitude, name and type of feature (e.g., road name), addresses for most streets, and other related information. The most recent version is the 2004 Second Edition TIGER/Line Files.

The files are not graphic images of maps, but are created through digitized data that describe geographic features. The Census Bureau uses such files to map their decennial census information and ensure there is no duplication of collected data. The maps, files, and data are also used by many local governments, agencies, and offices. Although available to the public, users must have GIS software that can import TIGER/Line file data.

## Forecasting

Forecasting is important to the comprehensive planning process. An inventory of existing conditions is important for making reasonable projections about how conditions may change, especially in the near future. The role of forecasting can be divided into three time horizons:

- Long range: more than four years (the election cycle for most local decision-makers)
- Short range: within one year
- Mid range: between long-range and short-range: over one year and less than four years

The most popular techniques for forecasting include trend analysis, cohort survival forecasting, housing needs projections, and small area forecasting.

*Trend analysis.* Trend analysis extrapolates the future by looking at past trends. It is based on the idea that the rate of past changes is likely to continue in the future, at least until a new trend emerges. In the example, population has been increasing at a steady rate over recent decades. Assuming that future growth will continue at about the same rate, the graph uses trend analysis and depicts a forecast of population levels projected out to the year 2020.

The limitation of trend analysis is that the future does not always follow the past. When a major change occurs, a tipping point can be reached, and the rate of growth or change can shift quickly. The trajectory of the curve may be altered significantly for many reasons. For example, when a major employer locates in a community, both employment and housing may increase significantly. New technologies can also alter growth patterns. For example, the development of air conditioning allowed residents in sunbelt cities like Phoenix, Arizona, to live comfortably even during very hot weather, contributing to a much faster rate of growth there compared to the national average.

Trend analysis uses aggregate data—data collected as a whole, rather than being broken into composite parts. Such information is general and may not indicate reasons causing a trend. More accurate forecasting rises from data broken into their component elements. Such disaggregated data are useful in cohort survival forecasting, which separates population information into various categories.

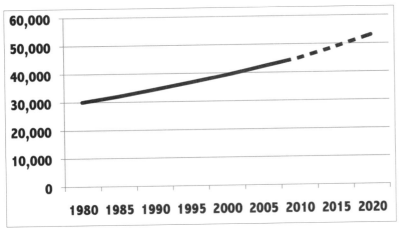

*4.8. Trend analysis applied to population growth for a hypothetical community*

*Cohort survival forecasting.* As noted, population changes happen through births, deaths, in-migration, out-migration, or combinations of these events. We can find which of these will have the most impact on population growth in a community by looking at it in terms of cohort groups. Cohort survival forecasting brings more detailed analysis to population change by subdividing the population according to age and gender. A large increase among the young married-with-children cohort will have very different implications from an increase among the middle-aged empty-nest cohort. A community should adjust its plans for provided services accordingly. The cohort survival method of forecasting is especially appropriate in larger communities, where census data are readily available in sufficient detail. In smaller communities, trend analysis probably is sufficient.

*Housing needs projections.* Housing is an important component of the comprehensive plan. To estimate future housing needs simply divide the projected annual population by the average population size per household. For example, if the population in five years is projected to be 60,000 and the average household has three individuals, the community would need 20,000 dwelling units. If 19,000 units were currently available, 1,000 new units would be needed in five years. This calculation is rough; a more accurate calculation would include the loss of some currently existing housing. Other considerations should include the types of housing needed (e.g., small apartments or larger single-family homes), the ability of local residents to buy or rent, and vacancy rates,

since not all housing units are filled all the time.

*Small Area Forecasting (SAF).* Small Area Forecasting (SAF) is a policy-planning model that evaluates the relationship of government policy to forecasts, and ultimately to costs and revenues, in smaller areas. Various policy alternatives are explored in terms of their potential growth and costs. Each is coupled with a forecast model to derive evaluation measures. This process of coupling growth scenarios with policy implications encourages public administrators to be part of the planning process.

The model in Fig. 4.9 exemplifies various growth scenarios based on government policies. Policy A describes a scenario where the local government encourages maximum growth, agreeing to expedite the process by providing infrastructure as needed for development, streamlining the issuance of necessary permits, and keeping development fees low.[3] Policy B assumes growth will continue along current trend lines, with past growth being used to predict future growth. Policy C looks at encouraging external development based on programs established by county, regional, or state government. Policy D limits and discourages further growth by recognizing a strong local interest in protecting the environment. It assumes residents prefer a smaller, more intimate community structure.

Each of these policies is processed using software incorporating national and regional economic conditions and predictions.[4] After a computer modeler inputs community inventory data, the model produces four separate forecasts, one for each policy. An evaluation is structured for each of these four scenarios. An inventory of existing land uses is compared against the amount of land recommended by planning standards. This defines the community's projected needs. For example, assume a planning standard recommends 10 acres of recreation land per 1,000 residents. If Policy A projected a final population of 8,000, the community would need 80 acres of recreation land to meet the standard. If the community currently has 65 acres, it should consider acquiring an additional 15 acres.

If undeveloped local land sells for $20,000 per acre, the community would need to set aside an additional $300,000 of capital funds for this purchase. However, if the community selects Policy D of low or no growth, it would not need to plan for any additional recreation land. SAF allows a municipal council to change existing policy to meet its desired evaluation and budget.

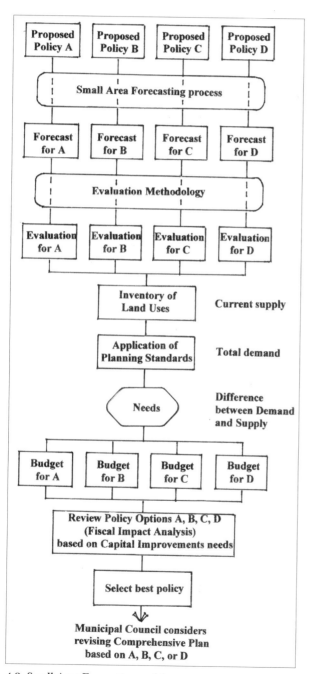

4.9. Small Area Forecasting model

| Variable | Approved Inputs 2009 | Source/Comments |
|---|---|---|
| **Residential Components** | | |
| **Single-Family Detached** | | |
| Number of Units | 57,407 | 2009 housing units |
| Household Size (Occupied Units) | 3.27 | FIC, 12/10/08 |
| School Age Children/New Household | 0.87 | 2008 School Census |
| Long-Run Vacancy Rate | 4.8% | Table A-8 |
| Long-Run Property Appreciation Factor (beyond inflation) | 0.5% beginning during 2011 | FIC, 7/13/09 |
| Property Value (New Units) | $545,186 | Table A-10 |
| **Single-Family Attached** | | |
| Number of Units | 31,328 | 2009 housing units |
| Household Size (Occupied Units) | 2.75 | FIC, 12/10/08 |
| School Age Children/New Household | 0.51 | 2008 School Census |
| Long-Run Vacancy Rate | 5.6% | Table A-8 |
| Long-Run Property Appreciation Factor (beyond inflation) | 0.5% beginning during 2011 | FIC, 7/13/09 |
| Property Value (New Units) | $402,307 | Table A-10 |

4.10. Summary of assumptions for residential forecast, 2009, Loudoun County, Virginia[5]

| Year | Forecasts by Scenario | | |
|---|---|---|---|
| | Low | Intermediate | High |
| *represents existing data | | | |
| 2000* | 6,134 | 6,134 | 6,134 |
| 2001* | 4,712 | 4,712 | 4,712 |
| 2002* | 5,976 | 5,976 | 5,976 |
| 2003* | 6,657 | 6,657 | 6,657 |
| 2004* | 6,593 | 6,593 | 6,593 |
| 2005* | 5,065 | 5,065 | 5,065 |
| 2006* | 3,061 | 3,061 | 3,061 |
| 2007* | 2,739 | 2,739 | 2,739 |
| 2008* | 2,391 | 2,391 | 2,391 |
| 2009 | 1,650 | 1,800 | 2,200 |
| 2010 | 1,700 | 2,000 | 2,300 |
| 2011 | 1,900 | 2,250 | 2,600 |
| 2012 | 2,000 | 2,400 | 2,800 |
| 2013 | 2,400 | 2,700 | 3,100 |
| 2014 | 2,500 | 2,815 | 3,200 |
| 2015 | 2,500 | 2,910 | 3,300 |
| 2016 | 2,900 | 3,240 | 3,700 |
| 2017 | 2,900 | 3,245 | 3,700 |
| 2018 | 3,300 | 3,500 | 4,000 |
| 2019 | 3,300 | 3,500 | 4,000 |
| 2020 | 3,300 | 3,500 | 4,000 |
| 2021 | 3,100 | 3,260 | 3,700 |
| 2022 | 2,900 | 3,065 | 3,500 |
| 2023 | 2,900 | 3,010 | 3,400 |
| 2024 | 2,400 | 2,610 | 2,900 |
| 2025 | 2,000 | 2,185 | 2,300 |

4.11. Alternative residential growth forecasts, Loudoun County, Virginia,[6] indicating peak growth in 2018–2020

This type of evaluation depends on planning standards derived from organizations in specialty areas. Standards typically exist for such elements as water usage and wastewater treatment facilities, fire and police services, schools, libraries, and other basic community services. Standards can also provide guidance on the type and size of commercial activities in shopping areas. Differing standards may exist for various organizations, so forecasters have to refer to a variety of sources during the modeling process.

The residential analysis and forecast undertaken by Loudoun County, Virginia, in 2009 began with a summary of approved assumptions. From these assumptions, Loudoun County planners applied residential planning standards to population growth projections, to forecast the number of residential housing units required to meet expected future demand. These projections enabled local officials to plan appropriately to accommodate anticipated growth in their county.

### Statistics

Statistical data derived from surveys can be used to draw inferences about the larger population. Statistics used for forecasting can be quite accurate when it accounts for various types of bias. Statistical methods can be used to make inferences in a variety of ways, among them: yes/no hypothesis testing (e.g., Do growth control measures reduce sprawl?); mathematical estimates (How many passengers used the metropolitan airport during the Thanksgiving weekend?); predictions of the future (How many students will be attending the local high school in 2015?); mathematical correlations (Do more downtown parking spaces result in higher retail sales?); or modeling of relationships (How much of northeast-to-southwest migration is due to [1] weather, [2] employment, or [3] other?).

Statistics can be used to examine causes of various phenomena. One way to do this is to view the effect changes in selected factors (independent variables) have on other factors (dependent variables). For example, a transportation study can evaluate the effect of adding restricted High-Occupancy Vehicle (HOV) lanes to a highway to see if it reduces congestion. The independent variable is the highway before and after the restricted lane is put in place (time period, weather, days of the week, etc., being held constant). The dependent variable, the level of congestion, is calculated to determine the impact of the change. This analysis can benefit future decisionmaking.

---

### An Efficient Approach to Data Collection: A Lesson from Rivertown

As planner for the community of Rivertown, you have been asked by the City Council to determine the number of recreational vehicles owned by residents. The vehicles may include bicycles, motorcycles, all-terrain vehicles, snowmobiles, and boats. This information will be used jointly with River Township to determine what recreational facilities should be funded and how extensive they should be. There are over 2,000 housing units within the city, including the college. To gather the information, it will take 10 student interns, each visiting 200 households, perhaps more than once if no one is home. Paying the interns $10 an hour, and assuming an average of one half-hour per household for making contact and conducting the survey, the total cost for this survey will be $10,000.

You ask your supervisor, Planning Director Burnham Daniel, for the funds. He responds that the cost is too high, and explains the value of "inferential statistics," where the final total is inferred from a random sample. Using this approach, a sample of the town's population represents the entire population. With addresses drawn randomly from a list of residents, it is possible to get a good estimate of the totals by surveying as few as 250 of the households. This reduces the overall cost to $2,500 and it makes Mr. Daniel much happier.

Will a random sample survey be totally accurate? No. Will it be accurate enough for making good decisions? Probably. Inferential statistics allow you to specify the amount of error, for example, saying, "There is a 95 percent probability that the predicted average number of RVs per household will be within 10 percent of the true value." It is a situation where you have obtained adequate information at a considerably lower cost while using proven survey statistical methods.

---

## Components of a Comprehensive Plan

A comprehensive plan consists of various planning topics as component parts, from land use to transportation to economic development and others as shown on the comprehensive planning process diagram (refer to Fig. 4.1). Major topics included in a comprehensive plan are summarized here and detailed in later chapters.[7]

### Land Use

Land use is the most important component, and a mandated topic, of a community's comprehensive plan. It provides a geographic base for all of the other elements and defines their spatial distribution. It includes maps designating the location and intensity of use of land for public and private uses, natural features and characteristics, and projected municipal services, such as sewer, water, schools, and transportation.

Land use categories generally include:

| | |
|---|---|
| Residential | Agricultural |
| Commercial/Office | Mining |
| Industrial | Woodlands |
| Mixed use | Vacant or open land |
| Institutional, Public/Private | Surface water |
| Recreational | Wetlands |

Planners often use a standard color system to designate land uses on a map. An example of this color coding system is found on the Land Use Plan for the City of Ypsilanti, Michigan, shown in Appendix D.

| *Standard color coding system* | |
|---|---|
| Low-density residential | Yellow |
| Medium-density residential | Light orange |
| High-density residential | Orange |
| Commercial | Red |
| Industrial | Purple |
| Public facilities | Blue |
| Open space | Green |

### Design

Design involves the incorporation of an aesthetic component into the process of planning, and emphasizes creative and innovative planning solutions. It includes careful planning of the public realm to complement development in the private sector. Good community design creates a balance between development and conservation by tying them together harmoniously.

### Housing

Providing enough housing is a primary need of every community. The housing section of the comprehensive plan has special significance to local residents because it directly affects everyone's life and property. It typically includes information on housing types, costs, and potential growth. Using an inventory of existing housing stock and demographic projections, a community can forecast future residential needs. For example, communities concerned about the availability of affordable housing can emphasize this need as part of their comprehensive plan by including provisions to help ensure that sufficient affordable and starter housing units are available in proximity to employment opportunities to meet the needs of a diverse population.

### Historic Preservation

Historic preservation's importance has become increasingly recognized in recent decades. The National Register of Historic Places recognizes structures of national significance. Local communities may provide protection of historic resources through establishment of regulatory local historic districts. Although many communities have such districts, preservation is not included as a component in many comprehensive plans. Since historic structures and districts are important to a community's heritage, culture, and economic development, planners should better integrate planning and preservation documents.

4.12. *Thomas Edison's winter home, Fort Myers, Florida, listed on the National Register of Historic Places*

### Economic Development

Many communities see economic development as a key consideration in future growth. Numerous strategies exist for achieving local economic development goals but they typically focus on businesses, tax revenues, and employment. To be most effective, expenditures should yield the maximum investment potential for the lowest cost. For the most favorable results, local economic development efforts should include analysis of state and federal policies and programs.

## Transportation and Circulation

Transportation systems are integral to the life of any community because there is a close link between transportation and land use. Planners should assess the needs for roads, parking, public transportation, park-and-ride facilities, bicycle routes or paths, pedestrian walkability, as well as environmental and aesthetic impacts of the municipality's transportation systems. Some comprehensive plans include separate sections for bicycle and pedestrian systems and for airports because of their diverse needs and significance.

Special consideration must be given to the impact of transportation improvements on a community's development and coordinating the content with state, regional, and local transportation agencies. A region's Metropolitan Planning Organization should be able to provide long-range forecasts of the area's needs.[8]

## Environmental Considerations

The environmental component of the comprehensive plan is built around a carefully researched and documented inventory, with maps, of a community's natural elements: soils, topography, water features, wetlands, floodplains, wildlife, agricultural lands, minerals, wooded areas and forest vegetation, groundwater recharge zones, and other resources deemed worthy of consideration and possible protection. Regional planning commissions can be a good source of information and may have already collected information useful for a local analysis. This section should indicate vulnerable areas in need of protection and address conflicts, or potential conflicts, resulting from development and include environmental assessment analysis.

## Other Components

The comprehensive plan can include other components not listed above. A Parks and Recreation section provides guidance on the need for additional facilities. Institutional uses can include public buildings, such as city

4.13. *Protected wetlands in an urbanized area, an environmental consideration*

hall, fire stations, and the public works garage. A Public Services section is a good place to compare costs of public infrastructure against benefits of new development. School planning is often excluded, since school needs are complex and may be handled by a designated school board. In this case, planners should coordinate with the board to forecast whether schools require expansion in the near future so planning for them can be done efficiently.

## Public Participation

Public participation is an important part of the comprehensive planning process and occurs throughout the development of the plan. Community involvement in the development of the comprehensive plan is quite different from that of citizen statements in public hearings relating to specific project proposals. Residents tend to become actively involved in confronting what they perceive to be an immediate threat to their neighborhood or business—for example, a proposal for a new gravel pit in a rural area may draw a large group of protesting residents concerned about water resources or heavy truck traffic on local roads. But reactions to a single issue typically are short-term. In contrast, community involvement in the development of a comprehensive plan has more long-term significance and impact. The public should be a full partner in shaping a document that will steer the overall future growth of their community. Most states require public participation in the creation of a comprehensive plan.

The concept of what constitutes the "public" can be viewed in a number of ways. Although planners may consider it important to have a large number of people attending public sessions, it is more important that attendees represent various significant population groups. A large number of attendees may look good in reports, but a smaller group that is diverse will be more effective in providing meaningful input, especially if the group is involved early in the process and stays involved.

Participation can occur in ways other than public meetings—by means of directed surveys, selective interviews, and focus groups dealing with single issues. What is important is that public participation does not happen at only one point in the planning process; it needs to be incorporated from beginning to end. Planners should never ignore the relevance of public ideas nor underestimate the public's ability to provide useful suggestions, and public input should never be considered an impediment to good planning or the outcry at the end may negate months of work.

## Goals and Objectives

An important step in the comprehensive planning process is to identify goals and objectives for the community. A goal is a statement of a future condition considered desirable for the community, an end toward which actions are aimed. For example, if the community desires physical growth, it can adopt policies to encourage that through promotion and annexation. Conversely, if it is more interested in stabilizing its size, it can select policies that will control and limit growth. Goals are the top of a functional pyramid, and are general in nature. They are supported by objectives, which give detail. If a goal is "Provide alternative means of transportation for all residents," "Provide on-call public transportation for elderly residents" could be an objective.

Public input is an important part of developing a community's goals and objectives. Such input may be solicited through public presentations with open discussion, visioning or charrettes (described in Chapter 5), or planning simulations. Open discussions with residents provide planners with perspectives regarding what the community wants to become. Such sessions should occur at the convenience of most citizens, typically during evenings or on Saturdays. In some situations, local experts with vested interests may be invited to express their feelings.

---

### Spotlight on Andover's Comprehensive Plan
This excerpt from the Comprehensive Plan for Andover, Massachusetts, illustrates how goals and objectives can be expressed in a comprehensive plan.[9]

*Land Use Goals*
Goal #1: A balance of residential, commercial, and industrial development is vital to the life of a community. The Town's Land Use Plan, through the expression of its recommendations in the Zoning By-law, Zoning Map, and Subdivision Rules and Regulations, should ensure that balanced growth occurs and that the health, safety, and welfare of the inhabitants of the Town of Andover are adequately addressed.
*Objectives:*
  1.1 Examine potential future development that will detrimentally impact natural and cultural resources in the Town, particularly in view of the marginal nature of much of the remaining undeveloped land. Implement any additions to existing regulations determined to be necessary to protect these resources.
  1.2 Examine existing and potential conflicts between land uses such as the provision of diversity in housing and the need for services or land uses currently prohibited or restricted by the Zoning By-law.
  1.3 Undertake a complete re-codification and revision of the Andover Zoning By-law to provide more clarity and definition in the regulations and to strengthen controls necessary for managing future growth taking into account the results of efforts undertaken to meet objectives 1.1 and 1.2 above.
  1.4 Computerize the building permit process and land use/zoning information to ensure the enforcement

of local and state regulations, and to help with the future analyses of land use issues and proposed growth control measures.

Goal #2: Anticipate and plan for the future of the Central area of Andover.

*Objectives:*

2.1 Develop as part of the overall Land Use Element of the Comprehensive plan a focused study of the Central Andover Area that would include an examination of future land uses and zoning including the advisability of proposing a transitional zone adjacent to the General Business Zone. The plan would be based on public input, existing land use, as well as traffic patterns and geographical features.

2.2 Develop a Central Business District Beautification Program, which would propose improvements to the streets, sidewalks, lighting, and other features of the Central Business District. The Plan should also address opportunities for participation in the development of these improvements by private landowners.

---

*Strategies*

Goals and objectives call for strategies, or specific proposals to accomplish an objective. A strategy identifies the how, where, when, and extent of action taken. It also may specify who is responsible and the cost. Planners should be prepared to establish measurable strategies to fulfill objectives. To use the example of on-call transit for the elderly as an objective, the strategy might be, "Purchase buses appropriate for on-call service and develop a plan for daily staffing." From goal to objective to strategy, each level states in more detail what should be done, from the general to the specific.

A tool developed in the 1960s that is commonly used for devising strategies, referred to as "SWOT," called for examining a situation's inherent Strengths, Weaknesses, Opportunities, and Threats.[10] This technique allows a group to evaluate what is good and what is bad in a community, based on both internal and external factors. Strengths represent attributes of the community that are helpful to achieve an objective, while Weaknesses are attributes that are seen as harmful. Opportunities are external conditions that help achieve the objective, while Threats are external factors that inhibit success.

The technique is used to evaluate how to utilize a community's Strengths and Opportunities, negate its Weaknesses, and defend against potential Threats. SWOT works well in brainstorming by encouraging discussion of new perspectives, policies, and strategies. Part of the formulation is the development and evaluation of alternative strategies.

*Plan Formulation and Adoption*

Community planners develop a final comprehensive plan to present to the public and to local officials, including the municipal council, planning commission, and other agencies affected by the plan, such as the local school board, parks and recreation board, utilities board, planning commissions in adjacent jurisdictions, and the regional planning agency. In states with townships, approval usually is referred to an elected board of trustees. When a consensus is reached on the plan's major provisions and agreed upon revisions made, resolutions are presented, votes taken, and the community's comprehensive plan is adopted.

Plans may be published in a number of forms. Most common is a booklet that includes background data, maps and graphics, policies, and the elements described in this chapter. The document should be brief enough to be readable by the general public. Online versions of the comprehensive plan are becoming more common as local officials and the public become increasingly comfortable with use of the Internet. An online document can include hot links to other relevant documents, allowing the basic plan to be relatively brief, but supported by related documents.

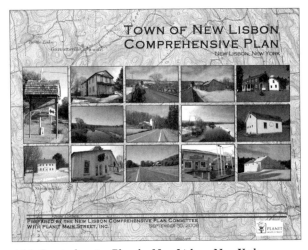

*4.14. Comprehensive Plan for New Lisbon, New York*

## Implementation

Although the adoption of a comprehensive plan does not guarantee change will occur as planned, a carefully considered implementation plan is the final step in the comprehensive planning process. After all, a comprehensive plan has no lasting value without steps for its implementation. Codes and ordinances may need to be amended to implement specified actions, such as updating zoning ordinances and maps. Funding for major projects like roads, sewers, and public facilities must be coordinated with a community's capital improvements program to ensure money will be available and budgeted when needed.

Three primary documents typically can be used to implement comprehensive plans. First, zoning ordinances define development districts and their allowable uses. Second, subdivision/site plan regulations place controls at the parcel level by specifying procedures of submittal, review, and approval of subdivision plats, often including review of environmental impacts such as erosion, sedimentation, and storm water management, the preservation of open space, and the location of proposed utilities. Finally, a capital improvements program gives guidance on public sector expenditures based on priorities and controls the timing and location of development.

The implementation of the comprehensive plan is affected by statutes and policies generated and administered by levels of government beyond the local community—federal and state environmental legislation, taxation legislation, economic assistance, unfunded mandates, grants, and other factors. Planners and local officials must keep abreast of these opportunities and constraints.

Although the power communities have to effect change directly is limited, officials and planners can influence such changes indirectly through education and persuasion. Publishing and distributing copies of the plan are the first step. Training city staff to encourage investors to develop in a way that reinforces the comprehensive plan, rather than putting up regulatory and administrative barriers for them, is an effective and no-cost strategy. Finally, promotion campaigns can attract businesses and developers.

### Spotlight on Scottsdale's One-Stop Planning and Development Office

The complexity of city government, with its review and approval procedures, can make implementing the comprehensive plan slow and cumbersome, but there are ways to streamline the process. The city of Scottsdale, Arizona, has made a special effort to provide easy service to its "customers," the residents, by establishing a One-Stop Shop that puts all agencies and departments involved with planning and project development review in one location. One front desk efficiently directs inquirers, whatever their needs, to the office that can assist. The offices include the following:

*Development Services.* Answers general development questions, assists in review of the comprehensive plan, accepts all necessary fees, and gives overnight plan review and permit service.

*Records.* Archives all maps and project files, and gives information on water lines, sewer lines, etc.

*Real Estate Services.* Handles all land acquisition questions, including for city uses, such as parks, roadways, etc., and leases and administers all city-owned buildings and properties.

*Project Review.* Reviews all final plans for construction and provides technical assistance.

*Project Coordination.* Provides coordination services for Zoning, Use Permit, Zoning Board of Appeals, and Development Review Board cases. Assigns one person who serves as the coordinator to shepherd each individual project through all these steps.

*Planning Commission.* Reviews projects and makes recommendations to the Council.

*Zoning Board of Appeals.* Hears all applications for variances from the provisions of the Zoning Ordinance.

*Building Advisory Board of Appeals.* Hears appeals from the staff's decisions regarding minor variances to the building code.

With one-stop shopping the public interest is still protected by having normal reviews of all projects, but the cumbersome process of taking a project through the halls of city government is considerably simplified and expedited, giving residents and others a better chance for a successful project.

## Review and Amendments

The comprehensive planning process appears to be complete after the steps described above have been accomplished, but planners should review and evaluate the community's plan in subsequent years to determine if it is fulfilling its purpose. Periodic meetings of the planning commission should be devoted to reviewing significant changes that have occurred in the community and assessing whether they have conformed to the plan. Planning staff should compile information from these reviews to assist in revisions of the plan at an appropriate time.

Amendments should be prepared by the office that created the original document, usually the planning department. The planning staff must research changes thoroughly to avoid conflicts with other elements of this or other plans. Proposed revisions then go to the planning commission, which solicits public input and makes a determination or recommendation to the municipal council. Any changes made go into effect only when formally adopted by the council or by the planning commission.

## Subarea Plans

Sometimes a district or neighborhood needs to be studied in more detail than is appropriate in a community's comprehensive plan. It may require more analyses because its unique or diverse character raises issues or problems not found elsewhere. For example, a downtown area, a waterfront district, or highway corridor may need planning approaches applicable to their situations. In these cases, it is useful to develop a subarea (or small-area) plan.

Subarea plans should include an introduction, an inventory of existing conditions, a vision statement and key strategies, a review of land use and circulation issues, development standards, and other topics similar to those found in the comprehensive plan. They may also include more detailed descriptions—design standards, special zoning, and/or traffic considerations. Input from the public and from stakeholders should be considered when developing the plan. Because a subarea plan is an extension of the comprehensive plan, it should include a description of its relationship to the comprehensive plan and other appropriate community planning studies.

### EXERCISE 3
### DEVELOPMENT OF A SUBAREA PLAN IN RIVERTOWN

*The area in the northwest corner of the city remains undeveloped. The parcels that make up this area are located directly west of the Reliance College campus and it is zoned an agriculture district. The City Council would like to encourage the development of this area for mixed residential and neighborhood commercial use. The property owner is amenable to a study to explore potential plans. The City Council has asked you, as the city planner, to develop a preliminary subarea plan for this district.*

*The plan should include a preliminary layout that includes the following features:*
- *single- and multifamily housing*
- *neighborhood commercial*

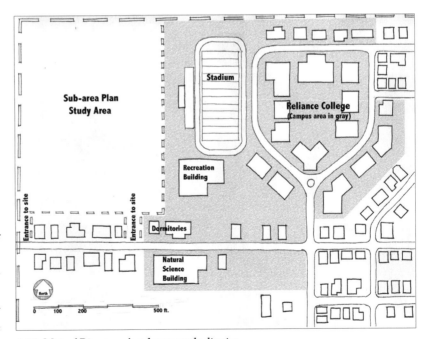

**4.15. Map of Rivertown's subarea study district**

- *public open space and amenities*
- *varied transportation links*

*Your report must include the proposed layout and a brief description (approximately 300 words) of its rationale. Consider how the college campus may benefit from land uses developed in this district.*

## Limitations of Planning

Planning cannot do everything. Local officials need to understand that the development of a comprehensive plan will not necessarily produce changes quickly. It will, however, provide a framework and set the direction for change. Most development comes from the private sector, not from local government. The city can institute public sector work according to its own schedule, but must wait for the private sector to respond when and if it is ready.

## Summary

The comprehensive plan, or master plan, should be the foundation for a community's decisions about its future. It is a document that provides guidance for land use and development within a community. The comprehensive plan is initiated by locally elected officials who work in conjunction with members of their community's planning commission and planning department.

The first step in developing a comprehensive plan is the collection of data and creation of an inventory of existing planning elements, including information on existing resources and facilities to recognize a community's assets and weaknesses. Forecasting techniques can help determine a community's future needs and priorities. The formulation of a comprehensive plan should include goals, objectives, strategies, and means of implementation, as well as a provision for periodic plan review. Three primary actions are available for implementing the comprehensive plan: zoning ordinances, which define land use districts and allowable land uses within each district; subdivision/site plan regulations, which place controls on land parcels through procedures of submittal, review, and approval of subdivision plats; and a capital improvement program to guide funding priorities.

A comprehensive plan takes considerable effort and should include input from every segment of the community, from city officials to residents to business owners and even neighboring communities that may be affected. Individual neighborhoods or districts of the city may be planned separately through the development of subarea plans. Separate plans may be created for specific elements, for example, transportation or recreation. Planners must recognize the significance of the interconnectedness of elements to be certain that the plan maintains the welfare of the entire community.

# 5

# PLANNERS AND THE DESIGN PROCESS

## The Importance of Urban Design to Planners

Although it is difficult to separate the definition of good design from good planning, good design emphasizes creative and innovative planning solutions. Design involves the incorporation of an aesthetic component into the process of planning. Good design does not happen by luck or happenstance, it is a conscious act practiced by professionals who understand its qualities. Good design presupposes that in spite of the complexity inherent in communities, it is possible to bring to them physical order and a pleasing character.

The design process may feel uncomfortable to some planners, since it requires a different perspective. Design looks for new solutions; it is commonly believed that most people are more comfortable with old problems than with new solutions. Design has been defined as "the *imaginative* jump from present facts to future possibilities."[1]

Christopher Alexander, a noted architect and urban design theorist, spent years studying patterns of city design. In his book, *A New Theory of Urban Design*, he recognized the importance of organic "wholeness" at every scale, from the scale of the city to the neighborhood to individual projects. "This quality," he wrote, "does not exist in towns being built today. And indeed, this quality *could* not exist, at present, because there isn't any discipline that actively sets out to create it. City planning definitely does not try to create wholeness. It is merely preoccupied with implementation of certain ordinances."[2] Alexander challenged planning practitioners to accept responsibility for the design not of individual projects but of "whole" communities.

Urban design often is overlooked in the education of planners, but planners play a significant role in the phys-

ical creation of communities. Architects and developers are responsible for the design of buildings, but planners conceptualize the spaces between and around these structures. All are integral to the development process. Architects might argue for the primacy of buildings in community design, but planners could counter that the spaces between buildings are just as important because these spaces are part of the public realm, which comprises public open space and privately owned exterior space used by the public.

Which should be designed first—open space or buildings? In the United States private property owners initiate the development process through construction of buildings in locations of their choosing. These individually designed buildings often have no significant relationship to one another (so-called plop architecture), suggesting that a building is "plopped" on a convenient site, the next one on an adjacent site. Each is seen as a separate project with little recognition of the larger context surrounding them.

Giving design of the public realm priority results in a more desirable urban context. Public areas should not be treated as residual spaces, but as special places that bring focus to the patterns of community life. In this scenario, the public realm is designed first and can then be used to delimit the appropriate placement of privately owned buildings. In his book, *Rural by Design: Maintaining Small Town Character*, Randall Arendt advocates this course, which conserves the interconnected open and natural spaces; the green infrastructure becomes a pattern into which developed spaces can be designed and gently fit.[3] Planners should not settle for doing the best they can with spaces left over by architects and developers. Planners should lead the way by initiating design of the public realm.

## Historical Perspective

Looking at the past can provide an understanding of the role planners can play in the design and development of the public realm. The following three key developments are exemplary and we discuss them in turn. Riverside, Illinois, was among the earliest communities to be designed as a whole. A new suburban town, its layout illustrates important elements of community design and planning. A few decades later, the City Beautiful Movement was based almost entirely on the idea of design. And in the 1980s, the New Urbanists picked up the mantle of urban design, emphasizing the importance of walkable, diverse, and sustainable development.

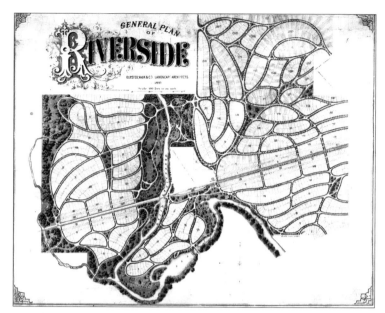

5.1. *Plan for Riverside, Illinois, 1869*

### Riverside, Illinois

Riverside, Illinois, is a landmark in the history of town planning in the United States. Designed in 1869 by Frederick Law Olmsted, the designer responsible for so many American parks and city plans (see Chapter 2), much of the beauty of the Riverside plan can be attributed to its landscape and environmental sensitivity.

In 1863, the Chicago, Burlington & Quincy Railroad came through an area just outside Chicago. Five years later, an eastern businessman brought together a group of associates to form the Riverside Improvement Association. This group decided to take advantage of the railroad's presence and bought an attractive 1,600-acre site where the line crossed the Des Plaines River. They in turn hired Olmsted to create a plan for their new city. The goal was to develop "a perfect village in a perfect setting."[4] The woods and river gave important amenities to the site and the railroad brought transportation convenience, connecting it to booming downtown Chicago.

Olmsted's plan for the new town fit the site's natural contours perfectly, creating curving streets and wooded open spaces. The plan included a Grand Park system comprising several large parks and 41 smaller parks and plazas sited throughout the community. It preserved the floodplain, riverbanks, and two open areas of upland to make scenic areas available to all residents. Gaslights illuminated curving streets that eased the grade of the slopes. The streets as public space and houses as private land formed a transitional area between the public and private realms, contributing to a beautiful design aesthetic.

Unlike unplanned towns, Riverside combined the best qualities of suburban residential living with urban convenience. Frank Lloyd Wright, Louis Sullivan, William Le Baron Jenney, and other prominent architects drew plans for houses that still stand in the village. It is graced by a striking Romanesque village hall built in 1895 and the Burlington's charming stone railroad station constructed in 1901. Riverside, designated a National Historic Landmark in 1970, remains a very desirable residential community, one of the best examples of community planning in the country.

### Chicago and the City Beautiful Movement

Large American cities in the nineteenth century were dirty, congested, polluted, and unhealthy. They were the products of the early industrial age, when factories were built with little regard for their impact on the quality of the environment. Their proud, dirty character is represented in Carl Sandburg's well-known poem, "Chicago."

## CHICAGO
by Carl Sandburg

Hog Butcher for the World,
Tool Maker, Stacker of Wheat,
Player with Railroads and the Nation's Freight Handler;
Stormy, husky, brawling,
City of the Big Shoulders:
They tell me you are wicked and I believe them, for I have seen your
    painted women under the gas lamps luring the farm boys.
And they tell me you are crooked and I answer: Yes, it is true I have
    seen the gunman kill and go free to kill again.
And they tell me you are brutal and my reply is: On the faces of
    women and children I have seen the marks of wanton hunger.
And having answered so I turn once more to those who sneer at this
    my city, and I give them back the sneer and say to them:
Come and show me another city with lifted head singing so proud to
    be alive and coarse and strong and cunning.
Flinging magnetic curses amid the toil of piling job on job, here is a
    tall bold slugger set vivid against the little soft cities;

Fierce as a dog with tongue lapping for action, cunning as a savage
    pitted against the wilderness,
    Bareheaded,
    Shoveling,
    Wrecking,
    Planning,
    Building, breaking, rebuilding,
Under the smoke, dust all over his mouth, laughing with white
    teeth,
Under the terrible burden of destiny laughing as a young man
    laughs,
Laughing even as an ignorant fighter laughs who has never lost a
    battle,
Bragging and laughing that under his wrist is the pulse and under
    his ribs the heart of the people,
Laughing!
Laughing the stormy, husky, brawling laughter of Youth, half-naked,
    sweating, proud to be Hog Butcher, Tool Maker, Stacker of
    Wheat, Player with Railroads and Freight Handler to the
    Nation.

Chicago had become the second largest city in the country (hence its nickname, "Second City"). But its growth was based on trade and production. Its residents wanted to be recognized as a cultured society, fully equal to sophisticated New York City. So Chicago decided to host an international exposition in 1893 celebrating the 400th anniversary of the arrival of Columbus in the New World. The goal was not to present new technologies, although many new technologies were evident, but to put on a display of grandeur never seen before in this part of the world. Daniel Burnham, the prominent architect and planner, headed a team of 10 selected designers who decided on a common scheme. They deemed Classicism the architectural style to best represent the concept of an ideal culture. The result was a vision, referred to as the "White City," that excited virtually every visitor who came to the exposition.

*5.2. World's Columbian Exposition, Chicago, 1893*

The fair's impact was tremendous. Its architecture inspired municipal leaders across the country to remake their cities in a similar mold. In St. Louis and Cincinnati and Detroit, and even in New York City, the new City Beautiful movement persuaded local leaders to support the construction of grand public buildings, spaces, and avenues. Local leaders were convinced that beautification would improve many of a city's ills and that good civic design would establish their city's eminence. As planner Peter Hall put it, "The City Beautiful movement represented a deliberate and conscious attempt to impose on America's greatest cities the kind of heavily formalistic urban reconstruction that Haussmann had carried through in Paris."[5]

The City Beautiful movement was not only supported by local governments but also by local business associations, which at that time were primary movers and shakers for city improvements. Business leaders believed that beautification would bring more visitors, and thus be good for business. Burnham appealed to this belief to sell his bold 1909 *Plan of Chicago* to the city's Commercial Club, which was paying for his services. He wrote: "No one has estimated the number of millions of dollars made in Chicago and expended elsewhere, but the sum must be a large one. What would be the effect upon our retail business at home if this money were circulated here? What would be the effect upon our prosperity if

*5.3. Daniel Burnham, Plan of Chicago, 1909*

the town were so delightful that most of the men who grow independent financially in the Mississippi Valley, or west of it, were to come to Chicago to live?"[6]

The Chicago plan of 1909, one of the most significant and ambitious proposals of the City Beautiful movement, incorporated the most significant city planning principles of the time. It was a comprehensive plan that incorporated most of the city. It looked to the future, with integration of traffic circulation on wide boulevards and overpasses at critical points. It called for improvements to Chicago's waterfront area and a system of parks and wildlife preserves that still define much of the city's landscape. Burnham's plan was a tour-de-force and is considered "the single most important offshoot of the City Beautiful movement."[7] As Burnham famously wrote, "Make no little plans, they have no magic to stir men's blood and probably themselves will not be realized. Make big plans. . . ."[8]

The Chicago plan illustrated the positive impact of good design and the relationship between beauty and commerce. It showed that cities should be planned, and that they should be planned by professional planners. Although the importance of this achievement for the new profession of city planning cannot be overstated, it is significant that the plan was never adopted officially by the city, since officials viewed it as a product of the private sector.[9]

The inherent problem of the City Beautiful approach to planning was that it did not address deeply rooted urban problems such as poverty, the pressures of immigration, poor housing, and overcrowding. It concentrated on the design of public spaces in prominent locations, but ignored the problems in the streets behind. Worst of all, it was expensive. Tremendous sums of money were spent on public art museums, courthouses, and parks—structures that remain the most attractive features of many cities. However, these public projects often left few resources for more mundane projects. It was a visionary movement, but its vision obscured reality, and it was doomed to a quick fall from favor. By 1915, the City Beautiful movement had largely run its course.

## New Urbanism

In the 1980s, a new movement brought the importance of physical design as a major tool of community planning again to the fore. Known as New Urbanism, it arose from the visionary work of a number of architects and planners across the United States, key among them the husband-wife team of Andres Duany and Elizabeth Plater-Zyberk through their planning firm, Duany Plater-Zyberk (DPZ). A "neotraditional" philosophy of planning, this movement followed, not coincidentally, on the heels of the environmental and historic preservation movements that began to take shape in the 1970s as a reaction to too much growth, too fast, with too little planning.

Duany and Plater-Zyberk began with a study of small towns located throughout the South. They examined intently the characteristics of older neighborhoods, forming opinions about what made them desirable, and from this analysis they devised ways to incorporate traditional planning principles in "new urban" projects. They suggested that planners "must return to first principles, laying out brand-new towns according to old-fashioned fundamentals, with the locations of stores, parks and schools precisely specified from the outset, with streets that invite walking, with stylistic harmony that avoids the extremes of either architectural anarchy or monotony."[10]

In their plan for Seaside, Florida, Duany and Plater-Zyberk first showcased their concepts. They began with the radical proposal that Seaside be designed as a low-rise traditional community, rather than as a high-rise condominium development typical of Florida coastline developments. They used the choicest beachfront real estate as public space and incorporated beach pavilions and a public overlook. The plan had streets radiate from the town center to define neighborhoods, each with its own character, but connected through pedestrian-friendly streets and alleys. The houses at Seaside observe a rigorous design code through a pattern book that includes specifications for front porches, rooflines, setbacks, details, and color. Within the code, however, property owners are free to choose individual designs. The result is order within diversity.

At Seaside, the concept of urban patterning became a viable approach to community design, as recognized by Christopher Alexander and Jenny Quillien, who wrote about Duany's work, "The scale is pleasant—and so this one architect (he would call himself a planner)—has asserted his design awareness over more than a thousand buildings, and has done so in a way that he can be proud of. To manage to have an effect on a very large num-

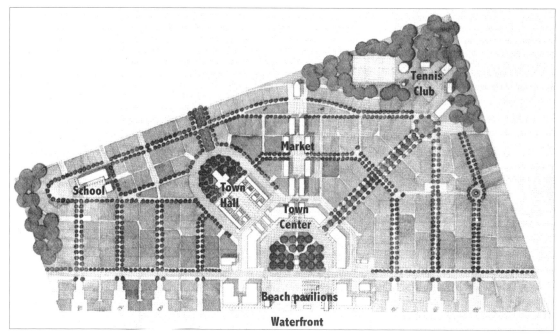

5.4. *Plan for Seaside, Florida, established in 1979*

ber of buildings, without personally designing them, and yet to be concerned with the *architecture*—to achieve a certain coherence, scale, and pleasantness in them, together with sensible patterns carefully controlled—all that is an amazing achievement."[11]

Out of these first steps grew an influential New Urbanist planning movement. In 1991, a private non-profit group in Sacramento, California, the Local Government Commission, invited a group including Andres Duany, Elizabeth Plater-Zyberk, Peter Calthorpe, Elizabeth Moule, Stefanos Polyzoides, and Daniel Solomon to develop a set of community principles for land use planning. Named the Ahwahnee Principles (after Yosemite National Park's Ahwahnee Hotel, where the group met), the group presented a series of statements to mitigate what they saw as problems that resulted from poor planning practice. (See Chapter 9 for the principles.)

However, New Urbanism has its critics, as typified by this writer from *Architecture* magazine, who suggests such a lifestyle is not appealing to most Americans: "Like the Modernists before them, New Urbanists believe they can change human behavior through design. Postwar car-dependent suburbs, once regarded as the realization of the American Dream, are to New Urbanists the roots of an alienated, wasteful, isolated society. Give Americans a traditional neighborhood, New Urbanists reason,

and they will behave like neighbors. Give two-income, two-car families a walkable grid of narrow streets, sidewalks, and corner stores, and they will rid themselves of one car. Give suburbanites a mix of housing types, from condominiums to rowhouses to detached houses, and a mix of people will occupy them. Give homeowners front porches, and they will eschew the TV, the air-conditioning, and the Internet, and talk to each other."[12] In spite of criticism, however, New Urbanism has contributed much to the dialogue on good planning, and its advocates support the principle of incorporating design as an essential element of community planning.

## Key Principles of Urban Design

Creation of a pleasing physical environment ultimately comes from professionals who are trained and experienced in good community design. The public sector's role is to set guidelines for good design. With the right encouragement, the private sector will follow. High-quality design of the public realm allows a community to be proactive, rather than reactive, and creates a pleasing environment. Good community design creates a balance between development and conservation, tying them together harmoniously. A community's planners should play an important role in achieving that end.

Urban design should be considered a process that extends over a longer time span than architectural or landscape design. While its two sister disciplines are project oriented, urban design is community oriented, and subject to the complexity inherent in working in that context. Rather than seeing a project completed in 1 to 3 years, community design projects may take 10 or 15 years before being fully realized. Also, the process encompasses diverse concerns, including land use, transportation, and social and economic goals.

The key principles of urban design can be most easily understood and appreciated by considering three different scales at which these principles are applied in practice—the scale of the city, the district or neighborhood, and the individual project. At the scale of the city, urban design looks at design elements important to the entire community. At the scale of districts or neighborhoods, relevant elements define character at a more local level. At the level of individual projects, urban design concerns itself primarily with relationships of particular structures to the street and to each other.

### Design at the City Scale

Design at the city scale focuses on elements important to an entire community. Cities benefit from density; good urban design encourages compact form that promotes interactions and where the private and public realms overlap. For example, privately owned restaurants may expand their seating onto public sidewalks in warm weather, or high-rise office buildings may include at street level public lobbies that contain a variety of retail, service, and passive recreation areas. When the distances among various uses are reduced, bicycles can make a viable alternative to motorized vehicles and walking can be an acceptable means to travel between destinations.

Public spaces encourage urban vitality if they contain activity nodes used during day and evening time periods. A lively public space allows residents to encounter each other as civic equals, each citizen free to interact in his or her own way. This is an important element in building a sense of community and social capital. Boston's Quincy Market, for example, is a vital urban public space. Bostonians from throughout the city come to enjoy its festival marketplace, which includes retail shops and restaurants, offices, and a large plaza with spaces for sitting, standing, and walking. Well-designed

*5.5. Quincy Market, Boston*

community spaces should group buildings in proximity to form the walls of urban-scaled "outdoor rooms." Too often, cities mistakenly permit new buildings to be built as single structures separated from each other by a sea of parking, but the highest property values are found where constrained open spaces have been created.

Urban researcher William ("Holly") Whyte, who conducted studies of how people used outdoor spaces in New York City, found that most spaces in the public realm were underused, even in a dense urban environment like Manhattan. He saw the "over-crowded city" as a myth. He argued that the street and the sidewalk are critical places of social interaction. Pedestrians do not look for solitude; the spaces people most enjoyed were the ones that were most intensely used. He wrote: "The street—particularly in the center city—is among the greatest of our cultural legacies. It is the river of city life. It gives the city continuity and coherence. It defines its scale. But it is under attack. . . . People tend to sit where there are places to sit. But what is just as important as a good place to sit is what you see from it. The prime places are those with full views of the main show, the street. . . . The elements of a good city space, then, are basics, and it is interesting to note how many of them are natural—people to watch, sun to bask in, trees to sit under, water to splash in and listen to. Nowhere does nature seem so important to people as in the city."[13]

Europe offers many famous examples of great public spaces, but there are also notable examples in American cities: Union Square in San Francisco, Pioneer Square in Seattle, Boston Common in Boston. Millennium

5.6. *Crown Fountain, Millennium Park, Chicago*

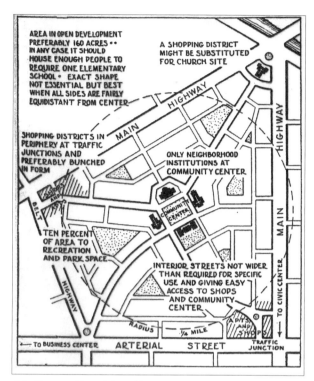

5.7. *Clarence Perry's Neighborhood Unit Concept, 1929*

Park in Chicago is a good example of an exciting urban space; one feature of the park interacts with the public by shooting water out of the mouth of a 50-foot-tall image of a projected face that cycles through 1,000 different images, with each face representing one of Chicago's citizens.

### Design at the Neighborhood Scale

Design at the scale of the city is essential to create a successful urban environment; design at the neighborhood level is equally important, though it can have different priorities and qualities. Two primary physical features help establish a sense of place—an identifiable center and clearly defined edges. People should know when they have arrived at a distinguishable district, and each district and neighborhood should be comprehensible in scope.

In 1929, Clarence Perry developed a scheme based on the optimal physical size and land use relationships for a "neighborhood unit", which he defined as a residential area approximately one-half mile across, surrounded by major streets with commercial land uses at their intersections.[14] His ideal neighborhood centered on an elementary

school and community center. This idea of the school as the center of community life was given further support in the 1960s with the planning of the new town of Columbia, Maryland (discussed in Chapter 2).

Mixed land uses and building types benefit neighborhoods. Business areas gain from incorporating residential and open space; residential neighborhoods from including businesses, particularly neighborhood stores. Housing that mixes owner-occupied and rental units helps ensure a diversity of residents. As with planning elements at the city scale, neighborhoods should have the best available land set aside for public uses, especially parks, squares, and passive and active recreation.

At the neighborhood level, planners must consciously create walkable environments; walkability enhances the sense of community. As two Canadian planners have written: "Isn't it time we build cities that are more child-friendly? . . . One common measure for how clean a mountain stream is [is] to look for trout. If you find the trout, the habitat is healthy. It's the same way with children in a city. Children are a kind of indicator species. If we can build a successful city for children we will have a successful city for all people."[15]

The layout of residential neighborhoods should follow good design principles. Ideally, parcels should minimize the amount of on-site infrastructure, such as streets and utility lines, that is required. A layout should have the smallest amount of street frontage practical to minimize the length and therefore construction costs of streets. Streets should be double-loaded, with frontage on both sides, for reasons of economy and environmental impact.

Housing units can provide more common open space at less cost if they are clustered. In a traditional layout, 85 percent of the land area is devoted to lots and 15 percent to the street. In comparison, in a typical cluster plan 50 percent is given to common open space, 40 percent to lots, and 10 percent to the street. A townhouse development is even more efficient, with 65 percent open space, 25 percent lots, and 10 percent devoted to a street.

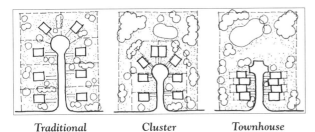

*Traditional*      *Cluster*      *Townhouse*

*5.8. Traditional parcels compared with cluster and townhouse layouts*

The layout of the streets in a new development needs special attention. Traffic should not be confined to one major arterial street because this creates congestion. Routes should be diffuse, with many linkages to surrounding areas. Although mixed-use developments may require varying street types, residential areas are safer when traffic is slow-moving, best promoted when streets are not too wide and are designed to accommodate pedestrians and bikers. For better safety, intersections should be at right angles and provide good views in both directions. For night safety, well-lit and easy-to-understand signage is desirable.

### Design at the Project Level

Design is significant for individual projects because it can actually save money for property owners in the medium to long term. A well-designed environment keeps its value over time.

Design at the project level starts with context—the project's relationship to its surroundings, including adjacent buildings, the street, and public spaces. A building's relationship to a street, and to buildings on the opposite side of the street, can be guided by recommended height-to-width ratios. In major cities, a comfortable ratio may be as much as 1:1, that is, if the distance from building front to building front is 100 feet, then the appropriate height of buildings is up to 100 feet (8 to 10 stories). In medium-sized and small cities, the ratio may be as low as 1:5, that is, a 20-foot height for a 100-foot separation. As a general rule, the ideal height-to-width ratio around public spaces is 1:3. Greater separation loses the visual sense of an enclosed space and causes it to be less well defined.[16]

A building's relationship to the sidewalk is also relevant. Studies have shown that building entrances are the most successful at ground level. Even a few steps above or below sidewalk level discourages entry by pedestrians (and may not conform to requirements of the Americans with Disabilities Act). Street-level commercial and public building frontage should be visually permeable, with inviting entrances and windows that show interior activity. The most successful pedestrian streets are those with many openings and visual connections. Long blank walls that contain few windows or doors (as is often the case with monumental buildings), featureless parking areas, and vacant lots discourage pedestrian traffic, so should be avoided in any area where walkability is desired.

At the project level, weather and environmental factors are important elements of design. North/south orientations for windows are best for this purpose. Good design ensures that a new building does not inadvertently block solar access for existing buildings and considers local weather conditions. Severe wind patterns can form on the downwind side of tall structures and make an unnecessarily uncomfortable environment for pedestrians. The use of properly designed overhangs, setbacks, or screen walls can mitigate such potential problems.

In residential areas traditional features such as tree-lined streets reinforce a sense of community. Front porches or stoops close to the sidewalk encourage interaction between homeowners and their neighbors, even if it is only a friendly hello as they walk by. Porches that are too close to the sidewalk may make residents feel a loss of privacy, but porches too distant from the sidewalk discourage informal conversation. Neighborhoods designed with alleys as service links make the front of houses appear welcoming and provide parking in the rear, making streets

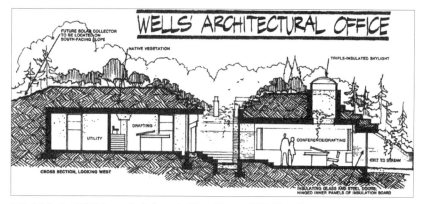

5.9. *Malcolm Wells's earth-sheltered office, Cherry Hill, New Jersey*

more pedestrian-friendly. Alleys allow services such as trash pickup and deliveries to be located out of view.

In an era of increased awareness about the need for sustainability, new design approaches are needed. Architect Malcolm Wells advocated the construction of new projects not on undeveloped land, but on abandoned or underutilized, previously developed sites. His "earth shelter" (or berm) houses employ passive solar concepts that restore sites to a natural beauty as they are being developed. "The best building site," he wrote, "is ruined, tortured, dying land. There's a lot of it. It sometimes goes for rock-bottom prices. And it offers us a chance to witness life-miracles as it slowly heals its wounds. The asphalt becomes chunks of riprap for erosion control, the subsoil begins once again the slow transformation to topsoil, green plants appear, sharp winds and industrial noise are moderated by vegetation, and instead of looking elsewhere for your view, your site becomes the view."[17]

### The Use of Design Guidelines

One way of encouraging good design is through the adoption of design guidelines for development projects. Design guidelines can encompass the city as a whole or may be based on various districts within the community, for example, downtown, waterfront, or mixed-use. Some comprehensive plans incorporate design guidelines, while other communities adopt pattern books to assist citizens in developing designs compatible with the character of a neighborhood or district.[18] Developers and architects often feel that design guidelines inhibit their freedom. If developed properly, however, they provide an excellent tool to ensure that a builder's vision is compatible with the community's goals and desires.

Community members who are concerned about architectural and open space design and want local government to be involved in a review process can appoint to a design review committee individuals qualified to make such aesthetic judgments. Design guidelines can be difficult to create and enforce, since by their very nature they involve a level of subjectivity, or taste. Often guidelines are based on a policy of mandatory review and voluntary compliance that does not bring full regulation, but does give some level of evaluation and exposure before other city agencies grant final approvals.

Design guidelines and review have worked well in a number of cities. Boulder, Colorado's downtown community has been increasingly concerned about growing competition from suburban shopping malls. To counter this problem, the city established design guidelines for the downtown to improve the quality of its developments. A citizen's board was established to review all proposed downtown projects. The Advisory Board reviews the exteriors of projects and site features with a construction value of $10,000 or more in the nonhistoric area. (Historic districts are reviewed by a separate commission.) Although the review of projects is mandatory, compliance with the board's recommendations is voluntary.

In Portland, Oregon, downtown projects are subject to approval by the city's Design Commission. The review includes a public forum for discussion of a project's merits. Developers seem to favor this, since they get public reaction in a controlled, organized environment, rather than in the unpredictable arenas of public hearings and media coverage. In 2003, the commission began a voluntary design advice option that allows developers to get feedback on designs early in the process. Many developers feel the expense for this service is cost effective for them, as it tends to make the more expensive full review process go more smoothly. One section from Portland's *Central City Fundamental Design Guidelines*, for example, says, "Maintain and extend the traditional 200-foot block pattern to preserve the Central City's ratio of open space to built space. Where super-blocks exist, locate public

## 3. PROPORTION

The characteristic proportion (the relationship between height and width) of existing facades should be respected.

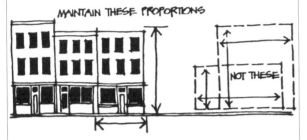

## 4. RELATIONSHIP TO STREET

The new facade should have a relationship to the street which is consistent with its neighbors.

## 5. ROOF FORMS

The type of a roof used should be similar to those found on adjacent buildings. On Main Street, this means a flat roof not visible on the front facade.

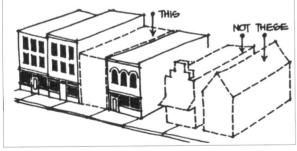

5.10. Sample downtown design guidelines, from Preservation Design Manual by Preservation Urban Design, Inc.

and/or private rights-of-way in a manner that reflects the 200-foot block pattern, and include landscaping and seating to enhance the pedestrian environment."[19] The publication's photographs illustrate how this has been accomplished in existing blocks.

Scottsdale, Arizona, has a design review board. The city's *Development Guide* prescribes that the board's agenda includes but is not limited to architectural review, site planning, and review of proposed developments as they relate to the surrounding environment and the community. The board is composed of one city council representative, a planning commission member, and five individuals who have backgrounds in design, architecture, or development. It has effectively established a consistent design format for new development based on a southwestern adobe design style. Some of the city's residents have criticized the design review process because they believe it stifles creativity and may result in a pattern of homogeneous design. Most Scottsdale residents, however, seem well satisfied with the designs that have been built. Recent projects have been able to achieve significant diversity and still comply with the approved design palette. The city's *Downtown Plan Urban Design and Architectural Guidelines* include many examples of features appropriate to Scottsdale and states that "The primary purpose of these Guidelines is to influence the general character of new projects so Downtown will preserve its present qualities as it develops."[20]

### Spotlight on Austin's Downtown Design Guidelines[21]

The city of Austin, Texas, gives a good example of what a complete set of design guidelines for a downtown includes and how to use them for very specific purposes. The city's *Downtown Austin Design Guidelines* includes sections on downtown boundaries, streetscape, plazas, buildings, districts, and the downtown. This excerpt from the guidelines, the section on the design of plazas, includes recommendations to provide public seating.

*Recommendations for Plaza Seating:*
- Provide one linear foot of seating per perimeter linear foot of the plaza.
- Provide for a variety of seating locations to accommodate the needs of various sitters.
- Place seating in shaded areas as well as in sunny areas. Shade may be created by trees, trellises, canopies, umbrellas, or building walls.
- Place seating where sitters can watch passersby.

- At least 50 percent of recommended seating should be secondary, in the form of steps, planter seat walls, retaining walls, or mounds of turf.
- Seating wall heights should be approximately 16–18 inches.
- Provide benches that are wide enough to serve many needs.
- Provide some linear or circular seating that encourages interaction.
- Provide backless benches, right-angle arrangements, or movable chairs and tables to accommodate groups.
- Provide seating materials that are inviting and that do not damage clothing.

## The Design Process

The design process was captured in a set of guidelines put forward by Bryan Lawson, who noted there is no infallibly correct process for designing; it involves finding, as well as solving, problems.[22] Lawson posits that design inevitably involves subjective and ethical value judgments based on experience. One cannot simply go step-by-step to a good solution; one must rely, to some degree, on inspiration, innovation, and creativity. Moreover, the urban designer is not an independent artist, but must work within the framework of a need for action. Lawson noted that design is not an end in itself; it is a creative tool used to achieve important community goals that may not be able to be obtained in other ways. The process should examine what can and should be, rather than what is. Community design never leads to completion; it is a continuing process that adjusts over time to changing circumstances.

### Steps in the Design Process

The design process may require inspiration and creativity, but it can proceed in an orderly way. It begins with research, the collection of useful data, relevant codes, and appropriate maps. The review of technical requirements establishes project parameters, and funding possibilities suggest an appropriate budget.

The context, or surrounding area, must be considered. It may be documented through a visual survey in the form of plans, photographs, and sketches with notes of any unique features or characteristics. From the analysis of these data, appropriate design ideas can be generated. Inspiration comes from looking at what is already there with a fresh perspective.

After this initial analysis, preliminary ideas can be formulated to graphically illustrate a proposal for review by others. Conceptual design may start with a schematic form known as a bubble diagram, which illustrates relationships among various uses. Each of the programmatic spaces is shown in a bubble whose size indicates the relative size of the space needed for the use. Diagrams like this are useful for exploring alternative schemes. Variations in the sizes and interrelationships of the bubbles allow early ideas to be evaluated before more detailed representation of structures and site is undertaken.

After review, evaluation, and adjustments lead to an

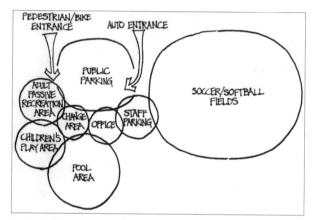

*5.11. Bubble diagram for a community's municipal pool and recreation facility*

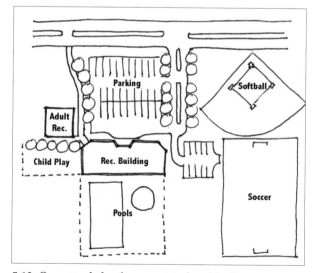

*5.12. Conceptual plan for a municipal pool facility*

acceptable schematic proposal, a project proceeds to a conceptual plan that indicates structures, open spaces, roads, parking, and other elements in sketch form. This allows reviewers to understand the planning of space more clearly so they can provide detailed responses to the proposed design.

## Spotlight on New Village, Pennsylvania

The illustration below shows a plan for the development of New Village near Uniontown in western Pennsylvania, a project initiated and sponsored by The Rensselaerville Institute in Rensselaerville, New York. The proposal illustrates a mixed-use community of approximately 200 housing units with community facilities.

The design process for New Village began with an advertisement in the local newspapers that solicited individuals interested in planning their own community. The resulting group of future residents began to work together as a seminal community: they established covenants, selected a site, and over the course of months developed a plan for their new community. The project was developed with the assistance of various professionals, who included architects, a planning consultant, an engineering firm, and the Institute.

The New Village plan illustrates many aspects of

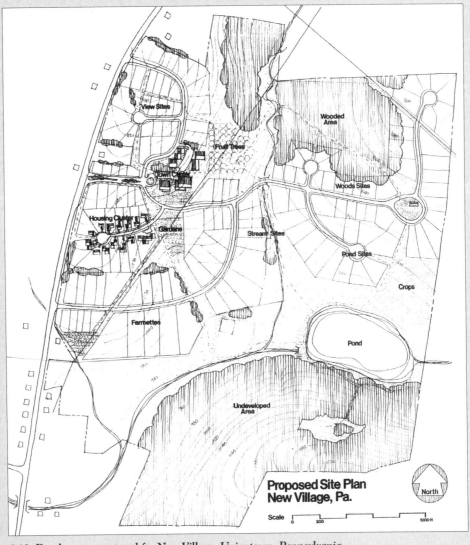

*5.13. Development proposal for New Village, Uniontown, Pennsylvania*

*5.14. Groundbreaking for New Village community, later named Springwood*

*5.15. View of Mt. Morris, Michigan, drawn using Google SketchUp*

good planning. First, the site is on a south-facing slope, which allows good solar access to most of the units. Second, a short boulevard gives access to the town center, the location of a community building (the first structure to be built), a small store, an incubator office (a facility offering assistance and facilities on a temporary basis for new businesses), a day care facility, and other small commercial structures. Next, housing parcels throughout the site vary in size and type, including traditional lots, cluster housing, stream and pond view sites, wooded sites, and larger farmettes, allowing a mix of residential patterns. Finally, the plan designates common areas—an orchard, gardens, a large woodlot, a recreation pond.

### The Use of 3D Graphics

Traditionally, preliminary concepts were drawn by hand, but three-dimensional (3D) graphics software is becoming increasingly popular for this purpose. It is easy to use, fast, and visually effective because it provides considerable detail and realism in a form easily understood by a layperson, making proposed developments available for public review and discussion.

Google's SketchUp software, for example, can be downloaded from the Web, free. SketchUp begins with a box that the user can alter to create a box representing an individual structure's massing. Photographs can be applied to this box to create a realistic 3D image. SketchUp software interacts with Google Map online software, so users can attach these 3D images to real-world coordinates. In addition, Google's 3D Warehouse stores and makes available free of charge images created by individuals from around the world, with a wealth of 3D images available.

Microsoft Photosynth offers a different approach: it combines dozens, and in some cases hundreds, of photos of a building, scans them for points of convergence, and creates 3D photos made from these composites. In contrast with SketchUp, Photosynth is not a modeling application but a photo-enhancement application, using multiple photos of structures supplied by users and compiling them into 3D images. Both can give realistic 3D versions of spaces and buildings, but the software uses completely different technologies to create these images.

## Envisioning a Community's Future

A number of methods are commonly used to encourage public input into the community design process. Each method offers a different perspective, but all are intended to partner professional expertise with the judgment and local knowledge of community leaders and citizens.

### Visioning

Visioning is a community exercise in which participants imagine what they would like their community to become. Visioning deals with aspects of planning for the future, including social and economic as well as physical considerations.

Visioning sessions typically are led by trained facilitators. A discussion might begin with a question such as, What would your community be like in 10 or 20 years if you had the power to make it any way you wanted? Participants then brainstorm and all the ideas that emerge are recorded. Once the array of ideas is assembled, small groups can discuss, evaluate, and build on them, with working groups taking responsibility for gathering additional information to determine which ideas have long-range merit. These concepts are then presented to the public for further comment. Photos, sketches, and drawings help to refine the concepts into proposals, with the ultimate goal of producing a vision statement that represents the community's consensus.

Visioning may take place in one session or involve a series of sessions over months. Some cities have opened visioning offices where the public is invited to discuss ideas as they are formulated and citizens are encouraged to add input as ideas develop. To lead toward implementation, communities should set benchmark dates and use a checklist to mark their progress.

### Charrettes

The word "charrette" is derived from the French for "small cart" and refers to a cart laden with drawings that was pushed through the studios when final projects were due at the famous architecture school, Ecole des Beaux-Arts, in Paris. The term was adopted by planners with a new meaning to refer to a process of facilitating public participation in the physical design of a community project, such as a park or town square, in a short time frame (one and a half to three days). The charrette first gained favor during the 1960s, when citizen participation became important to planning and a framework was needed for their input during the design process. It continues to be used as an expeditious means to gain ideas on community design from residents, city officials, local business owners, and other stakeholders who represent varying perspectives on community issues. All participants are encouraged to speak and present design ideas during

*5.16. Community design charrette in progress, Cary, North Carolina*

a charrette; their ideas are interpreted graphically by professionals who quickly sketch them. Since the process accommodates diverse points of view, it can lead efficiently to compromise and consensus building. All parties feel they share authorship of plans that emerge from a charrette, which encourages a cooperative, rather than adversarial, climate.

Because a charrette is intended to be a one-time process, it is important to have it function properly from its opening, guided by someone who has experience with these types of interactive activities. The American Planning Association's "Planning Advisory Service MEMO" suggests various keys to planning a successful charrette.[23]

### R/UDAT Process

The Rural/Urban Design Assistance Team (R/UDAT, pronounced *roo-dat*) program, sponsored by the American Institute of Architects, assists communities that need and desire professional urban design help in the form of a multidisciplinary team of architects, planners, landscape architects, and economic development experts. These professionals work with local planners, officials, and residents to ensure that all voices in a community are given a hearing.

Typically, in a four-day intensive workshop, the invited professionals first listen to local participants discuss the problems and potentials in their community. The R/UDAT team then develops and distributes a document during the workshop period that describes strategies to be refined and implemented by the local community. The report reflects the community's concerns and aspirations, and recommends a vision for the future, including specific action items and timetables. The R/UDAT program encourages team members to return within a year to review progress and give follow-up advice on implementation.

## EXERCISE 4
### NEW TOWN DESIGN
### NEAR RIVERTOWN

*Morris Moneta, a developer with a national reputation, has been buying parcels of farmland and is now ready to begin planning for a new town in Chippewa County, just west of Rivertown's River County. His goal is to create a complete new town for a population of 5,000 residents. His design objec-*

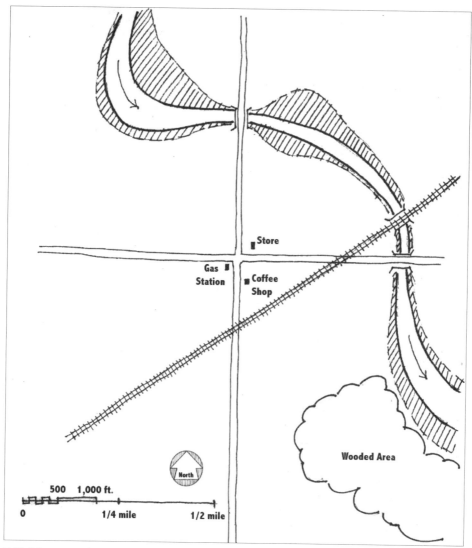

5.17. *Moneta site base map*

tive is to consider ideal land use relationships when planning this community.

The map illustrates the approximate area of undeveloped land now owned by Mr. Moneta; it includes a river, railroad tracks, and a mature-growth wooded area. At the crossroads of two, two-lane highways are an existing gas station, a convenience store, and a coffee shop/restaurant.

Because of your planning experience locally, you were contacted by Mr. Moneta. He has enlisted your professional expertise to develop a conceptual layout for his new town, and is interested in seeing your ideas based on good planning principles (as described in this chapter).

Using the map provided above, create a conceptual lay-out for a new town. (Enlarge the map as needed.) Your lay-out can be illustrated in the form of a neatly drawn bubble diagram, with specific locations indicated. It should show the following:

- a central business district
- three different residential districts (single-family, town-houses, apartments)
- a high school, middle school, and three elementary schools
- a water intake plant
- a wastewater treatment plant
- a library

- a post office
- police and fire departments
- recreation complex
- neighborhood parks
- three religious buildings
- an industrial park

Also include any additional land uses you consider necessary, such as a shopping center or mixed-use district of a composition of your choice.

Write a three-page rationale for your plan, addressing the following questions:

1. Why have you located given land uses in proximity to other land uses?

2. Why have you located some land uses farther away from other uses?

3. Where in your community would most people spend their time when they are not at home or work?

4. How does your plan allow for future growth?

To help you to prepare this layout, consider urban designer Bruce Liedstrand's review of what comprises "Fundamentals of a Good City."[24] Liedstrand's criteria describe factors important to community planning:

Intensity. A good city has intense enough development to support a rich urban life.

Diversity. A good city attracts people of diverse ages, cultures, and economic levels.

Public Realm. A good city has a rich public realm that serves as the community's common living room.

Centers. Good things are clustered in center cities and neighborhood centers, rather than being distributed randomly throughout the city.

Convenience. Everyday services are conveniently located for residents.

Walkability. Walking is a pleasurable experience that gives access to places and services.

Access. A good city provides access for its residents and visitors, which includes mass transportation, so people are not dependent on a car to get around. Cars are a useful transportation tool, but good cities do not make people depend on having access to a car.

Street Network. A good city has an interconnected, small-block street network that provides multiple access and egress points and helps disperse traffic.

Community Services. A good city provides police and fire protection, power, water, wastewater, communication, and public transportation.

In-ness. Buildings shape the space on the streets and other public places so that a person feels comfortable in the city, not outside looking at a series of objects.

## Summary

An attractive and pleasurable environment is important to good community planning. While architects design buildings, planners are responsible for the design of spaces in the public realm, and they can benefit from having design skills which complement their other areas of expertise.

Historical examples illustrate the importance of design in planning. In Riverside, Illinois, Frederick Law Olmsted created one of the country's most elegant and pleasing cities. In the early twentieth century, the City Beautiful movement grew from the idea that the more beautiful the public realm, the more pride its citizens will have in it and the more visitors it will attract. The contemporary New Urbanist movement renewed interest in design as a major tool of community planning through its focus on the use of traditional urban design principles and elements.

Although design is by nature a creative activity, there are key principles to guide the process. These principles apply at the scale of a city, a neighborhood or district, or an individual project. Steps in the design process include research, review of technical requirements, consideration of the context, the generation of conceptual design ideas, and development of a final design proposal. The adoption of design codes has gained momentum in recent years in many cities. When a community establishes design guidelines, developers and architects may object that their options are limited. If guidelines are written and drawn clearly and applied equitably, however, everyone involved in development can better meet community expectations based on the community's goals and desired urban form. Citizens can become involved in the design process through use of visioning, charrettes, or the R/UDAT process.

# 6

# URBAN PLANNING AND DOWNTOWN REVITALIZATION

## Understanding the Urban Fabric

Throughout history, the growth of human communities has occurred as a relatively continuous development of increasingly complex, ordered settlements. The first small settlements were established for hunter/gatherer groups. Advantages that came with growing crops and domesticating animals led to large and more specialized agricultural communities. As societies developed, towns based on trade were established at key locations, which meant more specialization and the development of a currency-based economy. Over the centuries, towns grew larger, attracting investment and industry, eventually leading to the complex human environments known as cities. A city is more than a collection of its inhabitants; it represents an urbanized way of life. The German urbanologist Ferdinand Tönnies (1855–1936) had a word for it—*Gesellschaft*, the pattern of life in cities: the word has a richness of meaning not found in the English vocabulary.[1]

Rural areas constitute 95 percent of the land area of the United States, but cities represent the greatest share of the country's resources of people and industry. What defines where the urban area ends and the rural area begins? In many parts of Europe, that is not a particularly difficult question to answer: the boundaries of towns are well defined. In America, by contrast, there is less control of such growth boundaries and development seems to wander into the hinterlands without defined edges, which produces sprawl.

Cities have been described as the engines of change because they stimulate economic and social progress. They are characterized by agglomeration—the concept that activities benefit from being carried on near other similar activities. For example, Detroit's shipbuilding industry spawned the early automobile industry, bringing hundreds of auto manufacturers to the region during the new industry's early years, as well as thousands of small ancillary industries supplementing the larger auto producers. This agglomeration of businesses made Detroit a major metropolitan economy during the twentieth century. Other cities hosted other industries, for example the textile industry in Lowell, Massachusetts, the fashion and garment industry in New York City, the movie industry in Los Angeles, and the computer industry in Palo Alto and Mountain View, California.

Urban societies are strong because their inhabitants live and work together with the support of rural-based production, sharing resources as basic as land and water or as sophisticated as education and the arts. Some cities have been planned for rational growth, but many of them have grown and evolved spontaneously with no real planning.

Traditionally, the central city was the most recognizable element of the urban pattern because of its higher density of development and the height of its buildings. Economist William Alonso describes the classic concept of urban land use and land value that begins with a Central Business District (CBD) at the urban core; as the city spreads outwards, the density of businesses gradually decreases.[2] Thus central commercial areas are surrounded by residential areas with agriculture beyond. Land values have followed this pattern, with the most valuable and expensive land located in the CBD, and decreasing in value with increasing distance from the center.

However, this model is no longer valid for many cities, since some have sprouted new commercial nodes

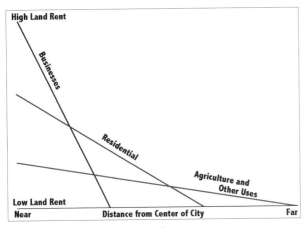

6.1. *Alonso's model of urban land use*

at the urban fringe. Writer Joel Garreau refers to these urban areas as "edge cities" because in many places these new development districts, located largely at intersections of interstate highways, have grown to the extent that the resulting city on the edge has business activity and residential development of greater density and value than its central city.[3]

## Qualitative Considerations in Urban Development

Many Americans choose to live in large urban areas that provide a wealth of resources and diversity. Some individuals find the complexity of life in a large city disconcerting, but they are able to cope with the intensity by finding their own niche within the larger metropolitan area. Large cities are broken into an array of smaller communities—ethnic, religious, social—and supporting organizations, and the greater diversity in cities makes it easier for individuals to find others with similar interests.

Planners play an important role in the process of urban growth. Urban areas fulfill both economic and cultural needs, and planning for cities should recognize the significance of both. However, often growth is seen only in quantitative terms, that is, growth in population, greater industrial production, more retail square footage, additional residential developments. What is not so obvious is that urban growth should also be seen qualitatively. Europeans in small towns and large cities are less enamored of growth for the sake of growth. The northern Italian hill town of Siena, for example, popu-

lation 56,000, attracts visitors from around the world not because of its size, but because of its special urban character. The focus of the city is the Piazza del Campo, first established in the 1200s as a marketplace for the surrounding villages. The town has retained the vital marketplace character for many centuries, and its piazza remains one of the most beautiful and best utilized civic spaces in Europe.

6.2. *Piazza del Campo, Siena, Italy, recognized in 1995 by UNESCO as a World Heritage Site*

Venice similarly focuses on a central square, the Piazza San Marco (St. Mark's Square), which provides an important entrance from the Grand Canal to the city's core. Its carefully positioned structures integrate three important aspects of any good city plan—physi-

6.3. *Piazza San Marco, Venice, Italy, with the Companile at center, the cathedral and Doge's Palace to the right; the National Library, Civic Museum, and office buildings are at left and in the background.*

cal, cultural, and economic. The Campanile tower visibly roots the space, both within the plaza and beyond. St. Mark's Cathedral, with its domed roof, is the city's most important cultural icon. The city's economic base is represented by the palace of the Doges, or merchants, located directly on the Grand Canal, historically the most important transportation link for the city's trade and a major contributor to its wealth.

Kevin Lynch, of MIT, conducted research on how residents in the United States understood their cities by asking individuals to draw maps of their city on a blank sheet of paper. As he described in *The Image of the City*, he found that their images exhibited five common elements: paths (streets, sidewalks, trails), nodes (focal points of activity), edges (perceived boundaries, such as water, walls, structures), districts (larger areas with some perceived identification), and landmarks (strongly identified objects that serve as reference points). Lynch's surveys revealed that cities with a balance of these five features—or strong "imageability"—were preferred urban environments. For examples, Bostonians drew maps with all five characteristics well represented, while the maps of Los Angeles described a city whose image consisted primarily of paths (roads and highways).[4]

Although some American cities have retained a central plaza as a major amenity (for example, San Francisco's Union Square), most cities in the United States do not provide significant civic open spaces in their core. It can be argued, however, that streets and sidewalks, where businesses, pedestrians, and automobiles are juxtaposed, are the American equivalent of the European

public plaza and serve many of the same functions. America is a dynamic society, not a static one, and our public realm reflects this.

## The Role of Downtown Retail

Commerce is one of the primary functions of all cities. Industries provide jobs; retail stores and restaurants bring life, vitality, and personality to the urban scene. The nature of retail business is one of constant change.

*6.5. Cheap Cash Store, Uniontown, Pennsylvania (circa 1900), illustrates how the image of retail business has changed in the past century*

Each era brings significant, and sometimes surprising, shifts in retail patterns. Historically, these changes have been brought about by a succession of innovations:

> packaging in containers of fixed sizes and weights (1840s); standardized methods of sorting, grading, weighing, and inspecting (early 1850s); fixed prices (1860s); standardized clothing sizes (early 1880s); periodic presentations via catalog (1880s); the buffet-style restaurant (1885) and the cafeteria serving line (1895); fully automated vending machines (1897); standardization through franchising (1911); drive-through auto service stations (1913); self-service store layout (1916); . . . packaging that 'sold itself' (late 1920s); 'fair trade' enforced price uniformity (1931); and wide selection of competing brands displayed on open shelves (1934).[5]

*6.4. Union Square, San Francisco, California*

The downtown department store was a modern commercial phenomenon. From the 1880s to the 1920s, it provided something new—a convenient one-stop shopping establishment: "In department stores, buyers of goods learned new roles for themselves, apprehended themselves as 'consumers,' something different from mere users of goods."[6] There was also a social element. The department store provided post-Victorian women a safe and convenient place to comparison shop in a pleasant environment. Shopping in grand emporiums glorified a new ethic of consumerism and embodied the success of the American economic system.

In the 1920s, Jesse C. Nichols, a real estate developer responsible for developing much of the area southwest of Kansas City for upper-income housing, recognized the increasing importance of the automobile to the new suburban lifestyle. Country Club Plaza was opened in 1922, probably the first center designed for shopping by use of the car. Located at a nexus of roads that Nichols had built over the years for his housing developments and near a trolley line, almost half of its space was devoted to streets and parking; it included one of the country's first parking garages. With 250 shops at Country Club Plaza, some of them branches of established downtown stores, Nichols made the suburban shopping center a direct competitor to the traditional downtown as a center of retail activity—a trend that has impacted cities ever since.

In 1931, Highland Park in Dallas became the prototype for suburban shopping centers as a commercial typology. All the retail activity was located in a single place, not divided by public streets, and managed by a

6.6. *Country Club Plaza, Kansas City, Missouri*

single owner, who established a uniform image for the entire complex. Northland Center, built two decades later in Southfield, Michigan, a suburb of Detroit, is generally considered to be the country's first regional mall. J. L. Hudson's, the huge downtown Detroit department store, decided to open a branch 8 miles north in this new suburban complex, where it was surrounded by a hundred smaller shops and nearly 10,000 parking spaces. Northland Center featured auditoriums, a bank, post office, infirmary, sculpture, fountains, lavish landscaping, even an office for lost children. Soon, Hudson's abandoned its downtown store, signaling the beginning of the inevitable shift of downtown retail to new suburban centers. (Coming full circle, Northland Center was demolished in 2005 and replaced by individual chain retail stores.)

Malls have continued to grow. Mall of America, just outside Minneapolis, opened in 1992. It employs 11,000

6.7. *Mall of America, Minneapolis, Minnesota*

people year-round and sales there contribute $1.8 billion to the state's economy each year. With 520 stores and 86 restaurants, it is a major shopping center that competes aggressively with downtown retail.[7] Even larger is Edmonton Mall in Alberta, Canada, with 5.2 million square feet of floor space and over 800 stores, 19 movie theatres, 110 eating establishments, and 5 amusement areas.

These malls, with all services collected in one common location, have put countless small independent retailers in traditional downtowns out of business, except for those who fill niches in the local market. Further competition to downtowns has come from commercial strips, which service shoppers by providing convenient in-and-out basic retail services directly along the roadside.

6.8. *Strip commercial district, Myrtle Beach, South Carolina*

Given the significant impact of new malls on existing communities, planners should consider measures for regulating mall siting and construction. Planning consultants Zenia Kotval and John R. Mullin suggested a mall should not be allowed by right; it should be granted only under a special permit that includes criteria related to the environment, traffic, fiscal impact, and community character as well as the potential effect on downtown, assuming full build-out of the entire property. A new mall should be governed by a site plan review, and provisions for buffer and open space, design, landscape requirements, and land use covenants should be established and enforced. The mall developer should be expected to pay for relevant technical and legal assistance required by the community.[8]

The rapid growth of these forms of retail has created many problems planners need to understand, including the following:

*Too much square footage.* The amount of retail store square footage has grown faster than the growth in population and consumer spending. One study estimates that the United States has 20 square feet of retail per capita compared to 2 square feet in Europe.[9] Many existing shopping centers have been abandoned as a result of oversupply and as new retail follows development at the urban fringe.

*Copycat imaging.* Retailers have made a habit of copying retail leaders in merchandise, layout, marketing, and service, obscuring the distinctiveness that in the past differentiated one retailer from another.

*Price sensitivity.* Growth in the retail industry in the first decade of the twenty-first century is primarily a result of making price more important than all other aspects of merchandising. Quantity sales are therefore needed to make minimal profit margins and many traditional retailers whose businesses were built primarily on quality and service have been forced out of business. With service no longer a goal, stores do not earn customer loyalty.

*Greater gap between big stores and start-ups.* Beginning in the early 1990s, a large gap began to develop and grow between large, high-performing retailers with sound management practices and the balance of the retail environment. Although this trend varies, in many communities it has discouraged start-up businesses and new entrepreneurs, leading to the control of commerce by a few big corporations.

Further, economic blight—loss in market demand brought by changes in competition or other socioeconomic factors—physical blight, and the aging and lack of maintenance of commercial structures have led to abandoned retail districts. Brian J. L. Berry has defined a number of reasons for commercial blight: changing technology; when older businesses do not accommodate changing markets; a lack of shopper convenience or inadequate parking; and external factors, such as incompatible adjacent land uses or environmental or social deterioration in the surrounding area.[10]

Planners can help communities develop strategies for encouraging redevelopment of overbuilt commercial districts with high vacancy rates. One is to require businesses to post a bond when submitting an application for a new building; the bond protects the community against the costs if the business subsequently abandons its building. In Buckingham Township, Pennsylvania, for example, "as part of the land development agreement . . . provisions shall be made for the removal or adaptive reuse of the structure by the applicant should the facility not be used for a period of 12 consecutive months. Financial security may be required by the township."[11] In Charlotte, North Carolina, city planners added to the zoning ordinance two provisions: (1) a developer must provide the financial means to tear down a building if their tenant store closes and remains empty, and (2) so-called big boxes (large stores owned and run by a corporation) must be part of a larger, mixed-use development of stores, offices, and apartments. Under the first provision, developers must put a designated amount of money in an escrow account for a specified period of time. If the structure is abandoned or destroyed, the local government can use the funds to mitigate loss of tax revenue caused by the vacant structure.[12]

## Downtown Revitalization

As many American cities lost their traditional center businesses to new developments on the city's edge, planners began to consider what could be done about it. Could downtown businesses compete directly against major discounters and chain stores in an attempt to recapture their retail dominance? Could they evolve into new kinds of retail centers, with businesses that do not compete directly with the discounters and chains, but are complementary to them? Should downtowns abandon their traditional retail role entirely and become service centers relying increasingly on office and financial functions for their viability? Or are downtowns obsolete; should they be allowed to die a natural death, as have other elements of nineteenth- and early-twentieth-century cities?

It seems we are not ready to render downtowns obsolete. A number of revitalization programs have been instituted, from the Main Street Program of the National Trust for Historic Preservation, to the Downtown Development Authority program, to Tax Increment Financing (TIF), to Business Improvement Districts (BIDs)—not to mention various programs established by local governments and merchant associations. From the 1970s to the 1990s, planners proposed new ideas to revitalize older downtown retail as well as failing industrial and residential areas. In some cities, traditional downtown functions were replaced with new types of businesses that bring a fresh vitality. Clothing and hardware stores may have moved to the suburbs, but restaurants, gift shops, entertainment, and loft apartments have filled the voids. Downtowns have had to reinvent themselves to remain viable and many of them have made the shift successfully.

The revitalization of downtowns makes sense for many reasons. Downtowns offer:

*Existing infrastructure.* Downtowns already have streets, sewer and water lines, gas and electricity, and a central location. It is wasteful to discard this existing infrastructure and build a new one at the city's edge. From both the economic and the environmental standpoints, it is a poor decision to discard our downtowns rather than recycle them.

*Community focus.* Downtowns provide a focus and a sense of identity for communities. Without such a community center, to borrow a phrase from Gertrude Stein, "There is no there there."[13] Where a community focus is lacking, it is difficult to get local support for projects and activities. As American society becomes more mobile and transient, the need for a place with which one can identify becomes increasingly important.

*Greater diversity.* Downtowns can have greater functional diversity than new centers built on the city fringe. Their mix of retail stores, banks, public agencies, local government offices, historic areas, and cultural and educational institutions, supported by public transportation, gives them viability.

*Employment opportunities.* Vital downtowns are centers of employment, and workers are regular and continuing users of other downtown businesses. A thriving downtown depends on a diverse, dynamic mix.

*Residential life.* At one time, residents moved away from their places of employment, resulting in a major disconnect of two of the most important aspects of American life: time spent at home and time spent at work. But starting in the 1970s, the downtown areas of New York City, Los Angeles, Seattle, and San Diego began to exhibit steady city center growth and cities across the country followed in the 1980s and 1990s.[14] For many, the good life can better be enjoyed by not living separated from their workplace, but by living near it in the center city. The individuals attracted to downtown tend to be educated, professional, and without children, what author Richard Florida has called the "Creative Class."[15] Among these are actors and artists, musicians and dancers, photographers, and writers, as well as professionals in health care, business and finance, law, and education.

To accommodate the influx, cities are increasingly reusing older buildings and adding sensitive infill of new buildings. In Milwaukee, for example, the largely disused riverfront area downtown has been given new life. Its Riverwalk system links many of the older industrial and commercial buildings along the river into alternative uses as restaurants, clubs and bars, with residences on the upper stories.

6.9. Riverfront redevelopment, Milwaukee, Wisconsin

In San Diego, Horton Plaza was converted from an underutilized downtown core into an exciting six-block, three-story retail area, with open spaces, bridges, towers, sculptures, fountains, and landscaping. And in South Boston, redevelopment of the waterfront area has brought major changes to this "last frontier" of the city.[16] An $800 million convention center is now fully booked, and more than 1,600 new hotel rooms and many new restaurants have brought life to a formerly down-at-the-heels district.

## Spotlight on Baltimore's Inner Harbor[17]

Urban revitalization can involve years of planning and implementation, especially when it involves large projects. The history of the Inner Harbor area of Baltimore illustrates the impact of decades of forethought and work by many individuals and organizations.

During the 1700s and early 1800s, Cheapside Wharf was the bustling mercantile center of Baltimore. Shipping agents, ship chandlers, grocers, copper and tin manufacturers, leather workers, and furniture makers lined its streets. In 1904, the Great Baltimore Fire destroyed more than 140 acres of prime business land, and many merchants could not afford to rebuild.

Fifty years later the Inner Harbor industrial district had declined terribly. Derelict warehouses testified to a once thriving commercial center. Cars were abandoned on deserted streets in deteriorating neighborhoods. As the City of Baltimore put it, "It was perceived as a city with a great past and no future, and if you made it, you were moving to New York or Philadelphia or Chicago."[18] When O'Neill's Department Store closed in 1954, J. Jefferson Miller, then executive vice president of the Hecht Company department store and director of the Retail Merchants Association, persuaded a group of business associates to look into what other cities were doing to cope with the loss of downtown as a retail hub. Their conclusion was that merchants by themselves could not bring a turnaround. The group formed a Committee for Downtown and recruited members from utilities and banks and other property owners, while 100 executives formed the Greater Baltimore Committee. The two groups secured the services of David Wallace, a nationally known planner and architect whose mission was to develop a comprehensive plan for downtown.

The first effort was Charles Center, an office development on a 33-acre parcel between the existing retail and financial districts and, in 1959, the City Council adopted Charles Center as an official urban renewal area. The downtown business community and city government became partners in revitalization efforts.

In 1964, Wallace produced a plan that provided basic guidance for a 30-year, $260 million effort to redevelop the edge of the city's inner harbor to bring the public to the water's edge. The Greater Baltimore Committee launched a public education campaign and voters approved $2 million in bonds to finance the first steps in the redevelopment of the district.

The first new Inner Harbor attraction was the restored USS *Constellation*, one of the oldest ships in the Navy, placed in 1972 at Baltimore's newly rebuilt Pier I. To draw people to the district, the City Fair—an annual September celebration—was moved to the Inner Harbor the next year. During the nation's bicentennial celebration, Baltimore hosted the Tall Ships, a flotilla of replicas of early sailing vessels. People from the city and beyond flocked to the Inner Harbor to see the spectacle. The harbor area was becoming a regional attraction.

New buildings rose: the United States Fidelity and Guaranty Company building, Baltimore's tallest, was completed; the Christ Church Harbor Apartments, senior citizen housing for low- and moderate-income people, was occupied. The IBM building, Maryland Science Center, and the Harbor Campus of the Community College all opened.

The city was only halfway through its 30-year plan, and the goal of turning the Inner Harbor vision into reality would still cost millions. The federal government provided funding through the Community Development Block Grant (CDBG) and Urban Development Action Grant (UDAG) programs.

Yet the Rouse Company's proposal to build two pavilions of shops and restaurants, called Harborplace, along the Inner Harbor promenade met with opposition. Baltimoreans feared a large commercial development would eliminate the open space along the water's edge. Businesses in Little Italy and South Baltimore, two of the city's most stable neighborhoods, feared their shops would suffer, and Baltimore's African American population did not see the proposed upscale shops and restaurants as appropriate to their needs. Developer James Rouse responded by committing to include minority firms in the building of the pavilions, to hire minorities after it was built, and promised the city careful attention to design and a high tax return. In 1978, the Harborplace proposal passed with 54 percent of voter approval and its doors opened in 1980 to a record noontime crowd of over 50,000.

6.10. *Harborplace Plaza, Baltimore, Maryland*

The glass pavilions of Harborplace, filled with an eclectic mix of retail and restaurants, illustrate the turnaround of the Inner Harbor. Ultimately, more than 90 developers and millions of dollars were involved in Baltimore's revitalization. In the years following the opening of Harborplace, more than a dozen new developments were added, including a second Rouse development, The Gallery at Harborplace. And in 1992, near the Inner Harbor, Oriole Park at Camden Yards, the home of the Baltimore Orioles, opened on the site of a former railroad center. In recent years the Inner Harbor has become an iconic landmark of the city, and its attractions bring over 16 million visitors each year.[19]

Planning played an important role in the revitalization of Baltimore's city center. The city says, "We started out with a first-rate comprehensive plan which we enacted in phases. Save for a couple of minor changes, we stuck to the plan."[20]

## Engines of Revitalization

There are many organizations and agencies that have been established to assist in efforts at downtown revitalization and center city redevelopment. Although they vary in the reasons for their existence, they often overlap in the services provided. Following are described some of the most common of these agencies.

### Redevelopment Agencies

Much of the success of a revitalization program depends on the individuals and agencies responsible for encouraging and funding such efforts. One of the most common and successful organizations is a community's redevelopment agency, which has the specific power, granted by one or more municipal authorities, to promote economic growth. The city entrusts the redevelopment agency with specific responsibilities for projects in designated districts. The powers of a redevelopment agency vary from state to state and community to community, but typical powers in its charter include the authority to acquire property to eliminate blight or obsolescence or to provide land for public facilities. The agency may demolish, construct, or reconstruct streets, utilities, parks and playgrounds, repair or rehabilitate older structures, or dispose of acquired property at fair market value.

A redevelopment agency usually does not have the power to construct administrative, police, or fire buildings, or publicly owned facilities that are part of a capital improvements program approved before the establishment of the agency. The redevelopment agency may work on projects that already have been approved for redevelopment expenditures or survey areas that are being considered for project status but are not yet approved by the city.

## Spotlight on Hunters Point Shipyard, San Francisco Redevelopment Authority

Hunters Point Shipyard is located in the bay area of southeastern San Francisco. The 500-acre facility was a naval shipyard from World War II until 1974 and was a major source of employment for the area. After 14 years of study, the City of San Francisco Redevelopment Agency proposed a plan for a $900 million cleanup and conversion of the facility to residential use, to feature new homes and parks, and employment opportunities for local residents.

Now called Bayview Hunters Point, the project has moved ahead with a new light rail service connected to the Caltrain line, Portola Place housing development and several affordable housing developments, a new police station, and a new waterfront park. Many other projects are in various planning stages.

6.11. Hunters Point Shipyard, San Francisco, 1970s

6.12. Bayview Hunters Point revitalization proposal, 2008

### Financial Institutions

Banks and lenders are essential to revitalization efforts. In an increasing effort to satisfy their stockholders, financial institutions have looked for opportunities providing the highest rate of return, sending their investment money to other regions and even to other parts of the world. These lenders ignore their responsibility to the community in which they are based and from which most of their business comes. Yet they have the resources to provide core support for their municipality's economic development programs.

The federal government's Community Reinvestment Act of 1977 (revised in 1995 and 2005) encourages local banks and thrifts to offer credit and services to their communities in an equitable manner by evaluating institutions based on their community involvement.[21] This legislation was aimed at providing affordable housing and eliminating prejudicial treatment in mortgage lending, but the act is more expansive in its administration. Some banks and lending institutions have responded by opening new branches in underserved areas, expanding services, and creating more flexible underwriting standards.

The housing meltdown of 2008 changed many of the rules of residential financing. According to a 2009 article in the *Wall Street Journal*, 23 percent of U.S. homeowners owed more on their mortgages than their properties were worth.[22] Without a substantial recovery, these owners have no equity available from their primary asset, limiting their ability to plan for the future. Planners must recognize the long-term implications of this situation.

## Business Improvement Districts

Business Improvement Districts (BIDs) are another mechanism for funding general improvements to a business district. BIDs use fees from member businesses to fund services in the BID district beyond what a city normally provides. The services may include security personnel (if there is concern about crime in the district), additional street cleaning, maintenance, or paying for joint promotional programs. Typically, the local government collects the fees and distributes them to the BID for defined projects.

BIDs, established through the petition of a majority of property owners in a commercial district who see the value in combining resources, are enabled through state legislation and are being used in most states. They are usually structured as nonprofit organizations, although they may be constituted as a public agency. As examples, the Alliance for Downtown New York, Downtown D.C. in Washington, the Fashion District in Los Angeles, and the Center City District in Philadelphia are BIDs. Many medium-sized and small cities also have BIDs.

## Downtown Development Authorities

Downtown Development Authorities (DDAs) are intended primarily to prevent and correct deterioration of existing business districts. They also promote economic growth, encourage historic preservation, and contribute to revitalization. DDAs provide communities with the necessary organizational, monetary, and legal assistance to carry out public sector initiatives alone or in concert with privately motivated development projects.

Similar to redevelopment agencies but focused more

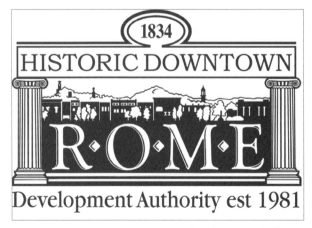

*6.13. Rome, Georgia's Downtown Development Authority placard*

on downtowns, DDAs study economic changes and the impact of metropolitan growth on the downtown district and plan, and develop and finance construction or rehabilitation that contributes to the economic growth of the downtown. Typically, a DDA prepares development and tax increment (TIF) plans (see Chapter 16) to submit to the local municipality for approval. The development plan describes the resources, location, and cost of public improvements projected to take place in the DDA district; the plan details the tax increment procedure, the amount of bonded indebtedness to be incurred, and the duration of the program. DDAs underwrite streetscape improvements, parking, underground utilities and other public infrastructure improvements, downtown marketing efforts, and downtown staff operations, to name a few. The DDA may sell, lease, convey, own, or dispose of property as both lessor and lessee and issue bonds for revenue-producing public facilities.

States utilize DDAs in various ways. Under Colorado law, local governments can establish DDAs and use tax increment financing for financial support. In Wyoming, authorities can "plan and propose . . . removal, site preparation, renovation, repair, remodeling, reconstruction, or other changes in existing buildings . . . which in the opinion of the board will aid and improve the downtown development area."[23] In Michigan, there are over 345 communities with DDAs, an indicator of the success of the program.

## The Main Street Program

In 1980, the National Trust for Historic Preservation established the Main Street Program to show that the rehabilitation of older commercial buildings could be an important part of a downtown revitalization effort. The original concept for the Main Street Program was based on three pilot projects that began in 1977 in Galesburg, Illinois; Hot Springs, South Dakota; and Madison, Indiana. Since then, the Main Street Program has become one of the most important and influential nationwide programs dealing directly with downtown revitalization. Designation as a Main Street state or city brings recognition to a community's efforts and ensures that the program's Standards of Performance are followed. Over 1,200 of these programs have been established across the United States. Main Street programs often are partnered with other downtown programs such as DDAs or BIDs.

Encouraged by the results of its pilot projects, the Main Street Program established a Four-Point Approach to downtown revitalization based on four key issues:

*Organization*. Various groups working in a downtown may have different perspectives on an approach to its revitalization. For example, the merchants' association may want to promote retail sales, the Chamber of Commerce create jobs, and city government provide municipal services. Without coordination, the separate agendas of these interest groups may not support those of the others (and, as a result, miss opportunities for synergy) or even conflict with one another. The Main Street Program organizes these varied interests into efforts with revitalization as their common goal.

*Promotion*. Many older downtowns have an image problem because they have deteriorated as residents have left them for shopping centers and malls. The Main Street Program has shown that joint advertising campaigns for downtown businesses, new logos, new signage, and special festivals attract people. Making the downtown a destination that offers a variety of pleasurable experiences can remake its image.

*Economic restructuring*. The Main Street Program looks for new and innovative sources of private and/or public funding for downtown improvements. It may enlist local banks to create a revolving loan program for rehabilitation work or use grants and loans from external sources for specific efforts.

*Design*. Good design downtown is a signal that a downtown is thriving. Organization, promotion, and economic restructuring are important to a successful overall program, but design provides the visual evidence. Residents can see that the downtown is improving when the streetscape gains plantings and furniture, storefronts are rehabilitated, and well-lit displays and special projects freshen the environment.

The National Trust Main Street Center office in Washington, D.C. (www.preservationnation.org/main-street), engages in many activities to benefit communities and individuals. It supports and coordinates a nationwide network of Main Street organizations and provides direct, on-site technical assistance and consulting services to towns, cities, and urban neighborhoods. It publishes a wide range of books and training materials including the *Main Street News*, available to its members. It offers professional training and certification programs through the National Main Street Institute and coordinates the annual National Main Street Conference on commercial district revitalization. Annual National Main Street Awards recognize revitalization successes.

### EXERCISE 5
### RIVERTOWN TOMORROW

*Rivertown's City Council has decided to establish a Main Street Program to focus efforts on the city's downtown area and wants guidance on how it can use the program for revitalization. Various merchants have agreed to assist in this effort and would likely support any recommendations. Norman Tyler, manager of the First National Bank, said the bank would be willing to cooperate in the establishment of a funding program for downtown businesses.*

*Based on your knowledge of Rivertown, suggest four proposed activities that respond to each of the four points of the Main Street Program: organization, promotion, economic restructuring, and design. (Information about Rivertown can be found in the Appendices and earlier exercises.)*

#### Downtown Zoning
Conventional zoning is a regulatory tool, rather than an incentive to revitalization (see Chapter 14 for more on zoning). Historically, zoning's role has been to prevent incompatible land uses. Over time this role has produced zoning ordinances that may limit flexibility for planners and developers.

Zoning, however, can be used as a tool for downtown revitalization. For example, mixed-use zoning enables the blending of commercial and residential land uses. With mixed-use zoning, residents become customers for commercial establishments, and in turn local businesses provide convenient services for residents. In some areas, clean industries may also be allowed in mixed-use districts because they provide local employment.

**Spotlight on Washington D.C.'s Downtown Shopping (SHOP) District (an overlay zone)[24]**
The SHOP district in Washington, D.C., uses zoning as a tool to encourage a diversity of functions in its downtown. The SHOP zoning district, an 18-square-block area of downtown, originally was a response to lack of ground floor retail space in many office buildings being constructed there, with the result that entire blocks of the downtown had little retail activity.

6.14. *SHOP Zone, Washington, D.C.*

The zoning overlay (a set of regulations available as an option to the underlying zoning) required that at least 20 percent of the total floor area of new buildings be either retail or service uses, while the remaining floor area could be office or residential. This ratio was nearly four times the typical amount of space previously allotted to retail in downtown buildings, and in many instances meant that both the ground floor and the second floor of a building needed to be reserved for retail. In the calculation of floor areas, exceptions were allowed: department stores count as triple square footage credit because they are considered very desirable uses; theaters count double; minority or displaced businesses count one and a half of the allocation. The zoning also regulated entrances and display windows, and discouraged indoor atriums since it was determined that these popular spaces do not contribute to the vitality of the street outdoors. The SHOP program's rigorous technique to create mixed uses initially met with resistance from developers, but it was successful in restoring retail uses to this important downtown area.

Other cities have established specially zoned downtown districts similar to the SHOP zone. In Cincinnati, a local ordinance specifies that at least 60 percent of ground-level frontage must be retail; banks, travel agents, and airline ticket offices are not considered retail uses. Bellevue, Washington, encourages the establishment of neighborhood businesses operated by in-town residents. San Francisco requires that a mix of retail be established for both affluent and less affluent downtown workers.

Zoning does not fully protect against undesirable uses. For example, downtowns, especially in economically depressed areas, may face the difficult issue of where to allow sex businesses. City officials must balance the rights of citizens who feel the moral values of their community are at stake and business owners who claim their right to free speech is constitutionally protected. The courts have established that the location of sex-oriented businesses can be regulated, but they cannot be banned completely; they must be able to exist someplace within a community. Although citizens tend to see the establishment of these businesses as an issue that should be addressed on moral grounds, for planning purposes only land-use restrictions are viable. Two basic approaches to control sex businesses are available: the "divide and regulate" scheme that forbids sex businesses from locating too close to one another or to a residential district, and the "concentrate and regulate" approach, which limits all sex businesses to one area.

If legal restraints of sex-related businesses are based on the impact on the surrounding area in the same objective way as other businesses are regulated, a reasonable method of zoning can be developed. Traffic studies, crime statistics, tax consequences, and the effect on surrounding commercial and residential areas are means to address the issue and offer the opportunity for review and development of appropriate regulations based on good planning principles, rather than on emotional public reaction.

6.15. Sketch of Adult World bookstore

### *EXERCISE 6*
### ADULT WORLD BOOKSTORE IN RIVERTOWN

*Residents in Rivertown are furious about a newly established Adult World bookstore operated by local businessman Nipsy More. It is located in his former Sports World store on Station Street, next to Feldt's Toys and Games store. Ms. Ima Peeples, who lives directly behind the store, has threatened to take action: "I'll go right to City Council and give them a piece of my mind for allowing this," said Ms. Peeples.*

*Bookstore owner More, when asked about the business, explained that a new America Big-Box store located just west of the city's boundary had drawn customers from his sports store and he had to find a business that would have no competition. He felt he was within his legal rights to open the new store. City Council member Delores Lemma, who is opposed to the new use, explained that the city's zoning ordinance (see Appendix C) makes no reference to sex businesses; thus, they are not explicitly prohibited.*

*As the city's assistant planner, you are to write a memo to Ms. Lemma describing what the city might do to resolve this problem. You may research how other communities have addressed a similar situation. Suggest actions residents could take to influence either Mr. More or Ms. Peeples to reevaluate their stand.*

## Smart Growth

"Smart growth" is one of the most important current movements in urban planning; as one critic said, "Who can be in favor of dumb growth?"[25] Smart growth is defined as planning that encourages growth in center cities rather than on the urban fringe and advocates land uses that are walkable, bicycle-friendly, and well-supplied with local transportation. Smart growth concentrates on neighborhood schools, multifunction streets, mixed-use development, and a range of housing choices. It ties urban growth to long-range, regional planning. The national organization, Smart Growth America, is a coalition of national, state, and local organizations working to improve the ways in which American communities are planned. Members represent various interests, among them environmental concerns, historic preservation, neighborhood redevelopment, farmland and open space preservation, and alternative transportation.

Some states have taken significant measures to control growth and encourage better decisions about where growth should occur. Maryland's Smart Growth Areas Act of 1997 designated Priority Funding Areas (PFAs), both urban and rural, including areas already serviced with water and sewer, or areas where such infrastructure improvements are part of the community's plan. Areas outside PFAs are ineligible for either infrastructure or economic development assistance. The intention is to stimulate development in existing communities, rather than in new ones that would contribute to sprawl. Smart Growth rates development proposals on a point system, with favorable treatment for projects that have a high proportion of private to public dollars, are located in areas with relatively high unemployment, are linked to local employment and training providers, and contribute to public safety, welfare, education, and/or transit. An Illinois act, for example, gives a tax credit to businesses that locate in an area with nearby public transportation and/or affordable (workforce) housing. Companies also may qualify for credits by giving employees housing credits or providing shuttle services.

## Urban Growth Boundaries

Urban growth boundaries are designed to direct growth to lands designated for increased intensity and away from lands reserved for rural uses. Local governments can guide and promote growth within their urban boundaries in accordance with their comprehensive plan for significant periods of time—typically 20 years or more. Urban growth boundaries correspondingly protect farmland and open space from premature development, thereby enhancing the agricultural economy and promoting conservation.

Growth boundaries must be drawn carefully and with foresight, especially if there is no requirement for future review. The establishment of growth boundaries typically is a three-step process. First, the boundary lines must be mapped in conjunction with the community's comprehensive plan. Next, the voters need to approve the boundaries through an initiative or a referendum or through the municipal council. Finally, the community must work with adjacent jurisdictions that will be affected by the measure, ensuring cooperation with the spirit and intent of the action.

Growth boundaries have been used successfully in urban areas in Tennessee, Maryland, and Florida in the east, and California, Washington, and Oregon in the west. Several states mandate creation of urban growth boundaries. Boundaries on a regional scale frequently

are adopted with multijurisdictional cooperation, by voter approval and/or governmental action.

The first growth-limiting measure was established in 1972 in Petaluma, California, 40 miles north of San Francisco. Concerned about rapid development, the voters in Petaluma limited the number of new housing units to 500 per year, about half the number that had been built in previous years. They approved a growth boundary to control urban sprawl and minimize growing costs for building infrastructure. As a result, pastures and open space now surround the city and grain silos and creameries are important ties to the community's past. Petaluma boasts an attractive mixture of old and new, with a central city plan that commits the city to keeping older land uses from being crowded out.

Portland, Oregon, offers perhaps the best example of the use of an urban growth boundary. In 1973, a coalition of farmers and environmentalists and a supportive governor convinced the state legislature that

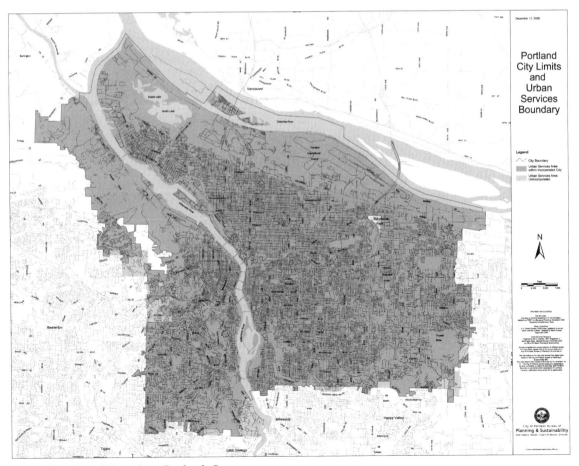

6.16. *Urban Growth Boundary, Portland, Oregon*

urban growth control measures would be the most effective means of protecting the state's natural beauty and ready access to open space. Under Oregon law, each city or metropolitan area in the state has an urban growth boundary that separates urban land from rural land.[26] By state law, the City of Portland is required to have a minimum 20-year supply of land available for residential development within its growth boundary. The status of the supply is reviewed every five years by the Metro Council. Portland's growth boundary is not static but is modified based on changing conditions. For example, in 2002 nearly 19,000 acres were added to provide for over 38,000 housing units, representing an increase in size of 9 percent since 1990, compared to an increase in population of 17 percent during that same period.

## Summary

Communities across the United States have evolved from small settlements along rivers to agricultural communities to centers for trade to large industrial cities and, finally, to postindustrial metropolitan areas. Urban areas occupy a small fraction of America's landscape, yet have become the location of the majority of residential, commercial, and industrial land uses.

Local government leaders and urban planners confront new challenges presented by significant demographic shifts and a long-term pattern of population migration from the center city to the urban and suburban fringe. The core of a city is its central business district (CBD). Most CBDs reached their peak of growth and economic vitality decades ago. During the last century, cities lost much of their primacy to suburban and rural transitional areas. Economic dependence on the central city declined as shopping malls and strip mall developments rose along major roads. Aging infrastructure such as streets, disused factories, and relocated or abandoned businesses contributed to urban flight. In response, most large city downtowns are reinventing themselves. Their existing infrastructure, including roads, sidewalks, and water and sewer lines, make them ready for redevelopment, and from the standpoint of sustainability it is desirable to utilize these existing developed areas rather than adding to sprawl. Yet, it is often cheaper to build on virgin land in the suburbs than it is to rebuild in an older urbanized area, so planners must help cities to find funding and develop incentives for builders and developers.

Many organizations are available to support revitalization plans to bring center cities increased economic development. Among these are redevelopment agencies, financial institutions, Business Improvement Districts, Downtown Development Authorities, and the Main Street Program. Special zoning provisions, Smart Growth programs, and Urban Growth Boundaries reinforce the vitality of urban core areas.

7

# HOUSING

## The Importance of Housing to Planners

Residential land use represents a major segment of urban and suburban communities. In addition to good air, water, and food, shelter is one of society's basic physical needs. Planners need to understand the various social and economic implications of a community's ability to provide for housing and homeownership. The provision of adequate housing is a highly personal issue—virtually every individual identifies with his or her own place of residence. Housing provides safety, security, and space for family activities. Its location establishes community links to schools, jobs, retail, social activities, and open space. The place an individual calls home also represents a public image and confers relative social status.

7.1. *Townhouses for sale in a new development, St. Louis, Missouri*

Much of a community's inherent wealth is tied up in revenues based on mortgages and construction, and from the taxes these generate, which impact public expenditures on schools, parks, utilities, and other public services and amenities. Thus, community planners should have a solid understanding of housing programs, both those financed by government and those financed by private lending agencies.

## Demographics of Housing

Housing has changed over time and from place to place. In 1900, the average American household had 4.6 people; by 1970, 3.1 people, and in 2008, 2.6 people.[1] The population of the United States now has passed 300 million, but the number of people per household has dropped dramatically because families have fewer children, marriages occur later, and there are more single-person households. Smaller households, coupled with the natural growth of the population, have led to a need for more housing units than in previous decades, a trend expected to continue throughout the twenty-first century.

Looking at cohort groups, that is, groups with similar characteristics, gives a useful perspective. The most significant group may be the baby boomer generation, those born from 1946 to 1954, which continues to skew almost every demographic chart. This generation, approaching retirement age, has triggered a significant shift in housing supply and demand, from homes for families to empty nester housing (couples with no children at home) and retiree housing. Elderly people are living longer and the percentage of seniors in the population is much larger than in previous decades.

These data provide a basis for formulating future scenarios. For example, as the baby boomer generation dies,

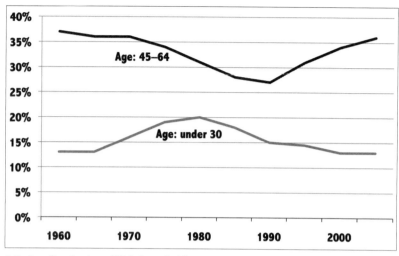

7.2. *Age distribution of U.S. households*

garbage receptacles, and it brought critical improvements to the health of the immigrant poor. In 1879, a second Tenement House Act promulgated stricter standards, requiring at least two toilets per floor and airshafts to provide interior living spaces with access to fresh air. The third Tenement House Act, enacted in 1901 and referred to as the "New Law," required permits for construction, alterations, and conversions, and subjected such work to inspection. In addition, it established a housing authority to ensure compliance. The New Law became the model for housing laws throughout the United States.

10 to 20 years out, the number of housing units available could increase significantly, reducing the cost of buying a house in locales where seniors are concentrated. Where more community residents become homeowners, the rental market may slow unless the community is attracting new residents to the area. These developments are somewhat predictable, but may be affected by new trends that are not yet apparent, such as changes in interest rates and the availability of mortgages.

Housing trends can be projected from the sample of households in the decennial U.S. Census of Housing. Selected households are asked questions about income, costs of housing, and the associated costs of plumbing facilities, fuel, heating equipment, and other expenses. These data, which provide detailed information on housing characteristics, are recorded at the census tract level as well as for larger units, such as towns, cities, metropolitan areas, and states.

## The Government's Role in Housing

### Tenement Laws

The first significant housing legislation in the United States was a series of tenement laws in New York City. The first act, the Tenement House Act of 1867, established a minimum design for tenement buildings being built speculatively to house an increasing influx of immigrants. The law mandated that tenement housing be equipped with ventilation, fire escapes, toilets, and

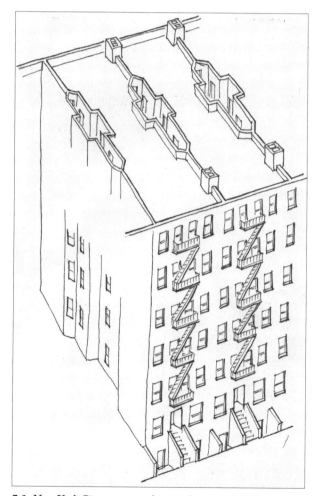

7.3. *New York City tenement house, showing airshafts*

## Mortgage Interest Deductions and the National Housing Act of 1934

The federal government has had an important role in housing for more than a century. Sometimes the impact has been indirect. In 1913, Congress initiated the federal income tax, and gave taxpayers the right to deduct interest payments on mortgages. The mortgage deduction was originally aimed at business expenses, since few individuals had home mortgages in 1913, but it became an important benefit of personal home ownership.

Other legislation followed. The National Housing Act of 1934 created the Federal Housing Administration (FHA) to provide low-cost housing and, by combining with the Public Works Administration (established the previous year), to provide jobs in construction. Bank loans had previously covered less than half the cost of a house, with the payback period a relatively short two to five years. The Act gave power to the FHA to insure home loans and to regulate the interest rate and terms of every mortgage it insured. The Act restored confidence in lending institutions that had been devastated by the Great Depression of the 1930s. Lending institutions were now willing to cover 80 percent of the cost of a house for 20 years, and subsequently 30 years, a policy that became a prime financial incentive for homeownership across the country. As many more Americans became able to purchase their own house, the single-family home became the prevalent form of housing. Single-family homes as a segment of the housing market increased from 44 percent in the 1940s to almost 70 percent in the 1990s. The National Housing Act also specified standards to ensure that new housing met a minimum level of quality in construction, materials, and room sizes.

World War II caused massive dislocation and redistribution of the American population as soldiers left home and workers moved to military-industrial areas in places such as southern California, Detroit, and Norfolk, Virginia. This relocation created severe housing shortages in these areas because housing starts dropped precipitously and construction of public housing virtually ceased during the war. Wartime employment coupled with very little to purchase resulted in high rates of personal savings. When soldiers returned from the war, married, and had children (the baby boom), a great pent-up demand for new housing was released. Government programs helped veterans buy housing through substantial subsidies; the Veterans Administration guaranteed home loans for new housing, including low-interest, long payback periods, and low down-payments. New home construction quickly grew to over 1 million units annually. Many who had previously been renters became homeowners.

## The Urban Renewal Program

The Housing Act of 1949 had two primary thrusts: to authorize funding for 810,000 units of public housing, with the stated goal of "a decent home in a suitable living environment for every American family," and urban redevelopment to eliminate blight found in many older large cities.[2] With heavy lobbying from the real estate sector, which saw public housing as competing with the private market, the Act emphasized instead the goal of "urban renewal," and the focus on slum clearance gained new momentum. Urban renewal policies established a process for using federal funds to assemble large parcels of urban real estate, clear them of unwanted structures, make appropriate site improvements, and sell the cleared sites to private developers at well below the cost to improve. The demolition part of this program was quite successful in many cities, but parcel sales to developers were not. Investors preferred to purchase unencumbered sites in newly developing suburban areas, since land was inexpensive, taxes were light, and the workforce had been moving there in ever-increasing numbers. Also, government policies encouraged the construction and purchase of housing in suburban areas. All this contributed, however unintentionally, to the decline of central cities.

A significant step for urban planning occurred with the passage of the Housing Act of 1954, an amendment of the 1949 act. Section 701 of the Act contained a provision for federal matching funds—a 50/50 match of federal and state money—to pay for the preparation of comprehensive plans with a housing element. Funding became available not only for new construction and demolition, but also for the rehabilitation and conservation of deteriorating areas. This shift in policy has had a major impact on today's housing policies, where rehabilitation rather than demolition is encouraged. Initially only cities with a population of less than 25,000 were eligible, but later this was amended to include larger cities, Native American reservations, and state governments. The federal government tied the plan to eligibility for grant funds earmarked for urban renewal. The Act precipitated a rash of comprehensive plans; planners rushed to gain contracts from local governments to produce planning documents. Many of the comprehensive plans created under this program were similar in content and lacked meaningful local identity; community leaders dutifully placed them on a shelf and ignored the content because the plans satisfied the qualification for federal housing grant eligibility, but offered minimal relevant planning recommendations for the local community.

The Urban Renewal Program received federal support through the 1950s and 1960s based on the assumption that clearing slums was a benefit in itself. As a result, 450,000 housing units per year were lost to the wrecking ball, reducing the number of affordable housing units available to the urban poor and destroying neighborhoods in the process. Only gradually did planners and local officials realize that social vitality had been eliminated in the name of renewal.

Urban renewal also was often highly discriminatory in its thrust. In Minneapolis, for example, the number of African American residents was quite small; a new highway constructed through the middle of the neighborhood in which they were concentrated caused many of these families to lose their homes. In Baltimore, the homes of 10,000 families were removed in the name of urban renewal; 90 percent of these belonged to African American families. The same story played out in cities from coast to coast. Many of the ethnic poor were moving to northern cities for new industrial jobs where they could not buy housing in white neighborhoods. This neglect contributed to the race riots of the 1960s, when frustration in black neighborhoods exploded in demonstrations, a situation which encouraged white flight to the suburbs.

### Housing and Civil Rights Acts of the 1960s

In the 1960s a number of civil rights acts addressed housing needs. The Civil Rights Acts of 1964 and 1968 established a policy of equal opportunity in housing to redress not just a lack of housing but the inability of minority families to afford adequate housing. In 1965, Lyndon Johnson's War on Poverty led to congressional approval of an Office of Economic Opportunity and the creation of a new federal agency, the Department of Housing and Urban Development (HUD), which was charged with coordinating all federal housing and redevelopment programs.

The Demonstration Cities and Metropolitan Devel-opment Act of 1966 transferred power and responsibility for administering housing and other programs from the federal government to local agencies. This effort to make the administration of the programs local was largely unsuccessful because local agencies were not equipped to handle such programs.

Nevertheless, during the Great Society of the 1960s, federal housing programs abounded. The Public Housing Act of 1968 set a 10-year goal to construct 26 million new low- and moderate-income housing units for HUD-qualified applicants. Public housing, first available as temporary housing for poor families during the Great Depression, by the 1960s had become permanent housing for a whole class of dependent families.

### Case Study: Pruitt-Igoe Project, St. Louis

The Pruitt-Igoe housing project in St. Louis is considered by many planners and government officials the most outstanding failure of public housing, and embodies the misguided federal public housing policy of the 1960s.

Pruitt-Igoe was St. Louis's answer to postwar blight. City planners had years before slated large portions of the center city for demolition. Under the urban renewal portion of the Housing Act of 1949, money became available and the city planned to construct an astounding 12,000 new units of public housing to house the displaced poor; 5,800 units were approved and constructed as Pruitt-Igoe. Pruitt-Igoe was really two projects; Pruitt was for blacks and Igoe for whites (although when problems arose whites quickly moved out and Igoe soon became less than 1 percent white). The plan included 33 identical 11-story buildings on a single site, on the theory that high-rise buildings would allow for large green spaces surrounding each structure.

*7.4. Pruitt-Igoe housing project, 1954*

At the time of its construction, the project was hailed as modern architecture's solution to social problems. The first tenants moved in 1954. The original plans called for a full community, including businesses, churches, and recreational facilities, but by 1956 the Housing Authority had depleted its fiscal resources. HUD, which had funded the construction, declined to support it further. St. Louis was left with the responsibility for fulfilling the plan.

The partially realized plan turned out to be a formula for failure. By 1959, Pruitt-Igoe had become a scandal. As one worker put it, "When one drives or walks in Pruitt-Igoe, he is confronted by a dismal sight. Glass, rubble and debris litter the streets, the accumulation is astonishing . . . abandoned automobiles have been left in parking areas; glass is omnipresent; tin cans are strewn throughout, paper has been rained on and stuck in the cracked, hardened mud. Pruitt-Igoe from without looks like a disaster area."[3] By 1961, the Pruitt-Igoe project area had the highest crime rate in the city, caused by the concentration of poor people in one place. The project became "a concrete shell where anarchy prevailed."[4]

Despite renovations, by 1968 the Housing Authority considered the project unmanageable and asked the federal government to take it over. With 75 percent of the units unoccupied by then, it was decided to demolish half the structures to reduce the density. A few years later, the remaining units were dynamited and Pruitt-Igoe came to an inglorious end.

Three primary theories have been advanced to explain the failure of Pruitt-Igoe and other similar high-rise public housing projects. The first theory suggests that the poor are irresponsible because, lacking employment or having low-wage jobs, they have not developed a sense of pride in property. The strategy for dealing with

7.5. Demolition of Pruitt-Igoe housing project, 1972

the problem, the theory holds, is to allow the poor to own their own housing through subsidy programs.

A second theory posits that high-rise buildings are the cause of the problem. Apartment blocks have repetitive, anonymous spaces with little relationship to the environment; monitoring spaces within and around the structures is difficult. This suggests that public housing should be built as low-rise units, where residents can monitor activities from windows, doorways, patios, and porches.

The third theory holds that housing projects become warehouses of the poor that undermine the dignity of their residents and isolate them from the rest of the community; the characterless atmosphere spawns depression and decay. The solution is to disperse public housing throughout the broader community so the poor are part of a larger, more affluent neighborhood that offers more support for residents.

Whatever the relative accuracy of such theories, they indicate how public housing needs to be addressed to rectify past mistakes. Providing properly designed residences for low- and moderate-income citizens in a manner that integrates, rather than isolates, them from the rest of the community eliminates the stigma which high-rise public housing engenders.

### The Housing and Community Development Act of 1974

The urban renewal programs of the 1940s and 1950s and the Great Society programs of the 1960s were less than successful. Urban renewal funds were most available to communities that could write the best proposals for grants, so funding frequently went to the wealthiest cities, which had the best resources to write winning applications. The cost of housing programs was rising, and the cost of fighting a war in Vietnam posed increasing financial difficulty funding both "guns and butter."

In 1971, President Richard Nixon proposed a new approach to community development through the Housing and Community Development (HCD) Act, which passed in 1974. In place of funding based on grant applications, the Act allocated funds directly to communities based on a pre-established formula for revenue sharing. Section 8 of the Act created a housing allowance program that permitted low-income residents to find their own housing and get federal support based on their income and rent. With this single program, which replaced many other programs, the federal government no longer needed to build housing, but could rely on the private sector to fill that need. The goal was to disperse the low-income population throughout communities, rather than concentrating them within a public housing project.

The HCD Act consolidated many housing programs into so-called block grants, which permit local governments to decide how best to use federal money for their needs, thereby linking them to overall community development projects. As a result, the Community Development Block Grant (CDBG) program became the primary means of government involvement and support for housing and community development.

During the 1980s, the Reagan administration further stressed reliance on policies instead of construction and shifted responsibility for satisfying housing needs to the states. The change in emphasis was dramatic: in the 1970s over 1 million federally subsidized housing units became available; by the 1980s there was just a trickle of new units. HUD's budget was cut during this period from $32 billion in 1981 to $9 billion by 1990. A controversial housing voucher program provided funding to cover the costs of families finding their own housing. In 1999, approximately 1.6 million households received vouchers that relied on a government budget of $7 billion. Through these efforts, there was a shift away from providing public housing for families toward continuing a program of providing housing primarily for the elderly.

The HUD-administered Housing Opportunities Program encouraged local governments to assume more responsibility for providing housing; it directed funding to local authorities, nonprofit agencies, and developers to initiate programs. Habitat for Humanity, a nonprofit, ecumenical Christian housing program that has built over 200,000 units around the world, largely through volunteer labor, is one result.

In Britain, 20 to 25 percent of the housing is in some manner government supported, and in other developed countries the percentage is well above 10 percent. In contrast, the U.S. government contributes less than 2 percent. One reason public housing does not have a more important role in the United States is an exceptionally strong free-enterprise ethic that looks upon public housing as "creeping socialism."[5] A degree of racial bias and discrimination lowers support for programs whose beneficiaries are likely to be largely African American and Hispanic. Other highly organized and well-funded opposition traditionally springs from various organizations with a vested interest such as the National Association of Real Estate Boards, the National Association of Home Builders, the United States Savings and Loan League, the U.S. Chamber of Commerce, the Mortgage Bankers Association of America, and the American Bankers Association, who benefit from private sector lending.

## Other Housing Issues

Planners and community leaders must understand a number of other issues related to housing when creating a comprehensive plan. Among these are homelessness, gentrification, and urban homesteading.

### Homelessness

The homeless are a relatively unseen population in American society. Homelessness does not refer only to people who lack housing, but also to those who live in transitional housing, or who spend most nights in supervised public or private facilities or in places not designed for, or ordinarily used as, regular sleeping accommodations for human beings. Homelessness has increased in recent decades, in part because of the growing shortage of affordable housing and in part because of an increase in poverty. In 2007, over 37 million Americans (13 percent) lived in poverty, 38 percent of them children under 18 years of age.[6] Homelessness may also be caused by a natural disaster, such as Hurricane Katrina, when the government proved ill-equipped to provide shelter

7.6. *Possessions of homeless stored for the day, Philadelphia*

to those who lost their own housing and did not have insurance or resources to find new housing.

People who are homeless by choice—because they wish to discard their physical attachments or remove themselves from society, or because they are social misfits—comprise a negligible portion of the population and generally require no special programs or services. Most homelessness stems from the inability to work, prolonged and severe drug and/or alcohol abuse or mental illness, or alienation from normal support networks such as family and friends.

A surprisingly high proportion of the homeless population are victims of the high cost of housing and a lack of living-wage jobs; this group is composed of unskilled workers who have been chronically unemployed, young people in transition in a new community or, most disturbing, single parents with children who have no other choice but to live in their car or seek shelter under a bridge. According to a 2005 survey, 42 percent of the chronically homeless were families with children, and they represent the fastest-growing group within the homeless population.[7] A 2007 study followed thousands of homeless people in New York City and found that they each used public services, such as hospital care and jail, valued at $40,000 per year. When half of the group was offered public housing, the costs per person dropped dramatically.[8]

In 1986, HUD established the McKinney-Vento Homeless Assistance Act. This Act offers additional funding to cities for programs that focus on the chronically homeless. As a result, many cities have adopted 10-year plans. Neighborhood opposition, known as NIMBYism—Not In My Back Yard—continues to impede success, but efforts by planners to address this community issue are important and necessary.

## EXERCISE 7
### LOCATING A NEW SHELTER FOR THE HOMELESS IN RIVERTOWN

*For many years the First Methodist Church has served as an emergency facility for Rivertown's increasing number of homeless. The trustees, believing the church can no longer afford to provide this service, have asked the city to accept responsibility for this social need. The homeless population may include people with a variety of problems—among them joblessness, substance abuse, and mental illness.*

*Rivertown's City Council held a public hearing to determine whether the homeless could be placed in individual residences or in a city-administered facility. They determined a new small facility was the best solution, and authorized funds for its construction.*

*As Rivertown's planner, you have been asked to recommend the location of a new shelter to house up to 20 individuals. You recognize that Rivertown's residents object to the idea of a homeless shelter near their home. Consider the following social factors to determine a workable location critical to the success of the project.*

- *The nearest medical facility is located 1 mile east of the city, in Erie Township.*
- *The First Methodist Church, located near Biltmore Avenue across from Walden Pond, has agreed to continue its breakfast program for the needy.*
- *Some of the homeless may be families with school-aged children.*
- *Public transportation currently provided by the city is limited to a small bus available on demand for a nominal fee.*

*Using the map of the city included in Appendix D, recommend a location for a shelter; in your report include a response to all of the concerns described above. (You do not need to consider current zoning.)*

### Urban Homesteading

A steady loss of affluent residents from old cities to the suburbs frequently results in a corresponding increase in abandoned and empty homes and a poorer population. Neighborhoods that were once contributors to community life and the tax base may become drags on both. One solution to attract a new generation of urbanites into these older, sometimes historic, residential areas is an urban homesteading program that allows low- and moderate-income residents to become homeowners. (The term "urban homesteader" also has been used to designate householders who live in cities but try to establish a natural and sustainable lifestyle by becoming as self-sufficient as possible.) Urban homesteading programs have been tried in a number of larger cities, including New York City, Baltimore, Pittsburgh, and Philadelphia, as well as some 90 other cities across the country. Most of the programs have been similar. Local governments that owned vacant houses (as a result of nonpayment of taxes or other reasons) offered these structures at a very low cost (sometimes for a nominal $1) to individuals who promised to upgrade the homes to meet building codes, pay property taxes, and live in the homes as owner-occupants for a minimum number of years. Once they fulfill the provisions of the program, they receive title to the property.

Local governments benefit from homesteading through increased property tax base due to higher property values. For example, in 1999 in Washington, D.C., over 2,000 people participated in a lottery for 68 boarded-up homes to be sold for $250 apiece. In return, buyers had to pledge to do the repairs and rehabilitation required to bring the structures to building code standards and to inhabit the homes for at least five years. In some cities, the programs grew by encouraging tenant associations to buy groups of buildings and share resources and management.

Urban homesteading may not be suitable for all community members who have housing needs: some residents do not have the skills to improve a code-deficient dwelling, while others may not have the resources to buy even basic building materials, such as lumber, roofing, or paint. But for those individuals or families who are able to take advantage of an urban homesteading program, it can encourage the rehabilitation of well-built housing at a very affordable cost. The Urban Homesteading Assistance Board, a national organization oriented toward affordable housing cooperatives, provides assistance in converting renters into homeowners.

### Gentrification

Many of a community's low- and moderate-income residents can afford to live only in areas of a city where rents are low. If these areas are revitalized through renovation and rehabilitation of the housing, with a resulting increase in property values, rents may increase and no longer be affordable. The resulting migration of wealthier residents into poor urban neighborhoods, displacing existing residents and transforming the character and quality of the neighborhood, is known as gentrification. As *Time* magazine put it, "Restored carriage houses and pressed-tin ceilings have seduced more children of the suburbs back to the city than mean, shiny apartment towers."[9]

This unintended side effect of a community's revitalization programs should concern planners and local government. It can be addressed by developing policies that allow low- or moderate-income residents to remain in established neighborhoods through programs such as low-interest loans that help them purchase and rehabilitate their residences or providing subsidies for rent.

## Alternative Types of Housing

### Gated Communities

The suburbs have always been attractive because they represent a lifestyle separated from the problems of urban centers. People move to the suburbs at least in part to find more privacy. Gated communities, starting in the 1980s, take the quality of separation one step further: they are not only more isolated, but also surrounded by walls and entrances monitored by security personnel. They are housing developments where permission is necessary to enter.

*7.7. Gated community, Scottsdale, Arizona*

There are now over 20,000 gated communities in the United States, many of them in the southwest and southeast because of their popularity with retirees. Populations within gated communities tend to be homogeneous, accentuating patterns of segregation that have always been part of our culture. Although families move to gated developments for the sense of community they seem to offer, studies have shown that feeling is no stronger, and often less strong, than in nongated communities.

### Co-housing

Co-housing, first developed in Denmark in the 1980s, provides a new form of residential community where owners have a private realm and a common realm. Ownership in a co-housing development is growing in popularity as more people become aware of it and more co-housing sites are being developed. The co-housing concept is based less on legal covenants than on social covenants. The primary purpose of co-housing is to encourage an innovative social environment.

Typically, co-housing includes 20 to 40 member families in private housing units clustered around a common courtyard. Member families share facilities such as a common dining area, social hall, workshop, offices, day care facilities, and recreational space. Driveways, roads, and parking lots usually are located on the outskirts of the development, with a pedestrian-oriented interior that is child-friendly. This design arrangement is especially useful if the co-housing development includes families with children.

Co-housing developments have a stronger sense of community and proprietorship if the residents' support network is designed as part of the plan from the beginning, and many communities involve future residents in the original design and planning. Co-housing can focus on the needs of special groups—for example, seniors who are concerned about accessibility and security. Glacier Circle in Davis, California, opened in 2006 as the first elder co-housing community in the United States. Other types of co-housing communities are being developed, among them eco-housing, which focuses on ecological concerns. Organic gardens, composting toilets, and other green systems are standard elements.

Co-housing developments may result from retrofitting an existing residential area—that is, utilize existing housing and adjust it to meet their goals. Fences may be removed, common facilities constructed, and existing streets redesigned. Development may be incremental and begin with two or three neighbors, gradually expanding as adjacent housing becomes available.

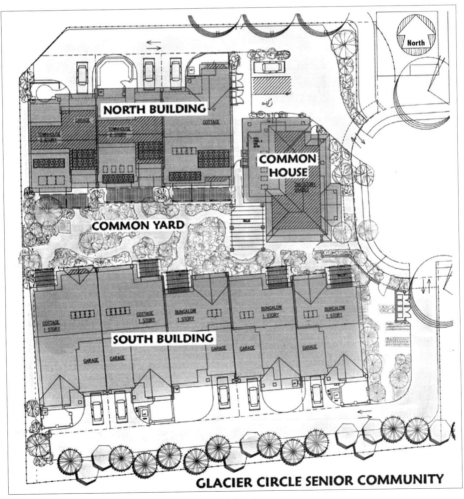

7.8. Glacier Circle elder co-housing, Davis, California

### Manufactured Housing

Manufactured, or prefabricated, housing can offer significant advantages to homebuyers. It is less expensive and easier to build than traditional housing. Most of the components are constructed in a controlled factory setting, where weather is not a problem, jigs can be installed for quick and accurate assembly, and tools are on hand. Such housing requires minimal onsite assembly of the component sections, which allows year-round construction with a constant, rather than seasonal, labor force. The assembly line system offers more quality assurance.

On the downside, manufactured housing has not been readily accepted by communities, who associate it with mobile homes, which are not built to the same standards and can be considered temporary housing units. Manufactured housing is opposed by powerful interest groups, such as the National Association of Homebuilders, an organization that protects the interests of the homebuilding industry, the builders, and its unions. Transportation costs are considerable because component parts may move across numerous jurisdictions, each with its own, and sometimes differing, requirements. The cost of approvals may also be high. Local building codes can mean a housing unit that is acceptable in one location is unacceptable in another, and required modifications reduce some of the efficiencies of the manufacturing process.

### Mobile Homes

Mobile homes evolved from the trailer industry. Realizing that many people were using trailers as permanent housing, the industry responded by building bigger units, increasing from 8-foot widths to 10-, 12-, and 14-foot widths; in some states, transport of 16- and 18-foot-wide units is allowed on highways. Lengths have increased from 45 feet to 85 feet. Currently, units can be expanded with double-side and triple-side units to satisfy selective buyers. Although technically movable because mobile homes by definition are built with wheels, many units never move after being located in a mobile home park or on a private site.

Planning for mobile home sites can be contentious. Many people oppose the location of these "parks" within their community, but legal precedent has established locations where mobile home parks can be developed. Among the issues for communities and planners is the disposition of the land if the owner of the park decides to sell and vacate it.

7.9. Mobile home park, Melbourne, Florida

### Inclusionary Housing

Inclusionary housing provisions (also called inclusionary zoning) require developers to offer a defined percentage of new housing at rates affordable to low- and moderate-income households. The term "affordable" needs to be carefully defined by local officials, since developers prefer to sell market-rate housing; lower-cost housing is not only less profitable but also tends to reduce the market value of adjacent housing. Some communities allow developers to contribute a given amount of money to an affordable-housing fund administered by the municipal government in lieu of providing affordable units in a development. This relieves developers of their obligation and places the responsibility to provide affordable housing on the local government. This cost of the developers' contribution is passed on to the buyer of the developer's market-rate homes.

In some communities, inclusionary housing programs are mandatory; in others incentive programs encourage developers to provide affordable housing. Incentives may include permission for higher building density or the easing of some normal requirements. In Montgomery County, Maryland, for example, developments of 35 or more housing units must include 12.5 to 15 percent that are affordable; affordability is defined as priced to be available for households in the lowest one-third of the county's income bracket. Between 1976 and 2003, over 11,000 affordable units were developed.

Steps planners can take to encourage inclusionary housing include inventorying a community's existing housing stock and using tax assessment data and census information to evaluate the needs of each segment of the housing market—renters, home-owning families, retirees, special needs individuals. With this information, planners can develop strategies within the comprehensive plan to accommodate community housing needs. Considerations include funding, available programs, available sites, and possible changes to codes and ordinances as incentives.

Affordable housing is in short supply in virtually all communities as a result of high land costs for large parcel size, high construction costs, reduced funding for housing from federal programs, complicated permitting processes for new construction, and opposition from local residents who want to keep home values high. Although local governments cannot eliminate most of these factors, they can promote more inclusionary housing through their policies and programs, making affordable housing a goal of their comprehensive plan. Local building departments can assist in achieving the goal by expediting the approval process for such units, giving lower up-front costs to developers, waiving impact fees (described in Chapter 16) and other costs, and making grants available for affordable-housing projects.

## Code Enforcement

Building codes protect residents from unsafe housing conditions. Codes are often administered in conjunction with ordinances and standards for health, safety, and welfare. The enforcement of housing codes is typically the responsibility of a municipality. Tenants can invoke code provisions to make landlords remedy unsafe conditions.

Code enforcement is an inexpensive way to keep the quality of neighborhoods intact and the tax base stable. It helps ensure that existing housing stock stays in good condition and is not lost to neglect or allowed to be haz-

ardous. If an uncooperative owner does not address violations, the municipality can take a number of actions, including fines, condemnation, or removing the structure's occupancy permit. It also may hire a contractor to correct the conditions and charge the owner with penalties that blemish the property title and must be settled before the property can be sold. In extreme cases, the local government can threaten stronger legal action and even take ownership of the property.

## Housing and the Private Sector

Federal, state, and local governments provide financing and subsidies and establish laws and regulations related to housing, but direct governmental involvement in the development and ownership of housing is relatively modest in the United States. The private sector plays a very large role. The ways community planners encourage private sector investment in housing can be quite different from the manner they support public sector housing. The largest and most successful housing projects have been through private investment, with government's role limited to giving favorable tax treatment, largely through mortgage deductions. Some of the factors that relate to private sector investment in housing are described below.

### The Economics of Housing

Housing is a major part of the national economy, and money spent directly on residential development can have a multiplier effect on a local economy in general. A 2008 California study found that for every $1,000 spent on housing construction, an additional $900 of industrial output resulted, and that for every housing job created, one additional job materialized.[10]

For example, if the sale price of a new house is $300,000, the total financial impact on the economy may be almost double that amount. This multiplier effect is considerably greater than the economic impact of growth in other sectors, for example, health care (50 to 80 percent), retail (57 percent), or finance (53 percent).[11]

Individuals and families can benefit financially from home ownership through tax savings that privilege ownership over renting. Mortgage interest payments and property taxes are tax deductible. For example, assume a couple purchases a home for $300,000 by paying 20 percent ($60,000) down and obtaining a 30-year mortgage of $240,000 at an interest rate of 7 percent. Also assume they pay property taxes of $4,000. The total annual tax deduction would be approximately $16,000. If the couple is in a 25 percent tax bracket, this yields a reduction in taxes owed of approximately $4,000 annually.

Another financial benefit of owning a home is the likelihood that it will increase in value over time. Tax laws assume other real properties decrease in value over time—for example, automobiles, boats—and give deductions on this basis. But for real estate the value increases, so although tax obligations are based on the assumption of a reduction in value, houses actually increase in value. Also, the value of a dollar deflates over time, so a fixed $1,500 per month mortgage payment may seem substantial in the first year but becomes less burdensome as years pass. At the end of a 30-year, fixed-rate mortgage, the impact on a family's budget of monthly payments will be substantially less in comparison to the impact for payments made in the first few years.

Mortgage payments can be considered a forced savings program similar to payments into a savings account, in that they increase personal net worth through equity value in the house. By comparison, rental payments are lost, add nothing to net worth, and may increase over time.

In recent years, the advantages of the savings inherent in a mortgage have been offset to some extent by the easy availability of home equity loans, which have allowed homeowners to borrow against the equity they have in their property, resulting in a deterioration of their mortgage-based "savings." Homeowners who are at least 62 years old can also qualify for reverse mortgages, a loan against your home that you do not pay back for as long as you live there, but again equity in your home is reduced over time.

## Foreclosures

As national, state, or local economies weaken, the number of foreclosures on homes tends to increase, sometimes quite dramatically, as happened in 2008, because homeowners could not make their mortgage payments. Such a significant economic downturn can cause the market value of a house to drop below the mortgage amount owed. Under those circumstances, selling a house is not practical, yet continued ownership may not be either—a losing situation for owners with mortgages they can no longer afford. The effects are well known:

lending institutions take possession of houses and evict the owners. A ripple effect throughout the community results in a growing number of vacant properties, a drop in city revenues, increased homelessness and crime, and a deteriorated community image.

Planners can help by recognizing this problem before it becomes unwieldy and developing strategies to minimize its impact by involving local lending institutions, local officials, and real estate professionals in making special provisions. Planners, especially those associated with community development or redevelopment agencies, should see this as part of their role in preserving their community's welfare.

## The "Teardown" Phenomenon

From the opposite perspective, as the value of housing increases in very desirable neighborhoods, buyers sometimes purchase a property with the intention of demolishing an existing house and building a new, larger house on the same site. This "teardown" approach sometimes results in the loss of satisfactory existing housing and its replacement with housing that may be out-of-scale or incompatible with the surrounding neighborhood.

Proponents of teardown argue that such new construction increases density in existing areas and is therefore beneficial. However, most such construction does not increase the number of people on a given parcel, only the square footage of the structure. The process generates more landfill, higher energy usage, and higher-cost housing. Limiting the size of a house does restrict a property owner's freedom and may prevent a property from reaching its highest and best use but city codes have long established that policies intended to restrict new development and ensure compatibility are appropriate and constitutionally valid. Regulating teardowns can be considered similar to setting building height and setback restrictions or instituting a design code because the character of a community is at stake.

### Spotlight on Winnetka, Illinois[12]

The Village of Winnetka, Illinois, is a built-out northern suburb of Chicago. It is a pedestrian-friendly, pre–World War II town with three commuter train stations, good for a town of 12,500. Because of its proximity to Chicago and excellent educational system, the village enjoys extremely high property values (the median sale price for

7.10. *House to become a teardown and replaced by a larger house, Winnetka, Illinois*

a single-family home in 2006 was $1,272,500), which are both a blessing and a curse for the community.

In the late 1990s, Winnetka began to experience a high number of residential teardowns because land value far exceeded the value of the homes occupying the land. Teardown homes purchased for an average price of $600,000 were replaced with much larger homes that sold for double—and even triple—that price.

Teardowns changed the character of Winnetka's neighborhoods, quietly removing many of the community's affordable housing options. The loss of modest single-family homes drove up the cost of condominiums and made rentals hard to find. A lack of housing options discouraged diversity. Senior citizens could no longer afford to stay in their homes or find acceptable alternatives; employees of local businesses could not afford to live where they work.

In 2008, Winnetka conducted an in-depth affordable housing study. Local officials concentrated on strengthening inclusionary zoning for multifamily properties, eliminating zoning language prohibiting affordable housing, and crafting a zoning ordinance requiring that a percentage of every developer's new housing units meet Winnetka's definition and standards for affordability. The study also considered the establishment of a community land trust, under which land would be held in trust by the community while improvements on it are made by individual owners. The result would be that appreciation is limited to improvements, rather than raising the value of an entire property beyond affordability.

## Summary

Shelter is a basic need of every individual. A home is also a major investment and the single most expensive purchase made by most families. Local government should ensure that every resident has access to at least minimal housing options. Successful housing programs result from a partnership of public and private sector activities and investments. Even though planners and local government officials control the location of residential development through a community's comprehensive plan and approval of proposed site plans, private developers provide the base of any community's housing stock.

Beginning with the National Housing Act of 1934, the federal government created a series of programs that have greatly influenced the supply of housing in the United States. These programs included the construction of public housing projects; support for private development of public housing; incentives for private sector housing, especially after World War II; the urban renewal program for redevelopment of urban sites; establishing the Department of Housing and Urban Development; and other significant legislation, policies, and programs.

Planning a successful housing program requires an understanding of the scope of the situation—the community's housing resources; supply factors, including available land, utilities, and potential financing; and what housing programs are available. The goal is to provide an array of housing options in terms of design, style, and price, and a supply of quality rental properties, public housing, and traditional housing options in urban, suburban, and rural areas to help ensure a diverse population base. In addition, communities must maintain the quality of their housing stock by having and enforcing housing codes to sustain the value of residential properties and their tax revenues, preserve neighborhoods, increase community pride, and create a place where people want to live, work, and play.

# 8

# HISTORIC PRESERVATION AND PLANNING

## A Brief History of the Preservation Movement

Historic preservation is now an integral component of community planning. However, in the United States interest in preserving historic resources was slow to evolve. One of the first preservation efforts in the country was to save Independence Hall in Philadelphia, where the Declaration of Independence, Articles of Confederation, and the Constitution of the United States were signed. Despite the site's historic significance, in 1816 a proposal was made to subdivide the site into parcels for sale. After a number of historical associations appealed, the city bought the structure and kept it from the hands of private developers.

Similarly, when local residents requested Congress to provide funding to preserve George Washington's deteriorating home, Mount Vernon, Congress refused to allocate any money. As a result, the Mount Vernon Ladies' Association was founded in 1853 to save the homestead through private efforts. The Association was the first preservation organization in the country and served as a model for other organizations involved in saving threatened landmark structures.

By the early twentieth century, Americans had begun to take a concerted interest in protecting natural features. In 1916, the National Park Service (NPS) was created in the U.S. Department of the Interior to establish federal parklands and eventually was given responsibility to administer programs to protect historic structures. Today, the NPS is the sponsoring agency for most federal preservation programs.

The first historic district in the United States was established in 1931 in Charleston, South Carolina, followed in 1936 by the Vieux Carré (old French Quarter) of New Orleans. Charleston and New Orleans became prototypes for other historic districts: in San Antonio, Texas (1939); Alexandria, Virginia (1946); Williamsburg, Virginia (1947); Winston-Salem, North Carolina (1948); and Washington, D.C. (1950). The regulatory powers available to an agency administering a historic district during those decades were quite limited.

The National Trust for Historic Preservation, a nongovernmental organization established in 1949, represents all segments of the preservation movement, both public

*8.1. Mount Vernon, Fairfax County, Virginia*

*8.2. Historic district, Charleston, South Carolina*

8.3. *Vieux Carré (old French Quarter), New Orleans*

and private. Public interest in historic preservation began to grow in the 1960s. Membership in the National Trust grew from 10,700 members in 1966 to 270,000 in 2008. The destruction caused by urban renewal and the interstate highway system and other massive public works projects of the 1950s and 1960s gave rise to public concern and led to the National Historic Preservation Act of 1966, undoubtedly the most important historic preservation legislation passed by Congress. Before it, preservation activities had focused on established landmarks and local historical organizations concentrated their efforts on museum-quality structures. Few neighborhoods had any kind of historic designation. The courts generally did not support local regulations that imposed aesthetic restraints on property owners, and local communities had almost no ties with preservation activities at the state and federal levels.

The 1966 Act changed the situation significantly with a number of key provisions. First, it established a National Register of Historic Places, which includes over 80,000 listings, to recognize properties of national historic interest, such as Ashland, the home of Henry Clay. Next, it transferred most of the federal government's responsibilities for preservation activities from the National Park Service, and much of its funding to newly established State Historic Preservation Offices (SHPOs). Each SHPO is responsible for surveying communities across its state and keeping records of designated historic properties. It processes nominations of properties for listing on the National Register. These are forwarded to the National Park Service for final approval and for its own state register as well. It reviews applications for tax credits to property owners who have rehabilitated privately

owned historic structures. Most important, SHPOs advise local governments on how to establish and administer local historic districts and create historic district commissions. They help to minimize conflicts and problems resulting from poorly established local districts. Finally, the Section 106 provision to the 1966 Act stipulated that federal funding of a private or public project could be withheld if the project would have a negative impact on a property listed on the National Register.

8.4. *Ashland, home of Henry Clay, Lexington, Kentucky, listed on the National Register of Historic Places*

The listing of properties on federal and state registers does not give protection to historic properties. Federal or state designation places no restrictions on what property owners can or cannot do with their structure. Historic properties are protected only through establishment of a local historic district ordinance. This power is reserved for local governments on the grounds that each community should determine what it considers historically significant, what is of value to the community, and what steps should be taken to provide protection. A local historic district commission (HDC) reviews proposed changes and may give approval based on the appropriateness of the work and its respect for the integrity of a building. The power of local government to protect historic properties against inappropriate changes has been tested in the U.S. Supreme Court. Most notable is the landmark Penn Central case in 1978, which decided that the New York City Landmarks Commission had the power to approve or deny a major addition to Grand Central Station, a designated historic structure.[1] Subsequent legal decisions firmly established the principle that local governments have the power to review and regulate changes proposed by owners of historic properties. For example, Miami Beach residents determined the art deco–style hotels and other buildings along Ocean Drive and nearby uniquely embodied their community's heritage. In 1976, they established the Miami Beach Architectural Historic District to preserve this character.

8.5. *Miami Beach Architectural Historic District*

## The Value of Historic Preservation

Studies have shown that designation of a historic district stabilizes or improves property values.[2] In older neighborhoods that have deteriorated, such designation protects against unnecessary demolition and inappropriate infill development and draws investment. When property values stabilize, owners feel it is safe to spend on necessary repairs or rehabilitation and banks are more willing to make loans. The market value of properties in historic districts appreciates at rates above the general local market; at worst, the value of historic properties tends to follow the trends of the overall local market. Being in a historic district helps ensure that a property's location remains desirable. For example, while the overall population in Washington, D.C., fell during the 1990s, the population within its historic districts increased. Likewise, when the business management association of Seattle's Pioneer Square district asked business owners why they chose the area, they found the leading reason was its location in a recognized historic district.

Historic districts also promote the character and image of a community. Rehabilitated buildings encourage diversity in economic levels, race, occupations, and education levels by allowing for a range of building opportunities. Historic neighborhoods are usually walkable areas where interaction among businesses, visitors, and residents takes place, forging a stronger neighborhood identity and a more cohesive community structure.

Preservation has been shown to be one of the most important factors in using tourism planning as a local economic development tool. A study in Virginia revealed that visitors coming to historic areas tend to stay longer, visit twice as many places, and, on a per trip basis, spend two and a half times more money than other types of tourists.[3] Preservation has continued to grow as a primary force in tourism development. Preservation contributes to local economies while producing few negative side effects. It preserves resources rather than using them, does not cause pollution, complements other parts of the local economy (e.g., retail), and provides local employment. Preservation also improves the image of an area, and therefore reinforces a community's quality of place.

In 2009, over 3,000 preservation organizations were actively engaged in public education, advocacy, and preservation and restoration projects of various types and sizes. The National Alliance of Preservation Commissions estimated there were more than 2,400 regulated historic districts in the United States and more than 35 university graduate professional and technical curriculums directly related to historic preservation.

### Spotlight on Pike Place Market, Seattle

In 1907, the city council of Seattle, Washington, created a public market known as Pike Place Market in the downtown area where farmers and fishermen could sell their goods. The market grew rapidly. It continued to prosper until World War II, when business declined. In 1941, the structures suffered from a fire, and, following Pearl Harbor, its many farmer-merchants of Japanese descent were interned. After the war, the market could not regain its prewar popularity; people were no longer interested in buying produce from small farms, new industries were taking over local farmland, and supermarkets attracted shoppers.

In 1963, the city's planning department formulated a plan to demolish the market and create a modern complex to be called Pike Plaza. It called for office towers, apartments, parking, and a small up-to-date market. The plan elicited strong opposition and a group called Friends of the Market succeeded in getting the

8.6. *Pike Place Market, Seattle, Washington*

issue of preserving the original Pike Place Market on the ballot in 1971. Their proposal won with 60 percent of the vote.

A 7-acre local market historic district was placed on the National Register of Historic Places, and a market authority was given 10 years and $150 million of private and public funds to restore and revitalize the market. Since then, the restoration and use of the market has been strictly controlled. An ordinance protects not only the market structures, but their architectural character. If a structural material needs to be replaced it must be replaced with a material of the same quality as the original material. Products sold must be either made or grown by the vendor. These provisions have helped to create the vital and bustling Pike Place Market of today, one of the primary destinations in the city of Seattle.

## Historic Preservation and the Comprehensive Plan

Comprehensive planning was formalized in the 1920s, as described in Chapter 4. This was decades before the Historic Preservation Act was passed in 1966. As a result, many planners do not view historic preservation as part of the regular planning process, but think of it as a separate function of local government. They consider historic districts to be overlay districts (an additional zoning requirement that is placed on a geographic area), since they are officially designated and regulated areas, but not integrated with either comprehensive planning or zoning documents. In a similar vein, local preserva-

tionists consider a preservation plan to consist simply of a survey and documentation of historic resources.[4] Planners should work to bridge this disconnect by making preservation planning an integral part of the comprehensive plan of any community with a historic area worthy of protection.

The American Planning Association's report, *Preparing a Historic Preservation Plan*, suggests 10 components that should be part of a historic preservation plan:[5]

1. A precise statement of the community's goals and policies
2. Definitions of its historic character
3. A summary of past preservation efforts
4. A survey of historic resources
5. An outline of the kind of survey that should be conducted
6. An explanation of the legal basis for protecting historic resources
7. A statement relating historic preservation to other local land-use and growth management tools
8. An assessment of the public sector's responsibilities toward historic resources
9. An outline of the incentives available to help preserve the community's historic resources
10. An explanation of how historic preservation relates to the educational system

Such an effort to better incorporate historic preservation into comprehensive plans should have the support of local preservationists, as explained in *Community Planning: An Introduction to the Comprehensive Plan*: "Most effective preservation plans exist in the context of a comprehensive plan, with the comprehensive plan providing the land-use and other contextual items for the preservation plan."[6]

## Financial Incentives for Historic Structures

Historic preservation helps local economic development in many ways. The cost of materials used for rehabilitation represents about a third of total project cost, while new construction represents more than 50 percent of the total cost. Moreover, money spent on buying new materials, a large part of new construction costs, goes to where products are manufactured, while money spent on labor, a large portion of costs for rehabilitation projects,

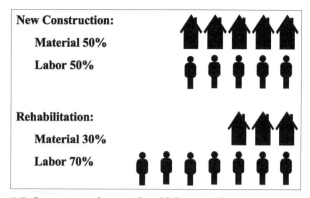

**New Construction:**

   **Material 50%**

   **Labor 50%**

**Rehabilitation:**

   **Material 30%**

   **Labor 70%**

8.7. *Comparison of material and labor costs for new construction and rehabilitation*

largely stays within the local community's economy. Work on a local historic building uses local resources and creates local jobs.

Local economies can use preservation to add value to products and resources. Historic buildings offer a unique experience not available anywhere else, and as a result value is added. A stay in an old art deco hotel in South Miami cannot be duplicated in any of the new high-rise structures that surround the district.

A significant financial incentive for owners of historic properties is the federal rehabilitation investment tax credit program, created by Congress in 1976 and supplemented by state tax credit programs. The federal program allows a tax credit to individuals based on 20 percent of the total cost of rehabilitation. In other words, if an owner spends $100,000 on the rehabilitation of a designated property, his or her personal federal income tax could be reduced by $20,000. As a result of this program, billions of private dollars have been invested in deteriorated properties. An example shows why. Consider two historic properties, one purchased for $400,000 and needing $100,000 of rehabilitation, the other bought for $100,000 and needing $400,000 of rehabilitation. Both projects will ultimately cost $500,000 and both will be worth the same when work is completed. But the owner of the first property earns a tax credit of $20,000 (20 percent of $100,000), while the second owner earns a credit of $80,000 (20 percent of $400,000). Whether or not an investor is interested in preservation, the advantage is clear. It is a wonderful case of a government program targeting the private sector to spend its money, not public funds, to improve communities through financial incentives.

Preservation easements provide another incentive to owners of historic properties, allowing private owners to take a tax deduction for designating some portion of their property to be protected from change in perpetuity—for instance, that the façade of their historic building can never be altered. Because this easement removes an ownership privilege for future owners, the value of the property may decrease. When the amount of the decrease in value is determined by a certified property appraiser, the owner can take a property tax deduction based on this amount.

## Establishing a Historic District Ordinance

A historic district ordinance allows for regulatory review of demolition and exterior alterations of designated structures. Owners of designated properties must gain approval before making changes from the local historic district commission. Ordinances may also include review of additions, maintenance and repair, and updating of structures to satisfy requirements of the Americans with Disabilities Act (ADA) of 1990. Historic ordinances are approved by the municipal council.

A historic district ordinance should satisfy three conditions: it should be well written, it should be needed, and it should be appropriate. It should not conflict with local zoning ordinances or building department regulations, which could result in owners acting on approval from one agency while being in conflict with another. Often, a historic district is established as an overlay but does not change the underlying zoning based on the existing zoning ordinance. A historic district ordinance may take precedence over other city ordinances if all affected agencies agree so.

### Local Historic District Commission Responsibilities
Local historic district commissions can be involved in many activities related to local history and preservation. Their powers are granted by local government and state law, although commissions often become involved in activities other than those specifically given through ordinance. The powers granted may include:

- Surveying and identifying historically and architecturally significant structures and areas
- Designating and protecting landmarks and their surroundings and landmark districts
- Reviewing applications for alteration, construc-

tion, or demolition of landmark buildings and all structures within a historic district

- Requiring affirmative maintenance of historic structures
- Making recommendations relating to zoning amendments and commenting on the local comprehensive plan
- Undertaking educational programs and activities
- Establishing standards and procedures for designation and development review
- Accepting funds from federal, state, and private sources
- Buying, selling, or accepting donations of property
- Exercising the power of eminent domain
- Accepting easements and other less-than-fee interests in property[7]

### The Secretary of the Interior's Standards

Many historic district commissions make determinations on changes to designated buildings using rehabilitation standards established by the U.S. Department of the Interior. First published in 1979 and updated regularly, the Secretary of the Interior's Standards serve as guidelines on what constitute appropriate changes to designated historic structures and what changes are inappropriate. The 10 standards include criteria for evaluating building use, design, repair, maintenance, and even archeology. The purpose of the standards is to establish consistency in approving proposed changes in historic districts so that commissioners, planners, and property owners feel the system is fair to all parties. The standards for rehabilitation, as stated in the 1995 revisions, are:

1. A property shall be used for its historic purpose or be placed in a new use that requires minimal change to the defining characteristics of the building and its site and environment.

2. The historic character of a property shall be retained and preserved. The removal of historic materials or alteration of features and spaces that characterize a property shall be avoided.

3. Each property shall be recognized as a physical record of its time, place, and use. Changes that create a false sense of historical development, such as adding conjectural features or architectural elements from other buildings, shall not be undertaken.

4. Most properties change over time; those changes that have acquired historic significance in their own right shall be retained and preserved.

5. Distinctive features, finishes, and construction techniques or examples of craftsmanship that characterize a property shall be preserved.

6. Deteriorated historic features shall be repaired rather than replaced. Where the severity of deterioration requires replacement of a distinctive feature, the new feature shall match the old in design, color, texture, and other visual qualities and, where possible, materials. Replacement of missing features shall be substantiated by documentary, physical, or pictorial evidence.

7. Chemical or physical treatments, such as sandblasting, that cause damage to historic materials shall not be used. The surface cleaning of structures, if appropriate, shall be undertaken using the gentlest means possible.

8. Significant archeological resources affected by a project shall be protected and preserved. If such resources must be disturbed, mitigation measures shall be undertaken.

9. New additions, exterior alterations, or related new construction shall not destroy historic materials that characterize the property. The new work shall be differentiated from the old and shall be compatible with the massing, size, scale, and architectural features to protect the historic integrity of the property and its environment.

10. New additions and adjacent or related new construction shall be undertaken in such a manner that if removed in the future, the essential form and integrity of the historic property and its environment would be unimpaired.[8]

The Secretary of the Interior's Standards are supplemented with publications explaining the principles behind each standard, and case studies of projects approved and not approved. The standards are used by State Historic Preservation Offices and the National Park Service to determine if rehabilitation work qualifies for historic tax credits, so owners who adhere to the standards can benefit financially.

## Spotlight on Union Station, St. Louis

When Union Station opened in 1894 in St. Louis, Missouri, the builders and designers little knew how important the building would become. St. Louis architect Theodore C. Link won the building's competition with a three-part design: headhouse, midway, and a vast trainshed. At completion, it was the largest train complex in the world and the busiest station as well. It covered 11.5 acres and contained 31 tracks. Between 1941 and 1945, 100,000 people passed through Union Station every day.

By 1969, the number of trains using Union Station had sunk to an all-time low. Although the project was designated a National Historic Landmark in 1970, the last train departed from the station in October 1978. Shortly thereafter, the structures were purchased for $5.5 million by a developer who proposed to renovate the transportation center as a pedestrian-friendly, mixed-use environment.

8.8. *Union Station, St. Louis, Missouri, 1894, with headhouse (station) in the foreground and midway and trainshed to the rear*

The project reopened in 1985 as the largest adaptive use project in the United States. The headhouse, originally housing ticket purchasing, waiting room, and a 70-room hotel, was renovated to house 67 shops and restaurants and the 538-room Hyatt Regency Hotel. The midway, which had been a covered passageway between the station and the trainshed, became two levels of shops. The renovated trainshed, in glass-covered elegance, holds two levels of shops and restaurants, an indoor lake, a plaza for entertainment, and another 469 hotel rooms.

Union Station is a redevelopment success. The most visited location in St. Louis, it receives more visitors than the Gateway Arch and the Anheuser Busch Brewery. It is a National Historic Landmark and is listed as one of the National Trust for Historic Preservation's Historic Hotels of America.

### Considerations When Establishing a District

Historic properties may be designated either individually or as part of a historic district. A district should be established when a group of structures has more importance and significance considered together than they have individually. The regulations for a historic district may apply only to designated historic structures or may also include review of changes to nonhistoric structures within the district. This is decided at the time of the approval of the ordinance. In some communities that do not fully support regulatory historic districts, so-called preservation-like conservation districts can institute ordinances that do not have full regulatory control over

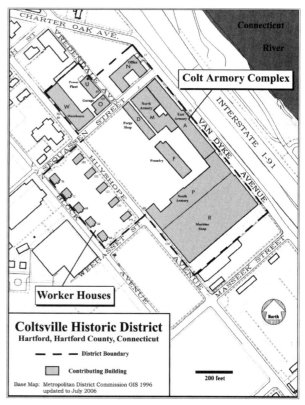

8.9. *Coltsville Historic District, Hartford, Connecticut*

individual changes to properties, but include more general guidelines.

Is the establishment of a historic district the best vehicle for protection? The formation of a district assumes that a common historic character permeates all parts of the area within its boundaries, including its buildings, its streetscape, even perhaps its natural features and open space. This may be appropriate when an assemblage of structures represents an architectural period or style—for example, a grouping of 1860s and 1870s Italianate storefronts or 1920s bungalows. Or it may comprise structures with a common use, like the Coltsville Historic District in Hartford, Connecticut, the historic site of the Colt Armory. The site was planned by Samuel Colt in 1855 for his firearm factory and served as a center for technological innovations in the industry well into the twentieth century. Mark Twain described it as "a great range of tall brick buildings, and on every floor is a dense wilderness of strange iron machines, a tangled forest of rods, bars, pulleys, wheels, and all the imaginable and unimaginable forms of mechanism."[9]

Alternatively, a district may be based on an important era in a community's history: buildings representing a mining or textile industry, for example. Rural districts too may represent the community's historically significant heritage, with farmsteads, barns, outbuildings, fencerows, and agricultural land preserved.

Finally, a district may be composed of noncontiguous sites or structures if they have a common theme. Examples include a community's historic resources that are scattered across a city, such as San Diego's Asian Pacific Thematic Historic District, established in 1987 to recognize 18 sites of historic association with the city's early Chinese, Filipino, Hawaiian, and Japanese communities.

### EXERCISE 8
### DELINEATE HISTORIC DISTRICT BOUNDARIES IN RIVERTOWN

*Rivertown's downtown area includes many older buildings, some of them important in the city's history. Local historian Clara Story has petitioned the City Council to have a historic district established to protect the area's historic character and the community's heritage. Owners of any buildings included in the district would be required to submit proposed exterior changes to their buildings to a historic district commission.*

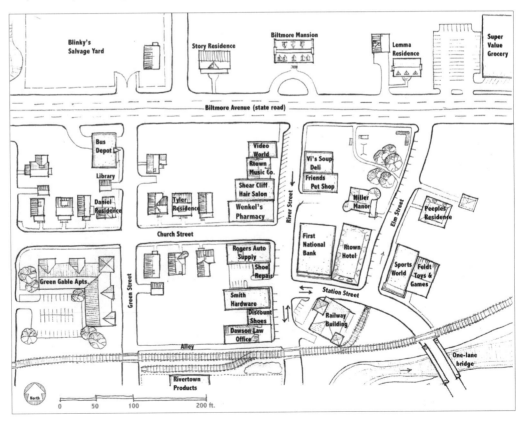

8.10. Buildings in and near downtown Rivertown

The Council has asked you, as the city's assistant planner, to review the buildings located downtown to recommend boundaries of a designated historic district. You must deliver: (1) a map of the downtown on which you have drawn proposed boundaries for a historic district, and (2) a memo that contains a rationale for the location of the proposed edges.

Be sure to consider these factors:

- A historic district should have integrity and be unified by common historical, thematic, or architectural characteristics.
- Residential and commercial areas typically require different ordinance provisions.
- Most of the structures within a district should contribute to its historic character.
- There may be future development of vacant land parcels.
- The district's boundary should not be overly complex in its delineation.

Additional maps of Rivertown and a bird's-eye sketch of the downtown area appear in Appendix A. You can access information on the buildings shown in and near Rivertown's downtown at:

http://cityhallcommons.com

For information on architectural styles:

http://www.emich.edu/public/geo/335book/335ch5.html.

For further information regarding the establishment of historic districts:

http://www.emich.edu/public/geo/335book/335ch4a.html

## Preservation and Sustainability

The United Nations has defined the term *sustainability* as "the ability to meet present needs without compromising the ability of future generations to meet their needs."[10] Sustainability in planning includes conservation of natural and built resources; historic preservation focuses on the preservation of the built environment.

Our communities' building stock is one of our greatest assets. However, currently the green building movement seems focused primarily on the construction of new energy-efficient buildings. It fails to account for each community's overwhelming number of existing buildings. It is important to recognize the inherent value in these existing resources. As architect Carl Elephante has written, "The greenest building is . . . one that is already built."[11]

It is obvious and profoundly true that to extend the useful service life of a community's building stock is common sense, good business, and sound resource management. Existing structures incorporate embodied energy, that is, the amount of total energy costs embedded in the original construction of the buildings. This is an investment that is lost if such structures are demolished. Removal of existing buildings incurs additional energy costs, including trucking away materials and increasing landfill where materials are deposited. Add to this the cost for a new building to replace the older structure, the construction of roads and utilities to service it, and the costs to manufacture new materials, and it becomes obvious that preserving older structures can be a good economic decision. The merging of community planning with historic preservation is necessary to fully capture the value of the existing building stock.

## Summary

Historic preservation has become increasingly important to American society in recent decades. It has grown from the work of a few dedicated individuals and historical organizations to an activity engaged in, at some level, by millions of citizens. Most communities now recognize the significance of the historic heritage represented in our built environment, and many have taken steps to ensure the protection of historic structures and other properties through designation and regulation.

The framework for preservation activities at the federal, state, and local levels was firmly established under the National Historic Preservation Act of 1966, which created a National Register of Historic Places and provided that each state establish a State Historic Preservation Office that is responsible for coordinating the administration of preservation efforts between federal and local levels. Under the 1966 Act, local governments are empowered to establish regulatory ordinances administered by local historic district commissions. These have the power to regulate changes to historic structures in designated historic districts. Inclusion in a regulatory historic district provides protection against inappropriate changes to properties, helps stabilize property values, and counters deterioration. It also makes owners eligible for financial incentives, especially through tax credits for rehabilitation costs.

Preserved historic character can boost a local economy, attracting tourists who tend to stay longer and spend more money. Most important, designation gives protection to a community's heritage and promotes a better image and pride for its residents.

In many communities there is little integration between preservation efforts and the comprehensive plan. Too often, historic preservation plans are prepared by preservationists, and comprehensive plans by local planners, each with little awareness of the activities of the other. Local planners need to better integrate the two activities.

# 9

# LOCAL ECONOMIC DEVELOPMENT

## Creating a Successful Economic Development Plan

Local governments are increasingly involved in local economic development efforts. This is a specialization that can be beneficial to community planners, who know how to spend a community's revenues but often are less skilled at attracting resources through creative, targeted initiatives. The economic climate at the time of writing is stormy, even at the community level. A changing global economy has brought greater international competition for low-wage industries whose operations have moved abroad. Less support from the federal government puts a greater burden on communities for development efforts. Locally owned banks and businesses cannot compete with larger corporate banks and national retailers and e-tailers, drawing away local investment capital.

To overcome these trends communities should inventory their assets (sometimes referred to as "asset mapping"), set goals and objectives, evaluate alternatives, and create an economic development program as a part of their comprehensive plan. Aggressive promotion of such a program is necessary to gain support and investment from the private sector. Economic development cannot simply be willed; it takes planning, patience, and commitment.

The first step in preparing an economic development plan is to compile an inventory that quantifies the total number of businesses by type and size and maps them to show spatial distribution. This is useful for assessing and analyzing the business environment, and reveals what kinds of business the community needs to supplement or complement what already exists. The inventory also helps planners to evaluate the business environment of a given community and compare it with that of surrounding communities.

The economic development planner should analyze the strength of the local community's tax base, which includes tax rates, assessed valuations, and bond ratings (the cost for a community to borrow money). Higher property taxes may bring in more local revenues, but they may also discourage investment. Local leaders should continually assess taxes to determine the right balance.

Any successful economic development program requires an adequate labor force with relevant job skills. Economic development goals should reflect strengths inherent in the community's existing labor force, for example, skilled construction, manufacturing, high-tech workers, service personnel and trade groups, or others. A community may build on a major institutional or governmental function, such as a large hospital or military base. Many communities have seen a significant shift in employment from manufacturing to service sector jobs. In others, tourism may provide the necessary economic stimulus. Comprehensive plans often do not include quality-of-place factors as part of economic development analysis, but amenities such as schools, recreation, museums, and hospitals are important in attracting investment.

Using information from sources such as the U.S. Census Bureau's Economic Census, planners can examine local economic data from the last 10 to 20 years to acquire historical perspective regarding their community's past performance and to make informed judgments about its competitive advantages and potential. Sector-specific reports are available in the North American Industry Classification System (NAICS), used by government for classifying businesses by type. Sectors of special interest in planning include retail trade, construction, real estate, and transportation. Firsthand data can be obtained by conducting surveys of local residents, shoppers, business people, and community leaders.

With the information collected, planners and community leaders can set goals and develop a clear set of objectives and strategies for implementing a successful program. It is important to recognize that programs are interrelated: improvements in one sector can spread to other sectors, with a multiplier effect that can improve the long-term impact on the community. A study conducted for the Economic Policy Institute showed that if 100 manufacturing jobs were created in a community, it would result in 291 additional jobs elsewhere in the economy. This compared to 154 additional new jobs from business services and 88 additional jobs in the retail sector. The report stated: The indirect employment (or *employment multipliers*) associated with jobs in any given industry results from three effects: *supplier* effects, *re-spending* effects, and *government employment* effects. Supplier effects are impacts that job creation or destruction in an industry has on supplier industries. For example, the closure of an automobile plant also affects (among other things) jobs in the steel industry that relate to supplying materials to the auto plant. Re-spending effects are the impacts that job creation or destruction in an industry has on those sectors where workers spend their paychecks. For example, when an automobile plant closes, it affects (among other things) the apparel industry that supplies the clothes workers from the auto plant purchase with their wages. Government employment effects refer to the taxes that support jobs in federal, state, and local government; if workers in private industries lose their jobs, this erodes the tax base that supports government employment.[1]

In deriving local economic development goals, a community can benefit from the thinking and experience of others. In 1991, some of the leading professionals in urban design—including Peter Katz, Andres Duany, Elizabeth Plater-Zyberk, Michael Corbett, Stefanos Polyzoides, Elizabeth Moule, and Peter Calthorpe—met to develop a set of community principles based on new and emerging ideas in community design and planning. They were written at the Ahwahnee Lodge in Yosemite National Park by these founders of the New Urbanism movement and revised as economic development guidelines in 1997 by the Local Government Commission.

The 15 items that comprise the Ahwahnee Principles emphasize sustainable development and quality of life, and span the economic, social, and environmental realms of responsibility.

## Spotlight on Ahwahnee Principles for Economic Development[2]

*Preamble*

Prosperity in the 21st Century will be based on creating and maintaining a sustainable standard of living and a high quality of life for all. To meet this challenge, a comprehensive new model is emerging which recognizes the economic value of natural and human capital. Embracing economic, social, and environmental responsibility, this approach focuses on the most critical building blocks for success, the community and the region. It emphasizes community-wide and regional collaboration for building prosperous and livable places. While each community and region has unique challenges and opportunities, the following common principles should guide an integrated approach by all sectors to promoting economic vitality within their communities, and in partnership with their neighbors in the larger region.

1. *Integrated Approach.* Government, business, education, and the community should work together to create a vibrant local economy, through a long-term investment strategy that:

- Encourages local enterprise
- Serves the needs of local residents, workers, and businesses
- Promotes stable employment and revenues by building on local competitive advantages
- Protects the natural environment
- Increases social equity
- Is capable of succeeding in the global marketplace

2. *Vision and Inclusion.* Communities and regions need a vision and strategy for economic development according to these principles.

Visioning, planning, and implementation efforts should continually involve all sectors, including the voluntary civic sector and those traditionally left out of the public planning process.

*3. Poverty Reduction.* Both local and regional economic development efforts should be targeted to reducing poverty by promoting jobs that match the skills of existing residents, improving the skills of low-income individuals, addressing the needs of families moving off welfare, and insuring the availability in all communities of quality affordable child care, transportation, and housing.

*4. Local Focus.* Because each community's most valuable assets are the ones they already have, and existing businesses are already contributing to their home communities, economic development efforts should give first priority to supporting existing enterprises as the best source of business expansion and local job growth. Luring businesses away from neighboring communities is a zero-sum game that doesn't create new wealth in the regional economy. Community economic development should focus instead on promoting local entrepreneurship to build locally based industries and businesses that can succeed among national and international competitors.

*5. Industry Clusters.* Communities and regions should identify specific gaps and niches their economies can fill, and promote a diversified range of specialized industry clusters drawing on local advantages to serve local and international markets.

*6. Wired Communities.* Communities should use and invest in technology that supports the ability of local enterprises to succeed, improves civic life, and provides open access to information and resources.

*7. Long-Term Investment.* Publicly supported economic development programs, investments, and subsidies should be evaluated on their long-term benefits and impacts on the whole community, not on short-term job or revenue increases. Public investments and subsidies should be equitable and targeted, support environmental and social goals, and prioritize infrastructure and supportive services that promote the vital-ity of all local enterprises, instead of individual firms.

*8. Human Investment.* Because human resources are so valuable in the information age, communities should provide lifelong skills and learning opportunities by investing in excellent schools, post-secondary institutions, and opportunities for continuous education and training available to all.

*9. Environmental Responsibility.* Communities should support and pursue economic development that maintains or improves, not harms, the environmental and public health.

*10. Corporate Responsibility.* Enterprises should work as civic partners, contributing to the communities and regions where they operate, protecting the natural environment, and providing workers with good pay, benefits, opportunities for upward mobility, and a healthful work environment.

*11. Compact Development.* To minimize economic, social, and environmental costs and efficiently use resources and infrastructure, new development should take place in existing urban, suburban, and rural areas before using more agricultural land or open space. Local and regional plans and policies should contain these physical and economic development planning principles to focus development activities in desired existing areas.

*12. Livable Communities.* To protect the natural environment and increase quality of life, neighborhoods, communities, and regions should have compact, multi-dimensional land use patterns that ensure a mix of uses, minimize the impact of cars, and promote walking, bicycling, and transit access to employment, education, recreation, entertainment, shopping, and services. Economic development and transportation investments should reinforce these land use patterns, and the ability to move people and goods by non-automobile alternatives wherever possible.

*13. Center Focus.* Communities should have an appropriately scaled and economically healthy center focus. At the community level, a wide range of commercial, residential, cultural, civic, and recreational uses should be located in the town center or downtown. At the neighborhood level, neighborhood centers should contain local businesses that serve the daily needs of nearby residents. At the regional level, regional facilities should be located in urban centers that are accessible by transit throughout the metropolitan area.

14. *Distinctive Communities.* Having a distinctive identity will help communities create a quality of life that is attractive for business retention and future residents and private investment. Community economic development efforts should help to create and preserve each community's sense of uniqueness, attractiveness, history, and cultural and social diversity, and include public gathering places and a strong local sense of place.

15. *Regional Collaboration.* Since industries, transportation, land uses, natural resources, and other key elements of a healthy economy are regional in scope, communities and the private sector should cooperate to create regional structures that promote a coherent metropolitan whole that respects local character and identity.

---

In his book, *The Rise of the Creative Class*, Richard Florida suggests that a new force for economic development has emerged in American cities.[3] He calls it the "creative class"—scientists, university professors, writers, artists, entertainers, architects, designers, and other cultural leaders and opinion makers, innovators, thinkers, and creative professionals who provide the initiatives and ideas for change that engenders new products. They are well-educated, young, independent thinkers who generate ideas or products that go beyond their typical job description.

This creative core, Florida believes, provides the primary stimulus for economic development. The more of this group in a community's population, the better its chances for new job and company creation. Florida posits that creative people should no longer be considered eccentric but mainstream, and communities would be wise to attract them.

## Evaluating an Economic Development Plan

Evaluation is a necessary part of the economic development planning process. It enables decisionmakers to determine whether planning efforts, projects, and programs have improved the existing situation and, if they have, by how much. The traditional objectives of evaluation are to ensure programs are efficient and equitable, qualities that have been called the "oil and water of economics" because they often are at cross-purposes and have disparate goals.[4] For example, funding for business development may be at the expense of support for social programs.

Various techniques can be used for program evaluation:[5]

*Checklists* assess a program against a list of criteria. Users consider trade-offs or provide a qualitative evaluation of effectiveness and level of satisfaction.

*Cost-benefit analysis* examines anticipated benefits of a program vis-à-vis its projected costs to determine whether the likely value created will be worth the investment in time, money, resources, and overall effort. The object of cost-benefit analysis is to identify projects where the benefits meet or exceed the costs. This condition is seldom evaluated in the public sector, since costs and benefits for community programs are difficult to define. For instance, what is the level of benefit of a downtown park or a recreation program? It may be ignored in constructing a cost-benefit analysis because it is not quantifiable. Contingency valuation, used to establish values that are hard to quantify, is based on asking people what they would be willing to pay for public goods or services to determine how to use limited resources. It is a technique used by major public agencies but has been criticized for its imprecision.

*Strategic choice* examines which programs have the greatest likelihood of success in a local political environment. Some programs are received more favorably by local officials and the general public, and this inherent interest and support can significantly affect a program's success.

*Cross-impact analysis* uses defined goals and activities to evaluate the likelihood of programs moving toward their established goals. A matrix illustrates the application of this technique to a central business district (CBD). Annual goals are ranged across the top. (In this example, all are evaluated as equally important; however, this type of analysis could also be weighted to

| Cost to City | Activities | Annual Goals | | | | | | |
|---|---|---|---|---|---|---|---|---|
| | | Increase per-business retail sales | Increase CBD share of area business | Increase local employment percentage | Increase pedestrian traffic | Reduce reported crime in CBD | Improve resident satisfaction with CBD | |
| Moderate | Annual downtown festival | X | X | | X | | XX | 5 |
| Low | Regular CBD promotions | XXX | XXX | X | XX | | XX | 11 |
| Low | Extended store hours | XX | XX | XX | XXX | XX | XXX | 14 |
| High | Improve parking, streetscape | X | XX | X | XX | XX | XX | 10 |
| Moderate | Improve city services for CBD | X | XX | | X | X | | 5 |
| Moderate | Establish retail incubator facility | XX | XX | XXX | X | | X | 9 |
| Low | Establish agreements with county | XX | XX | X | | | | 5 |
| | | 12 | 14 | 8 | 10 | 5 | 10 | |

9.1. Cross-impact analysis chart[6]

reflect the relative importance of each goal.) Activities relevant to achieve these goals are listed on the left, with the relative financial cost for each indicated as low, moderate, or high.

The relative connection of each goal and each activity is expressed by the number of Xs shown: an empty box indicates the activity would have no impact on the specified goal; one X signifies low impact; two Xs, moderate impact; and three Xs, high impact. Totals on the right of the matrix represent the impact of each activity, which can be compared to the relative cost of achieving the goal to derive its overall effectiveness. Totals at the bottom of columns represent the potential effectiveness of each goal, assuming a community initiates the listed activities.

Cross-impact analysis brings new perspectives to the evaluation of local economic development programs, and should include input from a variety of sources—for example, city officials, business owners, the public. Although based on educated "guesstimates," consensus, or other methods, the technique promotes discussion and consideration of the efficacy of various economic development goals.

### Market Segment Analysis

In any economic development study it is important to identify an area's primary market segments and develop a strategy for maximizing its commercial potential based on a defined market. Businesses in a commercial district can attract customers from varying markets. Some businesses attract local residents, while other businesses extend their marketing radius to a larger, regional area. Some may attract young families and older, conservative consumers.

Planners or community leaders may commission a marketing consultant to perform a market segment analysis to determine the percentage of various types of consumer groups living within a given area based on demographics. They might be characterized as "old money," "conspicuous consumers," "family-centered blue collar," "home-oriented senior citizens," and the like. Using information from a census database, analysts can compare the population in the target area with the region, state, or nation. For example, an index may be scaled so a score of 100 represents a proportion of the population similar to that of the United States as a whole; an index score of 25 would indicate relatively few people from that category are found in the area of analysis, while a score of 250 represents a proportion much higher than normal.

Market segment analysis generally is conducted by determining the boundaries of the trade area under analysis, inventorying its shopping facilities and competing businesses by square footages and North American Industry Classification System (NAICS) codes, and calculating sales leakage from the district from sales per household per year statistics from the U.S. Department of Commerce. The amount of floor area expansion in various business-type categories is calculated based on leakage and current sales. Finally, a survey of consumers gives an assessment of perceived conditions in the area.

## Other Economic Development Strategies

### Economic Development Committees

A study conducted by the National Center for the Revitalization of Central Cities looked at economic development for Atlanta, Portland (Oregon), Baltimore, New York City, New Orleans, Fort Worth, Minneapolis/St. Paul, and other cities. It identified the importance of

9.2. *Lowertown redevelopment area, St. Paul, Minnesota*

9.3. *Building developer and contractor discuss progress on a high-rise construction project*

planners and community leaders, including local bankers, utility executives, accountants, real estate brokers, attorneys, and small business owners, forming an economic development committee in their community. The research indicated the importance of maintaining good relationships between levels of government, whether city-state, city-county, or other.[7] Economic development programs can attract revenue from sources at all levels of government. The role of planners is to coordinate efforts and limit competition for resources. In the absence of such relationships, hostile action by a county council or state legislature can make the implementation of many local strategies difficult.

### Real Estate Investment

Encouraging local investment in real estate should be an obvious community economic development strategy. However, public sector planners are often seen merely as regulators of development, rather than promoters of appropriate development. To be effective, a community plan should not only establish regulatory controls but also deliberately provide incentives for desired new development.

Significant community advantages come from the promotion of real estate investment. It does not rely on direct public funding; although some public funds may be expended for support facilities, the bulk of the investment comes from the private sector. New construction and rehabilitation of older buildings are long-term investments in a community. Real estate is a commodity that stays in the community. Real estate investment improves not just the property where a project is located but the value of surrounding properties, a secondary benefit that contributes more than the initial value to the overall worth of a project. It brings increases in tax revenues and, therefore, more resources to invest in the community. Historically, most real estate has increased in value at a rate greater than inflation. Real estate appreciates in value, while federal tax regulations are based on its depreciation. This means that the tax obligation decreases over time, while the market value of the real estate generally increases. In sum, real estate investment represents a solid, long-term investment. Unfortunately, comprehensive plans and zoning provisions sometimes discourage real estate investment in a community through the regulatory guidelines they set for new development. Planners should work to provide sufficient flexibility to allow real estate investment proposals that contain substantial community benefits.

### Public–Private Partnerships

Public–private partnerships are designed to capitalize on the respective strengths of local government agencies and private sector entities. The public sector can offer incentives or resources; the private sector typically contributes the financial wherewithal. Public–private partnerships function best if the public agency uses its resources judiciously, and the private sector benefits from financial or other incentives. This cooperation should be encouraged by planners.

Public–private partnerships take a variety of forms. Local government can use tax revenues to provide capital for investment for private enterprises to stimulate the economy or run joint enterprises with private companies and contract with them to provide public services. Local government may lease on a long-term basis a facility owned and operated privately or sell one of its properties to a private investor, and then lease back the property at an agreed upon rate. Sale-leaseback gives the community the benefit of the sale plus new property tax revenues, while the owner has a reliable tenant. Such joint activities can have a significant impact on the community's capital improvements program and budget. (See Chapter 16 for more on capital improvement programs and budgets.) The arrangements should be simple to execute with a minimum of bureaucratic procedures.

### Business Incubators

Planners are in a good position to encourage the creation of small, entrepreneurial businesses to stimulate the local economy. Studies have shown most new jobs come from small businesses. For example, the federal Small Business Administration found that between 2003 and 2004 companies with fewer than 20 employees created roughly 1.6 million new jobs, while companies with 20 to 499 employees created around 275,000 new jobs; employment at companies with more than 500 employees shrank by 214,000.[8]

One way to help new businesses become successful is by establishing a community "incubator" facility. The purpose of an incubator facility is to provide basic resources that new business owners may not initially be able to afford. It typically provides office space, phone and Internet service, shared office equipment, temporary help, a small warehouse or manufacturing area, and other resources and services needed by start-up businesses. These are costly to provide on an individual

basis, but relatively inexpensive when shared. Incubator facility staff can provide assistance from the creative or concept stage to the promotion and distribution of a product or service. Research indicates that less than 20 percent of new businesses are still in operation five years, but more than 85 percent of incubator businesses are successful over the same time period.[9]

There are now over 1,400 business incubators in North America. Most are nonprofit organizations focused on economic development, with a strong emphasis on technology. Over half of them are sponsored and supported by either government entities or economic development organizations. Research conducted by the National Business Incubation Association (NBIA) found that for every dollar of public investment provided, incubator clients and graduates of incubators generated approximately $30 in local tax revenue. More than 84 percent of incubator graduate businesses stay in their communities and continue to provide a return to local investors.[10]

9.4. *Santa Fe Business Incubator facility, Santa Fe, New Mexico*

Bluenergy, developer of the Solarwind Turbine (a hybrid turbine combining wind energy with solar cells) exemplifies a young company that has been able to thrive and grow with support from its incubator facility, the Santa Fe Business Incubator. The incubator is a hub for business resources and links with other economic development organizations, and has received various national awards for its innovations. These include a "Client of the Year Award" from the NBIA and a "Community Development Excellence Award" from the U.S. Department of Housing and Urban Development.

### Tourism

Developing a strong tourism industry can be a highly beneficial strategy for a community, but it is not without challenges. Tourism injects outside dollars into the local economy. If businesses are locally owned, those dollars are recirculated in the community and make tourism an "export" industry whereby local businesses sell their goods and services to outsiders.

Successful tourism requires that a community offer an attraction that is viewed as a "destination"—that is, something that encourages visitors to come. Shopping and dining in a pedestrian-friendly environment are a draw. Historic sites and districts, as described in Chapter 8, are a draw, as are special attractions like the Garlic Festival in Gilroy, California; the nautical history of South Street Seaport in New York City; the music of the Grand Ole Opry and Opryland in Nashville, Tennessee. Visitors who stay overnight spend three to four times more than tourists who come only for the day, so evening activities are critical.

9.6. *Summerfest, Milwaukee, Wisconsin*

9.5. *Grand Ole Opry at Ryman Auditorium, Nashville, Tennessee*

The "4-times rule" states that to attract out-of-towners, activities should be able to provide visitors with enough things to see and do to keep them busy for four times the amount of time it takes to get there. A specialty restaurant may be a strong enough attraction for someone who needs to make only a 20- to 30-minute drive to get there, but if it takes an hour, there should be activities to occupy visitors for at least four hours. Thus, offering a special dining opportunity is not sufficient, since a meal takes only one or two hours' time, but combining eating and shopping at a large antiques mall or attending a half-day festival may serve as a sufficient draw.

Festivals are a fine attraction, whether the chicken broil of a small town or a large city marathon with cor-

CELEBRATE THE DIFFERENCE BETWEEN "U" AND "I"

9.7. *Promotion campaign for Arkansas Delta area*

porate supporters. Milwaukee's Summerfest, billed as the "world's largest music festival," started in 1968 and has grown into a major midwestern event, with annual attendance approaching the 1 million mark. Eleven stages along the shore of Lake Michigan provide venues for more than 700 performances continuously for 11 days. The festival's economic impact on Milwaukee comes to about $110 million annually, including more than $61 million in direct income and about $49 million in indirect income.[11]

Of course, such draws need to be adequately advertised and promoted. It helps to have a hook—a good logo, graphic, memorable phrase—and to sell activity rather than place. The emphasis should be on things to do, rather than on things to see. A scenic riverfront, being used by bikers, kids, and picnickers, with individuals, couples, and families enjoying and taking advantage of what is available to them at that location, is a dynamic picture likely to create stronger appeal than a downtown riverfront devoid of people. Visioning sessions with community leaders should seek to identify unique aspects of the area that will entice strangers to visit. Serving up one more quaint alpine village or "olde towne" antiques center may no longer be enough in today's highly competitive marketplace. Communities need to be more creative than ever before when developing a theme on which existing businesses can build.

The Internet is a powerful tool for marketing a community. Today, the Web is the primary source for people planning trips and vacations. A good Web site appears on the first page of search results, is visually appealing and easy to use, and is comprehensive.

Finally, tourism requires parking facilities. It is preferable to remove parking meters, which say, "Be careful; we are watching how long you stay and charging you for the privilege of being here." They encourage short stays appropriate for local and short-term visitors, but send a message inappropriate for tourists. Parking is an allocation problem: visitors should be given ample, easy-to-find parking, while employees should have reserved space in less visible, long-term areas.

## Spotlight on Navy Pier, Chicago

Navy Pier is a good example of converting an underutilized facility into a successful tourist draw. It is located on the Lake Michigan lakefront near downtown Chicago. Its 50 acres combine functions of the shipping business with recreational and entertainment activities that encompass parks, gardens, shops, restaurants, and a variety of entertainment opportunities. Navy Pier has 170,000

total square feet of exhibition space, 50,000 square feet of reception space, and 48,000 square feet of meeting room space. Many business conventions, art shows, and public festivals occur at the pier annually. Families can enjoy the Children's Museum, the Skyline Stage outdoor theater, Crystal Garden indoor park, and an IMAX theater.

The Pier opened to the public in 1916 and soon became a thriving public meeting place. It was a great success because it incorporated business with recreation. It was easily accessible to the public, enabling people to flock to the area. Navy Pier hosted the Pageant of Progress, which attracted more than 1 million visitors within a few days. During World War I, Navy Pier continued to be a popular destination, accessible by streetcar and offering theater and restaurants. It also functioned as a military information center. The 1920s were considered the pier's Golden Age: an estimated 3.2 million visitors frequented it annually. During the Great Depression, the pier was still popular, but it received far fewer visitors. In World War II, the city leased the pier to the Navy as a training site for 60,000 soldiers and 15,000 pilots, making it unavailable for public use.

After the war, the University of Illinois established a two-year branch campus at the pier, changing its identity and function once again. When the university abandoned its facilities, the site fell into disuse and became an eyesore—a symbol of the declining, decaying city. Efforts made by various government agencies to restore parts of the pier were unsuccessful. In 1989, the Metropolitan Pier and Exposition Authority obtained ownership and began a revitalization program, quickly redesigning Navy Pier into one of the country's most unique recreation and exposition facilities. By the end of

9.8. Navy Pier, Chicago, 2009

the twentieth century, 1 million people per month were visiting the pier and it is now considered Chicago's most popular year-round destination.

Navy Pier stimulated the growth of nearby residential development, and a plan for a riverwalk along the South Branch of the Chicago River that would become part of a continuous walkway from Navy Pier to Chinatown. This plan envisions carrying the pier's success into dilapidated parts of the city.

The renovations of Navy Pier came with many compromises. Structures that were part of the original core were demolished, losing the pier its listing on the National Register of Historic Places. However, the new Navy Pier is a success, attracting millions of visitors and the businesses that serve them.

## Casinos

Casinos provide a rather different but viable means of economic development. Although the United States has always had some form of gambling (it was well established in Mississippi River towns in the early 1800s), in the nineteenth century it came under attack for corruption and was prohibited, except in Nevada, which took additional steps and legalized most forms of gambling in 1931 in an attempt to increase tourism. In 1978, gambling became legal in the resort town of Atlantic City, New Jersey. Casinos have gained approval across the country from cities and towns that view the facilities as simple revenue generators with little public expense. A 2009 survey indicated two-thirds of the respondents felt gambling was important to travel and tourism, and three-quarters of travel agents agree that gambling facilities propelled local economies.[12] While casinos are "the only business where cash is the commodity" and may bring significant revenues into an area, the revenue-to-cost ratio is not always so positive as it may seem, and its connection with social problems of addiction is a downside to this economic bonanza.[13]

### Spotlight on Deadwood

In 1989, the community of Deadwood, South Dakota, decided to use gambling as a way to redevelop the town and its historic buildings. A former gold-mining town, it had been designated a National Historic Landmark, but its infrastructure was crumbling. Gambling was seen as a way to attract tourists to the town's historic sites while providing funds necessary to cover the costs for accommodating them. It was a controversial plan; as one resident commented, she did not want "the clean white linen of historic preservation washed with the dirty underwear of gambling."[14] The city did not have an adequate police force, housing, water, or sewerage to handle tourists attracted by the new slot machines. Deadwood officials had not had adequate time to prepare for the impact. Rebecca Crosswait, president of the Deadwood Historic Preservation Commission, said, "We wish we were more prepared. We need zoning for non-gaming and gaming areas. Parents are really concerned because gaming is so close to schools and churches and homes. . . You have to have a very good control system."[15]

In spite of the community's concerns, however, Deadwood became a successful gambling center, with three

*9.9. Casino Arizona, Scottsdale, Arizona*

*9.10. Deadwood, South Dakota*

dozen casinos and 3,500 slot machines. Through the end of 2009, Deadwood gamblers had bet more than $12.7 billion, with $123 million designated for local improvements.[16] The city's historic preservation officer noted, "Gaming has transformed Deadwood from a declining tourist town to a prosperous, vigorous community, and has ensured preservation of a unique historic landmark. It's been a successful wager."

### Sports Stadiums

One of the key strategies cities have employed to generate revenues is the construction of new sports stadiums. From 1997 to 2007, large cities across the country spent more than $16 billion on sports stadium construction and upkeep.[17] Local officials generally feel there is a rewarding economic spillover effect from such investment in new stadiums, since they generate tax revenues, direct spending by teams, new jobs, and ancillary benefits through concerts, festivals, and conventions. Successful sports franchises can be good for a community's image and attract local investment and tourism. To encourage such activities, public funds often are available for major sports franchises.

But planners and community leaders need to carefully consider whether these expenditures are in the public's best interest. The long term economic return to cities where stadiums have been built is not always clearly demonstrable: *Regulation* magazine found in 2000 that in 37 metropolitan areas in the United States, a professional sports environment "had no measurable impact on the growth rate of real per capita income."[18] As always, the best solutions occur when such a large-scale project is part of a more comprehensive redevelopment strategy.

## Organizations for Promoting Economic Development

### Planning Departments

A planning department can play a key role in the creation of a community's economic development plan. (Departments that focus on economic development are sometimes called the Department of Planning and Economic Development.) With data collected for the comprehensive plan and Geographic Information

System services, planners have access to a wealth of information on their community, which can be supplemented with additional economic information. Some planning departments encourage economic development by providing business assistance services, such as locations of development sites, sources of capital for expansion, hiring and training employees, and assistance in finding financial help through tax increment financing, tax abatements, or other available programs. For example, the Minneapolis Department of Community Planning and Economic Development lists 17 financial programs to assist in business development.[19] Planning departments can generate other information useful to businesses, such as offering guides to establishing a new business or for business growth; links to business associations; assistance in collecting employment, training, or recruitment data; and information on current development activities. A planning department can initiate proposals for special overlay economic zones to provide business incentives in designated areas of the community and administer loan programs. Obviously, the range of help a "full-service" planning department can offer is invaluable in a community's economic development plan.

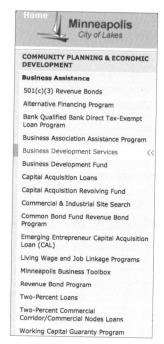

9.11. *Minneapolis's Economic Development Services*

### Business Associations

Business associations, formed by local business owners and merchants to coordinate their collaborative efforts, are another means of promoting retail and service enterprises. They are not regulators or enforcers, but promotional organizations that represent and speak for business owners, who have a stake in the survival and viability of the community. Planners have much to gain and little to lose by working cooperatively through a business association to enhance the commercial environment of a business district.

A program for economic development may come from within the business community, rather than from consultants or local officials. The business association's leadership board should include one or two local officials as members to encourage linkage between private and public interests. A business association's aim is to establish a set of general goals and specific objectives that encourage positive change rather than waiting for problems or circumstances to arise and then dealing with them.

### Chambers of Commerce

Local Chambers of Commerce typically focus on industrial growth and jobs. In many cities, they also are involved with retail businesses and downtowns and have been successful agents for economic development. These organizations represent a variety of business interests and programs, including fair tax policies, expanding and strengthening a community's infrastructure, and encouraging local governments to use resources for support of local businesses. Many local chambers encourage tourism and special events. The U.S. Chamber of Commerce lobbies for business interests at the national level and supports local chambers through various programs. For example, The Institute for a Competitive Workforce, which focuses on workforce development, and TradeRoots, a grassroots trade organization that helps communities assist small- and medium-sized companies to expand into the global marketplace.

## Economic Development Programs

The following discussion of programs relating to economic development is not all-inclusive, but gives an overview of programs at both the federal and state levels. Planners benefit from understanding these programs as potential sources of funding for community programs and projects.

### Federal Programs

*Community Development Block Grants (CDBGs).* As noted in Chapter 7, the Community Development Block Grant program is one of the most popular and successful of the programs of the U.S. Department of Housing

and Urban Development (HUD). Established in 1974 as part of the Housing and Community Development Act, the CDBG program gives annual grants to "entitlement communities"—larger cities and urbanized counties—to conduct activities related to local economic development, neighborhood revitalization, and community facilities and services. In 1981, revisions to the legislation allowed states also to give CDBG funding to non-entitlement communities, cities with populations less than 50,000, and counties with populations less than 200,000.

Communities may develop their own priorities for funding, rather than have the federal government define expenditures. This gives local governments considerable flexibility, but they must give priority to programs that benefit low- and medium-income residents, especially when funding from other sources is not available.

*Enterprise Zones.* Enterprise Zones, also referred to as Renaissance Zones or Empowerment Zones, can be established as a way to encourage special economic investment programs in an area needing renewal. The establishment of such zones often has led to economic revitalization. One of the most common incentives for Enterprise Zones is tax abatements for businesses that locate there. Connecticut, for example, allows an 80 percent tax abatement for five years and the state reimburses the local community for 75 percent of the lost revenue. Loan programs and job training programs may also qualify for tax abatement. Often the most effective incentive is simply the relaxation of normal regulations within the district to encourage investment, a strategy that encourages private involvement with minimal public cost.

*Small Business Administration.* The Small Business Administration (SBA) is one of the oldest of the federal support programs. Established in 1953, it aids, counsels, assists, and protects the interests of small businesses in recognition of their importance to the nation's economy. As previously noted, most new jobs are created not by large companies but by small businesses (the size of a qualifying business is based on its type). The SBA makes loans available directly to small businesses and acts as a guarantor for bank loans. One of the most frequently used of the SBA's loan programs is its 7(a) Loan Guaranty Program, which provides funding to small businesses that might not be eligible for loans through normal lending channels. The program's flexibility allows loans for a variety of purposes, including working capital, machinery and equipment, furniture and fixtures, and land and buildings. Under some circumstances, it can even be used for debt refinancing.

The SBA ensures that a fair proportion of government contracts go to small businesses, primarily through set-asides that make these contracts available on a predictable basis. The SBA has many regional field offices that work in partnership with a large number of public and private organizations. Nearly 20 million businesses have received direct or indirect assistance through the SBA since its inception in 1953. With over 200,000 loans in 2008, it is the largest single financial backer of U.S. business in the nation.

The Small Business Investment Corporation (SBIC) is a privately owned and operated company. The federal government uses it to sponsor public venture capital to small businesses, providing long-term loans using public and private funds. Typically, large loans are made available for up to 20 years for existing firms that have potential for rapid growth or expansion. Investments are regulated by the Small Business Administration.

The Small Business Innovation Research (SBIR) program provides support to small, innovative companies engaged in development and commercialization of new technologies. Through funding and other support services, the SBIR program makes it possible for small businesses to undertake significant research and development initiatives in the highly competitive new technology arena, covering the cost of research and protecting entrepreneurs from failure due to a lack of funding.

*Foreign Trade Zones.* Foreign Trade Zones (FTZ) can be established by communities to facilitate international trade in a local economy. An FTZ is an area located near a port of entry for goods, such as a port or international airport, where foreign and domestic merchandise is considered to be outside the country's customs territory and therefore free from duties and excise taxes, customarily collected when merchandise crosses the country's borders. No duty needs to be paid if the merchandise is re-exported without entering the United States. The FTZ thus serves as a staging area for international trade, allowing savings on items coming into the United States by deferring duty payments until they actually cross the customs boundary. No duty typically is collected for loss from transit. Merchandise containing foreign raw materials manufactured within an FTZ is subject to a lower duty rate. FTZs benefit local communities by providing jobs, adding to the tax base, generating trade contracts with other countries, and encouraging support businesses outside the trade zone.

There are currently 125 Foreign Trade Zones in the United States, some dating back to the 1930s. The El Paso FTZ No. 68 in El Paso, Texas, is a general-purpose zone that contains over 3,000 acres at 21 contiguous sites. Located adjacent to the El Paso International Airport, air transportation services are integral to its success. On the Texas–Mexico border, it has twin-plant operations with Ciudad Juarez, Mexico.

*9.12. El Paso Foreign Trade Zone No. 68, El Paso, Texas*

*Workforce Reinvestment and Adult Education Act.* The goal of the most recent Workforce Act (2003) is to provide opportunities for enhancing the general employment skills of the country's workforce as well as occupation-specific skills. This is accomplished through its one-stop career center systems. The Workforce Act encourages states to set up adult education programs and provide services that help individuals with disabilities become employable. The Act's broader goals include youth development programs connected to the private sector, postsecondary education and training, social services, and other economic development systems that enhance career opportunities.

*Economic Development Administration.* The federal government's Economic Development Administration (EDA) is especially relevant to planners. It provides support to planning organizations for development, implementation, revision, or replacement of Comprehensive Economic Development Strategies (CEDS). The EDA's Support for Planning Organizations program focuses on relatively short-term efforts to improve employment prospects in economically distressed areas. Eligible recipients may include community development corporations, economic development organizations, Native American tribes, and nonprofit regional planning organizations.

The EDA also has programs to provide investment capital for public works projects in distressed areas. The purpose is to upgrade a community's physical infrastructure to attract new business, encourage expansion of existing businesses, diversify the local economy, and support long-term private sector investment. The program's current emphasis is on developing clusters of associated industries in emerging work areas and creating a symbiotic environment for growth. Funding can support facilities such as water and sewer systems, industrial access roads, industrial and business parks, port facilities, railroad sidings, distance learning facilities, skill-training facilities, business incubator facilities, brownfield redevelopment, eco-industrial facilities, and telecommunications infrastructure improvements needed for business retention and expansion. Eligible activities include the acquisition or development of public land; improvements to a public works, public service, or development facility; and acquisition, design and engineering, construction, rehabilitation, alteration, expansion, or improvement of publicly owned and operated development facilities. Projects may also include infrastructure for broadband deployment and other types of telecommunications-enabling projects and technology infrastructure.

*Housing.* About 35 programs for housing are available at the federal level. Some of these are described in Chapter 7.

## State and Local Programs

*Land assembly programs.* One of the powers municipalities have for long-term planning is the ability to buy and sell land, typically for a public purpose such as creating a park or public facility. A community also can purchase parcels to assemble into larger parcels and then sell to the private sector. The public sector thus can play a key role in reducing land costs to developers by converting underproductive land that yields little in taxes into desirable parcels that may return much higher property tax revenues. Such a policy must be carefully considered, however, since properties temporarily owned by a municipal government are taken off local tax roles.

Municipalities acquire land in a number of ways besides outright purchase, for example, through foreclosure or by reducing or eliminating back taxes owed by the owner, as an incentive. Land may be donated, bringing the owner a tax deduction. The cost of land may be reduced through state and federal redevelopment programs. Land may also be taken through eminent domain procedures, but this may be a protracted and legally expensive process. (For example, see *Kelo v. City of New London, Connecticut* in Chapter 14.)

The key to successful land assembly is the same as any approach to property investment—location, location, location. Is a parcel near a major transportation link? Are complementary businesses nearby? Are there appropriate amenities? A good parcel in one of a community's growth paths becomes desirable to the community.

Planners can formulate policies to ensure this outcome. The first step is to inventory properties in the community, including publicly held parcels, to determine which do not contribute desired levels of taxation. Next, a redevelopment plan should incorporate properties ripe for purchase, assembly, and development. Potential environmental concerns should be addressed by a Phase I Environmental Assessment. (See Chapter 11 for Environmental Assessment procedures.) A land bank can be created. Land banks, parcels of land held for development, can be managed either by the local government or by a designated nonprofit organization.

The final step is to market the properties, using tax abatements, offering grant or loan programs, upgrading capital improvements through construction of sewer and water lines, or simply implementing a rapid approval process for new developments. If properly used, a land assembly program can work to the advantage of both developers and communities.

*University resources.* A community's local economic development efforts can include many partners. Increasingly, higher education institutions are helping to create jobs and revitalize local economies. Universities and colleges can provide a variety of resources, such as faculty expertise, student labor, internships, and economic analysis and recommendations. New buildings and other facilities attract people and resources in these districts and provide students as a customer base for nearby retail. The University of Wisconsin's Center for Community and Economic Development assists local communities with its Community and Economic Development Toolbox, a Web-based resource to guide them through the process of preparing for economic development action by carrying out economic analyses, offering economic development certificate courses, and publishing a monthly newsletter and articles on related topics.[20]

Local planners should work cooperatively with university personnel to determine how to improve the situation for the institution and the community. Both groups benefit by establishing formal ties.

## Evaluating Information and Generating Incentives

In planning, the problems that need to be addressed often are not obvious or clear; it is important to give them definition. If you do not know what the problem is, you cannot find a suitable solution. Ask yourself: Do I have the appropriate information? Have I used it as a basis for effectively defining alternative solutions? Did I evaluate those alternatives and select the best?

Once you have defined the problems, review the four basic tools communities and planners can use to solve problems, as outlined in Chapter 4:

- Tax incentives or disincentives
- Capital spending
- Regulatory powers
- Buying and selling property

(For additional information on regulatory powers and property transactions, see Chapter 14; on tax incentives/disincentives and capital spending, see Chapter 16.)

Many economic development proposals include a preponderance of ideas that cost a considerable amount of money to implement, in the belief that problems can be solved by spending. However, in reality cities have limited and tightly allocated budgets. Planners must find strategies that minimize spending the city's money and instead attract investment and funding from other sources.

Planners can encourage economic development by providing a vision for others of what can be accomplished. Economic development is most effective when the public sector gives appropriate incentives to encourage the private sector to invest. The job of the planner is to illustrate a community's possibilities for renewal,

building on its strengths. That sense of vision is the inherent fifth tool, and is possibly the most powerful one.

### EXERCISE 9
#### DEVELOPING A PRELIMINARY ECONOMIC DEVELOPMENT PLAN IN RIVERTOWN

*You are a member of Rivertown's Planning Department staff. Using the ideas in this chapter and the information on Rivertown contained in Appendix A, prepare a preliminary economic development proposal for the city for presentation to planning director Burnham Daniel. The proposal will be evaluated based on the following:*

- *Clarity of the statement of the problem*
- *Relationship of the proposal to the stated problem*
- *Appropriateness of the strategies recommended to encourage private investment with minimal public investment (remember: good planning can reduce costs)*
- *Relevance to the role of the planning department in this process*
- *Overall cohesiveness and clarity of the report.*

*If approved by Mr. Daniel, the proposal will be presented to members of City Council; other city agency representatives; Ms. Ima Peeples, president of Concerned Citizens of Rivertown; Norman Tyler, bank manager and representative of the Merchants Association; and other interested individuals.*

---

*Use the template below as a guide to overall organization and content.*

*Cover page:*
*Economic Development Plan for*
*the Downtown District of Rivertown*
*Prepared by _____*
*Rivertown City Planning Department*
*Date*

*Section 1: Problems Identified*
*The downtown district includes primarily retail uses but is adjacent to residential areas. Problems found in the district include:*

*Section 2: Potentials*
*The downtown district includes features on which an eco-*

*nomic redevelopment plan can be based. These sources of potential include:*

*Section 3: Goals*
*The goals of the economic development plan for the downtown district of Rivertown are to:*

*Section 4: Elements of the Economic Development Plan*
*Write a two- to three-page narrative presenting the important aspects of your economic development proposal. Explain how it addresses the goals for the area by addressing key problems and tapping key potentials. Include a map indicating clearly the areas tied in with your proposal.*

## Summary

A strong correlation exists between local economics and community revitalization and growth. All communities should develop a good economic development program to maintain their vitality and benefit private enterprise. Economic growth does not result from a natural evolutionary process, but rather from economic goals and objectives established and implemented by key individuals and organizations. The inclusion of an economic development plan as part of a community's comprehensive plan should be based on consideration of land use, social issues, and other planning elements.

Data collection and inventories provide the foundation for developing an economic plan. Market analyses help establish niches that may be attractive to investors. A strong and carefully considered economic development program can encourage public–private partnerships, teaming a local municipality with a private developer on projects that utilize the strengths and resources of both.

Many government economic development programs are available at the federal and state levels to assist local communities, and communities themselves can use their public spending, tax incentives, and regulatory powers such as zoning to create a positive environment of public sector–private sector cooperation. In this way, community growth patterns evolve from economic restructuring. So whatever path a community takes to remain viable, an economic development plan, with appropriate goals and strategies, must be part of it.

# 10

# TRANSPORTATION PLANNING

## Historical Development

Our culture has been affected significantly by changes in the patterns and technologies of transportation systems; in some ways we have become their servant rather than their master. It is not difficult to discern how transportation has affected American society, but the extent of the influence may be surprising. It is not hyperbole to say that the growth of the United States has been led by the development of its transportation systems from horse and wagons to the country's extensive interstate highway system to the latest high-speed trains and jet airplanes. The settlement patterns of the New World by Spanish explorers, French traders, and British settlers were based on new navigational skills of Europeans crossing the Atlantic in the sixteenth and seventeenth centuries. Each of these colonial powers established settlements based to some degree on their mode of travel: the Spanish traversed unexplored inland areas on horseback; the French established trade routes by water throughout areas of Canadian wilderness, the Great Lakes, and the Mississippi River watershed; the British settled the eastern coastal areas by sea routes and primitive roads. The development of western territories depended on opening new routes over difficult terrain. In the early nineteenth century, the National Road crossed the Appalachians; this first road west was soon followed by the Erie Canal, which provided a dependable water route from New York City to Lake Erie through a split in the mountainous divide. In the mid-nineteenth century, the transcontinental railroad crossed the Rocky Mountains and a rapidly expanding network of rail lines provided links to the Pacific Coast.

Interurban trolley service spread rapidly in the late 1800s and early 1900s. At the turn of the twentieth century, interurban railroads represented the best form of

transportation available in and between nearby cities. Once trolleys became electrified, passengers in the Midwest could ride them on interconnected lines for hundreds of miles—for example, from Cincinnati, Ohio, to Grand Rapids, Michigan.

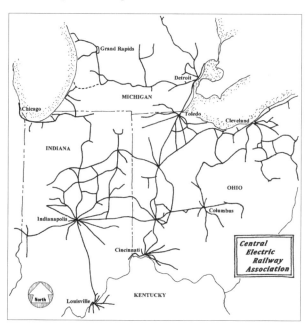

*10.1. Interurban network in the Midwest*

The dominance of interurbans began to slip in 1908, when Henry Ford introduced assembly line production of the Model T automobile. This inexpensive automobile gave more freedom and flexibility. Soon, many interurban companies were no longer profitable as the cost to operate them was too great for the smaller number of riders. The demise of interurbans was facilitated by officials at General Motors, who saw interurbans as direct competition to the sale of their automobiles. The increasingly powerful company bought many interurban companies and dismantled their systems by removing their tracks and replacing trolleys with gas-powered buses. By the 1930s, virtually all the country's interurban systems were gone. An industry that had satisfied the transit needs of most of the population had disappeared almost overnight.

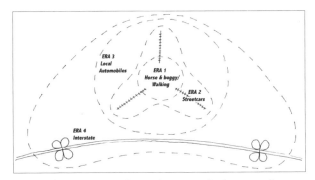
*10.2. Demise of the streetcar*

American cities developed along with their transportation systems in four distinct eras. Each tied closely with a new transportation technology and represents the extent of urbanized development allowed by the transportation speed of the time. Research has consistently shown commuters historically are generally willing to travel from 30 to 35 minutes each way from home to work.[1] Thus, the limit of the developed urban area is not based on distance, but on travel time.

*10.3. Urban expansion during four eras of urban growth*

The first era is that of the colonial city, based on the speed of the pedestrian and the horse and buggy—a walking speed. The cities' boundaries grew in a circular pattern based on how far people could walk from home to the town center, where they worked and shopped. The second era was represented by new urban rail systems of trolleys and streetcars and allowed families to live farther from the urban center. Cities expanded along the commuter rail lines, extended by the walking distance from the rails lines to home.

The third era was initiated by Henry Ford and his ubiquitous Model T, which made individualized transportation available to most citizens; newly paved roads brought comfortable and convenient transportation to everyone's back door. The automobile allowed for commuting from still greater distances, and along any streets. Cities grew in a circular pattern once again.

A vast system of interstate highways enabled the fourth era—a new growth pattern oriented to the locations of limited-access highway intersections. The intersections spawned new nodes of commercial development with easy access to the center city, and residential and industrial development followed to the urban fringe. Highways also provided intercity links.

## Impacts of Transportation

Transportation systems have many types of impacts on communities. Transportation and land use are closely linked. The intensified use of a parcel of land leads to increased activity, which creates a need for transportation to service it. Expanded accessibility encourages further development, which brings more activity, requiring additional transportation. Conversely, an increase in the capacity of a transportation system often fosters additional land uses. Thus transportation and land use directly affect one another, whether at a macro scale (whole urban areas) or micro scale (single projects).

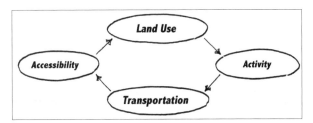
*10.4. Land use/transportation linkages*

Transportation systems also have significant effects on the environment, especially, as we now know, the deterioration of air quality caused by vehicle emissions. Although unleaded gas and more fuel-efficient engines reduce the level of pollutants emitted for each vehicle-mile, the benefits are moderated by the increased number of vehicle-miles traveled each year. Also, the construction of additional roads and development into urban fringe areas destroys natural wetlands. In the northern states, winter salt used to de-ice roads causes damage to soil and vegetation as well as concrete and steel. Noise pollution is another effect of vehicle use, and some communities have built miles-long walls to deflect highway noise from adjacent residential areas.

Transportation also has a direct effect on our national economy. Automobile manufacturers and parts suppliers, oil companies, construction companies, hotels, and travel and leisure industries are closely tied to our transportation systems. During downturns, advisers assert that a sluggish economy could most quickly be reinvigorated through major investments in new transportation systems, especially the construction of roads and bridges.

How dependent are we as a society on our transportation systems? An urban scholar from the mid-twentieth century, Lewis Mumford, questioned the priorities Americans have established: "Future generations will perhaps wonder at our willingness, indeed our eagerness, to sacrifice the education of our children, the care of the ill and the aged, the development of the arts, to say nothing of ready access to nature, for the lop-sided system of mono-transportation, going through low-density areas at sixty miles an hour."[2]

Should we sacrifice our cities to the god of the automobile, as Mumford describes, or see automobiles as providing previously unheard of mobility, convenience, and comfort, as suggested by urbanist Wilfred Owens:

The reason for preferring private over public transit is not, as often alleged, the perversity of the consumer or his ignorance of economics . . . the basic reason why most urban trips are made by automobile is that the family car, despite its shortcomings, is superior to any other method of transportation. It offers comfort, privacy, limited walking, minimum waiting, and freedom from schedules or routing. It guarantees a seat; protects the traveler from heat, cold and rain; provides space for baggage; carries extra passengers at no extra cost; and for most trips, except those in the center city, gets there faster and cheaper than any other way. The transit rider confronts an entirely different situation. He must walk, wait, stand, and be exposed to the elements. The ride is apt to be costly, slow, and uncomfortable because of antiquated equipment, poor ventilation (and service that is congested in rush hours), infrequent during any other time of day, inoperative at night, and non-existent in suburbia.[3]

We try to accommodate our need for better transportation by building more infrastructure, but with mixed results. Trying to resolve traffic congestion by adding more roads or increasing the size of existing roads has often not led to solutions, but instead has often created more problems. If more lanes are added to a road to relieve congestion, people will drive longer distances and make more trips until the wider roads are again filled to capacity (an effect known as latent demand). Roads built to increase capacity can encourage additional development along those routes, and traffic will increase until there is an even greater level of congestion. For example, 28th Street in Grand Rapids, Michigan, was originally built as a bypass route at the southern fringe of the city, intended to relieve traffic congestion within the city. However, because the new five-lane street provided easy accessibility, it became the most desirable location in Grand Rapids for new commercial development and quickly became the most congested corridor in the city and one of the slowest moving roads in the state. The linkage between a transportation system and its adjacent land uses was never clearer than here; the route did not relieve congestion, it created it.

*10.5. 28th Street, Grand Rapids, Michigan, 2009*

10.6. *Boston's "Big Dig" project under construction*

## Spotlight on Boston's "Big Dig"

"Big Dig" is the unofficial name of the Central Artery/ Tunnel project (CA/T), a mega-project that rerouted the Central Artery (Interstate 93) through the heart of Boston to a 3.5-mile tunnel under the city. The project included the construction of the Ted Williams Tunnel (extending Interstate 90 to Logan International Airport), the Zakim Bunker Hill Bridge over the Charles River, and the Rose Kennedy Greenway in the space vacated by the previous I-93 elevated roadway.

When originally built in 1959, the surface highway through Boston's downtown was planned to comfortably carry 75,000 vehicles a day. By the 1980s, it was carrying 200,000 vehicles a day, with stop-and-go traffic for 10 hours a day. The cost to motorists from congestion, including fuel from idling, elevated accident rates, and late delivery charges, was estimated at $500 million.

Plans were formulated to build a new highway underground through the heart of the city. In spite of its many complications, including cost overruns, delays, and poor execution, the project is considered by many to be a success. As Thomas Menino, the city's mayor during most of the construction, said, for the first time in half a century residents can walk from City Hall to the waterfront without trudging under a major highway: "Now we have a beautiful open space in the heart of the city. It knits the downtown with the waterfront. All those dire predictions by the experts didn't come true." And a study by the Turnpike Authority found the Big Dig cut the average trip through Boston from 19.5 minutes to 2.8 minutes.[4]

## Role of the Department of Transportation

The U.S. Department of Transportation (DOT) is the central agency for transportation programs at the national level. It offers many types of citizen services, from information on vehicle safety, scenic byways, airport conditions, and recreational boating sites, to the Department's Federal Highway Administration programs related to the national system of roads and highways.

One of the agency's responsibilities is administration of the SAFETEA-LU program (Safe, Accountable, Flexible, Efficient Transportation, and Equity Act: A Legacy for Users), which focuses on the federal surface transportation program. The legislation was originally passed in 1991 as the Intermodal Surface Transportation Efficiency Act (ISTEA), which gave increased attention to pedestrians, transit, and bicycle facilities. ISTEA marked the beginning of collaborative relationships with Metropolitan Planning Organizations, where transportation-related discussions occur in a broader context with more participating agencies (as noted in Chapter 3). Although the Transportation Fund still is used primarily for highway construction and maintenance, its Enhancements program allocates 10 percent of available funds for special programs that focus on safety, nonmotorized transportation—such as trails and bikeways—and the preservation of historic transportation-related properties.

For community planners, the activities of the DOT involve support for programs related to congestion relief; innovations in transit systems; highway programs, including road design; the Scenic Highways and Historic Covered Bridge programs; and similar services. Significant environmental requirements and a Safe Routes to School program have been incorporated in recent revisions to the act. The Transportation Planning section promotes consistency between transportation improvements and state and local planned growth and economic development patterns.

## Designing Infrastructure

### Street Hierarchy

Streets are the primary connectors in communities and their design and movement patterns are critical to their success as a tool of good planning. A schematic illustration of the hierarchy of streets shows how the relationships support traffic mobility and provide access to land uses. Arterial roads provide for the greatest amount of traffic. To achieve this, they may be developed as limited-access highways or four- or six-lane major streets that have controlled access from land uses along their length. This systematic control and restrictions on driveways, median openings, interchanges, traffic signals, and street connections is referred to as access management. Through such design control, arterials provide the greatest efficiency in traffic movement, but the least efficiency for access to sites.

Streets that feed into arterials are called collectors. They are designed to balance traffic efficiency and access. Collectors may have heavy traffic at times, but give fairly convenient, if controlled, access to land uses.

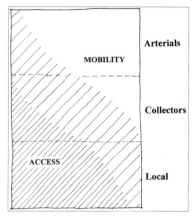

10.7. Road classifications relating traffic mobility to land use access

Most of the access connections to arterials are from such collectors. Local streets provide the greatest and most convenient access to all land uses, but at the cost of relatively slow speeds. The most frequent street type, local streets service the greatest number of individual sites.

Planning for urban traffic management can be counterintuitive. In many instances, the objective of traffic management should not be to handle traffic efficiently in terms of speed, but instead to be inefficient. Slow-moving automobiles contribute to street activity and liveliness, just as pedestrians do. As a *New York Times* article put it, "If you start looking, you start realizing that, gee, if you created less traffic flow, slower vehicles, you create more of a community and you increase the perception of safety and security. . . . Traffic engineers call this 'friction,' and friction in their eyes is bad. To us, friction is good."[5]

Planners can control traffic speeds through the width of streets and sidewalks, parking access patterns, and traffic signaling. Visual clues that alert drivers to take more care are known as "traffic-calming" measures; the most familiar is the speed bump, or speed table, a rise in the level of the pavement painted to be conspicuous. Other traffic-calming features include bulb-outs (a widening of the sidewalk at a pedestrian cross-walk) and narrowing of the street; intentional curving (chicanes); diverters, generally a landscape feature in the roadway which drivers must go around; and roundabouts, traffic circles that not only slow traffic at an intersection, but also handle more traffic with greater efficiency when used in proper locations.

The use of transportation systems—automobile,

10.8. *Traffic roundabout*

transit, pedestrian, and other—to promote linkages between popular activities is referred to as connectivity. Connectivity routes can bring life to spaces, and a deliberate pattern of linkages, including paths, nodes, and open spaces in and between districts. The connections between activity nodes vary based on the type of transportation utilized: automobile travel entails higher speeds and unpredictable routing; transit typically offers moderate-paced travel along defined routes; bicycles and pedestrians produce slower and free-form patterns of movement.

## Spotlight on Promoting Connectivity, Channahon, Illinois

A proposal for a new town center for Channahon, Illinois, was aimed at creating a street pattern to promote connectivity. The community connects to a state highway at its southeast corner. The community's main traffic axis pro-

vides easy orientation from this entry point through the site. Its focal point is a small central park that links various community functions. Biking and walking paths provide for non-motorized routes. The street pattern provides a variety of housing types and ensures that pedestrian and bike routes are present throughout the area.

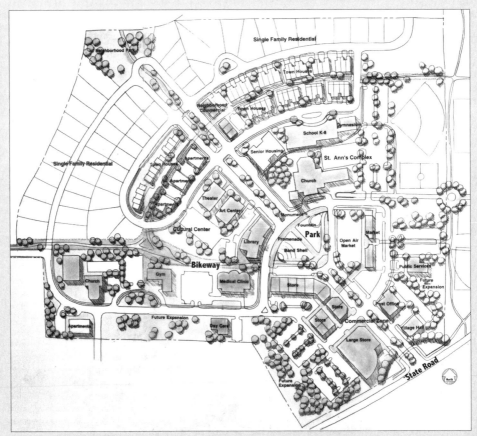

10.9. *Design competition entry for new town center for Channahon, Illinois*

The Federal Highway Administration and other traffic agencies and organizations support the design of roadways using an approach called context-sensitive design, which emphasizes that transportation facilities should preserve scenic, aesthetic, historic, and environmental resources while maintaining safety and mobility. These agencies encourage the involvement and collaboration of stakeholders, including residents, in such decisions.

*10.10. Highway art along Pima Freeway, an innovative solution that beautifies highways in Scottsdale, Arizona*

### Parking

Parking is a major design element for any transportation system that involves automobiles. Parking can occupy the largest portion of a commercial site plan. Suburban projects usually include land to accommodate this need; center city areas often do not have sufficient land available, and providing parking becomes a problem in revitalization efforts. Although some planners feel that parking has received too much attention as a tool of community revitalization—the primary strategy to create a successful commercial district is to have goods and services that are desired—it must be addressed nonetheless.

Some general guidelines for parking facilities are: (1) make the flow of traffic to parking areas readily apparent without excessive signage; (2) locate pedestrian walkways to and from parking such that there is minimal conflict with automobiles; and (3) allow adequate parking spaces near building entrances for handicapped persons.

In a parking lot, access lanes should be separated from parking lanes. There should be convenient drop-off locations for passengers. Access for trucks and service vehicles to building entrances and Dumpster locations should be separated from parking traffic. Many of these

standards are incorporated in the zoning ordinance, but all represent good design principles based on user convenience.

When large paved areas are necessary to provide sufficient parking spaces, these areas should be visually broken into smaller sections with landscaping, low walls, or other features; however, do not create areas that cannot be easily monitored for safety. Parking aisles should be no longer than 30 contiguous spaces. For better aesthetics, the edges of the parking lot should be screened so vehicles are partially screened.

Many zoning ordinances require parking areas to be sized for the greatest possible capacity: in retail areas this is typically considered the day after Thanksgiving and the Saturday before Christmas, the only days of the year when the lot may be filled. Many communities now are reconsidering such high requirements. Smaller parking areas reduce the amount of overall paved land, which minimizes loss of productive land area, heat buildup from asphalt, drainage problems, and environmental considerations. Conventional paved parking lots are impervious to rain water, causing rapid runoff, erosion, and flood damage during severe storms. New paving materials, such as permeable asphalt and concrete, allow drainage through the pavement and reduce potential site drainage and flooding problems. Adequate on-site drainage is essential; a retention or detention pond may be required.

The costs of parking are a major consideration. Surface parking lots are much less expensive to create than structures or underground parking. The cost of a surface lot averages $2,000 to $3,000 per space, while above-ground parking structures average $20,000 to $25,000 per space and underground parking $30,000 to $40,000 per space.[6] In spite of the high cost, above- or underground parking structures may be justified in dense urban areas, where land is expensive; elevator parking, although expensive, can also multiply the number of spaces on a given sized site, since cars are stored without the need for driving lanes.

The cost may be partially offset by planning for shared parking, where automobiles at different times of the day or week can utilize the same spaces. An estimate of parking occupancy rates for differing land uses has been derived for various day/time periods. This information is useful for calculating the extent of possible shared parking. For example, parking for office buildings is largely available during evenings and weekends, while the parking lot for a conference/convention center is planned for use at all times, making sharing impractical in most circumstances.

| Land Use | Mon-Fri. 8am-6pm | Mon-Fri. 6pm-midnight | Sat-Sun 8am-6pm | Sat-Sun 6pm-midnight |
|---|---|---|---|---|
| Residential | 60% | 100% | 80% | 100% |
| Office | 100% | 20% | 5% | 5% |
| Retail/Commercial | 90% | 80% | 100% | 70% |
| Restaurant | 70% | 100% | 70% | 100% |
| Movie Theater | 40% | 80% | 80% | 100% |
| Convention | 100% | 100% | 100% | 100% |
| Place of Worship | 10% | 5% | 100% | 50% |

10.11. *Parking occupancy rate table*[7]

Some communities offer Payment in Lieu of Parking (PILOP). Such a waiver for developers is based on the fact that the city will be responsible for providing parking as part of a well-planned parking system. Under a PILOP, parking is not a single land use, but is shared for multiple properties in close proximity. For example, the city may provide parking for a new development and tie it to municipal lots and structures, public transit, or other improvements for the general public. The municipal government benefits in two ways: it receives money from the developer (typically $3,000 to $10,000 or more per required space) to build parking facilities and these facilities generate additional revenue for the city from parking fees.

## Transportation Modeling

Transportation planning relies on computer modeling as a means to plan highways and other modes of transportation. Modeling predicts travel demand, a critical component in planning and setting spending priorities. The process incorporates factors such as public transit, land use and development issues, and air quality analysis. Planners need to understand the results of these models to develop proper transportation system recommendations. Travel demand modeling uses data derived from calculations of thousands of individual travelers making individual decisions about how, where, and when to travel.

The most widely known and used transportation model is the Urban Transportation Modeling System (UTMS). The four factors it incorporates to predict travel behavior are: (1) the number of trips generated from a zone of origin or attracted to a destination zone; (2) the likelihood of trips between specific origins and destinations; (3) the modes of transportation used (train, bus, car, bicycle, or walking); and (4) the routes traveled between origins and destinations. UTMS computer models support forecasts about the demand for transportation resources under different conditions and at different times of the year.

For example, if a major boulevard with heavy commuting traffic in the center of a city must close for an extended period of time for reconstruction, causing major congestion, transportation planners need to make decisions that will minimize disruption. The first step of the analysis is to determine how many vehicles typically used the street during its peak period. This information may be available through the transportation department; otherwise, before road closure a count can be conducted through use of a gross volume counter, an air hose laid across the lanes that uses air pulses to record axle counts (two pulses are assumed to be one vehicle).

Then planners determine trip origins and destinations by means of a random survey of people who use the route, to indicate statistically the number of vehicle trips from or to various origins and destinations. Alternatively, this information can be derived from analysis of the three most significant types of land use, residential (housing), commercial (shopping), and industrial (jobs). Residential areas are assumed to be origin zones, since most trips begin at home. Estimates of the number of trips generated typically are based on number of households, average number of persons per household, and number of vehicles owned per household; this information is available from census data. Industrial, office, and retail locations are assumed to be destination zones. The number of trips attracted to each may be derived from several factors, the most common being square footage of a facility or number of employees. The data on origins and destinations can indicate the percentage of current trips on the boulevard that are local and need to be adjusted at a local level and how many are more regional and must be modified more regionally.

The third step of the modeling process examines the mode of transportation used for individual trips. In the boulevard example, the great majority of the trips would be by automobile, creating the greatest congestion during a construction period. Therefore, if drivers are encouraged to take a bus for commuting, traffic problems would be reduced significantly. However, if the road is used by heavy trucks, possible substitute routes through local streets unable to accommodate their weight may not be suitable. In this case, alternative truck routes need to be identified.

| Travel Mode | Number of Commuters | Percent |
|---|---|---|
| Total workers | 128,279,000 | 100.0 |
| Car, truck or van | 112,736,000 | 87.9 |
| Drive alone | 97,102,000 | 75.7 |
| Carpool | 15,634,000 | 12.2 |
| Public transit | 6,068,000 | 4.7 |
| Bus or trolley | 3,207,000 | 2.5 |
| Subway or elevated railroad | 1,886,000 | 1.5 |
| Taxicab | 200,000 | 0.2 |
| Motorcycle | 142,000 | 0.1 |
| Bicycle | 488,000 | 0.4 |
| Walk | 3,759,000 | 2.9 |
| Other means | 901,000 | 0.7 |
| Work at home, no commute | 4,184,000 | 3.3 |

10.12. *Modes of transportation to work in the United States*[8]

The last step in the UTMS process focuses on the actual routes used. It assigns automobiles and trucks to the network of roads and streets they are likely to use during the construction period and transit passengers to their likely rail and bus lines. In the boulevard example, the outcome would determine which streets should be used as alternative routes during construction. Perhaps two of the local streets would be converted temporarily to a pair of one-way streets and an alternate truck route could be chosen. Using computer modeling, transportation planners can recommend what changes need to be made before construction begins.

Transportation planners use UTMS to do complex calculations that were impossible or prohibitive a few years ago. Such models, however, cannot solve all aspects of transportation planning. They do not deal with issues of environmental impact, energy use, or politics. However, these can sometimes be incorporated through the use of specially developed and applicable submodels.

### EXERCISE 10
#### TRANSPORTATION STUDY IN RIVERTOWN

*Rivertown's City Council recognizes a need to increase traffic capacity and reduce congestion on Station Street. The study area begins at River Street, continues across the one-lane bridge that spans the Eagle River, and extends to Elly's Mobile Home Park site and the entrances to a large, new, mixed-use development currently proposed for the Cartwright Farm just south of Toosters Swamp. (See Chapter 12 for a description of the Cartwright Farm proposal.)*

*The Council has asked its planners to collect information that a transportation consultant will require for modeling this situation. Based on the UTMS modeling system described above, prepare a list of the types of information required for each of the four steps in the process and explain how this information can be obtained. Use the template below to provide this information.*

*a = Information needed*
*b = How to obtain information*

UTMS Step 1
a _____
b _____

Step 2
a _____
b _____

Step 3
a _____
b _____

Step 4
a _____
b _____

## The Role of Public Transit

Public transit systems can play an important role in resolving transportation problems in American communities. These systems provide several options to enable residents to participate more fully in their community without the need for an automobile, a vital consideration for children, the nondriving elderly, individuals with disabilities that prevent driving, and those who cannot afford to own and operate a car. Public transportation not only can serve them, but it is more cost-effective than individual automobiles and can provide environmental benefits. An electric light rail system, for example, uses little electricity and so has a small carbon footprint.

The Federal Transit Administration (FTA) is the agency responsible for allocation of federal funding to support public transportation systems—buses, subways, light rail, commuter rail, streetcars, monorail, passenger ferryboats, and inclined railways. The FTA administers grant programs for metropolitan and statewide planning for multimodal transportation and assists with environmental analysis and review. In recent decades, many new versions of transit and multimodal systems have been developed.

### Modern Light Rail

In recent decades, cities have begun to adopt modern electric trolley systems called Light Rail Vehicles, or LRVs. They can move large groups of people rapidly and produce very little noise or air pollution, so they are environmentally friendly. Many of these popular and successful systems tie closely with bus routes, with coordinated routes scheduled to expand their service areas.

There are numerous examples of successful light rail systems. Portland, Oregon's Tri-Met system sets new ridership records every year. Washington, D.C.'s Metrorail system, a major means of transportation with almost 1 million riders per day in 2009, connects the nation's capital with neighboring communities in Maryland and Virginia.[9] Chicago's elevated railroad ("El"), which has been operating successfully since 1892, plans a major addition with a new light rail Circle Line that avoids the congestion of Chicago's "Loop" area. The San Diego Trolley opened in 1981 as the first modern light-rail system in California. With 53 miles of track, its routes extend from northern San Diego to the Mexican border at San Ysidro and carry over 35 million riders annually. Plans for future extension of the system are in place.

### Ferries

There are alternatives to ground transportation for public transit systems. Some coastal cities have relied for many decades on ferries for transporting commuters. The Staten Island Ferry in New York City, with five vessels in daily use, shuttles some 60,000 passengers per day. Alaska's Marine Highway provides transport to Alaskan cities so remote there are no roads to them. It is a year-round service connecting Bellingham, Washington, through the Inside Passage to other cities in Washington state and some of the largest cities in southeastern and southwestern Alaska, including the capital city of Juneau. Residents of Bainbridge Island, a bedroom community of 20,000, love their 35-minute commute to downtown Seattle on the Bainbridge Island Ferry, with its view of the skyline, the Space Needle, and Mount Rainier in one direction and the Olympic Mountains in another.

In San Francisco, the Golden Gate Ferry connects the city to Sausalito and Larkspur. The Key West Ferry connects the western Florida coast at Fort Myers to Key West with a three-hour crossing on a catamaran (otherwise a seven-hour car trip). The Maine State Ferry Service ties the mainland with many of the state's coastal islands as well as, seasonally, Nova Scotia.

*10.13. San Diego Trolley*

*10.14. Ferry, Seattle, Washington*

*10.15. Sketch of upgraded aerial tramway between Manhattan and Roosevelt Island, New York City*

## Trams

Two North American cities have used overhead cable car, or tram, systems to good advantage. Vancouver, British Columbia, has an overhead cable car system that comes into the center of the city and carries passengers to nearby hill areas. New York City's Roosevelt Island tram transports commuters from a new community located on an island in the East River via the only above-ground route across the water into midtown Manhattan.

## Individual Transportation Alternatives

### Bicycling

Forty percent of all automobile trips in the United States are less than 2 miles, a distance that can easily be biked in 15 minutes. Biking can be a viable alternative for many commuters. How can biking best be integrated into an overall urban transportation system? Bike lanes need to be well delineated, whether as part of the road or pedestrian system.

Bikeways are generally differentiated by type. A Class I route is: "A bikeway physically separated from motorized vehicular traffic by an open space or barrier within the right-of-way or within an independent right-of-way. These paths will also be used by pedestrians, skaters, wheelchairs, joggers and other non-motorized users." A Class II route is: "A portion of a roadway which has been designated by striping, signing, and pavement markings for the preferential or exclusive use of bicyclists. Bike lanes are one-way directional travel lanes, corresponding with the direction of vehicular traffic." A Class III route is: "A signed shared roadway which has been designated by signing as a preferred route for bicycle and motor vehicle travel. May be with or without paved shoulders and/or curbing. Bicyclists travel in the same direction as vehicles sharing the same side of the roadway."[10]

Other design elements to be considered are drive-

*10.16. Bike lane separated from road (Class I), Cambridge, Massachusetts*

*10.17. Bike lane integrated with road (Class II), Cambridge, Massachusetts*

ways opening into bikeways, which should be paved to prevent gravel from collecting at the edge of the road. Roadway curb drains should have grates that are perpendicular to the route of bikes, rather than parallel to them. Bridge walkways should be wide enough to allow bikers and pedestrians to pass each other when there is no other way to cross.

Communities that recognize the contribution of biking to a multimodal local transportation system accommodate bikers' needs. For example, buses and commuter trains can provide carrying racks for bikes so commuters can bike to the transit stop and travel by public transit to their job site, thus eliminating the need for a car. Oakland, California's "pedal-hopper" is one such vehicle.

10.19. "Pedal-hopper," Oakland, California

Some cities have made a serious commitment to the development of biking as a primary form of transportation. Seattle's bicycle and pedestrian program has six full-time employees and spends about $4 million annually on bicycle and pedestrian improvements. The city has a 150-mile integrated network of multiuse trails and a program to respond to public requests for improvements. In Cambridge, Massachusetts, four people are solely responsible for coordinating the extensive bikeway system. Boulder, Colorado, has a campaign to combine pedestrian, bike, and transit activities in an effort to reduce single-occupant vehicle trips.

Class I Bikeway: Independent right-of-way

Class II Bikeway: Designated bike lane on roadway

Class III Bikeway: Shared roadway

10.18. Bikeway classifications

### Walking

Walkability should be a goal of any urban or suburban transportation plan. When people can walk through their community, it fosters a sense of place and belonging because residents meet neighbors on a regular basis. Walking can bridge the isolation of suburban subdivisions. Furthermore, walking is the oldest, healthiest, and least expensive form of transportation. It is also a critical part of any effort to plan effective transit. A walkable neighborhood can survive without a public transit system, but public transit needs a walkable neighborhood.

Walkers need paths and destinations. Developments without sidewalks are an unsafe environment for walkers. Likewise, if there are sidewalks, but no logical places of origin or destination, they provide no incentive to people to walk; a sidewalk that does not lead anywhere is unlikely to be used. To be most effective, walking routes need to be prioritized around key locations, such as schools, civic buildings, shopping centers, transit stops, and senior centers.

A walkable community must be safe. Walkways should be a safe distance from moving traffic. Pedestrians should not have to walk adjacent to moving traffic; there should be a buffer zone between pedestrians and vehicular traffic. Parked cars can serve this purpose. The faster the traffic, the wider the buffer should be. Intersections, the place where most car-related pedestrian injuries occur, should be designed so pedestrians are as visible and their actions as predictable as possible. Crosswalks should be clearly defined. Raising the level of pedestrian crosswalks slightly can slow traffic at these points. The amount of pedestrian exposure to vehicular traffic can be reduced by creating refuge islands in wide streets or narrowing streets at pedestrian crossings.

In rural areas, wide shoulders along roads can serve as walkways and bikeways. A three- to five-foot-wide shoulder provides adequate safety in most circumstances, depending on the speed of traffic. With speeds of 50 miles per hour or more, wider shoulders provide increased safety. Changing the appearance of the shoulder by using a different paving material or painting the walkway a contrasting color adds safety. Special attention is required to address snow removal needs.

Montgomery County, Maryland, created an advisory board responsible for pedestrian safety and calls for a pedestrian impact statement to be included in all public or private projects. Local officials decided to improve pedestrian safety after suffering a period when there were more pedestrian fatalities than homicides.[11]

As noted earlier, pedestrians are a critical ingredient in a successful mix of downtown activities, and creating a comfortable environment for them, a few steps removed from the noise, heat, and pavement of city streets, is desirable. A University of Michigan study on downtown vitality found the best predictor of the health of a downtown is the number of pedestrians on the sidewalk.[12] In a Seattle survey, community leaders representing neighborhood businesses indicate that pedestrian activity is an important indicator of a thriving neighborhood business district.[13] The Riverwalk of San Antonio, Texas, provides an entire system of walkways and retail one level below the downtown grid, bringing recreational walking and increased business revenues for merchants.

10.20. *Riverwalk system, San Antonio, Texas*

### *Spotlight on Lakewood's Walkable Downtown*

Lakewood, Colorado, is the fourth largest city in the state, but it lacked a downtown, so residents instead frequented Belmar, a regional mall built in the 1970s. When the 1.4 million-square-foot mall failed in the mid-1990s, the city partnered with an investment team to convert Belmar's typical mall layout into a 19-block mixed-use, walkable downtown. Plans for the conversion included 1,300 residences, offices, a supermarket, a movie theater, parks, plazas, and a large events center. New streets extended through former parking lots, integrating the site with its surroundings. Existing buildings received new street-front small-scale facades to create visual variety and gradually Lakewood has developed its downtown.

10.21. *Conversion of the Belmar mall in progress, Lakewood, Colorado, 2005*

## Designing for Life

### Transit-Oriented Development

According to a study commissioned by the Federal Transit Administration, by 2025 nearly 15 million U.S. households will want to rent or buy housing near transit stops, doubling today's number.[14] Communities in which development is centered around a high-density core with a good transit system can offer residents an array of travel options that reduce dependence on any one mode. Demand for Transit-Oriented Development (TOD) will be highest in regions that have extensive existing transit systems, such as New York City, Boston, and Chicago, and those with growing systems like Los Angeles.[15] TODs include mixed land uses and a strongly pedestrian environment serviced by a transit terminal at a central location. The areas around transit stops are pedestrian-friendly and offer multiple destinations within walking distance. TODs marry land use and transportation functionally. As planner Peter Calthorpe puts it, "The environment in which transit is operated is no less critical to its success than the quality of service that is offered."[16]

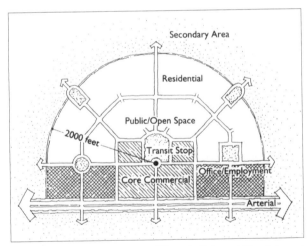

*10.22. Schematic illustration of Transit-Oriented Development*

TODs should include convenient retail, offices, food shopping, restaurants, above-first-floor residences, services, businesses, and entertainment. Businesses that do not promote pedestrian needs, such as auto dealers, car washes, fast food, or motels, should be discouraged. Development should be kept within 2,000 feet of the transit stop, a comfortable walking distance. Many non-commute trips can be captured within the TOD's stan-dard recommendation for mixed-use: 10 percent of land for public space, 30 percent for core commercial/employment, and 60 percent for housing. Planning TODs, even without existing transit, allows the possibility of adding more effective and less expensive transit later.

### Safe Routes to School

A 2001 consumer study found that 78 percent of people surveyed want a community where their children could walk or bike to a neighborhood school, while 19 percent preferred to drive them to a larger regional school.[17] Forty years ago, half of all children walked or biked to school; by 2009 that number had dropped to 1 in 10.[18] The discrepancy between how people want their children to get to school and how they actually get there was precipitated by the economics of building large school complexes; the result is that children do not have a close tie to a neighborhood school, and do not get the exercise of walking or biking, which probably contributes to the well-documented increase in childhood obesity.

The National Center for Safe Routes to School encourages communities to create safe ways for walking or biking to school through strategies that address safety and liability concerns as schools accept responsibility for making such programs successful. From a planning perspective, it means evaluating routes for safety and convenience, especially at busy intersections and crossings, and prioritizing improvements. In Burlington, Vermont, parents formed a walking group to shuttle young school children along a busy road supervised by a walk-leader. This "walking school bus" encourages many more students to walk and provides extra safety for those who do.

### Living Near Work

The two land uses of greatest significance to commuters are their home and their place of employment. Throughout the twentieth century, development patterns and lifestyle trends encouraged residents to live at a distance from their work, and home was separated from workplace by greater and greater distances. To address problems associated with transportation most directly, this mindset is where change must come, first in attitude and then in policy. If Americans were to live closer to their work, the change could have major impact on our communities, and it could lead to considerable savings. Such a shift in perspective has virtually no cost to the public sector and can lead to a richer lifestyle for most, because it can relieve commuters of wasted hours spent in heavy traffic and the costs of commuting. Moreover, it can regenerate cities and contribute to their sustainability.

Some people may see the policy of "Live closer to work" as the government telling them where to live or work. But the government has been doing that all along through its decisions on where roads are built, or sewer lines constructed, or zoning boundaries delineated, or schools located. For a century, myriad government policies have encouraged Americans to ignore travel costs to work or shopping destinations by providing a vast highway and road system. Government incentives such as mortgage insurance to build new housing rather than renovate existing housing, public services for suburbanizing areas, and similar programs served to support the expansion of development to rural areas, with little attention paid to existing center city land uses.

The policy of living closer to work does not mean residents must abandon the suburbs to return to the center city. Workplaces now are scattered across the map. In many cities, jobs have followed residents to the fringe, where land is cheap and regulations are light. It is fine to live in a suburban neighborhood if your job is in the same suburb. But if you work in the city, then it is best to live in closer proximity. This approach will not only lessen congestion and pollution but will also restore a stronger sense of community. Residents identify more strongly with a place where they both live and work.

Planners can encourage a shift in attitude and awareness. Walking to work, buying groceries from a neighborhood store, and letting children ride their bike to soccer practice rather than being driven represent a healthier lifestyle and a sustainable approach to the environment that is appropriate for the twenty-first century.

## Summary

The evolution of cities and communities in the United States has been closely linked to the development of its transportation systems. The change from eighteenth-century settlement roads and waterways to nineteenth-century railroads to twentieth-century automobiles and highways altered the lifestyles of Americans in major ways. There continues to be a strong relationship between land use, development, and transportation systems. Development stimulates demand for transportation routes; as transportation improves, more development follows. This cycle has a corresponding effect on surrounding land values.

Transportation planning is integral to virtually all aspects of community planning. It constitutes a major land use in urban areas. Community planners should work in cooperation with transportation planners to improve transportation systems while reducing congestion, pollution, and land use incompatibilities.

Transportation modeling is a method to predict future usage. Transportation management strategies, such as connectivity, context-sensitive design, traffic calming, and parking solutions are important aspects of planning. Various forms of transportation, including light rail and ferries, as well as bicycles and walking, may provide better solutions for communities. TOD, or transit-oriented development, a concept that encourages development around transit stops, has become recognized increasingly as a way to encourage better use of public transit. Ensuring safe walking routes to schools and encouraging living closer to work are essential life benefits to include in the development of a comprehensive transportation plan.

# 11
# ENVIRONMENTAL PLANNING

## The Environmental System

Environmental planning can be divided into two general categories—land cover and land use. Land cover is the physical presence of natural and man-made features in the landscape, such as fields, trees, water, and buildings in urbanized areas. Land use, as the name suggests, refers to functional aspects of what is on the land surface, such as farming, residential homes, or industrial sites. Land cover primarily represents the physical presence on the land, while land use includes how the land cover is used. Environmental issues can be discussed in broader terms, including policies, culture, history, behavior, and health. Planners need to understand the dynamics of these systems as they relate to the planned environment.

Environmental planning is relevant locally, regionally, and globally and spans many disciplines. Natural events, such as earthquakes, droughts, wildfires (natural or man-made), and major floods have short-term and long-term impacts on the earth's ecosystems and on communities. Local traditions, economics, and site amenities may influence the decision to establish communities in hazardous areas. When people occupy areas of known natural hazards, such as floodplains or eroding coasts, and continue to do so even after a major destructive event, planning can assist them to make appropriate decisions.

## Environmental Policies and Programs at the Federal and State Level

The federal government provides regulatory leadership and funding for national and state environmental legislation. Environmental programs include controls over air and water quality and solid- and hazardous-waste management. The federal government also provides relevant services to communities. U.S. Weather Service forecasts alert communities to prepare for weather emergencies by using new technologies and computer modeling procedures. The Federal Emergency Management Agency (FEMA) trains local residents and agencies to ensure that they are ready to respond quickly to a disaster and aids communities that have experienced disasters.

The federal government contributes substantially to sustainability through the design of its buildings. Executive Order 13123 of 1999, "Greening the Government through Efficient Energy Management," mandates the application of sustainable design principles to the siting, design, and construction of new facilities. The government now encourages the purchase of environmentally sound products, including bio-based materials, more energy-efficient electronic products, and the construction of high-performance buildings that are healthier and use less energy.

In the early 1970s, states began to introduce environmental regulations dealing with coastal protection, solid-waste management, hazardous-waste control, wetland protection, and inland lakes and streams protection. State enabling legislation gave local governments the right to develop comprehensive environmental plans and regulate proposed environmental activities through zoning and site plan review.

### Environmental Assessments and Environmental Impact Statements

The National Environmental Policy Act (NEPA) of 1969 requires that when a project has federal involvement an Environmental Assessment (EA) document must be prepared to provide sufficient evidence and analysis regarding its environmental impact. Project alternatives should be presented to aid in decisionmaking when there is an unresolved conflict in the use of resources. The EA must conclude either that there is a Finding of No Significant Impact (FONSI) or issue a Notice of Intent to Prepare an Environmental Impact Statement (EIS).

An EIS gives a critical examination of any potential environmental impacts from the proposed project and its alternatives. To determine whether an EIS is necessary the following criteria are evaluated: the extent of change in land use; compatibility with the surrounding area; the number of people affected; the impact on important natural resources, wildlife populations, or habitats; the effect on air or water quality; the effect on a designated historic property; imminent threat or hazard to the public. Some states have adopted similar regulations and procedures to deal with state-level activities.[1]

Development projects are generally reviewed through EIS, environmental assessment, or general permit processes, which are procedures established at the federal or state levels and conducted at the local level. Coordination meetings are held by a lead agency (e.g., department of transportation or city planning commission) along with representatives from review agencies. Projects that require an EIS generally necessitate fieldwork, sampling, and new data generation or modeling. They are administered in phases, described as follows:

*Phase I: Environmental Assessment.* An assessment of a site to determine whether it is contaminated is considered due diligence for any prospective property owner. An Environmental Site Assessment provides such information on an initial basis. A Phase I assessment, often performed by an environmental consultant, is conducted according to federal guidelines established by the American Society for Testing and Materials (ASTM) and All Appropriate Inquiry (AAI). The process involves reviewing the site's previous history and former uses to see whether hazardous materials could have been used (e.g., asbestos or lead from a paint shop). An on-site field survey of the site and surrounding area determines whether any contaminants might be present on the soil surface (e.g., iron slag from an old foundry site or abandoned oil drums). A Phase I assessment should include interviews with previous owners and local officials who may be able to provide firsthand information on the history of the site. The investigator also collects data from public safety officials, water and sewer maps, aerial photographs, and federal or state listings of any contaminated sites from previous assessments conducted on the site or on adjacent sites. If there is any likelihood of contamination, further testing is necessary. If the Phase I report contains no findings of possible contamination, a Phase II study is deemed unnecessary.

The costs of a site assessment and Phase I report are normal expenditures of development, since the findings may avoid costly complications and penalties as the site proposal moves forward. Sometimes existing owners are fearful of such assessment because in situations where serious contamination is found they may be liable for costly cleanup prior to sale of the site or facility.

*Phase II: Environmental investigation.* If the Phase I assessment indicates site contamination is possible, a Phase II investigation is necessary. In Phase II, samples of soil, water, and air are taken and analyzed at a laboratory to determine the location, type, and amount of environmental contamination. Concurrently, the investigator seeks the cause of the problem(s), the geographic distribution of the contamination, the direction of movement, its degree of concentration, and the extent of present and future risk to human life and other parts of the ecosystem. These are summarized in a report that details the findings and recommends cleanup alternatives. The report includes information on cleanup goals, future land use restrictions, the technology or combination of technologies needed for remediation, the risks associated with remediation, the selection of a strategy or strategies for implementation, and a calendar for measuring achievement.

*Phase III: Evaluation and remediation options.* Phase III assessment details a remediation plan that compares existing levels of contaminants against federal, state, and local requirements for various types of development. The amount of risk it allows depends on the type of contaminant, its amount and intensity, the physical characteristics of the site (e.g., does it slope toward a stream or river?), and the surrounding uses and population. The standards are stricter for redevelopment for residential use than for commercial or industrial uses.

Remediation of the site can be done through various methods, including capping contaminated soils with an impermeable surface that serves as a barrier (such as asphalt), neutralizing the soil chemically to render the contaminants harmless, or via phytoremediation—the use of certain plants capable of extracting heavy metals from the soil and concentrating them in their stems and leaves for easy removal. Sometimes the removal and transport of contaminated soil to a hazardous waste site and its replacement with clean soil is required.

Projects with small or insignificant environmental impact that receive a FONSI go through a shorter environmental assessment process—limited fieldwork, analysis of existing data, and the results of a literature review. General permit projects involve the repair and replacement of existing structures and facilities and determination of whether they are part of the routine management of natural resources as defined by the agency's mission statement.

### Spotlight on the Columbia River Crossing Improvement Project[2]

The Columbia River Crossing Improvement Project provides a good example of the use of an EIS. A project report describing the need for improvements to the existing I-5 crossing on the Columbia River connecting Portland, Oregon, with Vancouver, Washington, was prepared jointly by the Oregon Department of Transportation and the Washington State Department of Transportation. It explored various alternatives for bridge, highway, transit, freight, bicycle, and pedestrian improvements and strategies to reduce travel demand. A draft EIS was prepared for public and agency review. Based on public comment and a task force recommendation, the partner agencies proposed a replacement bridge with light rail as the Locally Preferred Alternative (LPA). A final EIS describes the additional analysis conducted on the potential community and environmental effects of the project. In 2010 the document was reviewed by agencies and neighborhood organizations before publication as a final EIS.

The Columbia River Crossing project report illustrates the content of a typical EIS. Its five chapters are titled:

1. Project Purpose and Need
2. Description of Alternatives
3. Existing Conditions and Environmental Consequences
4. Financial Analysis
5. Draft Section Evaluation

*11.1. Original Columbia River crossing, Portland, Oregon, to Vancouver, Washington, 2008 (top) and proposed crossing*

Chapter 3 of the report is focused on environmental factors and has sections titled: Land Use and Economic Activity, Neighborhoods and Environmental Justice, Parks and Recreation, Historic and Archeological Resources, Visual and Aesthetic Qualities, Air Quality, Noise and Vibration, Energy, Electric and Magnetic Fields, Ecosystems, Wetland and Jurisdictional Waters, Geology and Soils, Hazardous Materials, and Cumulative Effects. Together, these sections represent a comprehensive review of environmental impacts of the project.

## Environmental Planning at the Local Level

Buying and selling residential properties usually does not require an environmental assessment, although some lenders may require it as part of their approval process. A transaction screen is an evaluation that consists primarily of site reconnaissance and a review of historical municipal documents to determine whether there is any condition that might adversely impact the property. Common problems are septic systems and fuel storage tanks.

Developers of large projects typically assemble a team of professionals to conduct project planning that often includes, at least at the outset, an environmental specialist. The specialist's responsibilities may include examining site development factors—for example, slope, soil erosion, drainage systems, wildlife habitats, and land uses. The work involves issues such as wetlands or wildlife habitat, which can be handled individually, as well as considerations like storm water management, which require interdisciplinary training and work with engineers and public officials. Many environmental issues cross traditional disciplines.

### Brownfields

Brownfields are abandoned or underutilized properties, including former landfills, that cannot be improved or redeveloped without some degree of remedial action to stabilize or isolate problems they present, which may include chemicals or industrial wastes that were not properly disposed. These fall into four general categories of waste: (1) solvents, such as paint thinners and dry cleaning fluids, which come from garages, industry, homeowners, and dry cleaners; (2) heavy metals, including lead, chromium, cadmium, arsenic, and mercury, resulting from metal plating and finishing, manufacturing, and foundries; (3) petroleum contaminants such as gasoline and motor oil, found in underground storage tanks, gasoline stations, pipelines, and with homeowners; and (4) pesticides and herbicides, which are used by homeowners, farmers, manufacturers, and

11.2. The DuBois Brewery Company complex, DuBois, Pennsylvania: an industrial complex built in 1897, its operations ended in 1972; declared a brownfield site, demolition was completed in 2008 and the site prepared for a proposed new medical complex and women's health center

exterminators. Remediation may require minimal work or extensive, expensive reclamation of soils, thus causing otherwise desirable properties to be unsaleable and abandoned by their owners.

Some states and local governments provide public financial support in the form of tax reimbursements and/or tax credits for specified activities to individuals who are owners, investors, or lessees of brownfield property. The U.S. Environmental Protection Agency's Brownfields Economic Redevelopment Initiative can provide funding through initial stages of redevelopment; states can assist through tax increment financing programs. (See Chapter 16 for information on tax increment financing.) In other cases, private lenders are the sole source for capital necessary to demolish, excavate, remove waste, and rebuild. Regardless of who pays the bill, the cleanup of brownfield properties is closely monitored by the federal government and generally follows NEPA procedures.

Communities and planners must determine what agency oversees remediation within a given jurisdiction. A site cleanup may fall under the jurisdiction of the federal Resource Conservation and Recovery Act (RCRA), but since regulatory agencies vary by state, more than one agency may be involved. For example, in New York State, the State Environmental Quality Review Act (SEQRA) requires local government agencies to consider environmental impacts equally with social and economic factors. The California Environmental Quality Act (CEQA) requires all projects to have an environmental review. If environmental damage could have occurred, an Environmental Impact Report is required by the state, a process that can take six months.

## The Environment as Resource and Hazard

The environment can serve as a resource or threat; sometimes it is both. Different areas of the country may have distinctly different environmental concerns, each presenting unique challenges.

### Shorelines and Coastal Zones

The majority of Americans live near an ocean or a Great Lakes coastline. Land/water interfaces are considered desirable sites, but they can produce significant human and environmental problems that affect economic value. For example, coastal erosion and flooding may result

11.3. *Houses undermined by coastal erosion, Pacifica, California*

from inland activity that contributes to sediment loads, sending overflow over the adjacent land, especially at the mouth of rivers where velocity decreases and water discharges into the ocean. During storms, river water may be forced back inland. Resort communities and individual homes on islands are similarly vulnerable to erosion.

Over the years, severe storms have not only forced people to move, but have caused property to vanish into the ocean or Great Lakes. Spectacular photographs have recorded hilltop houses toppling from bluffs into the Pacific Ocean, Lake Michigan, and elsewhere.

Even inland, low-lying areas and river edges can be subject to severe weather damage. Such communities should formulate plans to manage the potential havoc a severe storm can wreak on their city. While the Army Corps of Engineers may have constructed physical barriers of steel and concrete, land use planners can offer other alternatives that are more cost-effective. The best solution may be to reduce human occupancy in hazardous areas, which communities can encourage by avoiding the extension of infrastructure to vulnerable areas. Where this is not feasible, planners can work with communities to carefully craft zoning ordinances that reduce the intensity of land use near the water's edge. Regulations should prohibit artificial land filling of offshore waters and restrict future development in highly vulnerable areas. They can require that native vegetation remain undisturbed and vegetation buffers be created. Building codes can be strengthened to include stronger flood-resistant walls and more secure roofing, and transportation planning can require measures to safeguard residents and property in inhabited areas.

11.4. *Building in a vulnerable shoreline area, Bald Head Island, North Carolina*

11.5. *Eastern Shore waterlands, Chesapeake Bay, Maryland*

Long-term sea-level change is an even larger problem; it is a gradual event that is being documented by many island and coastal nations. Higher sea levels may inundate cities, displace their residents, and disrupt society on an unimaginable scale. Planners and environmentalists can play a role in devising and implementing policies and programs to minimize the dangers of global climate change.

### Inland Floods

Rivers are one of the world's most important resources. Along with the fertile low-lying land near them, they have historically been the focus of early settlement. They provided drinking water, irrigation, a highway for people and goods, power, food, waste removal, and later tourism and local recreational activity. As land use intensifies in many areas, people place too much stress on these natural resource areas. Urban development creates vast areas of impervious surface (primarily roofs and pavement), which hinders normal water infiltration and accelerating storm water runoff. The result is increased soil erosion and sedimentation that reduces the capacity of rivers to carry water.

Floodplains are also areas of environmental concern. Floodplain areas, based on surveys completed by the Army Corps of Engineers or other qualified government agencies, can be delineated on maps to indicate the potential for flooding of a given magnitude. They are a useful source for planning land uses for a community's comprehensive plan and for developing zoning boundaries. It should be assumed whatever lies within the designated floodplain area may eventually suffer some degree of destruction. Engineers are asked to develop solutions to flooding through the construction of dams, dikes, and levees. These efforts help to alleviate small floods, but protecting a riverbank against flooding encourages use of the land for development along rivers and ultimately leads to greater losses. Each more intensive physical adaptation results in increasing expenditures.

A community's comprehensive plan should include an environmental component, which contains provisions preventing unneeded and inappropriate development in floodplain areas. The National Floodplain Insurance Program provides subsidized insurance to communities that comply with its provisions. To be eligible, the local government must regulate development in flood-prone areas and prescribe high standards for building codes. This includes zoning land uses, site plan constraints, proper land division, and the platting of large land parcels. For example, homes may be prohibited, while golf courses and passive recreation may be allowed. It is prudent to retain native vegetation and encourage greenbelts and buffer strips in these areas.

### Wetlands

Wetlands are land areas covered all or part of the year with water. They are located along shallow coastal areas or inland regions with surface depressions or in areas underlain by impermeable soils. Former glaciated areas have many wetlands; they are also found along some stream banks. They are characterized by extremely wet soils and distinctive vegetation, such as cattails and reeds, and are frequently home to waterfowl and amphibians.

Wetlands have significant value as storage areas for storm water and as collection points for sediments (as well as pollutants). They act as filters and holding zones for runoff and contribute to groundwater recharge. Without them, aquifers would begin to lose water and wells could become dry. Communities and planners can protect wetlands through local zoning and site plan review that regulate dredging or filling and prohibit development within a given distance of a wetlands area, and through the application of setback provisions and buffer strips.

### Spotlight on Hurricane Katrina and the Delta Wetlands

The natural and man-made defenses of New Orleans against storm surges and flooding proved to be sadly inadequate in the face of Hurricane Katrina in 2005. The lack of sufficient wetlands contributed to the devastation. In the Mississippi River delta, wetlands surround the mouth of the river where it empties into the Gulf of Mexico. These shallow areas are formed by silt that washes down the river and settles in the Gulf, and they serve as a natural defense by reducing the energy from high water coming on-shore from a storm. Each mile of wetlands will absorb 1 foot of storm surge coming in from the ocean.

New Orleans's wetlands, diminished by the con-

11.6. *Tidal wetlands with pedestrian walkway, Cape Cod, Massachusetts*

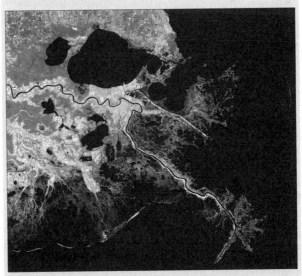

11.7. *Mississippi Delta wetlands area, New Orleans*

struction of levees and storm walls along the river's shore to channel the Mississippi, minimized the natural wetlands, and greatly reduced the city's first line of defense against storms. Some 25 to 35 square miles of wetlands were lost over the last decades, and in 2009 the Delta area was referred to as "the fastest-disappearing land mass on earth."[4]

The coastal area forms a hub of U.S. energy production, fishing, and shipping, yet is vulnerable to a variety of catastrophic events. On April 20, 2010, a BP oil rig in the Gulf of Mexico exploded and began spewing thousands of barrels of oil into the gulf every day, becoming one of the worst environmental disasters in U.S. history. One important lesson was that even an oil platform with multiple safeguard systems was not protected against catastrophic failure.

## Earthquakes

Earthquakes, commonly thought of as a West Coast phenomenon, occur not just in California, Oregon, Washington, and Alaska but in other parts of the United States. They can cause great destruction: buildings collapse, infrastructure fails, transportation stops. Fire and flooding may result. As with other natural disasters, planners need to be aware of the possible effects on communities.

Potential earthquake locations are well known. Fault lines have been mapped, along with related variables such as the type of subsurface materials present. Loose unconsolidated surface material will result in more dam-

11.8. *Damage from Loma Prieta earthquake, San Francisco, 1989*

age than bedrock. Liquefaction occurs when an earthquake reduces the strength and stability of saturated soil; maps show where liquefaction is expected. Maps can also indicate measures of surface movement, tilt and strain of underlying rock, in situ stresses, groundwater measurements, animal behavior, and other precursors, but efforts at prediction have been rudimentary. If evacuation is ordered, but an earthquake fails to occur, people are unlikely to heed the next warning, and moving large populations unnecessarily can produce social and economic chaos.

Planners and building inspectors may initiate zoning requirements and strict building codes to address the risks of earthquake damage. Zoning along fault lines should allow only low-intensity uses, such as open space for passive recreation and jogging, hiking, and biking trails. Building codes in earthquake-prone areas should have stringent requirements based on engineering analysis of what is necessary for structures to survive extended earth movement. Transportation planning also must take into account the possible need for safe evacuation and a means for relief workers and necessary materials to enter the devastated area.

## Sustainability and Planning

Sustainability focuses on the natural and the built environments, but it also is tied closely to social and economic concerns. The "3 Es of sustainability" are a prosperous economy, a quality environment, and social equity. The United Nations further qualifies the 3 Es by reminding us that "A sustainable society meets the needs of the present without sacrificing the ability of future generations to meet their own needs."[5] All land development should therefore include conservation measures.

### Spotlight on Sustainability in Chicago

Richard M. Daley, mayor of Chicago since 1989, initiated an environmental program that can serve as a model for other cities. Starting with a green roof at City Hall, the idea spread to public and private properties including police and fire stations, schools, and libraries, where 250 gardens now cover 3.5 million square feet.[6] These roof gardens aid in storm water management and modify the heat island effect in the city.

The city also encouraged sustainability by garnering

11.9. *Green roof on City Hall, Chicago*

local support for urban farmers' markets, increasing consumption of local foods grown organically. The program has brought millions of dollars into the local economy. A substantial amount of produce comes from neighborhood gardens, which the city helps by providing plants, materials, and technical assistance.

Mayor Daley is a strong advocate for land use planning. His planning staff has identified public and private lands that can serve open space functions and has plans to protect more than 100 sites by 2010, among them the 3,900-acre Calumet Open Space Reserve. More than 3,000 acres of this site are classified as brownfields, but much of the total acreage is to be reclaimed as reconstructed wetlands and marshes that are habitat for numerous threatened and endangered species. In addition, Chicago has a citywide brownfields initiative, with 1,000 acres of brownfields returned to productive use by 2007.

There are varying perspectives on sustainability. Architects view it in the context of building design—whether a structure is well insulated, has efficient heating and cooling systems, conserves construction materials, and is energy efficient. Environmental planners focus on the protection of open space and wilderness areas, bodies of water, air pollution, and climate change. Planners take a more holistic view, from the individual building level to the broad regional and international perspective. Their first step in developing a sustainability plan should be to review and modify communities' zoning ordinances to ensure they encourage sustainable activities and provide appropriate incentives. Some cities are proposing that new developments be carbon-neutral,

requiring the amount of energy used to be offset through better technologies or, for example, by planting more trees. Urban areas can benefit by converting vacant sites into urban agricultural usage; 1 acre of tended land can produce thousands of dollars worth of food. A community's comprehensive plan should contain goals, objectives, and strategies for sustainability and standards for comparing change.

## Spotlight on Planning and Climate Change Legislation, San Bernardino County

In 2007, San Bernardino County, California, was sued by the state's attorney general for not including global warming provisions in its new growth plan. The innovative suit held that global warming was the most significant issue facing the county and the world and that the state's environmental laws required that environmental impacts be addressed. A settlement was reached when the county agreed to establish a greenhouse gas reduction plan to identify sources of emissions and set reduction targets.

The San Bernardino lawsuit will echo through local government planning as environmental advocates insist that one of the solutions to climate change is a new approach to growth, development, and community planning practices. Some municipalities have included provisions in their new comprehensive plans calling for impact studies that examine greenhouse gases resulting from development and such issues as wildfire danger, habitat destruction, insect infestation, loss of groundwater resources, and the need to protect the health, safety, and welfare of residents.

## Summary

Federal and state governments assume a large role in environmental efforts. Federal departments and agencies provide assistance to communities threatened by natural hazards and human-generated environmental problems. The federal government is instrumental in data collection, forecasting, minimizing the impact of environmental events, and remediation and restoration of sites. Its many agencies include the U.S. Weather Service, Corps of Engineers, U.S. Geological Service,

Department of the Interior, and Federal Emergency Management Agency. Primary among federal legislation was passage of the National Environmental Policy Act in 1969, which gives protection to air, water, and land by requiring a statement of the effect of proposed projects on the environment. Two categories of reports include Environmental Assessments and Environmental Impact Statements, which provide information on potential negative impacts on environmental resources. Many of the environmental safeguards at the national level of government are mirrored at the state level.

Local environmental specialists analyze environmental impacts through a Phase I study to determine if there is site contamination. If there is a potential problem, a Phase II report is conducted to determine the type and extent of problem, and a Phase III study describes techniques for remediation. Redevelopment of contaminated sites, often referred to as brownfields, presents a challenge and opportunity for planners through the need for revisions of local ordinances.

Beyond site-specific concerns, planners must account for macroenvironmental events. They need to take preemptive measures to prevent human development in areas of known environmental risk. Chief among these are coastal areas and floodplains, but they also include earthquake fault lines and areas subject to severe erosion.

A community sets its development and land use goals in its master plan and zoning ordinances, but state and federal regulations also must be satisfied when environmental issues are considered. Planners should account for environmental resources, as well as natural hazard or disaster areas, and then apply appropriate zoning to implement the plan, even though many vulnerable areas are known for their amenities and are highly desirable for development. Planners should take a proactive approach to maintaining a sustainable environment.

12

# RURAL AND TRANSITIONAL LAND USE PLANNING

## Rural Land Use in the United States

The loss of open space is a major planning concern. Undeveloped land serves a number of necessary and desirable purposes. It provides on-site water for residents and farmers and acts as groundwater recharge zones for water wells. It is habitat for many species of native vegetation and wildlife. Trees and ground cover purify the air and stabilize the soil against erosion. Woodlands can be economically valuable when selectively cut for timber as part of a forest management program. Deer running across a meadow and sheep on a hillside pasture add a picturesque quality to the landscape.

Farms and ranches make up a large proportion of this country's open space. Our rich soils provide one of the world's most productive agricultural systems. Agribusiness corporate farms now dominate the nation's food-producing system, but family farms continue to meet consumers' desires for locally grown (and organic) food and cumulatively contribute to feeding America and the world. Agricultural activities also produce spin-off employment in processing, transportation, packaging, marketing, wholesaling, inspecting, and retailing food. This economic enterprise produces millions of tax dollars for state treasuries, while export of its products works to improve the American balance of trade.

Old farmsteads are part of the cultural heritage of the nation. Farms that have survived for more than a century may have living fence rows of trees and shrubs enclosing small fields once plowed by animals. Underutilized barns, windmills, glazed tile silos, and other remnants of an earlier age recall our past. Rural preservationists strive to prevent the removal of historically significant artifacts and advocate rehabilitation and adaptive reuse of these structures for living

*12.1. Old barns are part of America's rural heritage*

quarters, office complexes, dance halls, and other functions.

### Threats to Rural Land

Throughout history, the locations of settlements were selected for rational reasons. Sites with suitable topography and productive soils were chosen for farming, navigable waterways provided transportation routes, and easily developed land for community nodes were necessary for commerce. Eventually settlers established grain mills, feed stores, and farm implement businesses, which were soon followed by housing.

In the mid-twentieth century, land in the United States was still clearly differentiated as either urban or rural. However, World War II required the services of millions of the nation's men and women. Migrant industrial workers came to cities for war-related jobs and filled available housing. As military personnel returned after the war, they and their young families sought homes in newly developed suburbs. This influx created a need for additional development, and densely populated cities pushed many former urban residents outward to the periphery. Suburbanization and subsequent sprawl have continued undiminished, from Atlanta in the southeast to Seattle in the northwest, from rustbelt cities such as Pittsburgh to rapidly expanding sunbelt cities such as Phoenix. While such transitional areas provide homesites for millions of Americans, they have caused the loss of farmland and encouraged wasteful large-lot development. Suburban growth has given rise to a proliferation of single-use districts delimited mostly by developers' abilities to acquire parcels of land, often without consideration of the goals of community planning and design.

The continuing threat to rural land is severe. In the 1960s and 1970s, advocates of a nascent environmental movement, concerned about the disappearance of large quantities of agricultural land, influenced the federal government to address this issue. The resulting National Agricultural Lands Study concluded

*12.2. New homes replace farmland in Dallas County, Iowa, west of Des Moines*

that land conversion from agricultural uses, woodlands, and open space was occurring at an alarming rate. One million acres of prime agricultural land were being converted to other uses annually. According to a 2006 report by the U.S. Department of Agriculture, of nearly 2.3 billion acres total land area, land used for all agricultural purposes accounts for 52 percent, with grazing area (grassland pasture and range, cropland pasture, and grazed forests) composing two-thirds of that amount. About 94 million acres (4.2 percent of total land) were estimated to be rural residential areas. Urban land comprises 60 million acres, or 2.6 percent of total land area.[1] Thus, rural residential sites constitute a larger land area than all urban uses.

In addition, the financial impact of sprawl development is significant. An article in the *Sacramento [California] Business Journal* explained, "Sprawling communities need longer public roads, increase the cost of new water and sewer hookups by 20 percent to 40 percent, impose higher costs on police and fire departments and schools, and more. These costs are passed to business owners and residents through higher taxes and fees and sometimes through fewer public services. And in most cases, sprawling developments do not generate enough property taxes to cover these added costs."[2] In effect, urban communities subsidize suburban growth. The costs of sprawl in Los Angeles, Washington/Baltimore, and the San Francisco Bay area, the nation's highest, are estimated at $535 billion, $384 billion, and $378 billion, respectively, for the period from 2000 through 2025; on a per capita basis, Las Vegas spent $72,697 per person to pay for sprawl. As the authors of *Sprawl Costs* point out, shifting to more compact forms of development could save billions of dollars.[3]

### The Economics of Agricultural Land Use

Small farms are the most vulnerable to land economics because they do not enjoy the economies associated with large-scale farm production. Farm equipment is a major capital expense, and seeds and fertilizers are a major outlay. Small farmers also must bear the burden of paying for health care and retirement for themselves and their families. With the encroachment of suburbia, property taxes rise, which add to a farmer's overall expenditures. With such soaring costs, a farmer may be land rich but cash poor.

Farmers, who cannot or do not wish to remain in

agriculture by converting to higher value crops or other measures, sell their property for residential use and cash in on the developmental value of their land. Small farm fields that are 10-acre parcels or less are an appealing size for urban buyers and developers. This transition may be readily visible or subtle. For Sale and Acreage for Sale signs and farm auctions are signals.

*12.3. Acreage for sale*

As farmland gets converted to subdivisions, social problems can follow and place further stress on farm communities. In addition to causing a rise in local property taxes, new residents frequently find the sights, smells, and sounds of remaining neighboring agriculture unpleasant. They often expect city services to be available in the country, and the need for improved fire, police, water, and waste systems places a financial burden on the local community.

## EXERCISE 11

### DEVELOPMENT FOR THE CARTWRIGHT FARM IN RIVERTOWN

*A new industry is locating outside Rivertown and is expected to attract new residents. As a result, Moneta Development Corporation wishes to purchase the Cartwright farm, which is located within the city and just south of the river. Moneta is proposing a new mixed-use site to include between 60 and 70 townhouse units and limited retail and office space.*

*The small specialty crops farm is still run by its owners, Bob and Joan Cartwright, whose family has owned the property since 1868. They now are ready to retire and see the financial benefit of making their land available to a developer.*

*The proposed project will benefit the city with additional housing, attracting new residents who could add substantially*

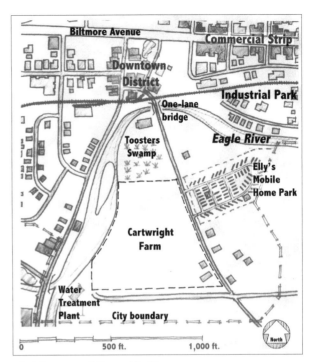

*12.4. Location of Cartwright Farm*

*to the city's tax base. Most residents are in favor of the project, but the following significant planning concerns must be addressed:*

*1. The one-lane bridge on Station Street is inadequate for increased traffic. A new two-lane bridge must be constructed.*

*2. Most traffic from the site would travel through the downtown district to Biltmore Avenue, a primary state road. The existing narrow downtown streets are not adequate to handle the increased traffic.*

*3. The public school system would need to be expanded to accommodate additional students.*

*4. The city council is concerned about funding necessary improvements.*

*5. The farm currently is zoned agricultural. The new development does not fit this category.*

*6. The property is only 5 feet above the river and is subject to flooding. Toosters Swamp, just north of the site, is a protected wetland. During the summer it breeds mosquitoes, which could be a nuisance to the new residents.*

*As the city's assistant planner, you have been asked by the city council to address these concerns. Determine what steps should be taken initially as part of the approval process, taking into account that projects of this size are not covered by the city's current comprehensive plan or capital improve-*

*ments budget. In a preliminary report of 500 to 700 words, discuss the overall impact on the community of the proposed development at this location. Make reference to costs and benefits, and explain how the council can best handle the concerns listed above. (It is not necessary to know the site design to address these concerns.) The council members anxiously await your assessment of the situation.*

### Annexation

Annexation, or boundary change, is the transfer of land from one political jurisdiction to another, usually from rural townships to adjacent cities as a result of an expanded population. It can provide for orderly growth and the extension of a city's services. It also enables a city to include within its taxing boundary the people who benefit from city services (e.g., water and sewer, fire and police protection, street maintenance) and amenities (e.g., libraries). School systems that have autonomy may be excluded from annexation if attendance zones are separate from political boundaries.

The role of planners in the annexation process is to provide information and make recommendations. The state government has the final authority as to whether new boundaries are approved, based on whether the majority of people involved will benefit from the change. Annexation is seldom accomplished quickly. It may be contentious, since residents and governments of both jurisdictions are affected. Those in the annexed area usually benefit from city government, but those benefits come with a price: property taxes often rise, zoning may become more restrictive, and owner obligations often increase. Nevertheless, an individual property owner may desire annexation and can submit a petition to annex a single parcel; if it is approved, the owner assumes the benefits and obligations of a resident of the new district.

## Planning in Rural and Transitional Areas

Planning for areas distant from cities was historically slow to evolve. Land was of paramount importance to settlers, and freedom to use it as they wished was embedded as a core American value.[4] The trend has continued. Farming communities often resist the idea of government regulation of land use and consider planning an unnecessary intrusion into their property rights. Since

more than 80 percent of America's population lives in or near densely populated urban zones, it is not surprising that planners are educated primarily to examine urban, rather than rural, issues. Consequently, even in places where it is clearly needed, rural planning tends to be limited to the conversion of farmlands at the urban fringe into suburban communities.

Landowners in rural areas have long been at odds with the federal government (National Forest Service, Bureau of Land Management, and the Environmental Protection Agency) over policies and regulations they feel have harmed their business operations and use of private lands, for example, wetlands and floodplains that cannot be developed and endangered species' habitats that must be protected. Yet, rural areas far from cities are also subject to development pressures and need varying degrees of protection. An area's physical geography can call for planning: mountains, deserts, and plains have factors such as slope, soil quality, and water availability

*12.5. Development in Larimer County, Colorado*

that limit land uses. Understanding rural communities, the dynamics of their economy, and geographical limitations will help planners recommend realistic policies and programs that are tailored to their circumstances rather than to urban conditions. Rural planning should balance the public good with the rights of property owners.

Planners in rural areas should accept that some land use conflicts are not physical, but philosophical, a result of lifestyle or point of view about the environment. Fortunately, not all rural residents are opposed to land use regulation; changing demographics are bringing about changes in outlook. As transportation and communication systems open remote areas to a new generation of settlers seeking open spaces and beautiful vistas, nature seems more worthy of protection rather than exploitation.

---

### Spotlight on the Experiences of a Rural Planner

The following correspondence is from a graduate of a planning program. He describes encounters with residents of a rural county in the Great Plains where he worked as their first planning professional.

*January 5:* "I have been here for a week now and thought that I would drop you a line. Currently I have a forty-mile commute in which I have to slow down more for buffalo than other motorists. This county is sparsely populated, but has many planning issues due to a rapidly increasing population and lack of land use ordinances. Many of the ranchers and landowners are splitting/subdividing their lands for sale to out-of-state retirees. Administering these land plats keeps our office busy. We do not have many tools to control the rate or direction of development. With virtually no zoning ordinance or building codes, the only tools at our disposal are septic-system design and approval and road design and access.

"We are trying to develop and adopt a zoning ordinance as well as update the comprehensive plan (a laughable two pages), but have been met with a lot of resistance. I have been warned of the existence of hanging trees within the county that await anyone coming here with ideas of change. However, I believe that with concerns about the newly erected cell tower in town people may be more receptive to land use controls."

*March 1:* "The County Board of Commissioners previously established a zoning committee and gave them the directive to write a zoning ordinance for the county. This committee has been in existence for nearly one year. As the liaison to the zoning committee I have had the opportunity to observe several of their recent working sessions. I have found that the committee is staffed with members who have opposing views on zoning. Much time is spent debating the necessity of zoning as opposed to developing a zoning ordinance, which is their charge. . . . Without a good comprehensive plan it cannot be determined if zoning is even necessary. The writing of the land use and zoning document is only the tip of the iceberg as far as adoption is concerned. Prepping the community for its introduction is a far more daunting task."

*March 13:* "'Zoning: the most feared six-letter word in the west.' I think this quote accurately describes the mentality of rural landowners in this part of the country. They are adamantly against any land use restriction being put upon their property for any reason. They seem to be comfortable in their shortsightedness and self-serving interests. In addition, they fear that any land use restriction is a ploy by the government to get more taxation from them.

"This evening I am handing the zoning document that I created for the county over to the zoning committee for their review and input. In addition, with the help of our GIS technician I have developed a map that delineates current land uses. This county is sparsely populated, with at least 50 percent of the lands being owned or controlled by either the federal government (national forests, prairies and parks) or state government (parks). My map designates all other lands as agricultural (the majority) or rural residential. I see no need for other designations at this point. However, I believe that even these few designations will incite negative reaction from the 'non-zoneists' who invariably claim their property rights are being taken."

*April 10:* "The comprehensive plan is a large and somewhat volatile undertaking. There are members of this community who are adamantly opposed to change or the threat thereof. I have to work around many sociopolitical issues and deep-seated fears of government intervention. I feel that for this initiative to be successful, I have to 'plan for the plan' and have to carefully and strategically introduce this community to the concept of a comprehensive plan. I want to garner support before introduction. The community, as well as the political leaders, needs to be educated to the fact that it is not harmful, nor does it mean that they lose their precious property rights."

## Mapping Rural and Transitional Areas

Once a city, township, or county government representing a rural area decides to develop a plan or update one that exists, planners begin by developing an inventory of existing land cover and land uses. Five broad land use categories are delineated: industrial, commercial, residential, agricultural, and open space. (These may become more specifically defined as required, but in the initial stage these are adequate.) The next step is to create or revise a comprehensive plan, including the establishment of goals for the community, incorporating input from its residents. These may include encouraging economic development; promoting low-density, clustered residential growth; and/or supporting agricultural, open space, and environmental values, or other goals.

### Topographic Maps
One of the important tools used by planners and developers, especially in rural and transitional areas, is the topographic map. "Topos" are maps produced by the U.S. Geological Survey for the primary purpose of showing surface land features. They depict the elevation of land above mean sea level by using contour lines. Such maps, often referred to as quadrangles, or quads, define the terrain. They are generally named after a prominent feature of the quad.

Longitude and latitude are expressed in degrees, minutes, and seconds of angular distance north and south of the equator and east and west of the prime meridian. While quads cover different land areas, planners typically use a 15-minute or 7.5-minute map, which shows areas that span 15 or 7.5 minutes of latitude and longitude. Township and range lines (resulting from the adoption of the Congressional Land Survey provision in the Land Ordinance of 1785 described in Chapter 13) are shown, including section numbers that are part of any individual property description. Scales in feet, miles, and kilometers appear as line segments below the body of the map. A second form of scale is the representative fraction, where 1 inch on the map represents a given number of inches on the earth, commonly 1:24,000.

A quad map for Washtenaw County, Michigan, shows conventional symbols that indicate physical and cultural features on the land surface (a color version of the quad is in Appendix D). Black squares or rectangles are buildings; wavy crosshatched areas (blue in the original) are water features; and shaded areas (red/pink in the original) are urbanized districts. Other symbols indicate wetlands (carrot-top) or wooded areas (scal-

12.6. Topographic quadrangle map, title corner, Washtenaw County, Michigan. The names of adjacent quadrangles are printed on each side of the map.

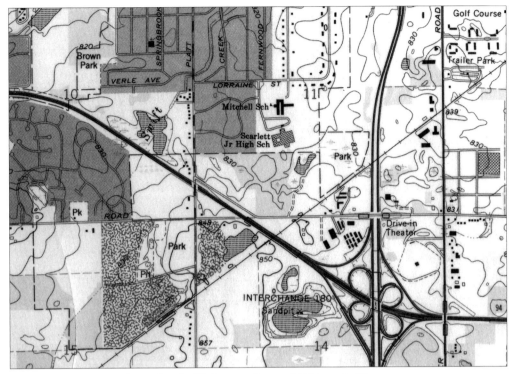

12.7. *Ypsilanti West quad map details, Washtenaw County, Michigan, 1983*

lop design). The square road patterns are boundaries of 1-square-mile sections that originated with the Congressional Land Survey. Section lines were often used as the location of early roads. An excellent orientation point is the highway cloverleaf that connects east/west I-94 and north/south U.S. 23. Both are limited-access highways.

The contour lines that appear over the map represent continuous points of elevation and indicate approximate height above sea level. When examined in conjunction with each other, the lines reveal the land's relative slope. On the map above, contour lines west and southwest of the cloverleaf are spaced relatively far apart, indicating flat land; the more closely spaced contour lines to the northwest indicate hillier terrain. Depressions on the land surface are denoted by short tick-marks pointed toward the center of enclosed contour lines, as illustrated by the sandpit southwest of the cloverleaf. Sand-excavation pits are common in proximity to highway intersections. They provide earthen material used by the Department of Transportation to construct overpasses and often fill with groundwater when the water table is high.

## EXERCISE 12
### INTERPRETATION OF CONTOURS IN RIVERTOWN

*The contour map of Rivertown on page 172 shows each contour line representing a difference in elevation of 5 feet. This map is used to determine slope. Using the scale shown in the lower right-hand corner, you can calculate the amount of slope: divide the vertical distance by the horizontal distance and multiply by 100. For example, a slope of 10 vertical feet to 10 feet horizontal (10/10 = 1.0 times 100) represents a slope of 100 percent; a ratio of 10 vertical feet to 50 feet horizontal is a 20 percent slope.*

*Based on the contour map, answer the following questions:*

*1. What is the lowest elevation and highest elevation of the Old Biltmore farmstead?*

*2. In what direction does the Eagle River flow?*

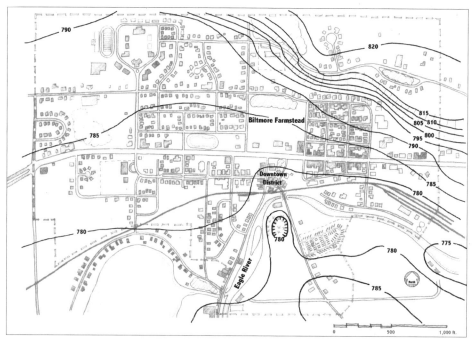

12.8. *Contour map of Rivertown. (Also refer to the city map shown in Appendix A.)*

*3. If the river runs normally at an elevation of 780 to 774 in the area shown on this map, draw a line representing the extent of damage if the river rose to 5 feet beyond its channel.*

*4. (a) Where in the city is land with the greatest slope located? (Indicate by designating the contours.)*

*4. (b) What is the percent slope at that location?*

### Aerial Photographs

Aerial photography is a useful tool for planners because aerial photos portray accurate visual images that complement maps used to conduct land inventories. Photographs provide land cover data, not land use data. An aerial photo shows the land cover of a wooded area, for example, but does not indicate the primary use of that woodlot (e.g., commercial forestry, wildlife habitat, recreation, or environmental values such as air purification). In a similar example, an aerial photo showing large buildings will not distinguish among warehouses, schools, office buildings, or multifamily residences, although a well-trained air photo interpreter may see clues to narrow the land use possibilities. Nevertheless, aerial photographs are relatively inexpensive and, when taken over years, can reveal significant changes in land cover. In addition, a stereoscopic image using two adjacent, overlapping photographs to create a three-dimensional effect can yield information about relative elevations. Increasingly, planners are also using tools such as Google Maps for aerial photo information.

Comparison of an aerial photo with the same portion of Washtenaw County shown in the quad in figure 12.7 illustrates how quads and aerial photos comple-

12.9. *Aerial photo, Washtenaw County, Michigan, 2007*

ment one another. The quad map shows the general features of a good map, that is, latitude and longitude, north arrow, scale, and elevations. Two noteworthy special features—a mobile home park at the eastern edge of the map and a drive-in theater near the highway interchange are shown. The more recent aerial photograph reveals the continued existence of the mobile home park, but the drive-in theater has been replaced by a large flat structure (a new multiplex theater).

Section 11 of the quad map (Fig. 12.9) shows a neighborhood school; to its immediate west is a multifamily attached housing development, such as is typically occupied by families with young children. To complement this information, the aerial photo shows two baseball fields and the school, which appear bordered by a small wetland to the east and a wooded area to the south. A thoughtful planner may see the potential of these areas to serve as outdoor laboratory facilities for the school.

## Soil Surveys and the Rural Comprehensive Planning Map

Soil surveys can be an excellent tool for rural planners in conjunction with topographic maps and existing land use maps. Produced by the U.S. Department of Agriculture's Natural Resources Conservation Service (NRCS), they are generally available through county offices. Trained soil scientists delineate soil types on aerial photographs and denote soil characteristics to a depth of 60 inches. A soil survey map that corresponds to the Ypsilanti West quad of Washtenaw County indicates soil types in this area. A complementary soil table gives information for a sample of indicated soil types.

The information can be related to several environmental concerns and to various types of construction and engineering practice. A soil survey may indicate suitability for on-site septic systems, the depth of the seasonal high water table, the capacity of the soils to

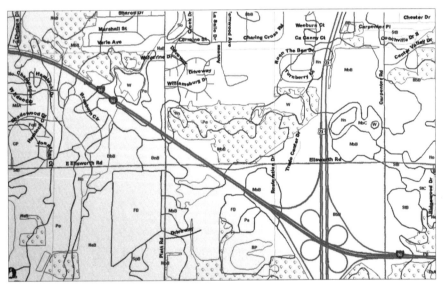

| Soil Code | Name | Slope | Agri. Yield (Corn/bushel) | Septic Limitation | Primary Use |
|-----------|------|-------|---------------------------|-------------------|-------------|
| **BbB** | Blount loam | 0–2% | 105 | severe | crops |
| | | 2–6% | 100 | severe | crops |
| **FoB** | Fox sandy loam | 2–6% | 85 | slight | crops |
| **Ho** | Hoytville silty clay loam | 0–2% | 110 | severe; flooding | crops w/ drainage |

*12.10. Soil survey map, Washtenaw County, Michigan, 1970, with a small sampling of soil types and characteristics*

shrink and swell, and other factors that affect construction of basements and foundations. As shown in the table below the map, the Fox sandy loam is the best soil for such use.

A soil survey map helps planners determine which areas have environmentally sensitive lands. A planner can compile a single map of wetlands and floodplains, steep slopes, and water recharge areas that would indicate lands to avoid for development. For example, highly organic soils may be the base for wetlands and relate to water infiltration rates that may correspond to the rate of groundwater recharge.

In addition to an environmental map, rural planners produce agricultural maps based on soil surveys to aid in agricultural planning by applying the average yield per acre under a high level of management for individual soils. A single map of high, moderate, and low crop yields per acre determines the best agricultural land. Likewise, homebuilding in rural lands is impacted by the soil's characteristics. Often, good agricultural land and desirable development land occupy the same areas. In these instances, a planner may decide to recommend that overlapping lands in proximity to existing urban clusters be planned for residential use, while those at a greater distance be planned for agricultural use. In the case of environmental lands, minimal conflict occurs because such lands retain the highest priority.

In the Washtenaw County example the most recent soil map dates from 1970, the topographic quad from 1983, and the aerial photo from 2007. Obviously, it is ideal to work with up-to-date information, but the cost of producing maps and surveys is high. Thus, while using data from different periods allows historical changes to be identified, it also calls for interpretation.

As a final map is being compiled for the comprehensive plan, all government-owned lands, recreational areas, airports, landfills, or other specialized uses should be located as part of the inventory. From this, the planner can derive information on preferred land uses. Even if agricultural productivity is low, other development uses can be undesirable because of the presence of fragile lands. A planned use should be indicated for every parcel in the jurisdiction. If land does not fit in any of the three major uses, it should be planned for secondary agriculture since no area on the map should remain undesignated.

## Build-out Analysis

A final stage of the planning process may be a build-out analysis, which portrays the maximum amount of development allowed under current codes and ordinances and illustrates a community at full capacity. A build-out analysis typically includes the maximum number of various types of housing units per acre, an estimate of the resulting population, and a projection of the maximum growth for commercial and industrial areas to determine if these are in balance with housing.

The two basic components of a build-out analysis are statistical models and maps. Statistics include the number and types of existing housing, minimum lot size necessary to construct a home, and land area available for future housing. Dividing the minimum lot size into the available acreage for housing yields the built-out calculation of the possible number of housing units. Similar calculations can be conducted for other land uses such as commercial and industrial. These calculations need interpretation because raw numbers can be misleading, but the exercise is informative and often surprising to planners and public officials.

The map component of the build-out analysis shows the impact on the entire community, as well as land areas adjacent to its boundaries, to evaluate any spillover effects. An overlay map of zoning districts indicates the level of possible development for each area, and shows parcels that could be developed but have not yet been developed, and underdeveloped areas that may be appropriate for redevelopment at a greater intensity.

Build-out analysis is most appropriate for communities experiencing rapid growth because it indicates where growth likely will occur if unchecked. Build-out analysis also may be requested by local government officials concerned about the level of demand for services and infrastructure and their relationship to the tax base. The analysis serves as an important indicator of whether existing codes and ordinances will actually lead to desired end results and suggests what adjustments are needed to prevent either overdevelopment or unwanted development. This information will help the community determine if changes to the comprehensive plan, zoning ordinance, or other documents, programs, or policies are needed. (Complementary analysis is described in the Small Area Forecasting discussion in Chapter 4.)

## Geographic Information Systems (GIS)

In the past few decades, the use of Geographic Information Systems (GIS) has become one of the most important technologies for planners. More than simply computer mapping, GIS combines maps with computer graphics and databases. This greatly expands land use analysis techniques. In 1969, Ian McHarg's *Design with Nature* described how spatial information could be better analyzed through the layering of maps with varying information; this could be applied to identify the suitability of parcels of land for different types of land use and development.[5] His overlay technique formed the basis of many complex analyses. It was laborious at that time, but the increased use of computer technology for spatial analysis and mapping has made overlay techniques both a practical and highly useful tool in the planners' toolkit today. If, as has been estimated, 80 percent of all government and business information has a spatial component, the use of GIS for spatial analysis is integral to good planning.[6]

Another landmark in the use of GIS for planning was the establishment of the Environmental Systems Research Institute (ESRI) in 1969. During the 1970s and 1980s, ESRI developed a core set of applications for GIS. The firm's ARC/INFO software was the first modern GIS software and still is considered the industry standard. By 1986, ESRI had adapted ARC/INFO to PC-based GIS workstations, making it readily accessible for most planning offices.

The use of GIS software requires varying levels of training. Some of the software (e.g., ARC/View) is user-friendly, but does not allow full interaction. Other software (e.g., ARC/INFO) offers a full range of interaction with its applications, but its use requires substantial training.

GIS software comprises three basic components—maps, databases, and analytical tools. The system's computer-generated layers can include many kinds of maps: slope (contours), elevation, soil types, drainage patterns, land cover, urbanized areas, utility lines, hill shade, and more. Databases integral to the software allow virtually any kind of information to be mapped through its association with the three basic elements used in maps—points (which can represent features like communication towers), lines (e.g., roads), and polygons (e.g., zoning districts).

Analytical software for GIS provides a rich information base for decisionmaking by planners and local officials. Software lets users interpret data and see relationships and patterns not possible with traditional maps, charts, graphs, or spreadsheets. GIS allows users to do what-if scenarios, studying relationships or patterns that would exist, assuming various future changes. This can be very useful in site location problems, such as deciding the impact of a new superstore on traffic patterns, or a new school on bus routes. The analysis can include as many, or as few, categories of information as desired. For example, the location of a new landfill site might include slope and drainage, wetlands or protected species areas, subsurface soil or rock layers, traffic patterns and road conditions, zoning categories, and proximity to residential areas.

Managing land records and tracking utility lines are the most common uses of GIS in the public sector. Applications useful to fieldwork can be coupled with Global

12.11. GIS layers indicating finished surface value, contours, elevation, and shading from hills

Positioning System (GPS) units to accurately locate positions. As one expert put it, "We have documented many success stories in which tasks that previously took hours or even days to complete are now being accomplished in minutes. This is a major trend that will continue as mobile technology continues its rapid evolution and more governments and utilities use it."[7]

GIS is especially useful in showing the dynamics of spatial change over time, such as the growth of housing or the loss of natural habitat, and in market analysis, such as determining the optimum location for a large commercial business. Databases of information used for land use analysis by local communities are readily available from federal and state government agencies and business and nonprofit sources. For example, the U.S. Census Bureau has data for zip-code areas, census tracts, and block units. Cities, counties, regional agencies, and states can supply demographic data, environmental conditions, political districts, zoning, transportation systems, and other statistics.

## Case Study: Evaluating Natural Features Using GIS

A project in Van Buren Township, Wayne County, Michigan, gives a good example of GIS analysis at a level that is easily understandable. The project was initiated to identify privately owned, undeveloped parcels with sufficient natural features to warrant their inclusion into the township's open space preservation program.[8] Using a GIS database developed for this purpose, individual parcels were evaluated based on their ecological potential for restoration. The highest-scoring properties had unique natural features, high-quality natural areas, and profuse native vegetation. These properties could fulfill essential ecological functions such as maintaining water quality and quantity, flood control, and soil stabilization and improvement. They also provide travel corridors for wildlife and refueling areas for migratory birds.

An aerial photo of the area shows a small but representative portion of the township included in the total study area: the shoreline of Belleville Lake, part of a golf course, a wooded area, a stream corridor, and various structures.

12.12. GIS base aerial photo, Van Buren Township, Wayne County, Michigan

12.13. Identified natural features overlay

12.14. Final GIS output showing prioritized parcels

From this aerial photo, a GIS land use layer was developed utilizing digitization of the boundaries and features of 100 parcels. The evaluation process began with the identification of land uses and their suitability as preserved open space. Parcels were rated based on overall size; presence of a stream corridor, wetlands, woodlands, wooded wetlands, grassland and shrubs; agricultural use; and percentage of developed area. Six parcels (light shading) with land cover and land use characteristics matched these criteria. Symbols represent woodlands, wetlands, and shrubs on some of the parcels (other characteristics were shown in color on the original map). Each of the parcels was rated, with the highest ratings indicating the best potential Open Space Program candidates.

Finally, the selected parcels were evaluated for connectivity, since adjacent parcels would allow for natural corridors. This evaluation noted the percentage of potential natural areas within one-quarter of a mile of a parcel and also the percentage of natural areas within 100 feet. Using the total scores for each aspect of the parcels, a final output indicated the priority of the sites for preservation.

Only 5 percent of the county's original forested, wetland ecosystem lands remain, but with analysis of the information provided by GIS, the township was able to make informed decisions about sites for their greenways program to shelter endangered, threatened, or existing plant and animal species. The 71 parcels in the entire township that received the highest rating were established as top priority. The township then created an open space plan, established funding mechanisms for planning and program development, property acquisition, and long-term management, and amended its comprehensive plan accordingly.

## Summary

Some 95 percent of America is considered rural land. It includes farming areas and open space that contain environmentally sensitive components and natural beauty. Some of the open spaces are not subject to significant forces of development, but when land use change is proposed, local inhabitants often actively resist comprehensive planning and land regulation. Community planners in rural and transitional areas must recognize inherent conflicts between the need to protect land resources and to safeguard the rights of property owners, and comprehensive plans must represent both.

Rural planning begins with mapping existing land use. Topographic quadrangle maps, aerial photographs, and soil surveys are good basic tools for locational information. Soil surveys mapped on aerial photographs provide soil characteristics placed on land cover photos. Layers of maps can indicate areas to remain as environmentally sensitive lands and those for future agricultural and construction/development uses. Build-out analyses give valuable information on the long-term impacts of current plans and ordinances and provide information for making informed adjustments to a community's comprehensive plan and growth policies.

Geographic Information Systems (GIS) is essential planning technology. GIS combines maps with computer graphics, databases, and analytic tools to greatly expand land use analysis techniques. It provides a quantitative and spatial portrayal of map layers that is sophisticated and increasingly popular as an analytic planning tool.

# IMPLEMENTATION OF
# THE COMPREHENSIVE PLAN

# 13

# EVOLUTION OF LAND USE CONTROLS

## The Basis for Land Use Law in the United States

The concept of landowners' private property rights and responsibilities is one of the cornerstones of American democracy: on those rights, arguably, sits American capital enterprise. Private property ownership characterizes land use law in the United States. Thus, planners in the United States must accommodate the power of individual property owners, who often contest loudly when public sector policies and regulations limit their control over their property, while protecting the public's interests.

John Locke, a British philosopher of the Enlightenment whose ideas influenced American revolutionaries, saw private property as the essential basis of a good society. He wrote: "The great and chief end, therefore, of men's uniting into commonwealths, and putting themselves under government, is the preservation of their property . . . The supreme power cannot take from any man any part of this property without his own consent."[1] However, this emphasis on property rights must be balanced against the needs of community. As stated by Chief Justice Roger Taney in 1837, "While the rights of private property are sacredly guarded, we must not forget that the community also [has] rights, and that the happiness and well being of every citizen depends on their faithful preservation."[2]

Property rights were particularly appropriate in early American planning because the abundance of land made individual control and proprietorship possible. In more heavily settled Europe, where land was scarce, government needed to be involved in its allocation and use. When Europeans expanded their landholdings through colonization to the seemingly limitless frontiers of America, they saw less need for government interference in development. Dissatisfied settlers could always pick up stakes and move west.

American land use law is also based on the Constitution. The Fifth Amendment establishes the principle that private property cannot be taken for public use without just compensation. The Fourteenth Amendment entitles every citizen to due process and equal protection under the law. Citizens expect proper notification and a public hearing before action that affects their property can be taken. The Fourteenth Amendment also ensures that government actions affecting private property must be reasonable, fair, and advance a legitimate public purpose.

## Early Land Use Patterns in North America

Land use patterns in North America were established early in the colonial period and reflected the different nationalities of the newcomers. The layout of early Spanish, French, and British settlements demonstrates the different approaches of each of these groups. Generally speaking, Spanish settlements were based on rules ordered by their king, French land divisions stemmed from trade considerations, while British settlements were shaped through adaptation to the local environment.

The construction of Spanish colonial outposts followed 148 rules known as the Law of the Indies promulgated under King Philip in 1573. This document is generally recognized as the first comprehensive set of requirements for the plan and design of colonial communities in the New World. Although there were variations, Spanish plans generally followed guidelines intended to aid settlers in determining the proper location for a town, the layouts of the streets and central plaza, and various building types. New settlements were located in areas with fertile soil and good water. Walls around the towns protected settlers against attacks; just outside, the land was cleared for agriculture and to prevent enemies from hiding as they approached. The grid street pattern within the walls was designed to provide monitoring of activities in the settlement. Primary streets met at a central public square large enough for horse parades by soldiers. Three primary building types were located around this central plaza—church, government, and market buildings—representing the three goals of Spanish colonialism, God, Glory, and Gold (the "3 Gs")—that is, converting an indigenous populace to Christianity, establishing Spanish domination in new areas of the world, and bringing wealth to the mother country.

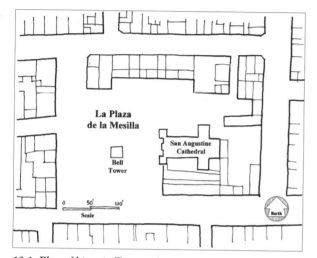

*13.1. Plan of historic Tucson, Arizona, a Spanish settlement*

In contrast, French settlers in the New World were not particularly interested in establishing permanent towns. They were interested in trade, especially the fur trade. They needed settlements with water frontage that was critical for exporting goods. French settlers laid out "long lots" (or ribbon lots), which gave each settler a narrow strip of land fronting a river or waterfront, which often became narrower as it was split through inheritance. The narrowness of the parcels meant that settlers lived close to each other, and this provided more security. Houses were built near the river and the land farmed inland. Long lots provided several uses through their length: from wet soils near riverbanks, to open lands for crops, to wooded areas for construction material. Roads often were built at the rear boundary of the lots, providing land transportation.

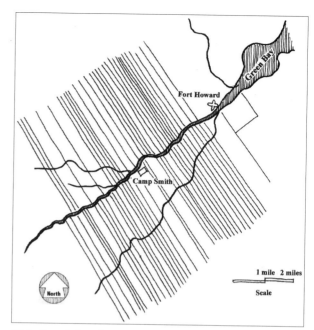

*13.2. French long-lot system from an early map of Green Bay, Wisconsin, 1821*

The British system of land allocation, known as metes and bounds, used natural features as reference points, relying on landmarks, angles, and distance for property boundaries. Thus, the Kentucky property where Abraham Lincoln was born was described as "Beginning with the Large White Oak 13 poles above the Sinking Spring, or Rock Spring, Running thence North 9 1/2 degrees East, 310 poles to a stake in John Taylor's field, thence South 89 1/2 degrees East, 310 poles to two Blackjacks, then North 89 1/2 degrees East, 155 poles to the beginning."[3] Such descriptions could present problems when features changed over time—trees dying or stones moved.

Most early towns arose in response to natural features, such as shorelines or rivers, and existing Native American trails. Many had no well-defined pattern. Each was unique and followed no regular guidelines.

There were various types of land regulations in colonial America. As early as the seventeenth century farmland ordinances gave protection from the overproduction of certain agricultural crops, most notably tobacco. Building ordinances required fireproof masonry construction and restricted the location of objectionable land uses within cities. In 1700, a Philadelphia ordinance called for every home to have one or more trees within at least eight feet of the dwelling.

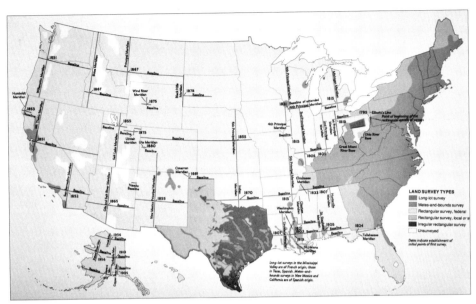

*13.3. Meridian/baseline systems in the United States*

Land was abundant, and the efficient sale of land enriched a meager U.S. treasury through collecting revenue from land sales with very little overhead costs. To expedite the process of surveying and selling land in the Midwest and West, the federal government established the Public Land Survey System, a series of meridians and base lines used as reference lines for land west of the original 13 colonies. In some states, such as Ohio, numerous meridian/baseline systems were established; in other states, such as Michigan and many of the Plains states, a simpler, single system was utilized. This system resulted in rapid settlement of lands, creating a tax base from the new revenues. As John Reps notes in *The Making of Urban America*, "Perhaps the rectangular survey pattern for the west was the only system that could have resulted in speedy settlement and the capture of a continent for the new nation."[4]

The law that had the greatest impact on early land ownership, perhaps, was a gridiron plan adopted by Congress for settlement of the West. "An Ordinance for Ascertaining the Mode of Disposing of Lands in the Western Territory," generally referred to as the Land Ordinance of 1785, described an efficient method for surveying land not yet settled.[5] By allowing

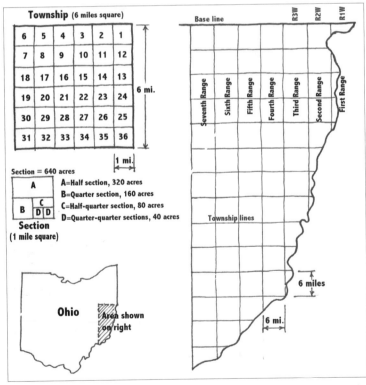

*13.4. The Land Ordinance of 1785 systematically allocated land parcels in the western territories.*

parcels to be easily mapped and recorded, it encouraged land sales, even from distant locations, and had a lasting impact on land use in midwestern and western states: "Today, as one flies over the last mountain ridges [of the Appalachians] from the east, one sees stretching ahead to the horizon a vast checkerboard of fields and roads. With military precision, modified only on occasion by some severe topographic break, or some earlier system of land distribution, this rectangular grid persists to the shores of the Pacific. America thus lives on a giant gridiron imposed on the natural landscape by the early surveyors carrying out the mandate of the Continental Congress expressed in the Land Ordinance of 1785."[6]

The Homestead Act of 1862 was a significant piece of land use legislation in the nineteenth century. It transferred land from the public domain to private ownership, and gave 160 to 640 acres of undeveloped land free to settlers who agreed to live on it and use it. The act opened the western territories for settlement and development. The Act required only that settlers file for a deed and improve the land.

A land grant program also contributed to settlement of the western territories by giving land to railroad companies. This began with the Pacific Railroad Act of 1862. Railroads received a ribbon of land (typically 10 miles wide) wherever they built a rail line, and they profitably sold land to new settlers, which encouraged small-scale communities to evolve along the railroad routes.

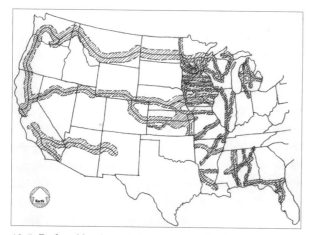

*13.5. Railroad land grants in western territories*

In the nineteenth century, government policies and court cases began to coalesce into a body of land use law. For example, in the 1820s New York City for-

bade gravesites in certain areas of the city and specified acceptable locations for cemeteries. Some cities, such as New Orleans, prohibited property owners from building slaughterhouses or ammunition factories in the city. Toward the end of the nineteenth century, Washington, D.C., placed height limitations on buildings to make the top floor of structures accessible for firemen with ladders. San Francisco enacted land use restrictions based on proximity to natural hazard areas after the devastating earthquake of 1906. In *Hadacheck v. Sebastian* (1915), the Supreme Court held that in Los Angeles an undesirable use (brick manufacture) could be regulated even if the business existed before the ordinance was passed.

Land use regulations continued to be established across the country in the twentieth century. In 1909, the first zoning board was created in Los Angeles. By 1916, the first comprehensive zoning ordinance had been adopted by the city of New York. Its purposes were to protect stable neighborhoods and prohibit undesirable uses there, and to promote commercial development in the center city. The impetus for this ordinance was provided by the encroachment of the sweatshop garment district into an upscale commercial/retail district along Park Avenue. This early zoning code had strong economic implications and protected high-valued property by regulating the use of land, the height and bulk of buildings, and population densities.

Problems arose as local and state governments sometimes made inconsistent determinations regarding land use issues. For instance, in Massachusetts single-family residential areas could prohibit multifamily uses, but courts in New Jersey and California ruled otherwise. In Massachusetts an ordinance allowed stores to be restricted from residential neighborhoods, but courts in Missouri and New Jersey did not agree. It became obvious that a better way was needed to confront the increasing problems of urbanization.

## Zoning as an Evolving Tool

To evaluate the impact of zoning ordinances over time, we must first examine the original regulations and the concerns they were meant to address. The concept of zoning fulfilled an obvious need to reduce the congestion that was a problem in many cities at the beginning of the twentieth century. During this period of intense urbanization, commercial areas were crowded with private dwellings, polluting industries were located in residential neighborhoods, and tall buildings crowded together without consideration for the blocking of air circulation and sunlight. City officials had no effective mechanism for controlling such development, and growth was haphazard.

A *Zoning Primer*, originally published in 1922 and revised in subsequent editions, compared zoning to one's own household. "Someone has asked, 'Does your city keep its gas range in the parlor and its piano in the kitchen?' That is what many an American city permits its household to do for it."[7]

WASTE IN CITY BUILDING!

[Illustration by courtesy of the Cleveland City Plan Commission]

Owing to haphazard city growth hundreds of perfectly good buildings go to the dump each year.

13.6. *An illustration in* A Zoning Primer *depicting the abandonment of good buildings because they were surrounded by inappropriate land uses, 1926*

The Standard State Zoning Enabling Act, also published in 1922, helped to establish a standard for zoning ordinances across the country. Although it served a public purpose, initially, the primary concern of zoning ordinances was to protect stable single-family residential districts against incursion of commercial, industrial, and even multifamily uses. These concerns were real. As zoning critic Richard Babcock has noted, "zoning caught on as an effective technique to further an eminently conservative purpose: the protection of the single-family house neighborhood. In spite of all the subsequent embellishments, that objective remains paramount."[8]

After the passage of the Zoning Enabling Act, zoning spread like wildfire in communities across the country; it had almost universal support. Its validity was established in a landmark Supreme Court decision in 1926, *Euclid*

*v. Ambler Realty Company*, which determined that zoning not only protected property values but was in the public interest as a means to reduce nuisance uses.[9] The question became: What determines a nuisance? Alfred Bettman, a zoning advocate who argued the *Euclid* case in front of the Supreme Court, said, "The zone plan, by comprehensively districting the whole territory of the city and finding ample space and appropriate territory to each type of use, is decidedly more just, intelligent, and reasonable than the system, if system it can be called, of spotty ordinances and uncertain litigations about the definition of a nuisance."[10] *Euclid v. Ambler*, almost by itself, led to zoning's becoming the most significant tool of land use planning yet devised.

It is not a coincidence that the concept of zoning came into being at the same time suburbs were first being developed. The construction of transit lines and the development of the automobile allowed middle- and high-income residents to leave the pollution, congestion, and density of the central urban areas and buy houses on a generous lot just outside the urban fringe. These homeowners, who saw their move as an escape, worried that the problems of the city would follow them to their new environments. Zoning gave them protection.

Conventional zoning typically divides land uses into four distinct classes: residential, commercial, industrial, and agricultural. Of these, residential is considered the highest class, and its protection is seen as most important. An illustrative hierarchical pyramid puts it at the peak, in a zone where nonresidential uses generally are not permitted. Commercial land uses come next in the hierarchy; here both commercial and residential uses are permitted. At the bottom of the pyramid, the industrial zone allows all three uses. (Agriculture is not included in the pyramid because it lies outside the areas of intensive land use that need

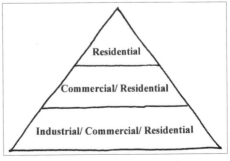

13.7. *Euclidean or pyramidal zoning diagram*

protection.) This type of conventional zoning is often referred to as Euclidean zoning, named for the landmark zoning case described above.

Euclidean zoning formed the basis of many early zoning ordinances. Although it protected residential zones from undesirable uses, it did not prevent residences from being built in commercial or industrial areas. Nor did it classify types of housing, commercial uses, or industry. Initially multiple-unit housing could be placed with single-family housing, and clean industries were rated no differently from smokestack industries. Later ordinances defined subcategories as zoning became more refined. For this reason, Euclidean zoning is not as common as it once was.

Zoning continued to be an important planning tool throughout the twentieth century. In midcentury, *Simon v. Town of Needham* (1942) and *Dundee Realty Co. v. City of Omaha* (1944) determined that zoning could be used to control minimum lot sizes and minimum floor sizes.[11] In the second half of the century, Ramapo, a New York City suburb, attempted to control growth by scheduling infrastructure improvements and the construction of public facilities. Under a new city ordinance, development permits would only be allowed as such improvements were completed and only after five essential services were provided (sewers; drainage; roads; a fire station; and parks, recreation, and public school sites). This allowed the community to manage both the size and timing of growth. The National Association for the Advancement of Colored People (NAACP) argued that this regulation was exclusionary because it discriminated against the poor, the young, and the old. In 1972, *Golden v. Planning Board of the Town of Ramapo* established that such controls were constitutional, upholding the right of the town to control growth.[12]

A significant and controversial case began in 1971 with *Southern Burlington County N.A.A.C.P. v. Mt. Laurel Township*, commonly referred to as *Mt. Laurel I*.[13] The New Jersey Supreme Court agreed with the argument that the township's zoning ordinance operated to exclude low- and moderate-income persons from obtaining housing in a community. The ruling was largely ignored by communities and developers, who anticipated a deterioration of property values. As a result, in 1983 the New Jersey Supreme Court issued

a judgment, known as *Mt. Laurel II*, which stated that each municipality had an obligation to provide a fair share of affordable housing and established guidelines for implementing low- and moderate-income housing. The state Supreme Court took an unusual step in assigning three judges to handle the most important issues. Three years later, the New Jersey Fair Housing Act of 1986 established a Council on Affordable Housing to determine the low- and moderate-income housing needs for each region and then assign fair share requirements for each community. The outcome of *Mt. Laurel II* also established the principle that exclusionary zoning, or zoning that excludes certain uses, is acceptable as long as a community is willing to pay the price for this exclusivity through additional fees.

Peter Marcuse, in the *Journal of the American Planning Association*, identified critical junctures in the history of planning when planners waived their responsibility. He contended that planners defaulted by not embracing zoning in the 1920s because they saw it as a threat to them professionally, and thus lost the opportunity to utilize zoning to rectify social ills, "which made zoning more a tool to protect real estate values than to improve the quality of place in democratic communities."[14] Zoning remains the most effective tool to implement land use plans. It offers a well-defined, court-tested, and respected system for regulating land use. Given a good comprehensive plan, zoning can be used to implement that plan.

## Summary

Community planning in the United States is based to a great extent on the nation's views about property ownership as codified in the Constitution and Bill of Rights and the ensuing evolution of land use law. The underlying philosophy was the right of landowners to do as they pleased with their land with minimal government interference while protecting the public's interests. As long as land was available for development, few Americans voiced opinions that would curtail this freedom.

The country's earliest colonial settlers adopted land patterns that guided development—the Spanish in the south and west, the French in the north, and the British in the east. The most significant land use legislation during the period of settlement of the western territories was the Land Ordinance of 1785, which established a survey system that promoted the efficient sale of parcels. Other important early legislation that dealt with the allocation of land included the Homestead Act of 1862 and the railroad land grants program of the late nineteenth century.

Limitations on land use began to occur during the nineteenth century. These were viewed as reasonable regulations, for example, preventing a munitions factory in the heart of the city. By the beginning of the twentieth century, additional regulations were common, especially in large cities where issues of health, safety, and welfare had become critical. In addition to the Sanitary Reform Movement, Open Space Movement, and the Tenement House Laws (discussed in Chapter 7), other regulations mandated physical requirements such as the height of buildings to enable fire control in tall buildings. Ordinances were developed to separate incompatible land uses. The turning point occurred in 1926 in *Euclid v. Ambler Realty Company*, when the U.S. Supreme Court upheld the constitutionality of zoning as a form of land use control. Since then, zoning ordinances have been the primary tool of implementing community planning.

# 14

# ZONING AND OTHER LAND USE REGULATIONS

## Conventional Zoning

Zoning is intended to regulate the use of private land for the common good. It establishes that the interests of private property owners must be balanced against the interests of the public. As R. Robert Linowes and Don T. Allensworth have written, "Zoning is the real power behind planning, and it is zoning that gives teeth to planning ideals and objectives. Planning as such cannot require that land be used in a particular manner, but zoning can."[1]

Zoning must serve a valid public purpose and be in accordance with an approved comprehensive plan. The same regulations must apply to all districts with similar zoning classifications. Zoning can show no discrimination or capricious intent and must not result in "taking" of a property (as described later in this chapter) or violate other laws or constitutional conditions.

The purposes of zoning typically include:

1. Promoting and protecting public health, safety, and general welfare.

2. Protecting the character and stability of residential, commercial, industrial, recreational, and agricultural areas and promoting the orderly and beneficial development of such areas.

3. Providing adequate light, air, privacy, and convenience of access to property.

4. Regulating the intensity of uses of land and lot areas and determining the area of open spaces surrounding buildings and structures necessary to protect the public health.

5. Reducing congestion on public highways and streets.

6. Protecting against fire, explosion, noxious fumes and odors, heat, dust, smoke, glare, noise, vibration, radioactivity, and other nuisances.

7. Preventing overcrowding of land and undue concentration of structures.

8. Conserving the taxable value of land and buildings.

9. Providing for payment of fees for zoning permits and setting penalties for violations.

Zoning separates land uses into categories based on two primary factors, physical (dimensional) and functional (use). Physical factors are regulated within each zoning district, including development density, minimum lot size, and building coverage, placement, and height. Also listed are use categories, such as residential or commercial.

Although ordinances may differ in structure and content from community to community, the primary components of an ordinance are text and a map. The text, which may contain tables and illustrations, details the provisions of the ordinance and provides standards for the districts. The map (or maps) shows the boundaries of zoning districts, which are usually drawn along street or property lines. There is no limit to the number of zoning districts that a municipality may choose to establish.

### The Zoning Ordinance

Carefully written, zoning ordinance text consists of a series of sections, articles, or chapters that explain zoning rules and set procedures for administering and applying the zoning ordinance in each district. Each word and comma has significance; for example, the word "shall"

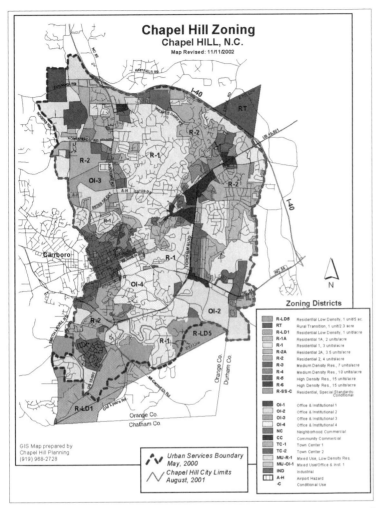

**14.1.** *Zoning map for Chapel Hill, North Carolina (an enlarged color version of this map is in Appendix D)*

The map contains the following labels:

**Chapel Hill Zoning**
Chapel HILL, N.C.
Map Revised: 11/11/2002

**Zoning Districts**

| | | |
|---|---|---|
| R-LD5 | Residential Low Density, 1 unit/5 ac. |
| RT | Rural Transition, 1 unit/2-3 acre |
| R-LD1 | Residential Low Density, 1 unit/acre |
| R-1A | Residential 1A, 2 units/acre |
| R-1 | Residential 1, 3 units/acre |
| R-2A | Residential 2A, 3-5 units/acre |
| R-2 | Residential 2, 4 units/acre |
| R-3 | Medium Density Res., 7 units/acre |
| R-4 | Medium Density Res., 10 units/acre |
| R-5 | High Density Res., 15 units/acre |
| R-6 | High Density Res., 15 units/acre |
| R-SS-C | Residential, Special Standards-Conditional |
| OI-1 | Office & Institutional 1 |
| OI-2 | Office & Institutional 2 |
| OI-3 | Office & Institutional 3 |
| OI-4 | Office & Institutional 4 |
| NC | Neighborhood Commercial |
| CC | Community Commercial |
| TC-1 | Town Center 1 |
| TC-2 | Town Center 2 |
| MU-R-1 | Mixed Use, Low Density Res. |
| MU-OI-1 | Mixed Use/Office & Inst. 1 |
| IND | Industrial |
| A-H | Airport Hazard |
| -C | Conditional Use |

GIS Map prepared by
Chapel Hill Planning
(919) 968-2728

Urban Services Boundary
May, 2000

Chapel Hill City Limits
August, 2001

established in its comprehensive plan. Thus, the introduction provides justification for the ordinance.

*Definitions.* Definitions provide a foundation for interpreting the regulatory statements contained in the ordinance. Definitions are important for public understanding of terms and to give legal meaning to the text. Such terms as *dwelling unit, essential services, floor area, ground floor coverage, home occupation, structure/use nonconformities, variance,* and others are defined. Even common words, such as *family* or *basement,* can be ambiguous and require a clear definition. Without such a common understanding, enforcement of the ordinance would be difficult, if not impossible, and court cases could result unnecessarily.

*Schedule of district regulations.* The schedule of district regulations is often the item of greatest concern to property owners because it determines what they can do with their property. The regulations may affect the amount of property taxes due for a parcel of land and a property's value at the time of sale. Land uses for each district typically are grouped and classified as permissible, special/conditional, or accessory. The primary uses are residential, "R"; commercial, "C" (office and retail); industrial, "I"; and agricultural, "A." These categories may be subdivided; for example, into single-family or multifamily residential ("R-1" or "R-2") or light versus heavy industry ("I-1" or "I-2") Other districts commonly found in zoning ordinances are conservation or open space, institutional, and mixed-use (which allows the blending of uses in certain areas of the community).

Statements of intent for each use in a district may also be included in district regulations. Property owners proposing a use not specifically defined in the district can better determine how a planning commission or zoning board is likely to evaluate their petition. For example, an archery range in an agricultural district may not be a listed use, but may be acceptable if it fits the statement of intent for the district.

There are three broad categories of use. Permitted uses do not require review or action by the planning

means that whatever follows it is mandatory, while the word "may" indicates permission to perform an act. Ordinances can be more or less complex, and their format and order may vary, but most contain the following elements.

*Introduction.* The introduction includes the title, date, purpose(s) of the ordinance, severability, and its legal authority. (Severability means that if any part of the ordinance is shown to be illegal or unconstitutional, it does not negate the remainder of the ordinance.) The introduction identifies the state's specific enabling legislation that empowers a community to adopt a zoning ordinance. A "Statement of Purpose" enumerates the reasons for the community to adopt the ordinance and links the zoning ordinance to the community's goals as commission or zoning board and may be given simple administrative approval by a local official. Accessory uses, for example, a detached garage on a residential lot with a house, are secondary to the principal use and can be treated administratively as principal uses. A use designated as special or conditional requires a more thorough examination, often involving a public hearing. For example, an intensive livestock operation, where numerous animals are concentrated in small feedlots, may need approval after review by the appropriate governmental agency. In this case, a community could, and should, express concern about waste material or animal odors and approval might be contingent on provisions for safety and welfare such as a limit on the number of animals or acceptable methods for handling waste.

Once the zoning district for a parcel of land is determined, the intensity of allowable development is the next consideration. Each district's regulations will include a subsection devoted to size, placement, and height of structures. For example, in an agricultural district the ordinance may require a minimum of 10 acres for a dwelling unit, while a suburban residential district might permit four houses per acre.

Area regulations include ground floor coverage (GFC) and floor area ratio (FAR). GFC is the amount of the site covered by construction, that is, the building footprint. GFC is measured as a percentage of the total lot area; it relates to the infiltration of snow/rainwater runoff on a site. A commercial district might have a GFC of 25 percent of the lot surface, for example, meaning the footprint cannot exceed this size.

FAR, in contrast, regulates the intensity of use on a lot and is tied to the traffic the use might generate, parking availability, and other concerns. FAR is based on the total area of all floors of a building divided by the area of the parcel. As shown in the example in Fig. 14.2, if the ground floor coverage of a building is 5,625 square feet (75 feet by 75 feet) and it is built on a 22,500-square-foot lot, the GFC is 25 percent. However, since this building has three stories of equal square footage per floor, the FAR would be 0.75, or three times the GFC.

Placement and height restrictions also are included in this section of the ordinance. Placement of a building on a lot is measured by setback provisions, that is, how far the building is positioned from a property's boundary lines. The provisions include minimum setbacks from the front, side, and rear boundaries. (Setbacks were established as early as the seventeenth century in Philadelphia to provide for future road widening and utilities. The provisions continue to serve these functions and also ensure a degree of privacy from adjacent properties as well as access to all portions of the parcel.)

The limit on the height of a building may be defined in feet or stories. As mentioned earlier, this provision was initially designed to allow fire departments to reach the top of a building with a ladder; later regulation became important to restrict shadows cast by buildings on their neighbors and to ensure air circulation.

In some ordinances, a distance requirement protects a less intense use from a use with greater intensity. For example, a minimum distance may be required between commercial and residential properties, or a transitional strip of vegetation may provide a barrier between the noise and light on a commercial area and nearby homeowners.

*Supplemental regulations.* Supplemental district regulations focus on specific items, for example, convenience storage facilities, or extraction operations such as sand and gravel mining—common in glaciated parts of the United States. An extraction plan might regulate hours and days of mining operation, depth in relation to the groundwater table, transition strips to separate mining areas from others, transportation for extractive products, fencing, restoration of the exhausted pit, and other relevant activities. Supplemental regulations, like regulations for special/conditional uses, try to minimize the impact of an activity on neighboring properties and infrastructure.

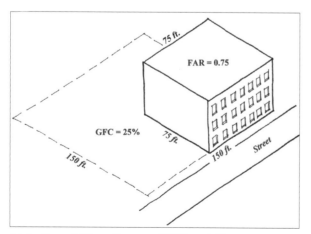

*14.2. Ground Floor Coverage (GFC) and Floor Area Ratio (FAR)*

*Parking.* Off-street parking and loading regulations are common for high-intensity uses, such as schools and churches and commercial and industrial activity. A parking standard sets the number of parking spaces required for a site's primary activity. For example, an ordinance requirement for a hospital may call for one parking space for each bed and one additional space for each two employees. In a commercial district, the parking standard may be related to the square footage of a building or buildings; one space may be required for each 200 square feet of a commercial building's floor area. Regulations may also include related design features such as turnaround areas (so vehicles do not need to back onto a street), lighting, ingress-egress, landscaping low enough to allow adequate visibility, or snow storage areas.

## EXERCISE 13
### PARKING REQUIREMENTS IN RIVERTOWN

*The Rivertown Zoning Ordinance (see Appendix C) describes parking standards adopted for the city. Use the ordinance to determine how many parking spaces are required for each of three potential projects:*

*1 A new clothing store of 3,000 square feet*

*2. A motel with 24 units and 5 employees and a sit-down restaurant for 36*

*3. An apartment building with 20 units*

*Sign regulation.* The regulation of signage can be contentious. Commercial property owners believe that bold, readily noticeable signs are necessary to the success of their businesses and that passersby find such signs

**14.3. Billboard blight in Los Angeles**

useful. Local residents, in contrast, generally see signs as an aesthetic intrusion, so it is not unusual for them to want close supervision of the number, size, and display of signs. Failure to regulate signage can create a jumbled, unsightly mess along a municipality's streets and main arteries.

Signs vary in nature from for-sale signs to political campaign signs to business advertisements. Regulations may control various aspects of signage—material, size, height, placement on a property, movement and lighting, maintenance, and the number of signs per business. Commercial signs cannot obstruct a motorist's view or resemble lawful traffic signs. Sign ordinances generally cannot regulate the content of a sign because the constitution protects the right of free speech, but hate messages and vulgarity can be regulated.

Confusion may occur about what constitutes a sign. Does a well-recognized logo without a name constitute a sign? Is an oversized American flag associated with a local business that draws attention a sign? Interpretations of the ordinance are usually decided by the zoning board of appeals or local courts.

*Site plan review.* Next to district regulations, the most important element of a zoning ordinance for individuals and corporations engaged in development activity is the site plan review. The zoning ordinance describes the process necessary for the required content and approval of a site plan proposal. The step-by-step site plan review procedure, usually coordinated by the community planner, begins with a preliminary site plan and ends with approval of a final site plan before building activity can begin. (See Chapter 15 for a full discussion of the site plan review process.)

*Administration.* A zoning ordinance needs to include a section on administration and enforcement, specifying the responsibilities and powers of the community's zoning administrator, who may be appointed by the local governing body to certify applications comply with zoning. Certification may be required before and after a request for a building permit, or at the time of the site plan review. The administrator checks the use in relation to the zoning district and the permitted, special condition, and accessory uses, and area and placement requirements. Once the development phase is complete, the administrator may conduct an on-site inspection to determine compliance with the site plan. When the project is complete, the zoning administrator may be part of a team that signs a certificate of occupancy, the final step before a building can be declared habitable. Thus, the zoning administrator is responsible for the day-to-day implementation of the provisions contained in the ordinance.

*Amendments.* Zoning ordinances are updated by amendment, typically written by members of the planning department or their private sector consultant. Any amendment should be consistent with the goals of the community's comprehensive plan. The amendments are then recommended by the planning commission and enacted by the elected local legislative body. Amendments should correct general deficiencies and ambiguities of an ordinance and should not be used to amend the status of single properties, an action referred to as spot zoning, which may not be a legal procedure.

*Variances.* A variance is a minor relaxation of the dimensional or use regulations of a property designed to avoid an individual hardship. Variances are allowed in the zoning ordinance when all of the following are found: the hardship is unique to a particular site, is more than just an inconvenience or an impediment to a higher financial return, would not harm the public welfare, and is not self-imposed. The variance must be the minimum accommodation necessary. In the strictest sense, variances should be allowed only when the problem is caused by a particular and unique aspect of the property, for example, with odd-shaped lots.

Variances may be allowed by the Zoning Board of Appeals (sometimes called the Zoning Board of Adjustment, or ZBA). Administrative decisions are appealed to the ZBA under terms of the state enabling act; legislative decisions are appealed directly to the courts. It is sometimes difficult for members of the ZBA to be completely objective in a determination, since they are dealing with local issues that may involve friends and acquaintances. However, members should be aware that if a variance is approved, the decision often acts as a legal precedent for future applicants, and the board may be compelled to approve similar applications or risk legal action. Thus, determinations of a ZBA can effectively modify an ordinance without the proper approval of the elected legislative body.

*Nonconforming uses.* When a zoning ordinance is enacted, some existing properties may not comply with the new regulations. Because the use or dimensional condition was pre-existing and legal, these noncon-

forming properties are "grandfathered." For example, an existing grocery store located in a district newly zoned residential would be allowed to remain. But if the owner of a nonconforming property wishes to change it substantially by enlarging, reconstructing, or converting it to a new use, the new regulations apply.

*Special and conditional use permits.* Owners may request a special or conditional use permit. (The terms "special use," "conditional use," or "special exception" generally are used interchangeably.) A conditional use is one that does not fit the zoning regulations unless appropriate provisions are attached. It is then permitted because it generally conforms to the community's comprehensive plan, is in the public interest in some way, and has been reviewed at a public hearing and found justifiable. For example, a day care facility in a residential district might be approved as a special use. The difference between a special use and a variance is that a special use is a legal use allowed in the ordinance, while a variance allows a use not permitted under the ordinance provisions, but granted because it meets justified hardships.

*Appeal.* If an applicant for a zoning decision can demonstrate that his or her petition meets all ordinance requirements, then the municipality must give approval. If approval is denied, the applicant can appeal. A typical ordinance outlines the responsibilities of the ZBA. Locally elected officials appoint the members (the number is specified in the ordinance) to interpret the meaning of the ordinance. The board acts as a local arbitrator for a narrow range of zoning decisions. They can interpret the wording, intent, content, and boundaries used in an ordinance, and act on variances, but they cannot change the ordinance.

### Enforcement

If a property owner deviates from the terms of a zoning permit, special land use permit, or variance, the violation is grounds for prosecution. Communities should fully enforce their zoning ordinance to keep its integrity as a document. Failure to enforce the ordinance even once sets a precedent for other property owners to ignore it.

### Due Process

The Fifth Amendment to the Constitution holds that no person shall be deprived of property without due process of law. The due process guarantee protects property owners from arbitrary actions of government at all lev-

*14.4. Poletown after construction of the General Motors plant, 2009*

els in two ways—substantive and procedural. The substantive aspect provides that government cannot take away something of value relating to a private individual's property without appropriate justification and compensation. This is relevant to zoning, which by its nature limits the rights of individual property owners.

If substantive due process deals with the *why* of actions, procedural due process deals with the *how*. It ensures that government will act in a fundamentally fair and reasonable manner when making decisions that affect citizens and their property and that citizens have a right to be heard, though not necessarily the right to prevail. Citizens must be adequately notified of actions that directly affect them and have the opportunity to attend and speak at proceedings. If a variance is necessary for a proposed new building, all property owners directly affected or in proximity to the site must be notified in writing about the action and the information should be published, for example, in the local newspaper. Both substantive and procedural due process cases are reviewed by the courts. Ordinances must incorporate appropriate provisions to ensure that due process is available.

## Eminent Domain

The American legal system permits the government to confiscate land in certain circumstances without an owner's consent. Through the concept of eminent domain, government may acquire private property for public use provided there is a purpose that benefits the citizenry and fair compensation (based on an objective appraisal of the property) paid to the owner. The most common use of eminent domain is for construction of utilities, government buildings, or public transportation.

Eminent domain can be instituted in spite of the objections of displaced property owners, although it can be controversial. A classic example is the seizure of land in 1981 for construction of a new General Motors manufacturing plant. The government exercised eminent domain to acquire the houses of 4,200 residents to make a large parcel of land available for expansion of facilities by General Motors in two communities, Detroit and Hamtramck, Michigan, in a private-to-public-to-private transfer of land ownership. The government's justification, or stated public purpose, was the project's potential value for economic development and job creation. The constitutional definition of the term "public purpose" was critical, since public use did not occur. Rather, an expanded interpretation of public purpose allowed the use of eminent domain for economic development and the benefit of a large private corporation.

Similarly, in 2005, in *Kelo v. City of New London* (Connecticut), the U.S. Supreme Court decided it was appropriate for government to use eminent domain to take land from private owners and make it available to a private developer, justified as improving a community's economic base and revitalizing a depressed urban area.[2] The lead plaintiff, Susette Kelo, representing 15 property owners, sued the city for misuse of eminent domain to allow construction of a hotel and resort as part of the city's comprehensive redevelopment plan. The courts decided in favor of the city, and the plaintiffs were paid for the purchase of their properties.

The fate of property located at the corner of Hollywood and Vine Streets in Los Angeles had a different outcome. In 2006, the Los Angeles City Council approved a $500 million project that included a 296-room hotel, upscale condominiums, and shops and restaurants. The project would displace some 30 existing small retail businesses, including the Bernard Luggage Company store, which had been at the location since the 1950s. The developer tried to buy the properties, but a number of the owners were unwilling to sell. Under California law, governments cannot condemn properties for

sale unless they are blighted, but blight is determined by local governments. Los Angeles's redevelopment agency determined the Bernard property was blighted because it lacked air conditioning and had insufficient parking. The city initiated a move to invoke eminent domain for purchase and demolition. However, the owner of Bernard Luggage, Robert Blue, fought back: "We survived all the hard times. We're all paying our taxes, we're all citizens, and we should all be treated equally. That's not happening when they take our business and give it to someone else."[3] Blue filed a lawsuit alleging a violation of his right to due process. After years in the court system, he was victorious, and the developers were limited to building their complex on three sides surrounding the store, which remained at its location. By 2010, however, although the business remains, the facade of the Bernard Luggage Building was incorporated into the design of Hollywood's new W Hotel.

Backlash against the broad interpretation of eminent domain have led to state referenda that limit the ability of public initiatives to take private land for private use in the name of economic development as a public purpose. By 2006, at least half of the states had passed this type of restricting legislation.[4]

## Takings

Property ownership includes what is often described as a bundle of rights and responsibilities considered inherent in ownership. A precedent-setting case, *Pennsylvania Coal v. Mahon* (1922), found that "while property may be regulated to a certain extent, if the regulation goes too far it will be recognized as a taking."[5] In some cases, the need for compensation is obvious. For example, if land is taken for construction of a new municipal facility such as a water treatment plant, property owners whose land was taken deserve appropriate compensation through an outright purchase by the government at fair market value. Similarly, when government action causes a significant impact on the value of a property, compensation is necessary. Such determinations are subject to legal interpretations, which may have varying perspectives. For example, courts have held that property owners have a right to light, air, and view from a property over the public street it abuts, but do not have a compensable right to be seen from the street, such as with street trees blocking the view of a retail store.[6]

*14.5. Bernard Luggage Company and other small businesses, (top); Bernard Luggage Building with restored façade, incorporated into new W Hotel complex, Hollywood, California*

In 1978 the decision in *Penn Central Transportation Co. v. City of New York* dealt with the rights of owners to develop a property versus the rights of cities to review and regulate development of a historic property.[7] Penn Central, the owner of Grand Central Terminal in New York City, had applied for permission to construct a 55-story addition over the building, which had previously been listed as a historic landmark structure. When the city denied approval for the addition based on the structure's historic designation, Penn Central claimed a taking and asked the City of New York for compensation for not being allowed to develop its property.

The court ruled that "there was no 'taking,' since the historic designation and resulting regulation had not transferred control of the property to the city, but had only restricted the appellants' exploitation of it."[8] When the owners argued there had not been due process in the historic designation of their building, the court responded that "there was no denial of due process because (1) the same use of the terminal was per-

mitted as before; (2) the appellants had not shown that they could not earn a reasonable return on their investment in the terminal itself; (3) even if the terminal proper could never operate at a reasonable profit, some of the income from Penn Central's extensive real estate holdings in the area must realistically be imputed to the terminal; and (4) the development rights above the terminal, which were made transferable to numerous sites in the vicinity, provided significant compensation for loss of rights above the terminal itself."[9] Only if the owner was kept from making a reasonable return (in New York City, a reasonable return was assumed at 6 percent per year at the time) could a taking be claimed.

In 1987, *Nollan v. California Coastal Commission* determined whether a partial taking could be claimed if part of the owner's rights were infringed upon. The Nollan family owned a piece of beachfront property. The state argued that a strip of land on the Nollan property was needed to "protect the public's ability to see the beach," as well as "assisting the public in overcoming the 'psychological barrier' to using the beach created by a developed shorefront." The court ultimately supported the argument of the property owner, ruling that requiring a portion of their beachfront property be given for public access was essentially a taking and that the owner must be compensated for it.

A U.S. Supreme Court case, *Tahoe-Sierra Preservation Council, Inc. v. Tahoe Regional Planning Agency* (2002), examined whether owners should be compensated if a temporary moratorium restricted their rights to develop for a certain period of time (in this case, 32 months).[10] The Court decided the moratorium did not constitute a taking because there is an inherent difference between the acquisition of property for a public purpose and the regulation of property.

Other cases give differing perspectives on the issue of takings.[11] Property owners have a right to a reasonable return for use of their land, but the Constitution does not guarantee that the most profitable use will be allowed, and courts continue to insist on a high threshold for compensatory taking claims. The Supreme Court has repeatedly held that the mere diminution of property value is insufficient to demonstrate a taking, a principle traceable to early zoning cases upholding the imposition of new zoning regulations that instantly decreased property values because of the loss of development potential.

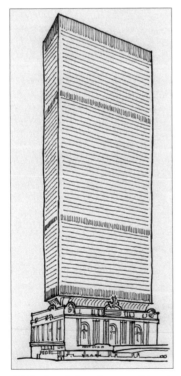

14.6. *Sketch based on architect's rendering of proposed addition to Grand Central Terminal, New York City, 1968*

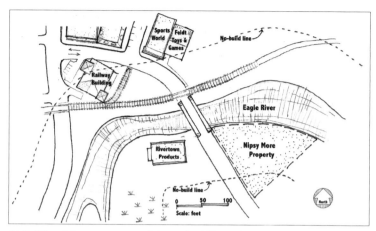

14.7. *Nipsy More property and the no-build boundary*

## EXERCISE 14
### A TAKING IN RIVERTOWN?

*The map delineates a property owned by resident Nipsy More just south of the Station Street Bridge. It is a beautiful location on the Eagle River and has long been considered a desirable investment. The property also is close to the downtown, where Mr. More owns two stores. Mr. More bought the property five years ago with the intention of building a residence on it. However, the city is concerned about flooding along the river and last year established a no-build zone extending 100 feet from the normal banks of the river. Based on the property's boundaries, this restriction does not allow the property to be used for any structure larger than a garage. If the city enforces its no-build zone, More asserts, he should be compensated for the loss of use of his property, and he intends to take the issue to court if necessary.*

*As the city's planner, you have been asked to look at legal cases that might have a bearing on this issue, especially the case of* Lucas v. South Carolina Coastal Council *(the decision is available online at http://lawschool.mikeshecket.com/ property/lucasvsouthcarolinacoastalcouncil.htm.).[12] Based on this case, prepare a report for the Rivertown City Council on whether these circumstances constitute a taking. Give a brief summary of the* Lucas *decision and discuss how the More situation is similar or different. Based on your findings, give your opinion as to whether the city would be responsible for compensating Mr. More if it enforces the no-build zone.*

## Zoning and the Comprehensive Plan

The relationship between planning and zoning became a major consideration in twentieth-century land use

law. In 1975, an Oregon court in *Baker v. City of Milwaukie* unequivocally accepted the primacy of the comprehensive plan. It ruled: "We conclude that a comprehensive plan is the controlling land use planning instrument for a city. Upon passage of a comprehensive plan, a city assumes a responsibility to effectuate the plan and conform prior conflicting zoning ordinances to it. We further hold that the zoning decisions of a city must be in accord with that plan."[13]

A growing number of planners consider the old policy of separating land uses through zoning as a regressive approach to regulation. According to Richard Babcock, author of *The Zoning Game*, "It was as a means of strengthening the institution of private property in the face of rapid and unsettling changes in the urban scene that zoning won such remarkable acceptance in American communities."[14] Today, mixed land uses are not seen as disadvantageous, but as progressive. Conventional zoning, which sets minimum or maximum standards and requirements, is largely quantitative and may not deal well with the more complex approach required to provide a more qualitative evaluation. Conventional zoning was not created to address urban design and quality of place issues that are increasingly seen as essential to the creation of inviting, healthy, and vibrant communities.

## Negotiated Alternatives to Conventional Zoning

Modern zoning promotes desired outcomes. Rather than merely protecting the status quo it should provide for growth management and social justice. As Jane Jacobs wrote, urban diversity may "sprout strange and unpredictable uses and peculiar scenes. But this is not a drawback of diversity. This is the point."[15]

Various types of negotiated zoning have been developed and adopted by some communities to bring more flexibility to the zoning process. Among them are Planned Unit Development, Incentive Zoning, and Contract Zoning, which can apply to individual parcels within an existing zone. The three are similar in nature and sometimes the names are used interchangeably.

## Planned Unit Development (PUD)

PUD bases approval of a proposed development on the intent of the standard zoning ordinance rather than on its specific provisions. Under PUD, developers can propose modifications that the community's planning commission or elected officials can approve either administratively or through rezoning. The intent of PUD is to encourage more options on site design and use, enabling an applicant to capitalize on a site's desirable features in ways that would be prohibited under the otherwise applicable zoning. The resulting mixed uses can encourage a greater sense of community (small commercial mixed with residential, for example, or a mix of single-family and multifamily residential). It also is intended to reduce the cost of infrastructure necessary to serve a new development while promoting land use efficiency, open space, and environmental protection. PUDs generally cover large areas and, as a result, are often developed in phases.

As an example, the Canandaigua Lakefront Development in Canandaigua, New York, is a proposal for an existing 33-acre lakefront commercial site. Although zoned Commercial Lakefront and Heavy Commercial, it was approved as a PUD project.[16] This change allows for a mixed-use plan based on community concerns and the market. In its first phase, the project includes 334 residential units, 55,000 square feet of retail, office development, and wellness center. Phase II adds 14,000 square feet of new retail to an existing retail center.

## Incentive Zoning

A local legislature can provide zoning incentives to land developers in exchange for specified community benefits. Incentive zoning permits more intensive development than ordinarily would be allowed under the zoning ordinance; the incentives are established as part of the ordinance and can be given in exchange for items such as open space or parks, affordable housing, day care or elder care, or other specified physical, social, or cultural amenities. When such a feature cannot practically be provided directly by individual developers, the municipality can provide the alternative of cash payments to be held in a trust fund and used exclusively for the community benefit specified.

## Contract Zoning

Most zoning regulations apply uniformly to all properties in a designated zoning district. Contract zoning allows authorities to negotiate with a property owner on a particular property. The owner agrees to a given set of restrictions that apply only to that parcel in return for modification of existing regulations. This gives both the owner and the zoning authority some flexibility based on the assumption that negotiation is in the public interest.

Contract zoning may be found to be illegal by some courts. For example, the State Supreme Court in Wisconsin found in 1970 that a contract made by a zoning authority to zone, to rezone, or not to zone was illegal because a municipality may not surrender its govern-

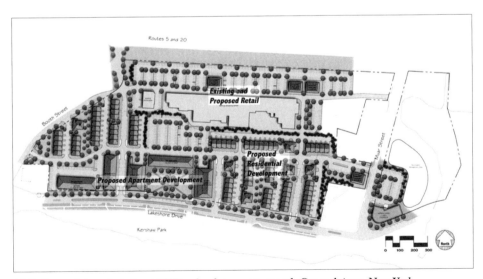

14.8. *Canandaigua Lakefront PUD redevelopment proposal, Canandaigua, New York*

mental powers and functions or inhibit the exercise of its police or legislative powers.[17] The courts could be held responsible for enforcing the contract over time, mixing the responsibilities of two branches of government. In contrast, the State of Michigan approved legislation to allow contract zoning. Amendments to public acts in Michigan permit counties, cities, villages, and townships to approve rezoning subject to conditions offered by a landowner. Michigan planner Phillip McKenna expressed some concern: "This latest legislation is changing the face of zoning as we have known it. Overriding the community plan is now easier than before. Communities need to be alert and may need to establish procedures and amendments to maintain the integrity of districts."[18]

## Performance Zoning

Conventional zoning specifies the use of land within districts; performance zoning specifies the intensity of land use that is acceptable. In other words, it does not regulate the use of a parcel, but the impact of a proposal on its surrounding areas. Performance zoning requires less administration, since variances, appeals, and rezonings often are not necessary. It also gives more flexibility to a municipality and developer and allows a greater range of land uses, as long as their impacts are not negative. It offers the opportunity for innovation and the incorporation of new technologies that may not be accommodated under provisions of conventional zoning. Performance zoning has been shown to be more effective in the preservation of natural features, since it evaluates a proposal's impact on the natural environment as well as the built environment.

This inherent flexibility of performance zoning is, however, also a disadvantage. In traditional ordinances, land uses are absolutes—they either are allowed or not allowed. In performance zoning, uses are determined by calculations based on a variety of factors, so administrators must be more adept at making appropriate and fair determinations to avoid legal challenges. Performance zoning relies significantly on communication between the public and private sectors to evaluate its requirements.

Studies have indicated the best approach for communities is probably a combination of conventional zoning and performance zoning. An ordinance includ-

ing components of performance zoning can encourage collaborative rather than confrontational planning, conditional approval of developments, and flexibility to allow quicker approvals and new design and building technologies.

*Spotlight on PLACE, Zoning Without Boundaries*[19]
PLACE (Proximity Location Analysis for Community Enforcement) is an alternative zoning approach similar to performance zoning in that it is zoning without boundaries. Its purpose is to allow a community to change, grow, and reinvent itself over time, rather than be limited to a fixed set of zoning rules. PLACE replaces conventional zoning districts with the concept that new land uses may be located near compatible uses and opposing uses should be separated. So-called associated uses complement, support, and provide benefits or services to other uses in the community; when combined and connected, they form the essential building blocks of community life. Opposing uses are those that cannot be placed near each other for reasons of health, safety, or welfare. For example, sex-oriented businesses could not be located adjacent to schools, nor airports adjacent to residential neighborhoods. Under the PLACE zoning concept, such opposing uses would be required to be set apart a minimum safe distance.

## Form-based Codes

Form-based codes represent a new approach to zoning: they focus less on the land use of property and more on the physical design of its structures and spaces. The Form-Based Codes Institute defines these codes as a way to "foster predictable built results and a high-quality public realm by using physical form (rather than separation of uses) as the organizing principle."[20]

Form-based codes deal with the outward appearance, size, and scale of buildings in relation to one another and the relationship between building facades and public spaces. These codes tend to be prescriptive (that is, building lines state exactly where the front of the building must be placed, instead of stating a minimum setback). They also rely more on graphics to illustrate code provisions and less on text. The form-based code approach does not

Conventional Zoning:
Based primarily on use

Form-Based Codes:
Based more on form and design

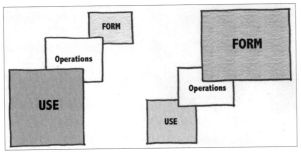

*14.9. Conventional zoning compared to form-based codes*

just regulate a site; it ties the site to the public realm, the streetscape. Building height is defined in both minimums and maximums, instead of only maximums, to ensure that a building is tall enough to define the streetscape, but not so tall that it overwhelms other adjacent buildings. Form-based codes may even include architectural standards, stipulating materials, design vocabulary, and quality. In a business district, this could include guidelines for doors and windows of a certain size and pattern along the sidewalk, window articulation on upper floors, and other details. In residential areas, they may require front porches or limit street-oriented garage doors. Landscape standards typically are a prominent component of form-based codes, since the placement of trees, walkways, and other features directly affects appearance. Because of their strong emphasis on physical design, form-based codes have been referred to as "architect's zoning." Some states do not have enabling legislation providing for form-based codes, although in some areas these codes are being developed without specific enabling legislation.

Form-based codes may present problems. Administratively, they can be compared to design standards or guidelines (typically, standards are regulatory, guidelines are not), as described in Chapter 5. These have proved to be problematic in some communities because the subjective nature of regulating aesthetics leaves more room for interpretation of what constitutes good design. However, regulation of aesthetics is not without precedent. Many communities have historic district commissions empowered to approve projects based on design compatibility. Form-based codes are oriented to this same end, but in all areas of a community, not just in its historic districts.

Form-based codes tend to cost more to write than conventional zoning ordinances because they have more complex standards. Planners need to spend more time and effort to complete a detailed inventory of their community's existing urban form, accommodate additional public involvement, and do the design work that goes into creating the graphically oriented plan and code. This type of zoning code tends to be more involved than a zoning map since form-based codes describe requirements as three-dimensional space.

## Religious Land Use and Institutionalized Persons Act

Citizens have sometimes disagreed about whether churches and other religious institutions should be permitted in residential districts. Edward Bassett, an early urban planner, who wrote the first comprehensive zoning ordinance in the United States (in New York City in 1916), said, "When in 1916 the framers of the Greater New York building zone resolution were discussing what buildings and uses should be excluded from residence districts, it did not occur to them that there was the remotest possibility that churches, schools, and hospitals could properly be excluded from any district."[21] A doctrine known as the "New York rule" established that "churches cannot be absolutely excluded from residential areas."[22] A few states, however, follow the "California rule," allowing municipalities to exclude religious buildings from residential areas under some circumstances.

In an attempt to resolve differences, in 2000 Congress passed the Religious Land Use and Institutionalized Persons Act (RLUIPA), (pronounced "Reloopa") which established a stronger base for the exercise of rights of religious bodies.[23] RLUIPA recognized that there are issues beyond the placement, building, and use of houses of worship. Although they may make claims based on free exercise of their religious rights, religious organizations should be subject to zoning provisions pertaining to health, safety, and welfare. For example, local governments have attempted to regulate the size and location of churches with more than 2,000 weekly attendance, or megachurches. Such churches often provide more than traditional services, including activities such as stock investment sessions, weight loss clinics, even fast-food restaurants, which can significantly impact a community's infrastructure on land exempt from local property taxes. Megachurches have invoked RLUIPA's general rule that "No government shall impose or implement a land use regulation in a manner that imposes a substantial burden on the religious exercise of a person, including a religious assembly or institution, unless the government demonstrates that imposition of the burden on that person, assembly, or institution— (A.) is in furtherance of a compelling governmental interest; and (B.) is the least restrictive means of furthering that compelling governmental interest."[24] In many cases, courts have given megachurches the freedom to be big without penalty, but recent cases are interpreting it more narrowly. The U.S. Supreme Court has not yet adjudicated any cases relating to RLUIPA.

## Rural Zoning

Rural zoning is less complicated than urban zoning because there are usually fewer zoning districts and fewer divisions within each district. The main categories of rural zoning are agriculture, open space (resource conservation), and residential. Small areas of industrial and commercial uses may support the tax base. Since land use is less intensive than in cities, land values are usually lower. When more intensive land uses are proposed, landowners or local officials may initiate rezoning. It is not unusual for agricultural districts near urban areas to be considered as holding zones that await rezoning to more intensive use when developers are ready to build.

Planners for rural areas generally have a different set of issues from urban planners. The most common ordinances allow some residential development as a permitted use on agricultural land, which increases the value of the land. Local governments that are concerned about farmland preservation may implement exclusive agricultural zoning, which does not permit nonfarm development.

Although exclusive agricultural zoning districts usually are found in agricultural areas where land use change is not expected, occasionally a commitment to preserve agricultural land occurs in areas where population density exerts pressure for nonfarm development. Crook County, Oregon, for example, created exclusive agricultural areas known as Exclusive Farm Use (EFU) zones, where subdivisions could be developed only with difficulty and under strict review. Utah County, Utah's agricultural zone, was reserved narrowly: "With the exception of utilities and public facilities that must pass through the zone, commercial agricultural use of the land is protected by relegating non-farm uses to other zones and limiting the zone to farm and farm-related uses."[25]

Rural zoning ordinances may allow higher density growth near hamlets or rural towns than in the surrounding agricultural areas. For example, when classified as rural residential, ¼-acre minimum lot sizes may be used in or near a town or hamlet, depending on whether sewer lines are available or septic systems are necessary. Farther away, larger lots are required: 1-acre lot sizes surrounded by 2-acre lots, then 5-acre lots, and, farthest from the town, 10- or 20-acre parcels may be required to build a home. In areas of large-scale agricultural use, the minimum size may be as large as a 640-acre section of land.

Several zoning techniques based on density requirements are available to preserve large blocks of agricultural land and/or open space. Most farmland owners want the opportunity to sell as many development-sized parcels as possible. Often, the smaller the size, the higher the purchase price per acre. Since a section of land is 640 acres, one-fourth of this is 160 acres, and one-fourth of that is 40 acres (referred to as ¼-¼ zoning). A single 40-acre parcel is a viable size for traditional livestock and crop farming, and farmers would be more inclined to lease 40-acre fields than smaller-sized ones under multiple owners. Consequently, in ¼-¼ zoning, sellable parcels are 40 acres, meaning that 16 homes could be constructed on a 640-acre section.

Another option, cluster zoning, combines a degree of urban density with more traditional rural growth. Again, an example is helpful. If a zoning ordinance allows one dwelling unit per 10 acres, on 160 acres of land 16 units could be constructed. Using cluster zoning, the 16 units could be constructed, for example, on 32 contiguous acres, while the balance of land, 128 acres, would be maintained as common land open space. The open space is protected in perpetuity by use of deed restrictions agreed to by the 16 new homebuyers as part of a homeowner's agreement.

Sliding scale zoning is a compromise between preserving agricultural use and open space as exclusive land use and giving landowners limited development value. Conventional zoning for residential development in agricultural districts is stated as dwelling units per number of acres, for example, one unit per 5 acres. Using sliding scale zoning, density depends on the size of the original parcel and is established geometrically instead of arithmetically. For example, regulations may permit one dwelling unit for each 5 acres, two dwelling units for 15 acres, three dwelling units for 30 acres, four dwelling units for 80 acres, five dwelling units for 160 acres, six dwelling units for 320 acres, and seven dwelling units for farmland exceeding 320 acres. It is possible to construct the wording of the ordinance to cluster the seven dwelling units on 20 acres; consequently 300 acres would remain in agricultural or open space use. Conventional zoning would allow many more units; with one unit allowed per 5 acres, a farmer who owns 320 acres could divide it to accommodate 64 dwelling units—57 more than under sliding scale zoning.

### Conservation Easements

Conservation easements are legal limitations intended to protect and preserve desirable agricultural land, environmentally sensitive land, important open spaces, and historic properties. Under a conservation easement, a landowner can make a charitable donation or sale of development rights to a government or nonprofit organization, such as a land trust/conservancy, in return for tax relief and the satisfaction of realizing the land will be preserved. Easements are individualized and may entail forgoing the right to construct structures for profit. The landowner retains ownership and can sell the land or bequeath it to heirs, but subsequent owners must abide by the restrictions attached to the easement. Farm owners can continue to farm and make improvements as stipulated in the conservation agreement. Tax advantages may be in the form of state and federal deductions and/or lower property and estate taxes.

### Purchase of Development Rights

Purchase of development rights (PDR) is one mechanism used to create or transfer a conservation easement. Under a PDR agreement, landowners sell the rights to develop their property to an appropriate administrative body and a deed restriction is placed on the land. The value of the development rights is based on the difference between the fair market value of the land with and without development rights. For example, a 100-acre parcel may have a fair market value of $500,000 including development rights, but may be worth only $200,000 if only agricultural use is permitted. Thus, the development rights are worth $300,000. With a PDR, the landowner would receive tax benefits (also reduced property tax) or direct payments based on the $300,000 development value.

While a PDR agreement preserves a property's use, the deed may allow for change under extreme circumstances determined by the administrative body. Owners rarely exercise such escape clauses, but they provide protection for them. For example, if a large area surrounding the farm is developed, impeding its operation, the local government may recognize the need to allow a change in land use.

PDR programs are expensive and local governments and land trusts have a limited amount of money to spend. But in communities that recognize the importance of agricultural land or open space as part of their comprehensive plan, ballot initiatives to increase millage rates to support a PDR program have been successful.

### Transfer of Development Rights

Transfer of Development Rights (TDR) is another form of restricting an owner's use of property for development purposes, one that shifts the cost to the private sector. More complex than a PDR, TDR entails purchase of development rights by individuals or corporations. It allows a developer to transfer permitted development density from a district where development is unwanted to an area where development is acceptable or even encouraged.

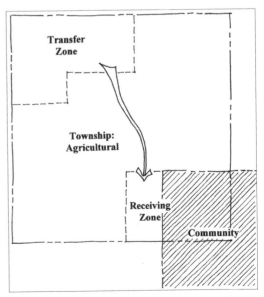

*14.10. The Transfer of Development Rights (TDR) process*

For example, a community's comprehensive plan might indicate that good quality agricultural land should be protected in one part of its jurisdiction, but that residential development is needed near a city in another part. Through a TDR, the government provides an incentive for farmers in the agricultural area to give up development rights on their property to a purchaser who gains the rights to build more houses than the zoning district permits in a designated receiving area. The development rights can be bought and sold on the real estate market. The end result is that the farmer profits from selling the development rights of the TDR to a private sector developer who then is able to increase the number of dwelling units on property he/she owns in the urban fringe that is in proximity to urban services.

TDRs also can be used in urban areas. For example, if a property's air rights (space above an existing building where development is permissible under zoning) cannot be used because the building is a protected historic building, a TDR would allow the owner to sell these air rights for use at another property within a designated receiver district. This sale of rights compensates the initial owner and, at the same time, gives the rights purchaser a greater development opportunity than allowed by code. The city gains additional revenues while protecting its architectural heritage.

---

### Spotlight on Maine's Open Space Tax Law

Maine enacted a Farm and Open Space Tax Law in the 1970s.[26] It gave farmers preferential taxation for preserving open space, farms, and forests by reducing property taxes for such uses. In 1993 the state legislature issued guidelines for the credit:

| | |
|---|---|
| Ordinary open space | 20% reduction |
| Land used for forestry or farming (and protected from future development by permanent easement) | 50% reduction |
| "Forever wild" open space (noncommercial only) | 70% reduction |
| Bonus for allowing public access | 25% additional reduction |

---

## Summary

Zoning is one of the planner's most effective tools. Its primary purposes have been to protect a community's health, safety, and welfare by separating land uses that are incompatible and preserve the value of private property. State governments have constitutional authority to regulate land use, yet they commonly transfer this responsibility to the local level through enabling legislation. Although traditional zoning ordinances are similar from community to community, there can be some variation: their structure may be complex in large metropolitan areas and relatively simple in small jurisdictions.

Zoning is an effective implementation tool of local governments because it is well defined, court tested, respected, and commonly used in communities across the United States. When a community wants to shape its future, it needs a comprehensive plan to serve as a guide for development, with a zoning ordinance as the primary enforcement tool for the plan. A zoning ordinance has two primary components, a map showing boundaries of the various zoning districts and text describing the provisions within each zone.

In addition to zoning land uses, the government can take private property when its procurement has a larger community interest. Roads, schools, and other public needs must be met, and American courts support the government's power to take actions such as the condemnation of property and eminent domain as a means to acquire necessary land in the public interest. When a provision in an ordinance becomes too restrictive, it can be deemed a taking, and the government is required to compensate property owners for the loss of ownership or reasonable use of their property. This preserves a balance between government restrictions and private property rights.

There are a number of alternatives to conventional zoning, including planned unit developments, incentive zoning, contract zoning, and performance zoning. Form-based codes focus less on the land use of property and more on the physical design of its structures and spaces. Programs such as conservation easements, purchase of development rights, and transfer of development rights can give flexible options to complement zoning regulations.

# 15

# SUBDIVISIONS, SITE PLANS, AND SITE PLAN REVIEW

## Subdivisions

Subdivision (or platting) of land occurs when a property is split into smaller parcels. The process and the products of platting are intended to provide uniformity and orderly layout of land and require that it be suitable for building sites and public improvements. Subdivision acts ensure proper surveying and legal descriptions of the property and describe how plats may be amended in the future. Such regulations include practical measures, such as providing proper access to lots and parcels, ensuring adequate drainage of the land, controlling development in floodplain areas, and reserving easements for utilities.

The process of platting land is subject to review by local and possibly state government agencies. Subdivisions affect the community because more intense development has the potential to disrupt established land use patterns and to require the extension of city services. However, property owners benefit from splitting land into smaller parcels since its value as a group of separate parcels is typically greater than its value as a whole.

Historically, individual lots were surveyed and drawn as a group to allow land speculators to sell lots from a plat book, rather than survey each plot individually on site. Before subdivision standards had been established, many developments were built by investors not concerned with providing adequate public services. The approval of plats led to more uniformity and efficiency, not only in the sale of land, but also in its assessment and collection of property taxes. The 1928 Standard City Planning Enabling Act (SCPEA) changed subdivision regulations from simply a process for recording land divisions to one of approving such proposals based on conformity with a community's comprehensive plan and zoning. The act included provisions assuring good planning through the "arrangement of streets in relation to other existing or planned streets and to the comprehensive plan for adequate and convenient open spaces of traffic, utilities, access of fire fighting apparatus, recreation, light, and air, and for avoidance of congestion of population, including minimum width and area of lots."[1]

Although subdivision acts are legislated by states (or in some cases through municipal charter), submissions must meet specified requirements in local ordinances and regulations. Some subdivision regulations establish a minimum number of new parcels (e.g., five) before a development is subject to subdivision act regulations. Many states have adopted their own subdivision acts based on the federal act, SCPEA. They often add provisions for open space, parks, schools, roads, and improvements. Local governments may also add impact fees (see Chapter 16) to cover costs for additional uses such as school facilities and open space near the subdivision.

### Subdivision Requirements

The first step in obtaining approval for a subdivision is to submit a preliminary plan. The plan minimally indicates property boundaries, boundary dimensions and size for each numbered parcel, and any dedicated street rights-of-way or easements. The plan also should contain a soils report, information on water supply (public line or a well), and provision for wastewater treatment. Local requirements may specify additional information: descriptive text, a financial analysis, the relationship of the plat to adjacent properties, an environmental assessment, and a traffic impact study.

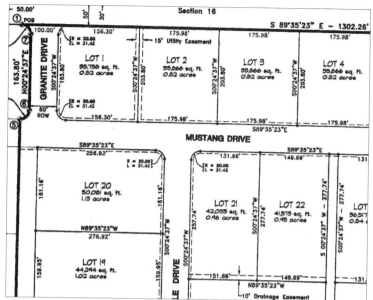

15.1. *Sample subdivision plat from Rock Springs, Wyoming, illustrating the main features of a preliminary plan*[2]

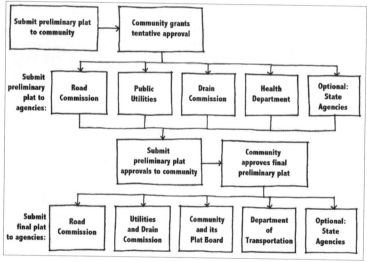

15.2. *Sample subdivision approval process*

Preliminary plats usually are reviewed first by the planning department of the local government. The planning staff or consultant forwards the documents to other departments and agencies for comment, collects these comments, and submits a package with the plan, planning department review, other comments, and a recommendation to the planning commission. A typical subdivision approval involves review by many agencies. Some areas require county and state-level approval of plats before final acceptance by the community, espe-cially if they are adjacent to or impact government land.

### Site Condominiums

Site condominiums are a variant type of development that differs from subdivisions in their form of ownership. Only a portion of the parcel is individually owned and maintained; other portions are owned in common, typically by a condominium association through a board of directors elected by the owners. Individually owned areas are called Exclusive Areas; Limited Common Elements are areas for use by individual owners but commonly owned (such as backyards); and General Common Elements are used and maintained by all owners. For example, in a multifamily condominium the homeowner may have full ownership and control over only the interior of the individual unit. Hallways, lobbies, building exteriors, and lawns are limited common elements. Private streets, recreation facilities, and other amenities are owned by the condominium association. The local government may take responsibility for some aspects by agreement, for example to maintain streets or roads and public safety within the development.

Condominium ownership may have various land uses—single-family detached or attached residential, offices, retail, marinas, or even hotel rooms or group housing facilities. These do not require state approval because they remain one property and are not subdivided. This typically saves developers lengthy review time and significant up-front cost.

A condominium board makes decisions regarding the property based on an agreement established when the site condo project becomes a legal entity. Owners pay a mandatory regular fee to be members in the association, which pays for common maintenance, repair, improvements, and other expenses. Condo associations usually restrict building modifications and common area land use. Since they are private entities, their decisions are not subject to the Open Meetings Act (see Chapter 3).

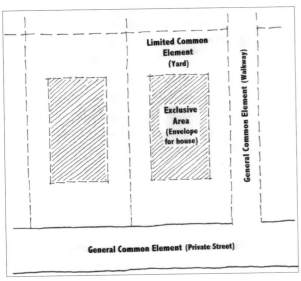

15.3. *Site condominium elements*

## Site Plans

The purpose of platting is to describe how large properties can be divided into smaller parcels. In contrast, a site plan depicts the elements of a single parcel and shows many more features, described below. The plan contains a series of large-size engineering drawings showing details of required information. When approved by the local municipality, it becomes the official record of what will be built.

### Site Plan Requirements

The requirements for a site plan are presented in detail in the local zoning ordinance or a stand-alone legal document. Planners carefully review drawings presented by the developer's engineers. Generally, they include the following information in graphic or tabular form:

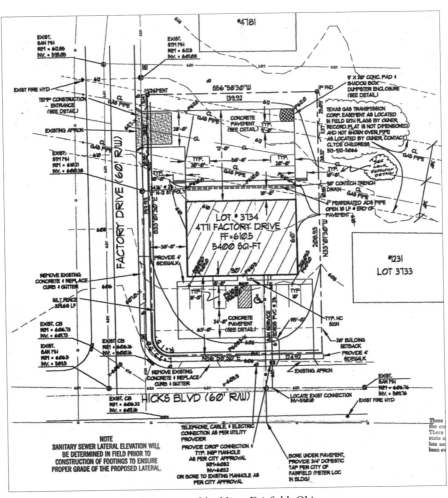

15.4. *Portion of a site plan of commercial building, Fairfield, Ohio*

1. North arrow; scale (usually no smaller than 1 inch equals 50 feet); descriptive legend; total acreage of the site; name and address of the applicant; address of the surveyor, engineer, landscape architect, or professional planner involved in the development of the site plan; the professional seal of the preparer; and the date prepared or last amended.

2. Property dimensions, legal description of the property, existing or proposed deed restrictions or previous zoning approval limiting the property, and, in the case of a condominium development, the proposed master deed. Correct legal boundaries are essential to prevent disputes with neighbors or land use regulating agencies. Also included is a drawing indicating the distance of proposed structures from rear, side, and front lot lines.

3. The zoning of the site and of all adjacent property and the location of buildings or structures within a designated distance (e.g., 200 feet) of the parcel's outside boundaries.

4. The location of abutting streets and proposed alignment of streets, drives, and easements serving the development, and the location of all roads and other access points within 200 feet of the parcel. This allows review of potential traffic conflicts and circulation patterns, for example, sight distance from hills and curves.

5. The location and design of off-street parking areas, including type of surface materials, maneuvering lanes, service lanes, off-street loading spaces, and other service areas within the development.

6. The location of proposed buildings and their intended uses, as well as floor area, building height, and lot coverage.

7. The location of water supply lines and the location and design of wastewater systems and solid-waste disposal facilities (including trash receptacles and Dumpsters). All utility lines must be indicated along with the location and specifications of any proposed above- or below-ground storage facilities for any chemicals, salts, flammable materials, or hazardous materials as well as containment structures or clear zones required by government authorities.

8. Water courses and water bodies, including surface drainage. Discharge or impact to these natural features will need to be reviewed and potentially reduced or prohibited. Information on drainage, erosion, sedimentation and controls, and grading, including areas within a 100-year floodplain or regulated wetland areas on the site.

9. The location of significant trees and other vegetation; proposed landscaping, buffer strips, greenbelts, berms, fences, or walls may be required. The designation of natural features allows planners to preserve significant trees or other important natural resources.

10. A location map at a smaller scale indicating the relationship of the site to the surrounding land use.

11. An environmental assessment.

12. A traffic impact assessment.

13. Additional information may be required for a conditional or special use permit. For example, a rifle range may require information on safety procedures and noise abatement or an adult bookstore proposal, on the proximity of schools and churches.

## Site Plan Review

The site plan review process is a necessary function of public sector planners. It may be considered a planner's most important day-to-day task. The review process is similar to review of subdivisions, but in the case of site plans the state government is not involved. Such a review ensures that a proposed development adheres to all legal requirements and balances the property owner's rights for use of a property with those of neighboring property owners and the community. Site plan review typically is required for multiple-family residential, commercial, and industrial projects. Review may be necessary when there is a proposal for a new use on a site, an expansion, or for changes to circulation patterns and parking lots. In most situations, only a minimal review and approval is required for single residences. Review is not required for remodeling of an existing structure where neither the size nor use is changed (although building permits are usually required), but may be required for large accessory structures.

A preapplication meeting between the developer and the planning staff is optional, but it can facilitate the application process. The developer presents the location and general scope of a project. Discussion includes its conformance to the goals and objectives of the community's comprehensive plan and policy and political issues that may affect the approval. This allows the developer to make appropriate adjustments before incurring an extended waiting time and the expense of engineering.

When a preliminary site plan is submitted, the municipal planner determines if it meets land development codes and ordinances relating to use, intensity, density, height, and setback requirements for proposed structures. (In some cases, it is appropriate to consider factors that might not be specified in the zoning ordinance, for example, the adequacy of buffers between incompatible uses and the connectivity between developments, although such items may be difficult to require if not explicitly specified.) The planner will determine whether it becomes necessary for the community or the developer to provide public improvements, such as road expansion, sewer line extensions, or even park development. If so, a decision should include whether such improvements, and the costs associated with them, are in the community's best interests. It may be appropriate to consider a site plan in the context of other community plans, such as those for downtown revitalization, neighborhoods, various types of overlay plans, or capital improvements. The reviewers may impose reasonable conditions based on other plans. If not specified in a municipal legal document, the reviewer must be prudent and not try to set a precedent.

An environmentally sustainable plan respects existing site characteristics and topography that may be the result of centuries of ecological evolution. Good planning generally means positioning buildings parallel to contours to minimize disruption and maintaining natural drainage patterns wherever possible. Large parking lots divided into landscaped sections minimize the extent of continuous impermeable surfaces. A site's storm water run-off should be accommodated within a property's boundaries, since most codes do not permit drainage patterns to be altered beyond the site. A storm water retention pond (to hold water) or detention pond (to detain and release water) will minimize problems after heavy rains or snowmelt and can provide a satisfying visual amenity. A landscape plan should use naturally occurring species. Nature's method of trial and error has shown which trees and planting materials are most suitable for development. Appropriate landscape features can take many years to develop as nature intended.

In most cases, the planner forwards proposed site plans to other departments where staff is asked to respond within a relatively short time span (two to three weeks) so the coordinating planning staff person can consolidate and coordinate the comments and prepare a full report for the applicant in a timely manner. This can be a complex task, with the following reviewing agencies pertinent in a typical city:

Building/Engineering Department
    Construction specifications
    Sewer and water
    Off-street parking
    Fences
    Soil erosion
    Sedimentation control
    Storm water retention
    Signs and outdoor advertising
    Landscape and screening
    Community Development Block Grant Department
    Housing assistance plan
    Fire Department
    Fire Department standards
    Historic District Commission
    Historic preservation
    Parks and Recreation Department
    Street tree escrow regulations
    Any park dedication

Planning Department
    Zoning ordinance
    Resolution regarding public improvements for new developments

Solid Waste Department
    Refuse

Transportation Department
    Traffic impact
    Street curb cuts

### EXERCISE 15
### JOLLY BURGER RESTAURANT PROPOSAL FOR RIVERTOWN

*A site plan has been submitted to the city of Rivertown for construction of a fast-food drive-through restaurant with limited indoor seating on a vacant site on Biltmore Boulevard. The proposal includes a building, 80 by 35 feet, designed to have up to eight employees working at one time.*

*Your assignment as community planner is to review the Jolly Burger preliminary proposal. List items that do not meet the zoning ordinance. Also identify design features that represent poor planning practice in general, whether or not part of the zoning ordinance. Special attention should be paid to the project's impact on adjacent properties, especially the*

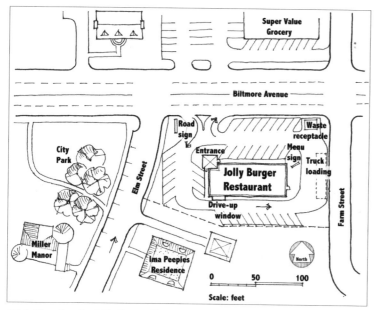

15.5. Site plan for Jolly Burger Restaurant

home of Ima Peeples, who lives just south of the site and who is president of the group, Concerned Citizens of Rivertown.

The following information was submitted along with the plan as shown:

- Name of applicant: Jolly Burger Corp.
- Name of property owner: Nestor More, 420 W. Church St., Rivertown
- Building: 1-story restaurant, 35 feet by 80 feet, at corner of Biltmore Avenue and Elm Street.
- Drives minimum 9 feet wide per lane, parking spaces at 60 degrees, dimensions as standard. Finish surface to be asphalt.
- There are no site easements.

You should review the Rivertown Zoning Ordinance, found in Appendix C.

## Planning Commission Approval

If a project successfully passes the staff's internal site review process and it is sufficiently complex or controversial, it may require more than administrative approval; it may require review by the planning commission. The commission examines it for technical requirements and solicits the community's input on the proposal. Part of this process is a public hearing where citizens are allowed to make comments for or against the proposal. A public hearing on

an application should be scheduled as soon as possible (e.g., 45 days after submission, with a final determination within 30 days from that time, although large cities or complex projects may take longer; this period is usually set by the state enabling law). The commission's determination may be approval, approval with specified conditions, or approval denied. Any decision other than full approval should be accompanied by a report on the specific reasons for the decision. The planning commission's determination may overrule the planning staff's recommendation if justifiable and appropriate reasons are given and clearly noted for the record.

In some communities the planning commission's approval is final; in other communities the commission's action serves as a recommendation to the municipal council, which has the final vote on approval. The council may vote counter to the commission's recommendation where justifiable reasons exist. However, typically neither the commission nor the council has the power to grant variances of ordinance requirements.

## Performance Guarantees

To save money, developers may attempt to renege on some aspects of an approved site plan—neglecting landscaping, sidewalks, utilities, roads, lighting, and other similar improvements. Zoning ordinances can be written to require that some form of performance guarantee be included before the final site plan is approved. The purpose of this guarantee is to assure compliance by the developer with terms contained in the site plan and that the developer adheres to the drawings prepared for approval. In essence, the developer's money is held in trust to be used by the local government if there is a default on the agreement. The amount of the performance guarantee is based on the costs associated with each necessary physical improvement. The performance guarantees may take the form of surety bonds, cash in an escrow account at a bank, or letter of credit. In some instances the property value becomes a base for a performance guarantee. When the developer satisfies the terms of the final site plan, he/she is released from the performance guarantee and, when actual money is involved, it is returned with the accrued interest.

After an approved project is under construction, a planner should make periodic inspections to determine whether the builder is complying with the approved site plan. For example, has the developer planted the required number of trees? As the work proceeds and concludes, as-built drawings are prepared to officially recognize any approved variations from the original plans. If a water or electrical utility line is not installed where located on the original drawings, the new location will be noted as part of the official record. If work is completed that does not follow the approved plans or approved changes, there needs to be an established enforcement policy to allow action to correct any deficiencies. Responsibility for such enforcement often is given to the building department, since they have inspectors and penalty procedures. Further action, if necessary, would be taken by the municipality's attorney. When the work has been completed satisfactorily, the municipal inspector issues a Certificate of Occupancy. This permits the property to be inhabited.

### Approval through Litigation

A disturbing trend being used increasingly by developers has been referred to as "approval through litigation." Developers have found that the normal site plan review and approval process can be circumvented to some degree by threatening legal action against local government agencies early in the process. Members of planning commissions, historic district commissions, zoning boards of appeal, and other review agencies can be threatened with a lawsuit if a proposal is not approved. Since developers typically have deeper pockets than commissioners, who serve in an unpaid volunteer capacity, it is difficult for these individuals to challenge this threat. They reluctantly may give approval rather than face a long legal battle. This maneuvering of the approval process represents a disturbing scenario, since planning commissioners sometimes are tempted to respond to the threat of litigation simply by conceding.

A similar back-door method of gaining approval is through a consent agreement. In this scenario, a developer finds a reason to sue the city for a reason relating to the approval process, and takes the city to court. In court, the judicial authority establishes an agreement between the parties, often a compromise between the positions presented by the developer and the city. This takes precedence over the normal approval process and results in the developer receiving concessions through what is essentially a judicial amendment to the comprehensive plan or zoning ordinance.

## Summary

The subdivision of land is the process of splitting a large land parcel into smaller parts. Subdivision through platting gives information regarding the proposed division of a property into land parcels. A plat map indicates the location of lot boundaries, property size, shape, easements, and utilities. They become part of the legally recorded deed description. In contrast, site condominiums subdivide land based on individual ownership of a limited portion of a site and common ownership of the remaining area. Site condominiums may be preferred by developers because of an easier approval process.

An individual site plan gives details on the development of a single parcel. The site plan package includes engineering drawings depicting the site after it is developed and identifies many site features. Site plan requirements often are contained in the community's zoning ordinance. Review of site plan proposals by the community planner ensures that a development meets the community's legal requirements and also that the property owner's rights are balanced with those of neighboring property owners and the community at large. When reviewing a site plan, the planner should consult with staff members from other departments in the municipality; they typically include engineering, public safety, public services, street and road, and utilities. Large sums of investment capital can be dependent on the outcome of the process, so review by local departments and agencies should be fair, predictable, and result in development that follows the provisions of the comprehensive plan and zoning ordinance. The developer also may be required to provide financial assurance that construction occurs as approved. When approval is granted, the project moves to the construction phase. Completion and formal inspection result in a Certificate of Occupancy that gives authority to occupy the property.

## 16

# CAPITAL IMPROVEMENTS PROGRAM AND LOCAL GOVERNMENT FINANCING

## The Capital Improvements Program and Budget

The implementation of a community's comprehensive plan includes a Capital Improvements Program (CIP), sometimes called a capital facilities program, capital outlay plan, or other similar term. The CIP sets the amount and timing of expenditures for public projects and thus plays a critical role in community development. While zoning controls growth, capital improvements serve to guide where growth is designed to happen. To use a common metaphor, zoning is the stick that regulates development; capital expenditures provide the carrot for desired development by influencing the direction, timing, and pattern of growth. A community's capital improvements program is one of the planner's most important tools because the CIP guides the allocation of financial resources, provides timing for major projects, and enables coordination between all of a community's departments and agencies. Over time, publicly owned facilities need major repair, replacement, or expansion. Upgrading a community's capital stock requires significant financial investment, and a capital improvements programming encourages wise choices. The CIP should be based on the community's goals and objectives as defined in its comprehensive plan.

A CIP committee, typically comprising the community's administrator, budget director, staff planners, planning commission, and others, uses revenue projections and computer programs to explore various future spending scenarios. These data give forecasts of population and economic growth and anticipated revenues to determine the most likely and desirable long-term capital expenditures. It is the responsibility of the CIP committee to clearly define criteria on which assessment and selection of capital projects will be based. Projects

submitted for consideration need to be accompanied by accurate data showing that they meet the criteria so municipal departments and community agencies can plan their budgets and then feel assured they will receive the necessary allocations from the city at the designated time. (Note that some agencies have budgets outside of the capital improvements program and may have access to and control of other financing.)

If properly managed, the CIP helps local governments function efficiently. The process can ease political decisionmaking by providing a rationale for approving or rejecting requests for immediate capital expenditures. The CIP allows for an appropriate lead-time for large purchases when bond referenda or bond sales are necessary. It generally covers a five-year span, but should be reviewed and updated each funding year because priorities can shift.

Well-chosen capital improvements can promote redevelopment of existing properties, as well as new development. For example, a community may rehabilitate its town hall as part of a new community center complex, restore a historically significant public building, or build a publicly financed conference center to accomplish recognized community goals.

Capital improvements planning should guide the construction, purchase, or replacement of capital items— buildings, roadways, bridges, parks, utilities, landfill, heavy equipment, or any other investment that has a high cost and a useful life of many years. In contrast, items such as small equipment purchases, small paving jobs, minor sewer extensions, and playground equipment are considered part of the operational budget and are financed from current revenues, as are salaries and supplies and day-today expenses of the community. For example, the expenses for a new fire station would be part of the long-range CIP; the firefighters' salaries are included in the operational budget. The allocation of expenditures for a small community is likely to be different from that of a large community in terms of scale and available revenue. In a large city the purchase of a fire truck may be considered an operational cost because a purchase of this size is rather common. In a small community, however, it may be the largest single expenditure made for a number of years and, as a result, would be considered part of the capital improvements budget.

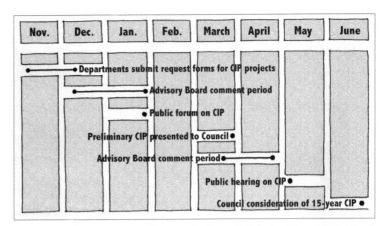

16.1. *Capital Improvements Program budget schedule for Chapel Hill, North Carolina.*[1]

Expenditures for capital improvements should be consistent with state and federal requirements, as well as locally approved policies and criteria. Guidelines typically may indicate CIP expenditures meet a minimum cost threshold (e.g., $50,000 to $100,000) depending on the size of the community; constitute physical improvements that are long lasting; exclude expenditures considered to be operational, maintenance, or recurring; and add to the value of the infrastructure of the community.

A CIP can improve a community's credit rating and help it to avoid sudden changes in debt service requirements. Investors in municipal bonds tend to look more favorably on communities that have a CIP. If bond financing is selected for a capital improvement project, the community may realize significant savings on interest.

The CIP process generally involves several steps, starting with the planning department conducting a full inventory of all properties, resources, and assets. This includes a review of previously approved projects to determine if they are completed and whether any funds are available for new purposes. Planning staff meet with municipal department heads and others who influence project selection and develop a policy framework that includes goals, objectives, and priorities. These will focus the process and ensure that projects are not developed in a vacuum. Department heads are asked to submit requests specifying justification for funding projects. To be most effective, the process of collecting requests and evaluating them should adhere to a schedule. A review committee evaluates project requests based on forecasted future demand, current facility inventory and maintenance costs, and the desired level of services.

Capital improvement projects involve substantial funding, which must sometimes be obtained from a number of sources. Most capital funding is earmarked for specific purposes and cannot be transferred from one project to another. For instance, funds raised by a community's park rehabilitation and development tax must be used for the purposes stated when the millage was approved by voters.

Voting to accept a budget does not mean that the governing body approves all of the projects it contains, only that the CIP represents a reasonable interpretation of upcoming needs for the community. The uncertainty inherent in some revenue sources may alter the implementation schedule of the CIP, affecting which projects, in what sequence, are selected for construction. For example, if a community is awarded a state grant for improvements to its water supply system, it may move the project to an advanced position on the CIP priority list.

### Funding Capital Improvement Projects

Taxes, reserves, bonds, private enterprise with vested interests, and donations are revenue-generating sources for capital improvement projects.

*Property taxes.* All private property has value; consequently, annual property taxes generate revenue. The tax on property is calculated in mills: a mill is defined as $1 of taxes per $1,000 of property valuation (e.g., one mill on a $100,000 property would be $100) applied to the net property value. Millages are voter-approved taxes specifically earmarked for a particular purpose. Enabling legislation allows millage rates to change with voter approval.

*Reserve (enterprise) funds.* After a community sets

funding levels for capital projects, increased costs could result in a budget shortfall. Fiscally responsible communities accumulate reserve, or "enterprise," funds in advance for capital requirements (and sometimes for day-to-day operations). Reserve fund dollars, however, can only be used for projects defined in the particular fund.

*General obligation bonds and revenue bonds.* Municipalities can sell bonds where purchasers are, in effect, lending money to the community. Bonds for capital improvement projects provide money in the short term, while the lenders benefit over time. Their investment is repaid from taxes, with interest, over a given number of years, with their earnings tax-exempt. The advantage of bonds is that they offer communities a way to raise money quickly; the disadvantage versus raising general revenues from taxes is the obligation to retire the debt with interest.

There are two forms of bonds. General obligation bonds, authorized by a variety of state statutes, are the most flexible funding source because they can be used for any capital project. They are generally financed by property taxes, meaning that the community pays interest and principal to retire the bond debt. Voter approval is required. The amount subject to the community's state-imposed debt limit, calculated based on its financial rating, is an indication of its ability to repay money. Communities that coordinate new bond issues with the retirement of previous bonds minimize the need for property tax increases.

Revenue bonds are bonds sold for revenue-producing projects, such as water and sewer systems or parking structures. Revenue bonds depend on user charges and other project-related income to cover their costs. Unlike general obligation bonds, revenue bonds are not included in state-imposed debt limits.

Of the three main sources of funds for capital projects—taxes, reserve funds, or bonds—paying with cash-on-hand from taxes is the most straightforward and surest method. However, it may penalize current taxpayers who are covering the upfront costs for projects that will provide benefit well into the future. For example, paying for a water treatment plant from current funding would heavily burden current taxpayers, even though future residents would benefit for decades. Using saved money from a reserve fund may be a more equitable method, especially for well-established communities whose plans are predictable. For many high-cost projects, however, it is appropriate to borrow against future revenues through

bond issues. Communities must borrow conservatively, though, because costs will be met by revenues coming from the project, and failure to meet revenue expectations can impact their credit rating.

Sometimes seeking funding through other sources is more prudent. State revenues returned to local government, such as taxes on vehicle weight and gasoline, if not restricted to expenditures for transportation services, may provide an alternative source of funds. In addition, urban redevelopment funds or environmental restoration funds may be available for specified projects. Communities may also apply for grants, loans, and other subsidies from state and federal agencies. Some federal funds are tied directly to a specific program; in other cases, they are discretionary (within certain guidelines). Generally, communities have no direct control over the amount of money received under these programs and restrictions may be applied by the funding agency. Federal funds have been declining since the 1980s due to a significant shift in federal policies, with recreation, transportation, and housing programs receiving smaller amounts. However, communities can take advantage of grants and loans for capital improvements projects when they become available.

Capital improvements that benefit particular properties, rather than the community as a whole, may be financed by special tax assessments, that is, taxing those who directly benefit—for example, an assessment on center city businesses for downtown sidewalk and street improvements. In another scenario, developers may voluntarily contribute funds or carry out an improvement themselves so a project can go forward.

## CIP and the Community Planning Process

The CIP implements elements of a community's comprehensive plan, and, in turn, the comprehensive plan should influence its capital improvements program. The comprehensive plan has an approximate 20-year time frame, and this offers a valuable perspective on the mid-range 5-year CIP.

Every type of land use has a different degree of need for capital facilities. For example, the drainage requirements of projects depend heavily on use and scale. A single-story, detached residence may require only 70 gallons per minute (gpm) of drainage flow, a three-story, multiunit structure may require 5,000 gpm; a shopping center requires even more capacity for storm drainage of a large paved area. Thus, land use policies and the CIP are linked. Communities should not expand or upgrade infrastructure just because the comprehensive plan calls for growth: they should have reasonable assurance that private development will follow the construction of public works. This is particularly true when plans aim at developing industrial uses, such as zoning large parcels of land for industrial parks, hoping this will attract industry. Zoning for industry bears no costs to the community, but physical facilities require services. If prospective businesses are not willing to pay for the installation of utilities, the community must do so, but it risks significant expenses if the expected revenues do not materialize.

The development of a CIP takes time. Communities have numerous budgets for their various departments and agencies and these must be coordinated with the CIP. Planners can help educate municipal department heads about the advantages of adhering to the CIP process, and council members must insist that the municipality's administrators share their budget information. Department heads must understand that money not spent in one fiscal year will be saved for the following year's projects, rather than being usurped for the general operating budget; money not expended is not "lost."

## EXERCISE 16
## MODIFY THE RIVERTOWN CAPITAL IMPROVEMENTS PROGRAM

*Rivertown Capital Improvements Program, 2011–2015*
*Proposed Improvements*
*The following capital improvements projects have been included in the current program:*

- *Rehabilitate the city hall building*
- *Purchase a new fire engine*
- *Install wireless high-speed Internet connections to the city's northwest quadrant*
- *Develop the riverfront area as a city park*
- *Construct a median on Biltmore Avenue*
- *Reconstruct one-lane bridge*

*From your knowledge of Rivertown (see Appendix A for information), select from the three projects listed below what you would consider to be a high-priority project to add to the city's current capital improvements program. Determine the most appropriate funding year(s) for your selected project and insert the amount as an added expense in the current CIP budget. (Costs for any major expenditure may be carried over two years.) Shift the funding for all projects in the revised CIP so expenditures are approximately the same in each of the five years covered. Finally, give a rationale for your recommendation.*

*Potential new projects*
*1. Pay for cleanup of Blinky's Salvage Yard site. Cost: $210,000.*
*2. Move city hall from its current location to the former railway station; sell the current city hall building and buy the railway station. (Note: If this item is selected, eliminate the item "Rehab City Hall"). Cost for the entire project (buy the station, sell the current city hall building, and move) is estimated at $380,000.*
*3. Provide funding to establish an incubator-style business development facility in a vacant building in industrial park district. Cost: $190,000.*

*(Note: For purposes of this exercise, assume the costs for these items are covered in full by the city, rather than through external funding.)*

| Project Funding Years | | | | | | |
| --- | --- | --- | --- | --- | --- | --- |
| | Year | | | | | |
| Item | 2011 | 2012 | 2013 | 2014 | 2015 | Total |
| Rehab city hall | $250,000 | 000 | 000 | 000 | 000 | $250,000 |
| Purchase fire engine | 000 | $190,000 | 000 | 000 | 000 | $190,000 |
| Install cable | $90,000 | $70,000 | 000 | 000 | 000 | $160,000 |
| Develop park | 000 | 000 | 000 | $75,000 | $200,000 | $275,000 |
| Construct median | $65,000 | 000 | 000 | 000 | 000 | $65,000 |
| Reconstruct bridge | 000 | 000 | $250,000 | $290,000 | 000 | $540,000 |
| Total Annual Cost | $405,000 | $260,000 | $250,000 | $365,000 | $200,000 | $1,480,000 |

## Local Government Financing

Federal and state governments provide many types of financial support to local communities, but the lion's share of funding comes from local revenues. Communities have power to effect change through their local tax structure and should always be concerned about costs versus benefits of new development. If the costs of publicly provided facilities are greater than any new tax revenue generated, then the rationale to encourage new development must be questioned.

Tax programs should be designed to achieve specific purposes. Is a tax intended to raise money for general revenues, or is it to give an incentive or disincentive? For example, a high tax on casino gambling would discourage potential operators to locate in the community. However, if job creation is the goal, then relatively low business-entity taxes would encourage these entrepreneurs. If the community's goal is not to discourage casinos, but to optimize tax revenues from this source, then an appropriate tax rate might be different—high enough to maximize revenues but low enough not to discourage investors.

### Impact Fees

Impact fees can mitigate expenses caused by new developments. These fees may pay for capital improvements not directly part of a project but impacted by it, such as schools, parks, road improvements, libraries, road upgrades and traffic signals, and additional water and sewer. Although sometimes controversial and legally tenuous, impact fees recognize the responsibility of developers to contribute to community costs as a result of a project. When developers subsequently pass the fees on to their customers, however, this becomes an indirect form of user fee or special assessment. Some states give broad discretion to local governments regarding impact fees, while others restrict how the money can be spent, for example, only for roads associated with a project.

Impact fees offer predictability to developers, who are aware of them from the outset, and to local officials and planners who can anticipate additional revenue and may thus be relieved of the need to raise taxes to cover development costs. Impact fees may help to pay for development, but they are collected only once, while the costs of public services are ongoing and must be considered annually. Although impact fees work well in affluent areas, they do not serve well in economically depressed areas because they discourage investment. Decisionmakers must weigh such factors when developing their community's comprehensive plan.

### *Spotlight on Impact Fees in Florida*[2]

Florida is a national leader in the use of impact fees, and its legislature passed CS/CS/SB 360, referred to as the "pay-as-you-grow" growth management law. The legislation was meant to ensure that roads, schools, and water are available to meet the needs of the state's many rapidly growing communities. Among its numerous provisions, the legislation created the Florida Impact Fee Review Task Force, a 15-member advisory body, to survey the use of impact fees as a method to finance local infrastructure. From 1993 through 2004, reported impact fee revenues totaled nearly $5.3 billion, with $3.5 billion going to counties and most of the remainder to municipalities. The task force concluded that many Florida communities could not provide sufficient infrastructure to accommodate rapid growth, especially the need for affordable housing throughout the state, and impact fees were necessary.

### Tax-Increment Financing

One of the most successful and useful financial programs for communities has been tax-increment financing (TIF). It can raise property tax revenues in districts where assessments have stagnated or decreased in value. TIF benefits economic development planning because it enables cities to create special districts and make public improvements within those districts for the purpose of generating private-sector development. TIF allows communities to borrow against future revenues to pay for present public improvements on the assumption that properly selected improvements will generate sufficient new tax revenues from private investment to cover initial costs. TIF takes no revenues from other sources; it relies on revenues newly created through its implementation.

Local governments establish a TIF district by first delineating boundaries. This is an important decision, since property owners within the district may gain significant benefits not available to owners outside the district. Next, the council establishes an organization to administer the TIF. Responsibility for this may be given to an existing agency or a new one created specifically for this purpose.

TIF program funding depends directly on the program's success in increasing property values within the district. First, a base (initial) year for the program is established. Property tax revenues collected in that year continue to be collected at this base rate each year and are paid into the municipality's general fund. Each of the taxing jurisdictions that are part of the district (e.g., municipal, county, school district) continues to receive its share of taxes based on the original assessed value, just as though the district had never been created.

After the base tax is allocated to the community's general fund, any increase in property tax revenues within the district (the "tax increment") is allocated only for projects within the district. These funds go into a special account that is controlled by the TIF's administrative agency. The increment can be used for public sector improvements, to stimulate private sector projects, or to retire bonds issued for development in the district. Redevelopment in a TIF district is usually required by statute to follow a comprehensive plan or subarea plan, to prevent assorted development efforts from creating a patchwork of unrelated projects.

If the TIF district is established in a stagnant or deteriorated area, why will property tax revenues be expected to rise? One reason is that, in general, property values tend to increase over time, so some of the increment can come from normal property appreciation. Additional increase may result from investments from incentive programs established and promoted by the community or from an external government agency. However, a successful TIF district coordinates the program's base year with a development project within the district that initiates a substantial increase in property taxes. Without new development, there will be minimal TIF increment funds and thus little chance to improve the district. The timing of a project to "prime the pump" is critical.

TIF revenue can be used for a variety of improvements, public and private, if they aid the economic growth of the district and there

is state enabling legislation. In most instances public improvements within a TIF district can be partially or wholly funded with TIF revenues. Projects should be compatible with the community's comprehensive plan and its goals and objectives for long-term growth. For example, if affordable housing is a goal, the TIF can help finance housing within the district through a private developer, as long as similar incentives would be available to any other development in the district and the support is distributed equitably. Rather than outright aid, indirect support may be given to private property owners or investors through a loan program for projects within the district. For example, a common program is providing low-interest revolving loans for facade improvements for downtown commercial structures. Agencies that administer TIF funds may buy and sell land in the public interest. Through this type of assistance, undesirable parcels can be purchased, consolidated and/or improved, and sold as marketable properties.

In the example shown below, the base assessment for the district is $12 million. The taxes collected from this base amount are static and made available for the community's general revenues each year. The tax-increment amount is the cumulative total from new construction each year (cumulative construction) added to the annual appreciation (property appreciation). The increase in assessed property value above the base valuation (this year's assessment increment) is multiplied by the millage rate (0.011) to derive the tax increment amount for the year (this year's tax increment). This tax increment amount can either be spent by the TIF agency for improvements in the district or retained for future use.

| Year | Base Assessment | New Construction | Cumulative Construction | Property Appreciation | New Assessment | Present Assessment Increment | Present Tax Increment | Cumulative Tax Increment |
|---|---|---|---|---|---|---|---|---|
| 20xx | $12,000,000 | | | | | | | |
| 20xx | $12,000,000 | $500,000 | $500,000 | $360,000 | $12,860,000 | $860,000 | $9,460 | $9,460 |
| 20xx | $12,000,000 | $700,000 | $1,215,000 | $385,800 | $13,600,800 | $1,600,800 | $17,609 | $27,069 |
| 20xx | $12,000,000 | $1,000,000 | $2,251,450 | $408,024 | $14,659,474 | $2,659,474 | $29,254 | $56,323 |
| | **Assumptions:** | | | | | | | |
| | Projected construction: Year 1, $500,000; Year 2, $700,000; Year 3, $1 million | | | | | | | |
| | Cumulative new construction = all previous construction + new construction | | | | | | | |
| | Appreciation = increase in value over last year's assessment (assume 3 percent per year) | | | | | | | |
| | Current assessment = base assessment + cumulative construction + current year's appreciation | | | | | | | |
| | Millage: 1 mil = $1 per $1,000 of property value; assume 11 mils (.011) rate for example | | | | | | | |

*16.2. TIF calculation example*

## EXERCISE 17

### TAX-INCREMENT FINANCING CALCULATION
### FOR RIVERTOWN

*Rivertown has adopted a tax-increment financing district. Calculate the annual and cumulative tax-increment amounts for the next four years, using the following assumptions:*

    *1. The base property assessment in the district is $20 million.*

    *2. Property appreciation will be 3 percent per year.*

    *3. New construction is expected to be zero in the base year (year 0); $800,000 in year 1; $1,000,000 in year 2; and $2,500,000 in year 3.*

    *4. The millage rate is 10 mills.*

As noted, TIF programs can be a successful method to generate revenues for redevelopment in areas not otherwise able to attract investment without depleting general revenues. Developers view TIF as a way for a city to make a commitment to redevelopment through public improvements; citizens see it as a way to fund redevelopment from taxes collected in the redevelopment district without raising their taxes. Appointed individuals can control large funds developed through TIF capture, so elected officials need to have regular oversight since commitments are backed by the full faith and credit of the municipality. A TIF program also can lead to intrajurisdictional conflict. For example, a local school board may feel its rightful local property tax share is directed inappropriately.

When first introduced in the 1950s, tax-increment financing was limited to districts that did not have good access to capital from the private sector because of their poor condition. Since then, the program has been a successful financing method for many communities, and by the 1980s was broadened so that any area that needed development could be designated as a TIF district. The use of economic development goals as a basis for establishing a new TIF district may even extend to undeveloped farmland. In 2007, 49 states (Arizona is the exception) and the District of Columbia allowed some form of TIF and thousands of TIF districts are being used as a regular tool of economic development.

### Tax Abatements

Another form of development funding is tax abatement, which provides tax relief for a certain number of years to encourage businesses to build new or enlarged facilities. When the abatement period expires, the community benefits and taxes are assessed at their unabated value. Tax abatements give communities a means to encourage new investment in deteriorated areas and to compete for new businesses.

However, community planners and others should carefully consider the value of a tax abatement program in terms of cost/benefit. An abatement means giving away tax revenue for a period of time, and while businesses are happy to accept the tax relief, it may not be an important part of a decision on where to locate. It has been shown that businesses typically make location decisions primarily on market characteristics and potential profitability rather than taxes. Therefore, the best way to attract a business is to provide a good location and potential market for its goods. Also, at the end of the abatement period companies can threaten to leave a community for another location that will offer new tax abatements unless the first community extends the abatement period.

Tax abatement can actually have a negative effect since it burdens existing businesses that pay their full share of taxes, as illustrated by the views of Phil Gordon, mayor of Phoenix, Arizona, who wrote to the city's retail community in 2004: "The use of tax incentives to lure retailers to one city rather than another has resulted in inequities for existing retail businesses and a significant reduction in funds for vital public services. Ultimately, it does not generate wealth and does not produce good jobs. . . . And we do it at the expense of our existing retailers, our taxpayers and our neighboring cities. Giving away future taxes to retailers who will then compete against existing retailers in the same city isn't fair."[3]

### Site-Value Taxation

Among the problems cities have been trying to solve since the exodus of urban dwellers to the suburbs is lost revenues from vacant land that, in large cities, can amount to hundreds or thousands of parcels. The current property tax system rewards those who neglect their properties because it lowers their taxes; conversely, improvements to a property bring a larger tax bill. The question is how a city can reward those who build on or improve their property, rather than penalize them.

Site-value (two-tier), or land-value, taxation, a solution suggested in the nineteenth century, is designed to separate tax millage rates for land and any buildings on the land.[4] The rate on the land is higher to discourage speculators from holding a parcel for long periods of time; the rate on buildings (or improvements) is set lower to encourage better uses of valuable real estate and make development more attractive to the landowner. Site-value taxation is based on the principle that geographic location determines the value of the land and should therefore be the basis for property tax. Land located near a desirable feature would be more valuable than land without such a good location, whether or not it is developed. This would encourage people to develop idle land or improve underutilized land. Communities that enact a site-value taxation program must consider the boundaries of the taxation district carefully. It is important to only include areas where development is desired and exclude areas planned for farmland or open space.

### Fiscal Impact Analysis

How do communities know whether new development or capital improvements will provide additional revenues or result in a revenue deficit? If a project generates more revenue than it costs, its net fiscal impact will ease local financial burdens. If its service costs exceed revenues, it will necessitate a rise in taxes or a reduction in community services. Fiscal impact analysis is the tool planners use to evaluate this. It can determine what land uses benefit a community most—for example, whether a parcel should be designated or promoted for industrial use, retail business, or housing. Generally, commercial, industrial, and agricultural land uses provide more financial benefit than housing, since they need fewer services, such as schools and recreation. However, since workers need housing, new business development typically results in a demand for new residences, which can be an economic burden on communities. For example, a study from Dutchess County, New York, found that residential land cost an average of $1.25 in public expenditures for every dollar in tax revenue it created, and consequently resulted in a net loss. In comparison, agricultural land required an average of only 35¢ in expenditure per dollar of revenue.[5]

The best rationale for encouraging farmland to be converted to housing is that residences will attract growth as a positive revenue producer. It is generally favorable to encourage higher density levels in new developments because the cost of infrastructure is less

per structure. Analyses may show a large development with multiple uses is most beneficial. This cumulative approach optimizes the potential impact over time.

A number of methods are used to forecast the fiscal impact of operating costs and revenues. The most common is based on per capita values: it divides the existing total local budget by the existing population (or number of housing units) to calculate a per capita (or per household) cost for budgeted services. Based on any projected population change, expected new revenues are compared against per capita costs after development to determine if there is a positive or negative benefit to the development. (Excluded from this analysis are real property tax revenues, which are usually calculated separately.)

There are inherent problems with fiscal impact analysis that planners should recognize. Governments are not unique entities, and their functions often overlap. It is difficult to separate the fiscal impact of a project for a community from its impact on adjacent communities, townships, or counties. Similarly, the costs to provide services such as police or sheriff, 911, parks, utilities, and school districts are often shared between jurisdictions. An impact analysis that does not recognize these overlaps may be overly simplistic, ultimately inaccurate in its conclusions, and may lead to inappropriate recommendations.

### Privatization of Urban Services

Many communities use private contracting firms to do work that previously was the responsibility of the municipality. The goal of privatization is to save money and serve the public more efficiently. Privatized services typically include waste removal, vehicle maintenance, bus operations, day care, and recreation facilities. In some instances, privatization has been productive; in others, it has been less successful. Privatization encourages competition, as contractors bid for jobs, and although this can save money, it may lead to provision of substandard services by cut-rate contractors.

Another problem with privatization is that private contractors may not offer employees the same level of compensation, security, and benefits that municipal employees enjoy. Communities need to recognize the potential for resulting disruption from adjusting retirement plans, seniority rules, job classifications, and pay scales accordingly.

Indianapolis is a city that has explored the use of

privatized services. The city's garage mechanics union was invited to bid against private contractors in 1996. The union won the competitive contract and thinned its management ranks by 75 percent to cut costs, let its employees share in any profits from the new arrangement, and increased profits by absorbing the work of retiring employees. The city got a workforce that was much more efficient. The mayor at the time, Stephen Goldsmith, said, "I don't think privatization is particularly valuable as an end in itself. That's why in Indianapolis we prefer to say we've introduced competition rather than privatization."[6]

Sandy Springs, an unincorporated area near Atlanta, offers another example. In 2005, its residents voted in favor of cityhood, making it the seventh largest city in the state. At its incorporation, a governor's commission opted to outsource all city services except police, fire, and 911 emergency services to a private contractor. After an intensive proposal and interview process, the city selected a firm to provide services, including administration, finance, tax collection, personnel, community development and planning, parks and recreation, and engineering and traffic. The contractor then subcontracted with other firms as necessary.

The city saved an estimated $20 million per year on staffing and capital outlay compared to other traditional city management. Planning approvals that took eight weeks to process under the old system were completed in an average of three weeks. Through this community's unique public-private partnership with its city council, Sandy Springs has become a privatized city in most of its functions.

*16.3. Sandy Springs, Georgia, near Atlanta, outsourced its city services in 2005*

## Privatized Communities

One of the most significant recent trends is the privatization of residential communities, built as unincorporated entities and not subject to the same rules and regulations as cities and villages. In a privatized community a developer can establish a set of private services to replace what would normally be public services. Under privatization, property covenants replace legislative ordinances, ownership fees are a form of taxing, and, most critically, the municipal council is supplanted by a development association, which relieves the community of requirements for open meetings, public input, or representative government. Participation in community decisionmaking is based on ownership, rather than residency. In other words, the idea of "one person, one vote," a fundamental basis of American democracy, is replaced by "one dollar, one vote."

There are over 150,000 private-enterprise governments of some type in the United States. Joel Garreau looked carefully at this phenomenon in his book, *Edge City*, and concluded that "These shadow governments have become the most numerous, ubiquitous, and largest form of local government in America today. . . . The privatization of government in America is the most important thing that's happening, but we're not focused on it. We haven't thought of it as government yet."[7]

## Summary

It takes money to administer a municipal government. Communities have two primary funding obligations. The first is the general operation of the municipality, which includes basic services. Second are major projects, such as infrastructure construction and repair and the purchase of big-ticket items that are too costly to be included in a department's annual budget. For these items a capital improvements program is the financial tool used to make decisions. Although the CIP is not supported by the force of law as is zoning, it is just as significant in guiding development.

A capital improvements program and its corresponding budget are considered important tools to implement a community's comprehensive plan. The CIP guides the purchase or replacement of major capital items such as roads and streets, public buildings, parks, utilities, heavy equipment, or any high-cost item expected to be purchased in the foreseeable future. Although expenses may need to be paid over several years, expenditures should be reviewed annually.

Capital improvements projects can be funded through available cash, the use of funds set aside for future expenses, or by selling bonds. The most significant source for local revenues comes from collection of property taxes. Other sources include state and federal grants, fines and fees, income from local government property, and a variety of alternative tax programs, such as tax-increment financing. Some communities charge impact fees to cover capital improvements necessary for a new development. Shifting the financial burden to private developers by applying impact fees can relieve the community of a portion of development costs, but often this cost is simply passed on to the end user.

Other programs give local officials alternative financing strategies. Tax abatements give temporary tax relief for new businesses; fiscal impact analysis considers the overall impact of local expenditures; privatization of government services can bring financial efficiencies.

# APPENDIX A: THE RIVERTOWN SIMULATION

The fictional city of Rivertown was created for the purpose of teaching planning principles. It includes a rich environment with distinctive features of interest to a community planner. Because it presents detailed information on downtown buildings and fictional citizens, it is especially useful in creating exercises relating to downtown revitalization. It employs the teaching concept of "problem-based learning," based on the idea that we learn best not simply by acquiring information but by solving tangible problems that require the understanding and use of that information.

We have adopted Rivertown as our home community for purposes of the planning exercises given throughout the book. The exercises can serve as assignments in planning classes. They are based on a course on downtown revitalization taught at Eastern Michigan University, with each week of class time representing a year in the life of the community, allowing 12 to 15 "years" to pass over the course of a semester. Students can become active members of the Rivertown community, adopting roles of mayor, city council members, merchants, residents, and a young city planner. Students can see the long-term impacts of their decisions over the span of the course. The exercises are designed to be as demanding as the instructor wishes. They are even more productive learning opportunities when issues are discussed with visiting practitioners who provide feedback from their professional experiences. In addition to the included exercises, instructors are encouraged to use Rivertown to create their own exercises and discussion topics.

Online resources facilitate and enhance the simulation, with Web pages that provide background information on relevant topics that include case studies. These Web pages can be found by following links to the Rivertown Simulation at: www.cityhall-commons.com. To discuss how to use the simulation or for more information, instructors may contact Norman Tyler by email (ntyler@emich.edu).

## City History

Rivertown was an important stop for settlers heading across the Appalachian Mountains into the "western territories." Many historic farmsteads surround the city and merchants provided goods for the farmers. This resulted in considerable wealth for both farmers and businessmen in the mid-nineteenth century. Some of the older houses were elaborately decorated with ornate woodworking throughout their interiors. Outstanding is the Biltmore mansion, built by the family of the town's founder, Amos Biltmore. Located on the north side of Biltmore Avenue, it sits on a parcel in the center of the city. Rivertown also was home to Benjamin Cartwright, a local merchant who served for a short time as the state's governor. A historic plaque on a vacant site along Biltmore Avenue marks his birthplace. Rivertown was incorporated as a village in 1845, as a city in 1876. Over the years, it evolved into a diverse community with a mixture of housing and employment while retaining its "small-town" character.

## Layout of the City

Rivertown has a variety of neighborhoods and districts; see Fig. AA.1; a larger color map of the city is in Appendix D. Areas with significant character include the city's nineteenth-century downtown district along the river, a twentieth century commercial district along east Biltmore Avenue, an industrial park along the river on the east side bisected by railroad tracks. A middle/upper-class residential area west and northwest of downtown with larger lots has primarily owner-occupied housing. The section of the city east of the Old Biltmore Farm has smaller houses and numerous multi-family and rental units. Apartment buildings on the eastern edge include many small efficiency and one-bedroom living units with affordable rents. Elly's Mobile Home Park, located on Station Street just inside the city's southern boundary, provides housing largely for low-income families. Many of its residents were formerly transient farm workers, but now have located permanently in Rivertown. Reliance College, a small liberal arts college established in 1956 that enrolls resident and commuter students, is in the northwest corner of the city. Upper income residential neighborhoods are River Heights in the northeast corner of the city, and the northern shore of Bitterroot Lake just outside the city boundary in River Township.

Rivertown's major road is Biltmore Avenue, a four-lane state route running east/west through the center of the city. Both local and through traffic contribute to the avenue's significant traffic

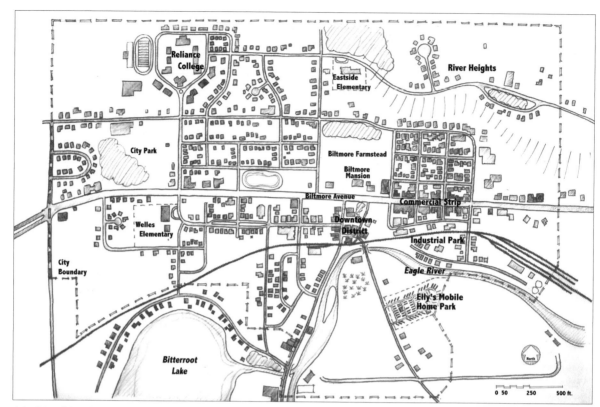

*AA.1 Map of City of Rivertown*

congestion. The downtown has two one-way streets, Elm Street and a portion of River Street; all other streets are two-way. Most residents coming downtown drive so traffic is congested on the narrow streets. Public parking is only on-street, and the older downtown district has no public parking lot.

## Buildings in the Downtown District

Rivertown's older downtown district was first built from the 1840s to the 1890s. The first buildings were constructed of wood, and in 1868 a fire destroyed many of the buildings on the west side of River Street except for the Dawson Law Building and the structure adjacent to it. After the fire, the damaged structures were rebuilt in brick. The downtown has a mix of healthy retail, struggling businesses, and vacancies; see Fig's. AA.2 and AA.3. The district shows signs of long-term deterioration and is in need of revitalization. A detailed description of the buildings in this district follows.

The First National Bank, at the corner of Station and River Streets, in the center of the downtown, has been a stabilizing influence in this district. Originally built by the bank as its headquarters, the building has been faithfully maintained inside and out since opening in 1912. Its interior marble detailing and elaborate bronze teller windows are in immaculate condition. The bank's board of directors is concerned about the condition of adjacent properties, which are bad for their image, especially the Rivertown Hotel.

The Rivertown Railway station is a focal point for the downtown district. Its durable masonry construction and slate roof are in good condition, though its exterior has received little regular maintenance. The building is no longer used as a station; the lower floor currently houses an antiques store; the rest of the structure is vacant.

The Rivertown Hotel was once a well-known building where many important visitors in the region stayed. Now sparsely tenanted, its inexpensive rooms on the second floor are rented by the night or week. There is a small coffee shop on the ground floor. The condition of the structure is marginally safe. Many of the upper floor windows are boarded and there is obvious structural damage. The extent of work necessary to rehabilitate the structure for rooms or apartments on the upper floors and commercial space on the ground floor is not known.

Miller Manor, situated behind the hotel, is a large Victorian-era home that has been converted to a single-room-occupancy rooming house. It needs exterior and interior repairs.

The Dawson Law Building is a well-maintained office building considered an architectural gem of the downtown. It has been used for law offices since it was built in the early nineteenth century. There have been few alterations, so it is one of the best preserved old buildings in the downtown area. The attorneys who currently lease the building plan to stay as long as the structure is properly maintained, but are concerned about the deteriorated

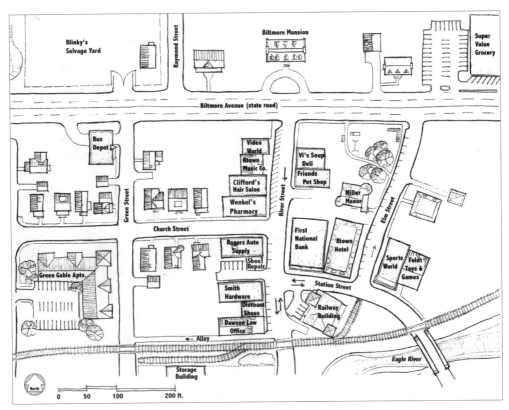

AA.2 *The downtown district*

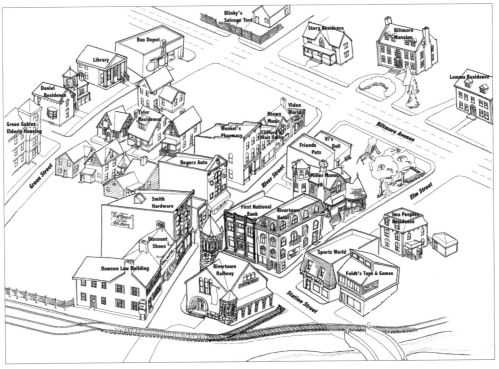

AA.3 *Perspective of the downtown district*

condition of the adjacent Discount Shoes building, which had a fire a few years ago and is now vacant. The structure is in very poor condition, with significant water damage around the roof and pigeons roosting in the attic. The second floor is unstable, a condition that should have been addressed by the city's building inspector, and the building is considered unsafe. The building's owner, Nipsy More, has indicated he will accept offers for its purchase.

The Smith Hardware Building has had a longstanding hardware business on the ground floor. The current tenant would like to remain in the space. The second floor has rented apartments. The third floor is vacant and needs roof repairs to protect the interior.

The small shoe repair building, located north of Smith Hardware on River Street, is a one-room shop of brick construction with no distinguishing characteristics built in the 1940s by an immigrant shoe repairman. Next door is the Webber Building. Rogers Auto Supply, a long-standing downtown business, occupies the ground floor. The second floor is a large open space used for storage; the third floor was used until the 1950s as a fraternal organization's meeting hall.

The Eagle Sports World building on Station Street has had many tenants over its history and is currently owned by businessman Nipsy More. The vacant second floor has been used for storage. Both the mansard-style front and first floor display windows were added in the 1970s. Next to it is Feldt's Toys and Games,

owned by Mr. Feldt, who enjoys sharing his passion for games with neighborhood kids. Built with plywood siding, the building is kept in good condition with normal maintenance.

Other businesses downtown on River Street include Wenkel's Pharmacy, Clifford's hair salon, Rivertown Music Company, Video World, Vi's Deli, and Friends Pet Shop.

## Other Districts

A second commercial district on east Biltmore Avenue includes most of Rivertown's remaining commercial establishments. Its mostly nondescript structures date from the 1930s and '40s. The vacant Bijou Theater is the only structure to be considered historically significant. The current city hall is in an undistinguished 1940s concrete block building in the center of the commercial district along east Biltmore Avenue. Also located in this district are the Public Safety Building, with the police and fire departments; and the downtown post office.

An industrial park along the railroad tracks and river on the east side of the city includes older brick and concrete block structures, most of them in use by various small businesses. They contain warehousing, small manufacturing, contractors businesses, and similar enterprises. The largest building, now vacant, was constructed in 1852 as the Eagle Stove Works.

Reliance College is a small liberal arts college located in the northwest corner of the city. It is best known for programs in

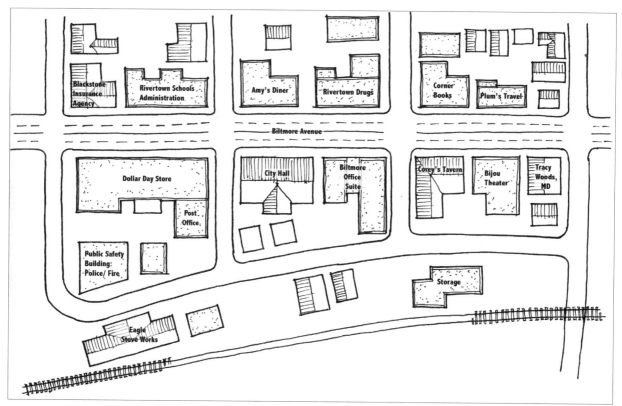

*AA.4 Biltmore Avenue secondary commercial district*

computer science, urban and regional planning, and Geographic Information Systems (GIS), and the campus has a surprising number of high-tech facilities. Its intermural football and conference basketball teams draw small crowds. The college's other public activities—its theater, bookstore, and library—attract primarily students; few local residents utilize the college facilities. Students live either in campus dormitories or medium- to high-density apartments on or near campus. They travel to Falls Mall in Erie Falls, a larger town 15 miles to the east, to shop and for entertainment rather than going to Rivertown's downtown.

Rivertown's middle school and high school students attend classes at a new educational complex one mile west of the city. They arrive either by school bus or by private automobile. Two elementary schools are located within the city. Eastside Elementary, the oldest school in the city, and Welles Elementary, located on the west side, are over capacity.

Rivertown's public facilities are located throughout the city. A large city park and recreation center is located on Park Street at Biltmore Avenue. It is used by Welles Elementary School for regular outdoor activities on school days and by many local residents on weekends and summer days. A number of small parks are located throughout the city, including a downtown park at the corner of Biltmore Avenue and Elm Street. One block west of the downtown, Green Gables Apartments was built with federal funding as senior citizen housing in the 1980s. It has a long waiting list.

Rivertown has no regular public transportation system, but has two small buses available on-call for residents. The bus depot still services an inter-city bus line; three buses a day provide connections throughout the region. The railroad no longer has any passenger service, but a few freight trains travel through the city each day. The Eagle River Railroad owns the train station and intends to retain the main line and its right-of-way for the foreseeable future.

The slow-flowing Eagle River is a prime amenity. It is deep enough for small watercraft and excellent for fishing. A large portion of the older downtown district is in the 100-year floodplain area. Bitterroot Lake feeds into Eagle River. The southern portion of the lake has thick clusters of freshwater algae during the summer and a muddy shoreline. The northern shore has a pleasing shoreline with sandy beaches.

## Environmental Concerns

There are some areas of environmental concern in the Rivertown community. The railroad right-of-way may be contaminated from its many decades of use by dirty steam engines. Tooster's Swamp, located within the south bend of the river, is a small wetland area with abundant native flora and fauna, but its standing water is a breeding place for mosquitoes. This brings complaints from residents. Blinky's Salvage Yard, just west of the Old Biltmore Farm and adjacent to city-owned spring-fed Walden Pond, is suspected of having contaminated soils. This brownfield site is owned by Herman "Blinky" Bunkmeister. He is no longer adding new materials but has not removed existing salvage.

## The People of Rivertown

*A number of influential people living or working in Rivertown are described below. They are presented to give a perspective on Rivertown's society, specifically as it relates to the downtown district.*

Burnham Daniel, recently retired from a position with the Chicago Planning Department, is the city's planning director. He lives in Erie Falls and works part-time for the city. He delegates daily planning responsibilities to an associate in an entry-level "Planner 1" position. You assume this role of his assistant.

Delores Lemma, known as Aunt Dee, has been an active member of the Rivertown City Council for four terms. She has been reelected every two years because she is popular with residents in her ward, which encompasses the downtown district and a portion of the west side residential area. She is a strong proponent of social programs and supports a shelter for the homeless. The project died for lack of funding.

Clara Story is descended from one of the early families in Rivertown, the Biltmores. She lives in a Gothic Revival house next door to the Biltmore Mansion. Ms. Story has long been involved with the Rivertown Historical Society, a non-profit educational organization that collects artifacts for a planned local museum. Its primary goal is to encourage historic districts in selected areas of the city, especially in the older downtown area.

Nipsy More, a local businessman and property owner, lives out of town but owns the Eagle Sports World store on Station Street and has operated this marginally profitable business for a number of years. He also owns the Discount Shoes building, vacant since a fire. He also owns an unimproved residential property on the south side of the Eagle River.

Ima Peeples lives with her 25 year-old daughter, Erma, in a Second Empire style house behind the Eagle Sports World store. She leads the Concerned Citizens of Rivertown, a loosely structured advocacy group that is irregularly active. Issues she is concerned about include parking on the street in front of the Peeples' house; trucks servicing nearby downtown businesses, especially the Sports World store; and expansion of downtown businesses. The group lobbied for the construction of a small park at the corner of Biltmore Avenue and Elm Street, which was built across the street from the Peeples' house.

Norman Tyler, manager of the First National Bank of Rivertown, the oldest and largest bank in the area, has lived in town all his life and is knowledgeable about the city's history and its current events. (In his non-fictional role, Mr. Tyler is author of this book and coordinates the online Rivertown simulation.)

Local organizations are active in community affairs. The Rivertown Merchants Association has promoted businesses throughout the city. Its activities include sales promotions, festivals, and other attempts to attract new business. The Eagle River Arts Alliance sponsors a successful arts and crafts festival each August on the island in the Eagle River, featuring a raft ride to the island. The First Methodist Church, three blocks west of the downtown, has run a breakfast program for needy residents and the homeless, staffed by community volunteers, since 1967.

# APPENDIX B: RIVERTOWN COMPREHENSIVE PLAN (ABRIDGED)

*Note: The following is an abridged comprehensive plan intended as a reference for the exercises in the text and is based on the comprehensive plan prepared by LSL Planning, Inc. for Chelsea, Michigan. This abridged version follows the format of a typical full comprehensive plan, but focuses on land use. Sections describing social and economic aspects of the comprehensive plan have not been included.*

## CITY OF RIVERTOWN COMPREHENSIVE PLAN

Adopted by Rivertown City Council, September 1, 2010

Table of Contents
    Chapter 1: Introduction
    Chapter 2: Demographics and Trends
    Chapter 3: Land Use

## Section 1: Introduction

### Description and Purpose of Comprehensive Plan

Rivertown's comprehensive plan is a guide for growth over the next twenty years. The plan was developed through evaluation of data, trends, the vision local citizens have for their community, and alternatives for development. The plan's underlying purpose is to guide the community's physical, social and economic growth. It addresses the intensity and arrangement of land uses for the benefit of the community overall, identifies areas that should generally remain the same, and provides a guide for areas that are planned to change through new development or redevelopment. In addition, the plan provides a framework for municipal facilities to support the desired land use pattern—streets, pathways, parks, utilities, and other city infrastructure. A link between land use and those facilities helps ensure wise allocation of public investments in capital improvements.

The plan provides policies and actions for community leaders to consider. This plan is a "living" document, and as such the planning commission should review the plan on an annual basis. This review should focus on the existing goals, evaluating which have been met and those that have not, and culminate in an implementation strategy. Some recommendations may require changes or amendments to the comprehensive plan, zoning ordinance, and/or the capital improvements program. Other changes can occur through a combination of municipal and private investments—new roads, pathways, park improvements, homes, stores, and industry.

## Section 2: Demographics and Trends

### Population Characteristics

A small Midwestern town, Rivertown has a population of 5,200 plus 900 students who attend Reliance College. Including farm families living on the city's periphery. The total population of the Rivertown area comes to about 7,500. The city currently has 530 single-family houses, 28 multi-family structures, and 39 commercial properties.

Many of the city's residents commute to other cities for work. The greatest number travel 15 miles east to Erie Falls, which has a population of 20,000. Residents also travel to Erie Falls to shop at Falls Mall, the largest shopping center in the region.

*Population Projection* According to the Regional Council of Government's 2030 Regional Development Forecast, the City of Rivertown's population is projected to increase by 38 percent between 2010 and 2030. The forecast uses a multitiered system of regional, district, and small area forecasts to predict housing, population, and employment for the region. The process takes into consideration land coverage and plans including current and future land use, sewer service areas, soils suitability, recreation and public lands, and flood-prone areas. Many of the surrounding townships are expected to grow at an even greater rate.

*Number and Size of Households* The number of households in the Rivertown area has continued to grow with a corresponding growth in population. The number of households has increased from 1,750 in 2000 to 1,990 in 2010. A decrease in the average household size mirrors national and statewide trends. The trend can be attributed to a number of factors including an increase in single-headed households and couples without children. The growing number of families choosing to have fewer children than past generations and the aging "baby boom" generation create more empty-nester homes, and a growing number of senior-oriented housing developments.

*Population Age* Two demographic groups are strongly represented. The large number of elderly living in the city are primarily older farm families who have moved into the city limits. The second group is the college student population. Students live primarily near the campus of Reliance College.

### Housing Characteristics
The majority of housing units were constructed before 1960. Other housing units, especially in the River Heights area, were constructed during growth spurts in the 1980s and 1990s. The median housing value for Rivertown is $159,800 (Census 2000). In 2000, the majority of housing units in Rivertown were single-family detached homes. In comparison to 1990, the percentage of detached homes has decreased in the wake of more duplex and multiple-family home construction. This trend reflects the changing household sizes and composition.

The majority of homes in Rivertown are owner-occupied. Vacancy rates remain low, while a slight decrease in owner-occupied housing and an increase in renter-occupied units occurred between 2000 and 2010.

### Local Economics
The median household income in Rivertown was $49,132 in 2010; River County's median household income was $51,990 and the state's median household income was $44,667. The surrounding townships share a relatively high household income. Only 4 percent of families in Rivertown reported incomes below the poverty level in 2000, as established through the Federal Office of Management and Budget. This is lower than River County's average of 10 percent and the state's average of 7.4 percent.

*Occupation and Industry* Management and professional jobs account for 27 percent of Rivertown's employment. Sales and office represent 20 percent of jobs, followed by service occupations (13 percent), construction and maintenance (8 percent), and production and transportation (6 percent). Education, largely at the college, accounts for 8 percent; 6 percent of the working population are currently unemployed. Much of Rivertown's history is based on farming, and 12 percent of its current residents have retained this occupation.

### Key Findings and Issues
Population and household growth in the city and surrounding area is expected to continue. With additional population come greater demands on community facilities, traffic congestion, and other impacts that can alter the character of the area. Careful planning and coordination with adjacent townships is needed to ensure that this growth occurs at a balanced rate and in a manner that respects the inherent qualities of the city.

As household compositions evolve, as the population ages, and as household sizes decrease, housing needs will change in the city. The typical single-family home and lot may not meet all these needs, and consideration should be given to providing a variety of housing options. The mature housing stock will continue to be an asset for the city because of the neighborhood character it provides, but will be a challenge in terms of continuing maintenance. In order to protect the character and value of these areas, renovations, expansions, and other reinvestment will need to be supported.

As newer neighborhoods have developed on the outer edges of the city, neighborhood connectivity has diminished. Where the opportunity for new development exists, stronger links between existing and new neighborhoods should be encouraged.

There is still potential for additional commercial and office development and redevelopment as the population grows and market demands increase. Consideration should be given to establishing design principles for future projects, and efforts taken to ensure that appropriate commercial establishments locate within the existing commercial districts. Future efforts should promote these districts, which currently have significant deterioration.

The Rivertown area has attractive natural features. The Eagle River is clean and provides good fishing. Nearby Bitterroot Lake is a motor-free 20-acre lake suitable for fishing and water sports. Walden Pond, located in the center of the city, is a spring-fed pond; however, contamination from an adjacent salvage yard is suspected.

The city currently provides minimal public transportation. Two on-call vans serve the entire city. They are available for anyone at a nominal cost throughout the day and evening, six days a week.

## Section 3: Land Use

This chapter outlines existing conditions, goals, and future recommendations for land use. It begins with a community planning framework that establishes an overall perspective of what Rivertown wants to achieve. Goal statements provide a more specific approach to realize the stated vision. Finally, each part provides detailed recommendations and management strategies to achieve these goals.

### Existing Land Use
*Existing Land Uses* The following summarizes the existing land uses within the city; the categories correspond to the Existing Land Use Map.

*Low Density Residential (LDR).* Low density residential, primarily single-family homes, comprises the largest land use area. Densities vary from one neighborhood to another, but the neighborhoods generally contain small- to moderate-sized lots typical of traditional Midwest cities. Most existing neighborhoods are integrated into Rivertown's urban fabric through grid pattern streets and a connected sidewalk system. Older housing stock reflects traditional neighborhood design elements. Homes display prominent front porches, varying architectural styles and details, recessed or detached garages, and shallow setbacks. These features have contributed to an intimate and admired neighborhood experience.

*Multiple Family Residential (MFR).* A variety of multiple family dwellings include apartment buildings, attached townhouses,

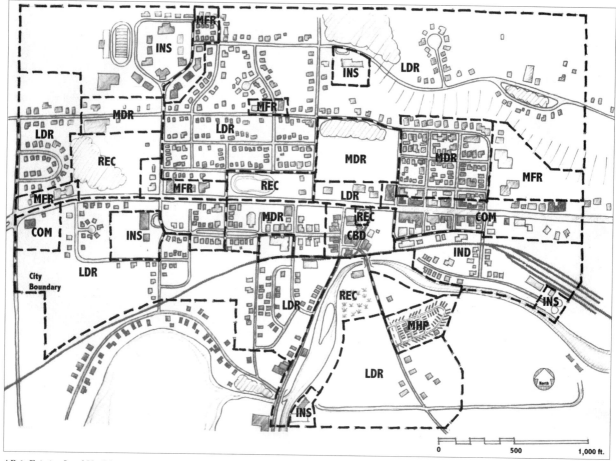

*AB.1. Existing Land Use Map*

two-story apartment complexes, a large new senior housing complex, and a limited number of second-story apartments above commercial buildings within the central business district. The existing mixture of multiple family unit types offers a variety of housing options for residents.

*Central Business District (CBD).* The nineteenth century downtown district near the Eagle River and railroad line is characteristic of small, historic downtowns with a mixture of uses—retail, restaurants, personal service establishments, office, and limited second-story residential—situated in a compact area. Many of the structures in the central business district are historically significant.

*Twentieth Century Commercial District (COM).* A second commercial district is located along Biltmore Avenue on the east side of the city. Built primarily in the twentieth century, it includes a mix of retail and office. None of the buildings is architecturally significant, except for the vacant Bijou Theater. Rivertown also includes limited strip commercial businesses along Biltmore Avenue at the eastern and western edges of the city.

*Industrial (IND).* Industrial land is located along the railroad tracks on the east side of the city, north of the river. Eagle Stove

Works is the main historic industry located in this area. Several properties and lots remain vacant. They offer new opportunities for industrial growth in this area of the city.

*Institutional (INS).* The largest institution in the city is Reliance College, a private undergraduate college. Other public buildings include the city hall, combined fire and police building, library, and post office. The nearest medical facilities are located in Erie Falls.

*Parks and Recreation (REC).* City Park is located on the west side of the city. The city also owns land along the north side of the Eagle River and surrounding Walden Pond.

*Other land use considerations.* The old Biltmore Farm is a large open space located in the center of the city, directly behind the Biltmore Mansion. Open space available for development is found in the River Heights district on the northeast side of the city and land adjacent to the college campus in the far northwest corner of the city.

Rivertown is generally surrounded by agricultural and large lot single-family residential land uses that represent a rural atmosphere. Land uses near Rivertown that influence land use patterns and traffic flows within the city include:

- Bitterroot Lake as a residential/recreation area
- A number of small to medium sized industrial uses east of the city on Biltmore Avenue (State Road 51)
- A new middle school/high school complex just west of the city boundary on Biltmore Avenue (State Road 51)

## Future Land Use Goals

As Rivertown and its environs face continued pressure for new growth, the community wishes to accommodate high quality development served by roads, infrastructure and municipal services that maintain the community's character as a small town. The comprehensive plan enumerates the following goals related to the overall vision for the community:

- To promote a balance of residential, commercial, industrial and institutional uses, located and arranged in a logical pattern which complements neighboring land uses.
- To encourage quality industrial, office, and commercial development to provide employment opportunities for residents and to diversify the tax base.
- To maintain a small-town environment bounded by a distinct rural setting, with coordinated decisions on land use, pathways, roads and utility provisions, through cooperative planning with the surrounding townships, the River County Road Commission, and other organizations.
- To ensure that new development and redevelopment conserve the most important features of the natural environment and stormwater quality.
- To accommodate new development or redevelopment as far as possible through the existing capacity of roads, municipal sanitary sewer and water systems, schools, parks, open space and recreation facilities, and city facilities/services or the concurrent construction of new infrastructure.
- To preserve and enhance community character through the creation of design guidelines and regulations for architecture, signs, lighting, pedestrian amenities, and traffic/

access management. Infill residential, either new homes or substantial expansions/renovations, should respect the character of the existing historic neighborhoods in terms of setbacks and building design.
- To direct industrial development and expansion to areas currently zoned as industrial along the railroad tracks.
- To maintain a distinct downtown as a city center that meets the shopping, civic, entertainment and recreational needs of current and future residents and visitors.

Because Rivertown's downtown is the focal point of the community, its historic qualities are a major factor in making the downtown a unique place. The plan's goals for the Central Business District are:

- To promote retention of existing businesses and encourage their expansion when consistent with other goals in the plan.
- To encourage new retail and commercial land uses in appropriate areas.
- To ensure that new infill development is compatible with the downtown's historic architecture, scale, proportion and character.
- To develop an updated marketing and promotional strategy for the downtown district.
- To promote future expansion of the central business district eastward along Biltmore Avenue.
- To improve the downtown by adding parking, pedestrian amenities, event areas and other elements that keep the downtown vibrant.
- To address the economic viability of the downtown through a diversified mixture of complementary commercial, office, residential and civic uses.
- To ensure that renovations of historic buildings in the downtown retain their historical and architectural integrity.

# APPENDIX C: RIVERTOWN ZONING ORDINANCE (ABRIDGED)

*The following is a partial zoning ordinance based on the zoning code for Manchester, Michigan. It has been significantly shortened for use in the exercises in this book. For example, only the district regulations needed for Rivertown exercises are described; they are limited to Commercial, Institutional, and Agricultural; Residential, Industrial, and Planned Unit Development sections are omitted. The ordinance is a useful foundation on which to base land use decisions in the exercises.*

## CITY OF RIVERTOWN ZONING ORDINANCE

*GENERAL PROVISIONS*
*Adopted January 10, 2002*

### 100. Short Title.

This section shall be known and cited as the City of Rivertown Zoning Ordinance.

### 101. Introduction.

(A) The purpose of this ordinance is to promote public health, safety, and welfare; to protect, regulate, restrict, and provide for the use of land and buildings; to meet the needs of the city's property owners for places of residence, recreation, industry, trade, service, and other uses of land; to ensure that uses of the land shall be situated in appropriate locations and have desired relationships; to limit the inappropriate overcrowding of land and congestion of population and other public facilities; and to facilitate adequate and efficient provision for transportation systems, sewage disposal, water, energy, education, recreation, other public services, and basic needs.
(B) The city is divided into districts with regulations designating land uses or activities that are permitted or subjected to special regulations.
(C) The purpose of this ordinance is to provide for the establishment of a Board of Appeals and its powers and duties to interpret the ordinance and the boundaries of its districts.

(D) The ordinance is also intended to enhance social and economic stability in the city and conserve the taxable value of land, buildings, and structures.

### 101a. Scope and Construction of Regulations

(A) No building or structure, or part thereof, shall hereafter be erected, constructed, reconstructed, or altered, and no new use or change shall be made to any building, structure, or land, or part thereof, except as permitted by the provisions of this ordinance.
(B) In interpreting and applying the provisions of this ordinance, the requirements shall be held to be the minimum for the promotion of the public health, safety, convenience, comfort, prosperity, and general welfare.
(C) Where a condition imposed by a provision of this ordinance upon the use of any lot, building, or structure is conflicting with a condition imposed by any other provision of this chapter, or by the provision of an ordinance adopted under any other law, the provision which is more restrictive shall govern.
(D) Nothing within this ordinance shall be construed to prevent compliance with an order by the appropriate authority to correct, improve, strengthen, or restore to a safe or healthy condition, any part of a building or premises declared unsafe or unhealthy.

### 102. Definitions

For the purpose of this ordinance, the following definitions shall apply unless the context clearly indicates or requires a different meaning.

BUILDING. A structure having a roof supported by columns or walls.

BUILDING SETBACK LINE. The line established for required setbacks forming the area within a lot in which a building may be located.

BUFFER. A landscaped area composed of living material, wall, berm, or combination thereof, established and/or maintained to provide visual screening, noise reduction, and/or transition between conflicting types of land uses.

COMMERCIAL USE. The use of property in connection with the purchase, sale, barter, display, or exchange of goods, wares, merchandise, or personal services, and the maintenance or operation of offices.

CONDITIONAL USE. A use that is subject to conditional approval by the City Council or Planning Commission. A conditional use may be granted only when there is a specific provision listed in this chapter. A conditional use is not considered to be a nonconforming use.

DWELLING, SINGLE-FAMILY. A building designed for, or occupied exclusively by, one family, but in no case shall a travel trailer, motor home, trailer coach, automobile chassis, tent, or other portable building be considered a dwelling.

DWELLING, 2-FAMILY. A building consisting of two dwellings.

DWELLING, MULTIPLE-FAMILY. A building consisting of three or more dwellings.

EASEMENT. A right given to another person or entity to trespass upon land that person or entity does not own for purposes of ingress, egress, utilities, drainage, and similar uses.

FLOOR AREA. The sum of the gross horizontal areas of the building measured from the exterior faces of the exterior walls or from the centerline of walls separating two buildings.

HOME OCCUPATION. An occupation, profession, activity, or use that is a customary or secondary use of a residential dwelling unit and which does not alter the exterior of the property or affect the residential character of the neighborhood.

JUNK YARD. A place, structure, parcel, or use of land where waste, discard, salvage, or similar materials are bought, sold, exchanged, stored, baled, packed, disassembled, or handled, including auto wrecking yards and used lumber, housing wrecking and structural steel materials and equipment, and establishments for the sale, purchase, or storage of salvaged or inoperative machinery and the processing of used, discarded, or salvaged materials, for any 30 consecutive days.

LODGING FACILITY. Any establishment in which individual units are rented to transients for periods of less than 30 days for the purpose of sleeping accommodations. The term shall include hotels and motels, bed and breakfast operations, but shall not include multiple-family dwellings.

LOT. A parcel of land, excluding any portion in a street or other right-of-way, of at least sufficient size to meet minimum requirements for use, coverage, lot area, and yards or other open spaces as herein required. A lot shall have frontage on a public street, or on an approved private street, and may consist of:

1. A single lot of record;
2. A portion of a lot of record;
3. Any combination of complete and/or portions of lots of record; or
4. A parcel of land described by metes and bounds.

LOT AREA. The total horizontal area within the lot lines of a lot, but excluding that portion within a street right-of-way.

LOT, CORNER. A lot with frontage on two intersecting streets.

LOT COVERAGE. The percentage of a lot area covered by the building area.

LOT DEPTH. The mean horizontal distance from the front line to the rear lot line; or in the case of a waterfront lot, from the water frontage line to the street frontage line.

LOT, DOUBLE FRONTAGE. A lot other than a corner lot having frontage on two more or less parallel streets. In the case of a row of double frontage lots, one street will be designated as the front street for all lots in the plat and in the request for a zoning compliance permit. If there are existing structures in the same block fronting one or both of the streets, the required front yard setback shall be observed on those streets where structures presently front.

LOT, INTERIOR. A lot other than a corner lot with only one lot line fronting on a street.

LOT LINES. Any line dividing one lot from another or from a public right-of-way, and thus constituting the property lines bounding a lot.

LOT WIDTH. The required horizontal distance between the side lot lines measured at the points where the required front yard setback line intersects the side lot lines. For lots located on the turning circle of a cul-de-sac, the lot width may be reduced to 80 percent of the required lot width.

MOBILE HOME. A detached portable single-family dwelling, prefabricated on its own chassis and intended for long-term occupancy. The unit contains sleeping accommodations, a flush toilet, a wash basin, a tub or shower, eating and living quarters. It is designed to be transported on its own wheels or flatbed arriving at the site where it is to be occupied as a complete dwelling without permanent foundation and connected to existing utilities.

MOBILE HOME PARK. Any parcel of land intended and designed to accommodate more than one mobile home for living use which is offered to the public for that purpose; and any structure, facility, area, or equipment used or intended for use incidental to that living use.

NONCONFORMING BUILDING. A building or portion thereof lawfully existing at the effective date of this ordinance, or amendments thereto, and which does not conform to the provisions of this ordinance in the zoning district in which it is located.

NONCONFORMING LOT. A lot lawfully existing at the effective date of this ordinance, or amendments thereto, with dimensions and size not conforming to the zoning ordinance.

NONCONFORMING USE. A use which lawfully occupied a building or land at the effective date of this ordinance, or amendments thereto, and that does not conform to the use regulations of the zoning district in which it is located.

OFF-STREET PARKING AREA. A land surface or facility providing vehicular parking spaces along with adequate drives and aisles for maneuvering so as to provide access for entrance and exit for the parking of more than two vehicles.

RESTAURANT. Any establishment whose principal business is the sale of food and beverages to the customer in a ready-to-consume state, and whose method of operation is characteristic of a carryout, drive-in, drive-through, fast food, standard restaurant, bar/lounge, or combination thereof, as defined below.

1. BAR/LOUNGE. A restaurant operated primarily for dispensing alcoholic beverages, although the sale of prepared food or snacks may also be permitted.
2. RESTAURANT, CARRYOUT. A restaurant whose method of operation involves sale of food, beverages, and/or frozen desserts in disposable or edible containers or wrappers in a ready-to-consume state for consumption primarily off the premises.
3. RESTAURANT, FAST-FOOD. A restaurant whose method of operation involves minimum waiting for delivery of ready-to-consume food to the customer at a counter or drive-through line.
4. RESTAURANT, STANDARD. A restaurant whose method of operation involves the delivery of prepared food by waiters and waitresses to customers seated at tables.

SETBACK. The minimum required horizontal distance between the building or structure and the front, side, and rear lot lines and specified natural features.

SITE CONDOMINIUM. A type of ownership in a development containing residential, commercial, office, industrial, or other structures or improvements in which each co-owner owns exclusive rights to a volume of space in a structure herein defined as a condominium unit as described in the master deed and common parts of the property are owned jointly.

STRUCTURE. A constructed or erected object, typically including such things as buildings, bridges, sheds, and decks.

VARIANCE. A modification of the literal provisions of the zoning ordinance granted when strict enforcement of the zoning ordinance would cause undue hardship owing to circumstances unique to the individual's property on which the variance is granted.

YARD, FRONT.
1. A yard extending across the full width of the lot, the depth of which is the minimum horizontal distance between the principal building and the front lot line, and measured perpendicular to the building at the closest point to the front lot line.
2. In all cases, the front lot line shall be considered to be that portion of the lot that abuts a public road right-of-way or private road easement.

YARD, REAR. A yard extending across the full width of the lot, the depth of which is the minimum horizontal distance between the rear lot line and the nearest point of the principal building.

YARD, SIDE.
1. A yard between any building and the side lot line, extending from the front yard to the rear yard.
2. The width of the required side yard shall be measured horizontally from the nearest point of the side lot line to the nearest point of principal building.

## 103. District Designations

This Zoning Ordinance includes the following districts:

(AG) Agriculture District
(R-1A) Single-Family Residential District, Low Density
(R-1B) Single-Family Residential District, Medium Density
(R-2) Multiple-Family Residential District, Low Density
(R-3) Multiple-Family Residential District, Medium Density
(MHP) Mobile Home Park Residential District
(C-1) Local Service District
(C-2) General Commercial District
(CBD) Central Business District
(I-1) Limited Industrial District
(I-2) General Industrial District
(PUD) Planned Unit Development District
(INST) Institutional

## 104. Zoning District Map

(A) The zoning districts as provided in Section 105 are delineated on the Zoning Districts Map of the City of Rivertown.

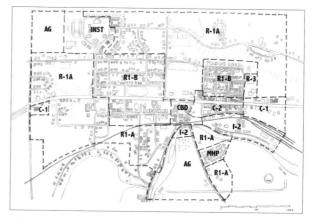

AC.1 *Zoning Districts Map of the City of Rivertown*

## 105. Zoning Districts and Regulations

### 105.1 C-1, Local Service District

(A) *Purpose.* This District is designed primarily for the convenience of persons residing in the city by providing office, limited retail, and business service uses that serve the adjacent and surrounding neighborhoods. It is the purpose of these regulations to permit development of the enumerated functions in a manner that is compatible with uses in the surrounding area. To these ends, certain uses are excluded which would function more effectively in other districts.

(B) *Permitted uses.*
1. Office buildings for the use of any of the following occupations: executive, administrative, professional, accounting, writing, clerical, stenographic, drafting, and sales;
2. Medical and dental office, including clinics and medical laboratories;
3. Banks, credit unions, savings and loan associations;
4. Publicly owned buildings, public utility transformer sta-

tions and substations, telephone exchanges, and public utility offices;

5. Retail office supply, computer and business machine sales;
6. Business service establishments such as printing and photocopying services, mail and packaging services, and typing and secretarial services;
7. Personal service establishments, such as barber and beauty shops; watch, clothing, and shoe repair; locksmith; and similar establishments;
8. Outdoor display of products or materials for retail sale or rental when accessory to a principle permitted use; and
9. A single-family dwelling and any use, building, or structure accessory thereto, established and existing at the time of adoption of this chapter.

(C) *Conditional uses.*

1. Private service clubs, social organizations, and lodge halls;
2. Funeral homes;
3. Multiple-family housing and/or apartment dwelling second floor and above;
4. Veterinary offices and hospitals, including accessory boarding, provided no outdoor exercise runs or pens are permitted; and
5. Bed and breakfast establishments.

## 105.2 C-2, General Commercial District

(A) *Purpose.* This District is intended to accommodate office, business service, and retail uses that serve a larger market than C-1 District, including the city and portions of the surrounding townships. The purpose of these regulations is to permit development of the enumerated functions in a manner that is compatible with uses in the surrounding area. To these ends, certain uses are excluded which would function more effectively in other Districts.

(B) *Permitted uses.*

1. All permitted and conditional uses allowed in C-1 Local Service District, with the exception of single-family dwellings;
2. Food services including grocery, meat market, bakery, restaurant, delicatessen and fruit market, and similar self-service units, but not including any business of a drive-in type;
3. Retail sales of drug and health care products, hardware, gifts, dry goods, notions, sporting goods, clothing, furniture, and appliances;
4. Radio, television, and electrical appliance repair, and shops of plumbers, electricians, and other similar services and trades;
5. Accessory uses, buildings, or structures.

(C) *Conditional uses.*

1. Bar/lounge serving alcoholic beverages and/or providing entertainment;
2. Fast-food restaurants;
3. Sit-down and/or carry-out restaurants; move to conditional uses

4. Laundromats and dry cleaning establishments; move to conditional uses
5. Planned shopping centers;
6. Lodging facilities;
7. Outdoor sales of manufactured products;
8. Sale of new and used automobiles, boats, mobile homes, farm machinery, and other vehicles;
9. Automobile service stations and washes;
10. Recreation and amusement services, including theaters, bowling alleys, roller and ice skating rinks, billiard halls, and miniature golf; and
11. Farm supply and feed stores.

## 105.3 CBD, Central Business District

(A) *Purpose.* This District is designed to provide for a variety of office, business service, entertainment, and retail uses which occupy the prime retail frontage, by serving the comparison, convenience, and service needs of the market area which includes the city and surrounding townships. The regulations of the CBD District are designed to promote convenient pedestrian shopping and the stability of retail development by encouraging a continuous retail frontage and by prohibiting automotive-related services and non-retail uses which tend to break up the continuity.

(B) *Permitted uses.*

1. All permitted uses allowed in the C-1 and C-2 District;
2. Newspaper offices and printing plants;
3. Post offices;
4. Private service clubs, social organizations, and lodge halls; and
5. Parks and playgrounds.

(C) *Conditional uses.*

1. Bar/lounge serving alcoholic beverages and/or providing entertainment;
2. Fast-food restaurants;
3. Theaters, when completely enclosed;
4. Recreation and amusement services, including theaters, bowling alleys, roller and ice skating rinks, and billiard halls;

## 105.4 INST, Institutional District

(A) *Purpose.* The public institutional designation is intended to provide an area for activities relating to the purpose of state and local governmental entities and semi-public institutions providing necessary public services and provide for continued operation and facilitate managed growth of existing major institutions within the city.

(B) *Permitted uses.*

1. Government buildings or offices such as fire stations, schools and colleges, hospitals, community meeting or recreation halls;
2. Libraries, museums, or similar cultural facilities;
3. Churches, hospitals, schools and colleges, and other public or semi-public institutions;
4. Public utilities, such as electrical, sewer, water, natural gas, storm water, telecom facilities and other similar uses;

(C) *Conditional uses.*

    1. Small-scale retail sales and services designed to serve the immediate surroundings;

### 105.5 AG, Agricultural District

(A) *Purpose.* The purposes of the agricultural district are to protect and promote the continuation of farming in areas with prime soils where farming is a viable component of the local economy, to promote the continuation of farming in areas where it is already established, and to separate agricultural land uses and activities from incompatible residential, commercial, and industrial development, and public facilities.

(B) *Permitted uses.*

    1. General farming, and horticulture, including necessary farm structures;

    2. Forestry uses;

    3. Production nurseries and greenhouses;

    4. Single-family residential;

(C) *Conditional uses.*

    1. Elementary schools and churches;

    2. Roadside stands for the sale of agricultural products;

    3. Intensive livestock

    4. Manure storage facilities.

    5. Agricultural marketing outlets

    6. Residential subdivision or site condominium developments;

## 106. Supplemental Regulations

### 106.1 Open Space

(A) *Gross acreage required.* When completed, a development shall have 20% of the gross acreage in the development devoted to open space, which shall remain in its natural state and/or be restricted to active and/or passive outdoor recreational purposes.

    1. The computation of designated open space shall not include: rights-of-way or easements designated for road purposes; areas within the minimum setbacks of a dwelling unit; land which is under water (lakes, streams, water courses, and other similar bodies of water); any area to be improved into a lake or pond; and/or more than 25% of the area of regulated wetlands.

(B) *Transition from adjacent parcels.* In order to provide an orderly transition of density when a cluster development abuts a single-family residential district of equal or lower density, the Planning Commission, at its discretion, may require one or more of the following measures: designation of open space along the common boundaries; screening in accordance with an area or row of lots of commensurate size as neighboring residential lots.

(C) *Density.* The number of dwelling units within any development permitted hereunder shall not exceed the number of dwelling units permitted in the zoning district in which the proposed development is located without application of the cluster housing option. The applicant must submit a concept plan that illustrates a site layout without the cluster option and all applicable ordinances and laws observed.

(D) *Setbacks.* Minimum setback requirements are established in a manner that permits variation in the siting of individual dwelling units in order to encourage creativity in design and compatibility with natural resource features. The minimum setback requirements for each dwelling unit shall be shown on the site plan as follows.

    1. In the case of single-family detached dwellings, the following minimum setbacks shall be applied:

*Minimum Yard Setbacks per Unit*

| Front | Rear | Total Front and Rear | Side: Least | Side: Total |
|---|---|---|---|---|
| 20 | 30 | 55 | 5 | 15 |

### 106.2 Landscaping

(A) *Landscape plan requirements.* A separate detailed landscape plan shall be required to be submitted to the city as part of the site plan review or tentative preliminary plat review. The landscape plan shall demonstrate that all requirements of this section are met and shall include, but not necessarily be limited to, the following items:

    1. Location, spacing, size, root type, and descriptions for each plant type;

    2. Typical straight cross section including slope, height, and width of berms;

    3. Typical construction details to resolve specific site conditions, such as landscape walls and tree wells used to preserve existing trees or maintain natural grades;

    4. Details in either text or drawing form to ensure proper installation and establishment of proposed plant materials;

    5. Identification of existing trees and vegetative cover to be preserved; and

    6. Identification of grass and other ground cover and method of planting.

(B) *Screening between land uses.*

    1. Upon any improvement for which a site plan is required, a landscape buffer shall be constructed to create a visual screen at least 6 feet in height along all adjoining boundaries between either a conflicting nonresidential or conflicting residential land use and residentially zoned or used property. A landscape buffer may consist of earthen berms and/or living materials so as to maintain a minimum opacity of at least 80%. Opacity shall be measured by observation of any 2 square-yard area of landscape screen between 1 foot above the established grade of the area to be concealed and the top or the highest point of the required screen. The plantings must meet this standard based upon reasonably anticipated growth over a period of three years.

(C) *Subdivision and site condominium landscaping.* Landscaping for single-family residential subdivisions and site condominiums shall be provided in accordance with the following requirements.

    1. *Street trees.* The frontage of all internal public or private streets shall be landscaped with a minimum of one tree for every 50 lineal feet, or fraction thereof.

2. *Required landscaping at the perimeter of parking lots.* Separate landscape areas shall be provided at the perimeter of parking lots in accordance with the following requirements.

   a. Parking lots that are considered to be a conflicting land use as defined by this section shall meet the screening requirements set forth above.

   b. Parking lots shall be screened from view with a solid wall at least 3 feet in height along the perimeter of those sides that are visible from a public road. The city, at its discretion, may approve alternative landscape plantings in lieu of a wall.

(D) *Screening of trash containers.*

1. Outside trash disposal containers shall be screened on all sides with an opaque fence or wall and gate at least as high as the container, but no less than 6 feet in height, and shall be constructed of material that is compatible with the architectural materials used in the site development.

## 107. Conditional Land Uses

(A) *Basis of determinations.* The Planning Commission and City Council shall review the proposed conditional use in terms of the standards stated within this ordinance and shall establish that the use and the proposed location:

1. Will be designed, constructed, operated, and maintained so as to (be harmonious) and appropriate in appearance with the comprehensive plan, existing or intended character of the general vicinity, and will not change the essential character of the area;

2. Will not be hazardous or disturbing to existing uses or uses reasonably anticipated in the future;

3. Will be an improvement in relation to property in the immediate vicinity and to the city as a whole;

4. Will be served adequately by essential public services and facilities or that the persons responsible for the establishment of the proposed use will provide adequately any such service or facility;

5. Will not create excessive additional public costs and will not be detrimental to the economic welfare of the city;

6. and will be consistent with the intent and purposes of this ordinance.

## 108. Nonconforming Uses, Structures, and Lots

(A) *Intent.* Certain existing lots, structures, and uses of lots and structures were lawful before this ordinance was adopted, but have become nonconformities under the terms of this ordinance and its amendments. It is the intent of this ordinance to permit the nonconformities to remain until they are discontinued or removed, but not to encourage their survival or, where discontinuance or removal is not feasible, to gradually upgrade the nonconformities to conforming status. Nonconformities shall not be enlarged, expanded, or extended, except as provided herein, and

shall not be used as grounds for adding other structures and uses of lots and structures which are prohibited. Nonconformities are declared by this ordinance to be incompatible with the structures and uses permitted in the various districts.

1. No nonconforming uses shall be enlarged or increased, or extended to occupy a greater area of land than was occupied at the effective date of adoption or amendment of this ordinance.

2. No nonconforming use shall be moved in whole or in part to any other portion of the lot or parcel occupied by the use at the effective date of adoption or amendment of this ordinance.

3. If the nonconforming use of land ceases operation with the intent of abandonment for a period of more than 6 months, any subsequent use of the land shall conform to the regulations specified by this chapter for the district in which the land is located.

4. Property losses due to fire or extreme natural events resulting in destruction of more than 50 percent of the property cannot be rebuilt.

## 109. Off-Street Parking

The purpose of this section is to ensure the provision of off-street parking facilities that are sufficient in number, adequately sized, and properly designed to meet the range of parking needs and demands that are associated with land uses now in place in the city or with land uses allowed by this ordinance.

(A) *Where required.* In all zoning districts, off-street parking facilities for the storage and parking of self-propelled motor vehicles for the use of occupants, employees, and patrons of the buildings hereafter erected, altered, or extended after the effective date of this chapter, shall be provided as herein prescribed. The space shall be maintained and shall not be encroached upon so long as the main building or structure remains, unless an equivalent number of the spaces are provided elsewhere in conformance with this ordinance.

1. *One- and two-family dwellings.* The off-street parking facilities required for 1- and 2-family dwellings shall be located on the same lot or plot of ground as the building they are intended to serve.

2. *Multiple-family residential.* The off-street parking facilities for multiple-family dwellings shall be located on the same lot or plot of ground as the dwellings they are intended to serve. In no event shall any parking space be located nearer than 10 feet to any main building.

3. *Other land uses.* The off-street parking facilities required for all other uses shall be located on the lot or within 500 feet of the permitted uses requiring the off-street parking, the distance to be measured along lines of public access to the property between the nearest point of the parking facility to the building to be served.

*109.1 Table of off-street parking requirements.*

The amount of required off-street parking space for new uses or buildings, additions thereto, and additions to existing buildings shall be determined in accordance with the table at the end of this document.

## 110. Site Plan Review

(A) *Generally.* The City Council shall have the authority to review and approve or reject all site plans (i.e., preliminary, final, and combined site plans), taking into account the recommendations of the City Planning Commission. Site plan review and approval is required in accordance with the procedures contained in this section prior to the issuance of building permits or commencement of construction for new structures and for additions or reductions that alter the size of the floor area.

(B) *Where required.*

1. Site plan review is required for all proposed uses and certain existing uses within the city where an alteration, addition, expansion, change, or conversion constitutes an increase or reduction to the existing structure or use of more than 500 square feet or 10 percent, whichever is less; or would require a variance from the provisions of this chapter, regardless of its size. Site plan review shall also be required prior to the paving of any off-street parking for any use for which off-street parking is required by this chapter.

2. Site plan review shall not be required for individual single-family dwellings or residential accessory storage buildings.

3. The city shall not issue a building permit until a final site plan has been approved and is in effect. A use, not involving a building or structure, shall not be commenced or expanded, nor shall the Zoning Administrator or duly appointed agent issue an occupancy permit for the use until a final site plan has been approved and an onsite inspection has been conducted.

4. No grading, removal of trees or other vegetation, landfill, or construction of improvements shall commence for any development which requires site plan approval until a final site plan is approved and an onsite inspection has been conducted.

(C) *Preliminary site plan.*

1. *Application.* Any applicant may submit a request for preliminary site plan review by filing with the Zoning Administrator completed forms, payment of the review fee, and 7 copies of the preliminary site plan drawing(s). The Administrator, upon receipt of the application, shall transmit only complete submittals of the preliminary site plan drawings to the Planning Commission prior to its next regular meeting. The purpose of the preliminary review is to confirm general compliance with city standards as well as to suggest changes, if necessary, for final site plan approval.

2. *Information required.* Each preliminary site plan submitted for review shall provide the following information:

   a. Property owner's and applicant's name and address;

   b. Scale, north arrow, and date of plan; Sheet size shall be at least 24 inches by 36 inches with plan view drawn to a scale of no greater than 1 inch equals 50 feet for property less than 3 acres or no greater than 1 inch equals 100 feet for property of 3 or more acres.

   c. Location, description, dimensions, and area of the site; zoning classification; and demonstration of compliance with lot area, width, coverage, and setback requirements;

   d. General topography and soils information and existing natural and manmade features to be retained, altered, or removed;

   e. Location, number, and dimensions of proposed buildings/structures; including floor area, number of floors, height, number, and type of dwelling units (where applicable);

   f. Proposed streets/drives; including general alignment, right-of-way, surface type, and width;

   g. Proposed parking; including location and dimensions of spaces and aisles, and surface type;

   h. Adjacent land uses, property owners, and zoning and location of adjacent buildings and drives/streets;

   i. Proposed phasing;

   j. Location and width of any easements on the site.

3. *Planning Commission action.* The Planning Commission shall make a recommendation to approve, approve with conditions, or deny the preliminary site plan within 60 days from the date of the Planning Commission meeting at which the site plan is first heard. The Planning Commission shall set forth the reason for its action in the record of the meeting at which action is taken. The time limit may be extended upon a written request by the applicant and approval by the Planning Commission.

4. *City Council action.* The City Council shall receive the recommendations of the Planning Commission and may approve or deny the preliminary site plan.

5. *Effect of approval.* Approval of a preliminary site plan by the City Council shall indicate its general acceptance of the proposed layout of buildings, streets and drives, parking areas, other facilities, and overall character of the proposed development. The City Council may, at its discretion, and with appropriate conditions attached, authorize issuance of grading and foundation permits on the basis of the approved preliminary site plan. The authorization, however, will be used only in those situations in which seasonable conditions, such as the onset of frost, or other severe time limitations might, in the City Council's opinion, unduly delay the commencement of construction until after the final site plan is approved. The City Council shall attach appropriate conditions to the authorization.

6. *Expiration of approval.* Approval of a preliminary site

plan shall be valid for a period of 180 days from the date of approval and shall expire and be of no effect unless an application for a final site plan is filed with the Zoning Administrator within that time period. The Zoning Administrator or duly appointed agent shall, within ten days of the date of approval of the preliminary site plan by the City Council, transmit a written certification of the approval to the applicant.

(D) *Final site plan.*

1. *Application.* Following approval of a preliminary site plan, the applicant shall submit to the Zoning Administrator seven copies of a final site plan as well as other data and exhibits hereinafter required, the review fee, and a completed application form. The Administrator shall transmit only complete submittals of the final site plan drawing(s) to the Planning Commission prior to its next regular meeting upon receipt of the following:

   a. Scale, north arrow, and date of plan;
   b. Location, description, dimensions, and area of the site; zoning classification; and demonstration of compliance with lot area, width, coverage, and setback requirements;
   c. General topographic application.

2. *Information required.* A final site plan submitted for review and approval shall contain all of the following data presented in a clear and legible format. Site plans shall consist of an overall plan for the entire development. Sheet size shall be at least 24 inches by 36 inches with plan view drawn to a scale of no greater than 1 inch equals 50 feet for property less than 3 acres or no greater than 1 inch equals 100 feet for property 3 or more acres in size.

   a. *General information.*
      1. Proprietors', applicants', and owners' names, addresses, and telephone numbers;
      2. Date of preparation, including revisions;
      3. Scale;
      4. North point;
      5. Location map drawn at a scale of 1 inch equals 2,000 feet with north point indicated;
      6. Architect, engineer, surveyor, landscape architect, or planner's seal;
      7. Existing and proposed lot lines, building lines, structures, parking areas, and the like, on the parcel and within 100 feet of the site;
      8. Centerline and existing and proposed right-of-way lines of any street;
      9. Zoning classification of petitioner's parcel and all abutting parcels; and
      10. Gross acreage figure.
   b. *Physical features.*
      1. Acceleration, deceleration, and passing lanes and approaches;
      2. Proposed locations of access drives, street intersections, driveway locations, sidewalks, and curbing;
      3. Location of existing and proposed service facilities above and below ground, including:
         a. Chemical and fuel storage tanks and containers;
         b. Water supply facilities;
         c. Sanitary sewage disposal facilities;
         d. Storm water control facilities and structures; and
         e. Delineation/location of all easements.
      4. Location of all structures with setback and yard dimensions;
      5. Dimensioned parking spaces and calculation, driveways and method of surfacing;
      6. Exterior lighting locations and illumination patterns;
      7. Location and description of all existing and proposed landscaping, berms, fencing, and walls;
      8. Trash receptacle pad location and method of screening; for commercial and industrial
      9. Transformer pad location and method of screening;
      10. Dedicated road or service drive locations;
      11. Entrance details including sign locations and size;
      12. Designation of fire lanes; and
      13. Any other pertinent physical features.
   c. *Natural features.*
      1. Soil characteristics of the parcel to at least the detail provided by the U.S. Soil Conservation Service, County Soil Survey;
      2. Existing topography with a maximum contour interval of 2 feet. Topography on the site and beyond the site for a distance of 100 feet in all directions should be indicated. Grading plan, showing finished contours at a maximum interval of 2 feet, correlated with existing contours so as to clearly indicate required cutting, filling, and grading;
      3. Location of existing drainage courses and associated bodies of water, on- and off-site, and their elevations;
      4. Location of existing wetlands;
      5. Location of natural resource features, including woodlands and areas with slopes greater than 10 percent (1 foot of vertical elevation for every 10 feet of horizontal distance).
   d. *Additional requirements for residential developments.*
      1. Density calculations by type of unit by bedroom counts;
      2. Designation of units by type and number of units in each building;
      3. Carport locations and details where proposed; and

4. Specific amount and location of recreation spaces.
   e. *Additional requirements for commercial and industrial developments.*
      1. Loading/unloading areas;
      2. Total and useable floor area; and
      3. Number of employees in peak usage.
3. *Standards for review.* In reviewing the final site plan, the Planning Commission and City Council shall determine whether the plan meets the following specifications and standards.
   a. The plan conforms to the approved preliminary site plan and with all Zoning Ordinance regulations.
   b. All required information is provided.
   c. The proposed use will not be injurious to the surrounding neighborhood and protects the general health, safety, welfare, and character of the township.
   d. There is a proper relationship between major thoroughfares and proposed service drives, driveways, and parking areas. Proper access to all portions of the site and all sides of any structure is provided. All structures or groups of structures shall be so arranged as to permit emergency vehicle access by some practical means to all sides.
   e. The location of buildings is such that the adverse effects of the uses will be minimized for the occupants of that use and surrounding areas.
   f. Natural resources will be preserved to the maximum extent possible in the site design by developing in a manner that will not detrimentally affect or destroy natural features such as lakes, ponds, streams, wetlands, steep slopes, soils, groundwater, and woodlands.
   g. Storm water management systems and facilities will preserve the natural drainage characteristics and enhance the aesthetics of the site to the maximum extent possible, and will not substantially reduce or increase the natural retention or storage capacity of any wetland, water body, or water course, or cause alterations which could increase flooding or water pollution on- or off-site.
   h. Wastewater treatment systems, including on-site septic systems, will be located to minimize any potential degradation of surface water or groundwater quality and meet county and state standards.
   i. Sites which include storage of hazardous materials or waste, fuels, salt, or chemicals will be designed to prevent spills and discharges of polluting materials to the surface of the ground, groundwater, or nearby water bodies in accordance with county and state standards.
   j. Landscaping, including grass, trees, shrubs, and other vegetation is provided to maintain and improve the aesthetic quality of the site and area.
   k. The proposed use is in compliance with all city ordinances and any other applicable laws.
4. *Planning Commission action.* The Planning Commission shall make a recommendation to approve, approve with conditions, or deny the final site plan within 60 days of the date of the Planning Commission meeting at which the site plan is first heard. The time limit may be extended upon a written request by the applicant and approved by the Planning Commission. The Planning Commission may suggest and/or require modifications in the proposed final site plan as are needed to gain approval. All engineering drawings and plans shall be reviewed by the City Engineer, Department of Public Works, and Fire Chief before a final site plan may be recommended to Council.
5. *City Council action.* The City Council shall receive the recommendations of the Planning Commission and approve or deny the site plan.
6. *Effect of approval.* Approval of a final site plan authorizes issuance of a building permit or, in the case of uses without buildings or structures, issuance of a certificate of zoning compliance.

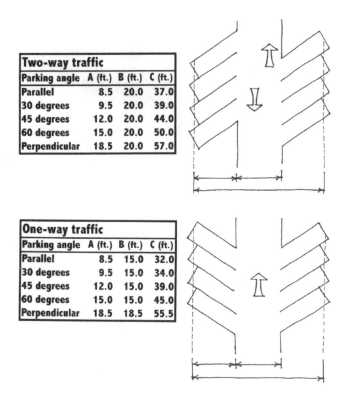

| Two-way traffic | | | |
|---|---|---|---|
| Parking angle | A (ft.) | B (ft.) | C (ft.) |
| Parallel | 8.5 | 20.0 | 37.0 |
| 30 degrees | 9.5 | 20.0 | 39.0 |
| 45 degrees | 12.0 | 20.0 | 44.0 |
| 60 degrees | 15.0 | 20.0 | 50.0 |
| Perpendicular | 18.5 | 20.0 | 57.0 |

| One-way traffic | | | |
|---|---|---|---|
| Parking angle | A (ft.) | B (ft.) | C (ft.) |
| Parallel | 8.5 | 15.0 | 32.0 |
| 30 degrees | 9.5 | 15.0 | 34.0 |
| 45 degrees | 12.0 | 15.0 | 39.0 |
| 60 degrees | 15.0 | 15.0 | 45.0 |
| Perpendicular | 18.5 | 18.5 | 55.5 |

*Note: "Parking Pattern" represents the angle of parking spaces in degrees. 1-Way and 2-Way represent the width of the driving lane based on whether it serves one-lane or two-lane traffic.*

| Use | Required Number of Parking Spaces Per Each Unit of Measure as Follows |
|---|---|
| *Residential Uses* | |
| Single- or 2-family dwelling | 2 Per each dwelling unit |
| Multiple-family dwelling | 2 Per each dwelling, plus 1 Per each 10 dwelling units |
| Senior citizen housing and senior assisted living | 1 Per each dwelling unit, plus 1 Per each 10 dwelling units; 1 Per each employee |
| *Institutional Uses* | |
| Churches | 1 Per each 3 seats based on maximum seating capacity in the main place of assembly therein |
| Private clubs and lodges | 1 Per each 3 individual members allowed within the maximum occupancy load as established by fire and/or building codes |
| Hospitals | 1 Per each 4 beds, plus 1 Per staff doctor, plus 1 Per each employee at peak shift |
| Convalescent homes, homes for the aged, children's homes | 1 Per each 5 beds, plus 1 Per each staff doctor, plus 1 Per each employee at peak shift |
| High schools, trade schools, colleges, and universities | 1 Per each teacher, plus 1 Per each 10 students, plus 1 Per each employee |
| Elementary and middle schools | 1 Per each teacher, plus 1 Per each 25 students, plus 1 Per each employee |
| Child-care center, or nursery schools | 1 Per each 5 students, plus 1 Per each employee |

| Day-care homes | 1 Per each employee and/or caregiver |
| Stadiums, sports arenas, and auditoriums | 1 Per each 4 seats based on maximum seating capacity |
| Libraries and museums | 1 Per each 500 square feet of floor area |

*General Commercial Uses*

| Retail stores, except as otherwise | 1 Per each 100 square feet of floor area specified herein |
| Supermarkets, drugstores, and other self-service retail establishments | 1 Per 150 square feet of floor area |
| Convenience stores and video stores | 1 Per 100 square feet of floor area |
| Planned shopping center | 1 Per 100 square feet of floor area for the first 15,000 square feet, plus 1 Per 150 square feet of floor area in excess of 15,000 square feet |
| Furniture, appliances, hardware, household equipment sales | 1 Per each 400 square feet of floor area, plus 1 Per each employee |
| Motels and hotels | 1 Per each guest bedroom, plus 1 Per employee, plus amount required for accessory uses, such as a restaurant or cocktail lounge |
| Fast-food restaurant | 1 Per each 125 square feet of floor area, plus 1 Per each employee |
| Sit-down restaurants | 1 Per each 3 seats, based on maximum seating capacity, plus 1 Per each employee |
| Taverns and cocktail lounges | 1 Per each 3 persons allowed within the (other than fast-food restaurants) maximum occupancy load as established by fire and/or building codes, plus 1 Per each employee |
| Garden stores, building material sales | 1 Per each 800 square feet of lot area used for the business provided for herein |
| Movie theaters | 1 Per each 4 seats based on the maximum seating capacity, plus 1 Per each employee |
| Wholesale stores, machinery sales, and other similar uses | 1 Per each 1,000 square feet of floor area, plus 1 per each employee |

*Automotive Uses*

| Auto sales | 1 Per each 200 square feet of showroom floor area, plus 1 Per each employee, plus 1 Per each service stall |
| Automotive repair facilities | 2 Per each service stall, plus 1 Per each employee, plus 1 Per each service vehicle |
| Gasoline stations without convenience store | 1 Per each pump unit, plus 2 Per each service stall, plus 1 Per each employee |
| Gasoline stations with convenience store | 1 Per each pump unit, plus 2 Per each service stall, plus 1 Per each employee, plus 1 Per each 100 square feet of floor area devoted to retail sales and customer service |
| Car washes (self-serve) | 1 Per each wash stall, plus 1 Per each vacuum station, plus 1 Per each employee |

# APPENDIX D

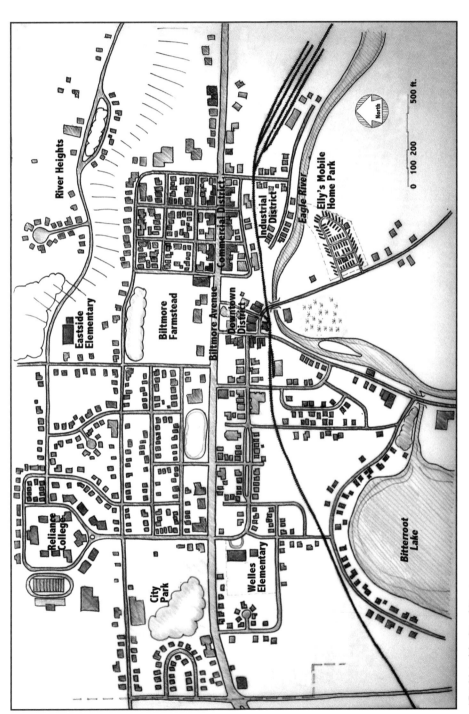

AD.1 *Map of the City of Rivertown*

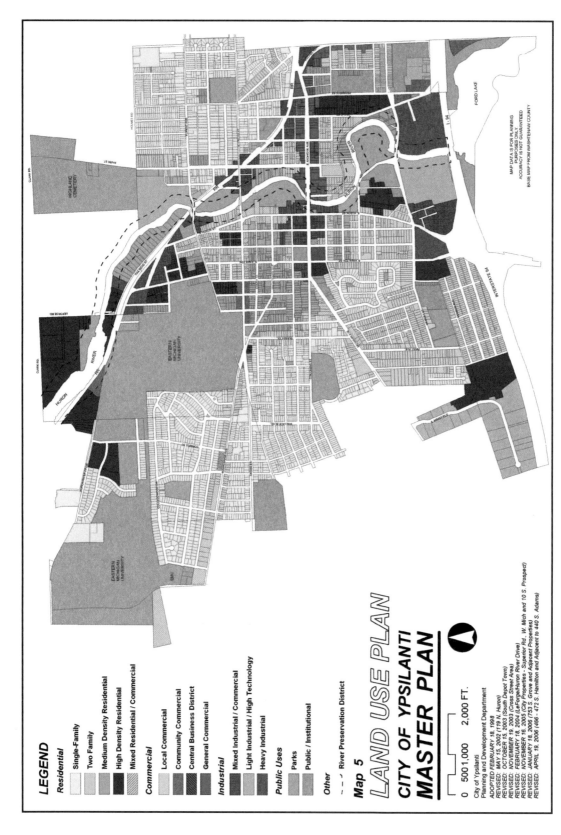

AD.2 *Land Use Plan for the City of Ypsilanti, Michigan*

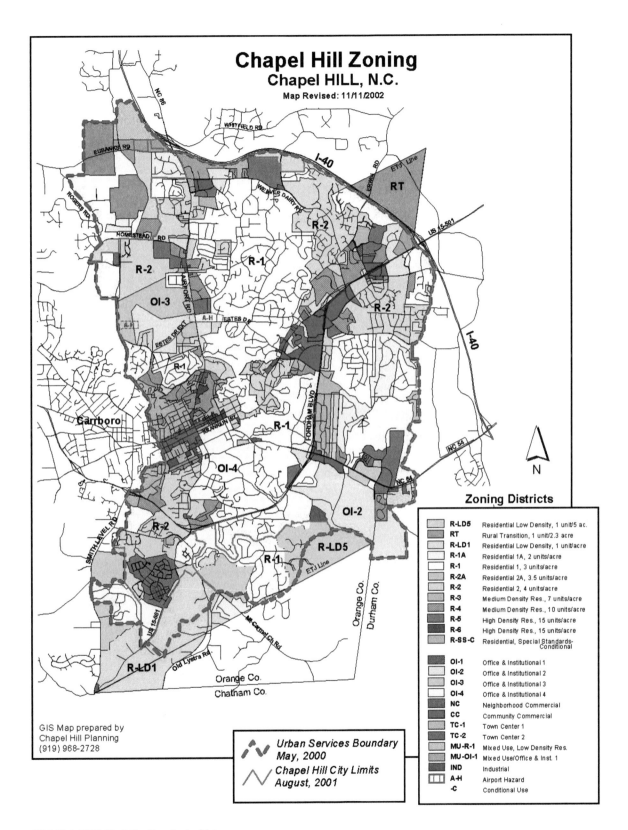

**Zoning Districts**

| | | |
|---|---|---|
| R-LD5 | Residential Low Density, 1 unit/5 ac. |
| RT | Rural Transition, 1 unit/2.3 acre |
| R-LD1 | Residential Low Density, 1 unit/acre |
| R-1A | Residential 1A, 2 units/acre |
| R-1 | Residential 1, 3 units/acre |
| R-2A | Residential 2A, 3.5 units/acre |
| R-2 | Residential 2, 4 units/acre |
| R-3 | Medium Density Res., 7 units/acre |
| R-4 | Medium Density Res., 10 units/acre |
| R-5 | High Density Res., 15 units/acre |
| R-6 | High Density Res., 15 units/acre |
| R-SS-C | Residential, Special Standards-Conditional |
| OI-1 | Office & Institutional 1 |
| OI-2 | Office & Institutional 2 |
| OI-3 | Office & Institutional 3 |
| OI-4 | Office & Institutional 4 |
| NC | Neighborhood Commercial |
| CC | Community Commercial |
| TC-1 | Town Center 1 |
| TC-2 | Town Center 2 |
| MU-R-1 | Mixed Use, Low Density Res. |
| MU-OI-1 | Mixed Use/Office & Inst. 1 |
| IND | Industrial |
| A-H | Airport Hazard |
| -C | Conditional Use |

Urban Services Boundary May, 2000

Chapel Hill City Limits August, 2001

GIS Map prepared by Chapel Hill Planning (919) 968-2728

*AD.3 Chapel Hill, North Carolina, Zoning Map*

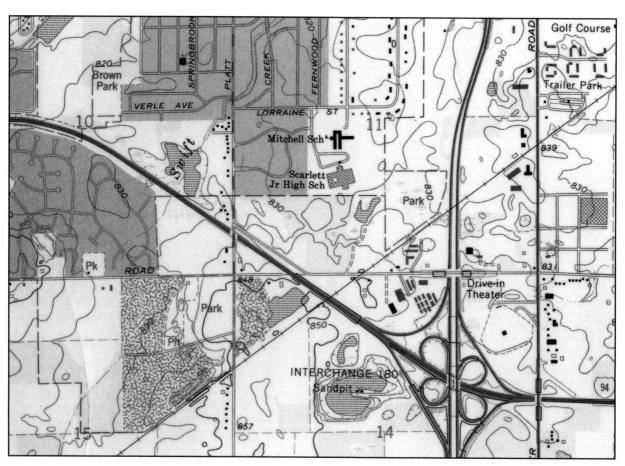

*AD.4 Quad Map of Washtenaw County, Michigan*

# NOTES

## 1. The Practice of Planning

1 Marty Nemko, "Best Careers 2009: Urban Regional Planning," *U.S. News and World Report* (December 11, 2008), http://www.usnews,com/articles/business/best-careers/2008/12/11 (accessed June 3, 2009).

2 Tara Kalwarski, Daphne Mosher, Janet Paskin, and Donna Rosato, "50 Best Jobs in America," *Money* (April 12, 2006) http://money.cnn.com/magazines/moneymag/moneymag_archive/2006/05/01/8375749/index.htm (accessed June 3, 2009).

3 "Occupational Outlook Handbook, 2008-09 Edition," Bureau of Labor Statistics, U.S. Department of Labor, http://www.bls.gov/oco/ocos057.htm (accessed June 3, 2009).

4 Anya Kamenetz, "Ten Best Green Jobs for the Next Decade," *Fast Company*, http://www.fastcompany.com/articles/2009/01/best-green-jobs.html (accessed June 3, 2009).

5 *Green Careers Guide*, http://www.greencareersguide.com/Urban-Planner.html (accessed June 3, 2009).

6 "The Lexicon of New Urbanism," 1999 (draft document available from Duany Plater-Zyberk & Company, Miami, Florida).

7 *Encyclopedia Britannica* online, http://www.britannica.com/EBchecked/topic/619445/urban-planning (accessed June 3, 2009).

8 Ann Markusen, "Planning as Craft and as Philosophy," *The Profession of City Planning: Changes, Images, and Challenges, 1950–2000*, Lloyd Rodwin and Bishwapriya Sanyal, ed. (New Brunswick, NJ: Center for Urban Policy Research, Rutgers, 2000), 264 and 265.

9 W. Paul Farmer, "A Planning Agenda, Post 2009," *Planning* (June 2009): 3.

10 American Planning Association, "Salary Survey Summary," www.planning.org/salary/summary.htm (posted June 2008).

11 See http://www.acsp.org/org/links_to_planning_schools.htm for a list of accredited planning programs.

12 Excerpted from a letter written to students by Rodney C. Nanney, AICP, principal planner for Building Place Consultants.

13 M. Christine Boyer, *Dreaming the Rational City: The Myth of American City Planning* (Cambridge, MA: The MIT Press, 1986), 27.

14 Leonardo Vazquez, "Overcoming the Comfort of Powerlessness," *Planning* (May 23, 2005): 60.

## 2. Conceptual Approaches to Planning

1 Edmund Bacon, *Design of Cities* (New York: Viking Penguin Inc., 1967), 108 and 109.

2 John W. Reps, *The Making of Urban America* (Princeton, NJ: Princeton University Press, 1965), 297.

3 Ebenezer Howard, *Tomorrow: A Peaceful Path to Real Reform* (London: Routledge, 2003 edition).

4 Le Corbusier, *Towards a New Architecture* (Mineola, NY: Dover Publications, Inc. 1986, based on 1931 translation by John Rodker), 95.

5 Quoted in Rem Koolhaas, *Delirious New York: A Retroactive Manifesto for Manhattan* (New York: Monacelli Press, 1997), 267.

6 See, for example, Robert Caro, *The Power Broker: Robert Moses and the Fall of New York* (New York: Vintage, 1975) and Hilary Ballon and Kenneth Jackson, *Robert Moses and the Modern City: The Transformation of New York* (New York: W. W. Norton, 2008).

7 Excerpt from *The World That Moses Built*, produced by Edward Gray (Obenhaus Films, Inc. 1988).

8 Suzanne Stevens, "A Look Back: Planner Ed Bacon," *Architectural Record* (November 22, 2005): 36.

9 Jane Jacobs, *The Death and Life of the Great American City* (New York: Random House, Inc., 1961).

10 Ibid., p. 3.

11 Norman Krumholz and J. Forester, *Making Equity Planning Work* (Philadelphia: Temple University Press, 1990), 51.

12 Norman Krumholz and Pierre Clavel, *Reinventing Cities: Equity Planners Tell Their Stories* (Philadelphia: Temple University, 1994), 3.

13 Norman Krumholz, "A Retrospective View of Urban Planning Cleveland 1969–1979," *Journal of the American Planning Association* 48, no. 2 (1982): 163.

14 Quoted in Robert T. Grieves and Peter Stoler, "He Digs Downtown," *Time*, August 24, 1981. http://www.time.com/time/magazine/article/0,9171,949385,00.html (accessed 24 December 2009).

15 John Friedmann, *Planning in the Public Domain: From Knowledge to Action* (Princeton, NJ: Princeton University Press, 1987), 38.

16 For an example of this approach, see Amy Gardner, "Tysons Plan Poised To Move Forward: Redevelopment's Scope, Pace Still Sticking Points," *Washington Post*, (August 12, 2008), www.washingtonpost.com/wp-dyn/content/article/2008/08/11/AR2008081102450.html (accessed September 24, 2009).

17 Tore Sager, "Teaching Planning Theory as Order or Fragments," *Journal of Planning Education and Research* 14,3 (Spring 1995): 172.

18 John Forester, "Judgment and the Cultivation of Appreciation in Policy-Making," *American Behavioral Scientist* 38, no. 1 (September 1994): 64.

19 Norman Krumholz, Janice Cogger, and John Linner, "Make No Big Plans . . . Planning in Cleveland in the 1970's," in Robert W. Burchell and George Sternlieb, *Planning Theory in the 1980's: A Search for Future Directions* (New Brunswick, NJ: Center for Urban Policy Research, Rutgers University, 1978), 39,

### 3. The Scope of Planning at the Federal, State, Regional and Local Levels

1 Marlow Vesterby and Kenneth S. Krupa, *Major Uses of Land in the United States, 1997* (Washington, D.C.: Resource Economics Division, Economic Research Service, U.S. Department of Agriculture. Statistical Bulletin No. 973), http://www.ers.usda.gov/publications/sb973/sb973.pdf (accessed July 7, 2009).

2 http://www.state.de.us/planning/aboutagency.html (accessed May 11, 2009).

3 Commission on Behavioral and Social Sciences and Education (CBASSE), "Governance and Opportunity in Metropolitan America," http://www.nap.edu/openbook.php?isbn=0309065534 (accessed April 12, 2010).

4 Myron Orfield, *American Metropolitics: The New Suburban Reality* (Washington, D.C.: The Brookings Institution Press, 2002), 107.

5 National Association of Regional Councils, "What Is a Regional Council?" http://narc.org/regional-councils-mpos/what-is-a-regional-council.html (accessed April 12, 2010).

6 The Riverdale City Planning Commission, Riverdale, Utah, http://www.riverdalecity.com/how_do_i/contact.htm (accessed September 24, 2009).

7 A good resource on the role of planning commissioners is: Albert Solnit, *The Job of the Planning Commissioner* (Chicago: APA Press, 1987).

8 Melvin Webber, "A Difference Paradigm for Planning" in *Planning Theory in the 1980s: Search for Future Directions* (New Brunswick, NJ: Rutgers University Center for Urban Policy Research, 1978), 157.

9 Clarence N. Stone, *Regime Politics: Governing Atlanta, 1946–1988* (Lawrence, KS: The University Press of Kansas, 1989), 3.

10 Quoted in Robert G. Dixon, Jr., "The Reapportionment Amendments and Direct Democracy," *State Government* (Spring 1965): 117.

11 Quoted in David Dillon, "Jane Jacobs: Eyes on the Street," *Preservation Magazine* 50, no. 1 (January/February, 1998): 39.

12 From notes taken at a presentation by Barbara Roelofs at the University of Michigan, 1983.

13 For more factors associated with email and Internet surveys, see Matthias Schonlau, Ronald D. Fricker, and Marc N. Elliott, *Conducting Research Surveys via E-mail and the Web* (Santa Monica, CA: Rand, 2002).

### 4. The Comprehensive Plan

1 Charles M. Haar, "The Master Plan: An Impermanent Constitution," *Law & Contemporary Problems: Urban Housing and Planning* 20, no. 3 (Summer 1955) (Durham, NC, Duke University School of Law): 353–418.

2 K. Dychtwald, *Age Wave: How the Most Important Trend Of Our Time Can Change Your Future* (New York: St. Martin's Press, 1990).

3 The model described here is a modification to a Small Area Forecast model developed in the 1970s by the Southeast Michigan Council of Governments.

4 Software commonly used for small area forecasting includes IMPLAN (www.implan.com), REMI (www.remi.com), and URBANSIM (www.urbansim.org).

5 2009 Fiscal Impact Committee Guidelines: Demographic, Economic, and Fiscal Assumptions and Forecasts (Loudoun County, Virginia, Loudoun County Board of Supervisors), 1.

6 Ibid, A-11.

7 For an excellent description of the elements of a comprehensive plan, refer to the Rhode Island "Handbook on the Local Comprehensive Plan" (Handbook No. 16, 2003) available online at http://www.planning.ri.gov/comp/handbook16.pdf.

8 Metropolitan Planning Organizations (MPOs) are agencies established to administer regional planning and funding for transportation projects.

9 Go to http://andoverma.gov/planning/ for the complete document

10 SWOT analysis was developed at the Stanford Research Institute.

### 5. Planners and the Design Process

1 J. Christopher Jones, *Design Methods: Seeds of Human Futures* (New York: Wiley-Interscience, 1970).

2. Christopher Alexander et al., *A New Theory of Urban Design* (New York: Oxford University Press, 1987), 2 and 3.

3 Randall Arendt et al., *Rural by Design: Maintaining Small Town Character* (Chicago: Planners' Press, 1994), 48–53.

4 Village of Riverside, "About Riverside," Riverside, Illinois, Web site, http://www.riverside.il.us/index.asp?Type=B_BASIC&SEC={DC4955B9-2DBD-4383-A011-14F34A625889}&DE=.

5 Quoted in Peter Hall, "The Turbulent Eighth Decade: Challenges to American City Planning," *Journal of the American Planning Association* 55, no. 3 (Summer 1989): 277.

6 Ibid.

7 John M. Levy, *Contemporary Urban Planning* (Englewood Cliffs, NJ: Prentice-Hall, Inc., 1994), 38.

8 Quoted in Robert A. Beauregard, "Without a Net: Modernist Planning and the Postmodern Abyss," *Journal of Planning Education and Research* 10, 3 (Fall 1991): 191.

9 For a fuller description of the development of the Chicago plan of 1909, see the Chicago Historical Society's Web site, "The Plan of Chicago," at http://www.encyclopedia.chicago-history.org/pages/10537.html.

10 Quoted in Kurt Andersen, "Oldfangled New Towns," *Time* (May 20, 1991): 52.

11 Christopher Alexander and Jenny Quillen, "The Vital Work of Andres Duany: A Commentary," at Pattern Language's Web site, www.patternlanguage.com/townplanning/duany.htm (accessed May 19, 2009).

12 Heidi Landecker, "Is New Urbanism Good for America?" *Architecture* (April 1996): 68.

13 William H. Whyte, "The Humble Street," *Historic Preservation* (January 1980): 34.

14 Clarence Arthur Perry, "The Neighborhood Unit," in *Regional Survey of New York and Its Environs, Volume VII: Neighborhood and Community Planning* (New York: Committee on Regional Plan of New York and Its Environs, 1929), 88.

15 Richard Gilbert and Catherine O'Brien, *Child- and Youth-Friendly Land-Use and Transport Planning Guidelines for British Columbia* (Centre for Sustainable Transportation, University of Winnepeg, Winnepeg, Manitoba, Canada: April 27, 2005), 25.

16 Andres Duany and Elizabeth Plater-Zyberk, *Lexicon of the New Urbanism* (draft, Miami, Florida: Duany Plater-Zyberk and Company, 1999).

17 Malcolm Wells, *Underground Designs* (Cherry Hill, NJ: Self-published, 1977), 72.

18 A description of Norfolk, Virginia's Pattern Book can be found at: http://www.norfolk.gov/comehome/norfolk_pattern_book.asp (accessed July 2, 2010).

19 City of Portland Bureau of Planning, "Central City Fundamental Design Guidelines" (April 1, 2001; updated November 8, 2003), 28.

20 *Downtown Plan Urban Design and Architectural Guidelines* (Scottsdale, AZ: City of Scottsdale Planning Resources, approved July 1986, updated March 2004), Preface.

21 Austin City Connection, "Downtown Austin Design Guidelines," City of Austin, Texas, official Web site: http://www.ci.austin.tx.us/downtown/downloads/dg060-072.pdf.

22 Bryan Lawson, *How Designers Think: The Design Process Demystified* (Burlington, MA: Architectural Press, Elsevier, 2005).

23 American Planning Association, "Planning Advisory Service MEMO," American Planning Association, Chicago, IL, August 1995.

24 Bruce Liedstrand, "Fundamentals of a Good City," at the Walkable Streets Web site: http://www.walkablestreets.com/city.htm.

**6. Urban Planning and Downtown Revitalization**

1 Ferdinand Tönnies, *Community and Society (Gemeinschaft and Gesellschaft)* (Edison, NJ: Transaction Publishers, 1988; first published in German in 1887).

2 Willliam Alonso, *Location and Land Use: Toward a General Theory of Land Rent* (Cambridge, MA: Harvard University Press, 1965).

3 Joel Garreau, *Edge City* (New York: Doubleday, 1991).

4 Kevin Lynch, *The Image of the City* (Cambridge, MA: MIT Press, 1960).

5 Robert A. Peterson, ed., *The Future of U.S. Retailing* (New York: Quorum Books, 1991), 54 and 55.

6 Alan Trachtenberg, *The Incorporation of America* (New York: Hill and Wang, 1982), 130.

7 Information from the Mall of America Web site: www.mallofamerica.com.

8 Zenia Kotval and John R. Mullin, "When the Mall Comes to a Small Town: How to Shape Development with Carrots and Sticks," *Small Town* (September/October 1992): 21.

9 Gibbs Planning Group PowerPoint, July 17, 2008, http://alexandriava.gov/uploadedFiles/planning/info/landmark-van-dorn/LVD2008_07_17cmp.pdf (accessed October 10, 2009).

10 Brian J. L. Berry, "Commercial Structure and Commercial Blight," Research Paper No. 85, University of Chicago, Department of Geography, 1963, as found in Michael Pacione, *Urban Geography: A Global Perspective*, 2nd ed. (London: Taylor and Francis, 2001), 253.

11 Sprawl-Busters.com, "Charlotte, N.C. Planners Want Demolition Bond for Big Boxes," http://sprawl-busters.com/search.php?readstory=973 (accessed March 6, 2009).

12 Ibid.

13 Gertrude Stein, *Everybody's Autobiography* (Berkeley, CA: Exact Change [Small Press Distribution], 2004), 289.

14 Eugenie L. Birch, "Who Lives Downtown? in the Brookings Institution's *Living Cities Census Series*, November 2005, 1.

15 Richard Florida, *The Rise of the Creative Class: And How It's Transforming Work, Leisure, Community and Everyday Life* (New York: Basic Books, 2003).

16 Stephanie Ebbert, "Waterfront's Not Yet Feeling Like Home," *Boston Globe*, June 29, 2008, http://www.boston.com/news/local/articles/2008/06/29/waterfronts_not_yet_feeling_like_home.

17 This case study was researched and written by Eastern Michigan University graduate student Denise Pike.

18 City of Baltimore Department of Planning, *The Inner Harbor Book* (1984).

19 Baltimore Development Corporation, *Inner Harbor Coordinator Annual Report* (2008), 6.

20 City of Baltimore Department of Planning, *The Inner Harbor Book* (1984).

21 *Community Reinvestment Act of 1971* (rev. 1995, 2005), Public Law 95-128, title VIII, 91 Stat. 1147, 12 U.S.C. § 2901 et seq.

22 Ruth Simon and James R. Hagerty, "1 in 4 Borrowers Under Water." *Wall Street Journal.* (November 24, 2009): A1.

23 Wyoming Urban Renewal Code, "Chapter 9—Urban Renewal," Article 1 (Urban Development), http://legisweb.state.wy.us/statutes/titles/Title15/T15CH9.htm.

24 Mark Jenkins, "Bringing Retail Back Downtown," *Urban*

*Land* (June 1989): 2–5. See also the Washington, D.C., Zoning Ordinance, Section 1703, "Downtown Shopping District (Retail Core)."

25 Duane Desiderio is quoted in an article by Gurdon H. Buck, "The Latest Buzz in the Land Development Cocktail Parties: 'Smart Growth,' 'Urban Sprawl,' 'New Urbanism,' 'The Village Districts'" (Palm Beach, FL: American College of Real Estate Lawyers, Spring 1999), http://www.acrel.org/Documents/Seminars/a000013.pdf.

26 Metro Regional Government, "Urban growth boundary," http://www.metro-region.org/index.cfm/go/by.web/id/277 (accessed April 17, 2009).

## 7. Housing

1 U.S. Bureau of the Census, http://www.census.gov/hhes/www/income/histinc/h11AR.html and http://www.census.gov/statab/hist/HS-12.pdf.

2 Alex F. Schwartz, *Housing Policy in the United States: An Introduction* (New York: Routledge, 2006), 1.

3 From Barry Checkoway and Carl V. Patton, *The Metropolitan Midwest: Policy Problems and Prospects for Change* (Champaign, IL: University of Illinois Press, 1991), 238.

4 Robert L. Green, *The Urban Challenge: Poverty and Race* (Chicago: Follett, 1977), 179.

5 Paul Knox, *Urban Social Geography: An Introduction* (New York: John Wiley & Sons, Inc., 1987), 223.

6 U.S. Census Bureau, "Current Population Survey: POV01: Age and Sex of All People, Family Members and Unrelated Individuals Iterated by Income-to-Poverty Ratio and Race: 2007," http://www.census.gov/hhes/www/macro/032008/pov/new01_100_01.htm.

7 Martin Kasindorf, "Nation Taking a New Look at Homelessness, Solutions," *USA Today* (October 12, 2005): A1.

8 Dennis Culhane, "Not Always What They Seem," *The Economist* (October 20, 2007): 46.

9 Kurt Anderson, "Spiffing Up the Urban Heritage," *Time* (November 23, 1987): 79.

10 Sacramento Regional Research Institute, "The Economic Benefits of Housing in California," (Sacramento, CA: Sacramento Regional Research Institute, 2008), 5.

11 Section written by Jill Morgan, Winnetka, Illinois, planner.

## 8. Historic Preservation and Planning

1 *Penn Central Transportation Company v. City of New York.* 438 U.S. 104, 98 S. Ct. 2646 (1978).

2 For examples of such studies, see Robin M. Keichenko, N. Edward Coulson, and David Listokin, "Historic Preservation and Residential Property Values: An Analysis of Texas Cities," *Urban Studies* 38, no. 11, (2001): 1973–1987; and Amy Facca, "An Introduction to Preservation Planning," http://www.plannersweb.com/wfiles/w191.html (accessed January 16, 2010).

3 Donovan Rypkema, "Economics, Sustainability, and Historic Preservation," National Trust Conference, Portland, Oregon, October 1, 2005.

4 Robert M. Ward and Norman Tyler, "Integrating Historic Preservation Plans with Comprehensive Plans," *Planning* (October 2005): 24.

5 Planning Advisory Service Report 450, "Preparing a Historic Preservation Plan," (American Planning Association, Chicago, Illinois, March 1994).

6 Eric Damian Kelly and Barbara Becker, *Community Planning: An Introduction to the Comprehensive Plan* (Washington, D.C.: Island Press, 2000), 5.

7 Christopher Duerksen, *A Handbook of Historic Preservation Law* (Naperville, IL: Conservation Foundation, 1983), 70.

8 *The Secretary of the Interior's Standards for Rehabilitation* (Washington, D.C.: National Park Service Technical Preservation Services, 1990), http://www.nps.gov/history/hps/TPS/tax/rhb/stand.htm.

9 Quoted in *Coltsville Historic District*, James C. O'Connell, National Historic Landmark Nomination, United States Department of the Interior, National Park Service, Washington, D.C., July 25, 2006, 19.

10 United Nations 96th General Assembly Plenary Meeting, *Report of the World Commission on Environment and Development* (42/187), December 11, 1987, 1.

11 Carl Elephante, "The Greenest Building Is . . . One That Is Already Built," *Forum Journal* (May 25, 2007): 1.

## 9. Local Economic Development

1 Josh Bivens, *Updated Employment Multipliers for the U.S. Economy (2003)* (Washington DC: Economic Policy Institute, 2003), 3.

2 The following material appears as revised and adopted by the Local Government Commission, 1997. From "Ahwahnee Principles for Economic Development: Smart Growth: Economic Development for the 21st Century: A Set of Principles for Building Prosperous and Livable Communities," http://www.lgc.org/ahwahnee/econ_principles.html (accessed March 17, 2009).

3 Richard Florida, *The Rise of the Creative Class: And How It's Transforming Work, Leisure, Community and Everyday Life* (New York: Basic Books, 2002).

4 Daniel Shefer and Lisa Kaess, "Evaluation Methods in Urban and Regional Planning: Theory and Practice" in *Evaluation Methods for Urban and Regional Plans: Essays in Memory of Morris (Moshe) Hill*, ed. Daniel Shefer and Henk Voogd (London: Pion Limited, 1990), 99.

5 Ian Bracken, *Urban Planning Methods: Research and Policy Analysis* (New York: Methuen, 1981), 74–79.

6 This Cross-Impact Analysis Chart is based on an example in a book by Thomas S. Lyons and Roger E. Hamlin, *Creating an Economic Development Action Plan: A Guide for Development Professionals* (Westport, CT: Praeger Publishers, 2001), 147–154.

7 Fritz W. Wagner, Timothy E. Joder, and Anthony J. Mumphrey Jr., *Urban Revitalization: Policies and Programs* (Thousand Oaks, CA: Sage Publications, Inc., 1995), 203 and 204.

8 U.S. Small Business Administration Office of Advocacy,

"Small Business Profile: United States," http://www.sba.gov/advo/research/profiles/07us.pdf.

9 University of Michigan, NBIA, Ohio University, and Southern Technology Council, *Business Incubation Works* (Athens, OH: National Business Incubation Association, 1997).

10 National Business Incubation Association, "Business Incubation FAQ," http://www.nbia.org/resource_center/bus_inc_facts/index.php (accessed March 21, 2009).

11 Elizabeth Hockerman, "The Business of Summerfest," BizTimes.com (May 25, 2007), http://www.biztimes.com/news/2007/5/25/the-business-of-summerfest (accessed March 20, 2009).

12 A. J. Maldonado, "Survey Shows US Tourism Driven by Casino Gambling," Online Casino Advisory, http://www.onlinecasinoadvisory.com/casino-news/land/survey-shows-casino-gambling-economically-important-42815.htm (accessed June 18, 2009).

13 Joanne Ditmer, "Gambling: A Tiger by the Tail," *Historic Preservation News* (August 1990): 1.

14 Tim Velder, "Deadwood Marks 20 Years of Bets," *Lawrence County Journal* (September 19, 2009): http://www.rapidcityjournal.com/news/local/top-stories/article_c02ec7bb-8a0d-5405-87e6-27f36378ecca.html (accessed October 27, 2009).

15 Ditmer, "Gambling: A Tiger by the Tail."

16 Velder, "Deadwood marks 20 years of bets."

17 Dave Zirin, "The Doming of America," CommonDreams.org, http://www.commondreams.org/archive/2007/07/08/2384/ (accessed March 20, 2009).

18 Dennis Coates and Brad R. Humphreys, "The Stadium Gambit and Local Economic Development," *Regulation* 23, no. 2 (2000): 18.

19 Community Planning & Economic Development: Business Assistance & Finance (sidebar menu on Business Development Services page of the City of Minneapolis's Web page), http://www.ci.minneapolis.mn.us/cped/business_development_home.asp (accessed March 20, 2009).

20 University of Wisconsin Center for Community and Economic Development, Community and Economic Development Tool Box, http://www2.uwsuper.edu/cedpt/index.htm (accessed October 27, 2009).

## 10. Transportation Planning

1 See U.S. Census Bureau, "American Community Survey," for latest data on commuting times, http://www.census.gov/population/www/socdemo/journey.html (accessed April 16, 2010).

2 Lewis Mumford, *The City in History: Its Origins, Its Transformations, and Its Prospects* (New York: Harcourt, Brace and World, Inc., 1961), 486, 509–512.

3 Wilfred Owens, "Automotive Transportation: Trends and Problems," *Land Economics* 26, no. 2 (May 1950): 204 and 205.

4 Steve LeBlanc, "On Dec. 31, It's Official: Boston's Big Dig Will Be Done," *washingtonpost.com,* December 26, 2007, http://www.washingtonpost.com/wp-dyn/content/article/2007/12/25/AR2007122500600.html?nav=hcmoduletmv (accessed March 22, 2009).

5 Martin Gottlieb, "Conversations/Fred Kent; One Who Would Like to See Most Architects Hit the Road," *The New York Times*, March 28, 1993, sec. 4, p. 7.

6 Derived from discussion on Cyburbia, http://www.cyburbia.org/forums/showthread.php?t=36546 (accessed January 26, 2010); City of Ferndale, Michigan, Parking Structure Feasibility Study, June 2009, http://www.ferndale-mi.com/Government/ParkingStructureFeasibilityStudy.pdf.

7 Derived from information at "Shared Parking: Sharing Parking Facilities Among Multiple Users," *TDM Encyclopedia* (Victoria Transport Policy Institute, July 22, 2008), http://www.vtpi.org/tdm/tdm89.htm.

8 U.S. Census Bureau, *Journey to Work 2000*, http://www.census.gov/prod/2004pubs/c2kbr-33.pdf (Washington DC: U.S. Government Printing Office, 2004), 3.

9 American Public Transit Association, Public Transit Ridership Report, Third Quarter 2009, http://www.apta.com/resources/statistics/Documents/Ridership/2009_Q4_ridership_APTA.pdf (accessed April 16, 2010).

10 Bikeways manual for Metropolitan Providence, Rhode Island: "Metropolitan Providence Bicycle Facilities Site Assessment Project" (PARE Project No. 02175.00, April 25, 2005), 8.

11 "Maryland Panel Issues Report on Enhancing Pedestrian Safety," *The Urban Transportation Monitor*, February 8, 2002, 3, 7.

12 Carol Sullivan, "Form and Function in Downtown Revitalization," Doctor of Architecture dissertation, The University of Michigan, 1986, 1.

13 "Sustainable Seattle," Sustainable Seattle, http://www.sustainableseattle.org/Programs/SUNI/researchingconditions/Streetlevelresearch/pedestriancounts/ (accessed May 22, 2009).

14 John Ritter, "Americans Discover Charms of Living Near Mass Transit," *USA Today,* November 18, 2004, http://www.usatoday.com/news/nation/2004-11-08-transit-cover_x.htm (accessed September 22, 2009).

15 Peter Calthorpe, *The Next American Metropolis: Ecology, Community, and the American Dream* 3rd ed, (New York: Princeton Architectural Press, 1995), 56.

16 Metropolitan Transit Development Board, "Designing for Transit," San Diego, CA, July 1993, 3.

17 Joel S. Hirschhorn and Paul Souza, "New Community Design to the Rescue: Fulfilling Another American Dream" (Washington, D.C., National Governors Association, 2001), 79.

18 James Corless, "Safe Routes to School," Surface Transportation Policy Project, www.transact.org (accessed May 22, 2009).

## 11. Environmental Planning

1 The information on NEPA, EA, and EIS is based on information from: http//www.fema.gov/plan/ehp/ehplaws/nepa.shtm (accessed December 15, 2009).

2 Oregon Department of Transportation and Washington State Department of Transportation, "Columbia River Crossing Draft Environmental Impact Statement" (May 21, 2008), http://www.columbiarivercrossing.com/FileLibrary/DraftEIS/DraftEISTableofContents.pdf (accessed November 15, 2009).

3 Information on the Chesapeake Bay Program submitted by Joseph A. Stevens of Stevens, Phillips & McCann, Centreville, Maryland, an environmental law specialist with offices in Maryland and Maine (September 2007).

4 "Our Common Future," a report of the World Commission on Environment and Development, 1987. Published as Annex to General Assembly document A/42/427, Development and International Co-operation: Environment, August 2, 1987. Retrieved November 14, 2007.

5 American Farmland Trust newsletter, Washington, DC, Spring 2007.

## 12. Rural and Transitional Land Use Planning

1 Ruben N. Lubowski, Marlow Vesterby, Shawn Bucholtz, Alba Baez, and Michael J. Roberts, "Major Uses of Land in the United States, 2002," in *Economic Information Bulletin No. EIB-14* (Washington, DC, U.S. Department of Agriculture Economic Research Service, May 2006), i.

2 "The High Costs of Sprawl," *Sacramento Business Journal*, November 14, 2005. Posted on Walkable Streets' Web site, http://www.walkablestreets.com/sprawl2.htm (accessed June 2, 2009).

3 Robert W. Burchell et al., *Sprawl Costs: Economic Impacts of Unchecked Development* (Washington, D.C.: Island Press, 2005).

4 For readers interested in the history, we recommend Conrad Richter's *The Awakening Land*, a trilogy originally published in 1940, reprinted by Ohio University Press in 1991.

5 Ian McHarg, *Design with Nature* (Hoboken, NJ: reprint, John Wiley and Sons, Inc., 1995).

6 Milo Robinson, "A History of Spatial Data Coordination," May 2008, 4. http://www.fgdc.gov/ngac/a-history-of-spatial-data-coordination.pdf (accessed November 8, 2009) and "Introduction: GIS—for Executives," part 2, http://www.richmondgov.com/departments/dit/docs/GISWebContent.pdf (accessed November 8, 2009).

7 Quote by Robert Samborski, executive director of Geospatial Information and Technology Association, from Ed Brock, "Report Shows Trends in GIS Technology Use," *American City & County* online, June 1, 2008.

8 This example, "Open Space Evaluation & Prioritization: Utilizing Geographic Information System Technology," was developed in 2003 for Van Buren Township, Wayne County, Michigan, by the Institute for Geographic Research and Education (IGRE) at Eastern Michigan University. It was prepared by Chris Lehr of Nativescape and Mike Dueweke of IGRE.

## 13. Evolution of Land Use Controls

1 John Locke, *The Second Treatise of Civil Government*, ed. J. W. Goug (1690; reprint, Oxford: Basil Blackwell, 1948), 62, 69.

2 *Charles River Bridge v. Warren Bridge*, 36 U.S. (11 Pet.) 420, 548 (1837).

3 Alan A. Lew, "Geography: USA," http://www.geog.nau.edu/courses/alew/ggr346/text/chapters/ch3.html (accessed May 26, 2008).

4 John W. Reps, *The Making of Urban America* (Princeton, NJ: Princeton University Press, 1965), 217.

5 *Journals of the Continental Congress* 375 (1785).

6 Reps, *The Making of Urban America*, pp. 216 and 217.

7 Advisory Committee on Zoning, *Zoning Primer* (Washington, D.C.: Department of Commerce, 1922), 1.

8 Richard F. Babcock, *The Zoning Game: Municipal Practices and Policies* (Madison, WI: University of Wisconsin Press, 1966), 115.

9 *Village of Euclid v. Ambler Realty Co.*, 272 U.S. 365 (1926). *Nectow v. Cambridge*, 277 U.S. 183 (1928).

10 Babcock, *The Zoning Game*, p. 4.

11 *Simon v. Town of Needham*, 42 NE2d 516 Mass. (1942), and *Dundee Realty Co. v. City of Omaha*, 13 NW2d 634 Neb. (1944).

12 *Golden v. Planning Board of the Town of Ramapo*, 285 N.E.2nd 291 (1972) (New York State Court of Appeals).

13 *Southern Burlington County N.A.A.C.P. v. Mount Laurel Township*, 67 N.J. 151 (1975).

14 Peter Marcuse, "Who/What Decides What Planners Do?" *Journal of the American Planning Association* (Winter 1989): 79–81.

## 14. Zoning and Other Land Use Regulations

1 R. Robert Linowes and Don T. Allensworth, *The Politics of Land Use: Planning, Zoning and the Private Developer* (Santa Barbara, CA: Praeger Publishers, Inc., 1974), 61.

2 *Kelo v. City of New London*, 545 U.S. 469 (2005).

3 Quoted in Justin Gelfand, "Say Goodbye to Hollywood," http://www.castlecoalition.org/index.php?option=com_content&task=view&id=132 (accessed May 28, 2009).

4 Margot Roosevelt, "This Land Is My Land," *Time* (November 6, 2006), http://www.time.com/time/magazine/article/0,9171,1552023,00.html (accessed May 29, 2009).

5 *Pennsylvania Coal Co. v. Mahon*, 260 U.S. 393 (1922).

6 Ivers v. Utah Department of Transportation, 154 P.3d 802 (Utah 2007); Regency Outdoor Advertising, Inc. v. City of Los Angeles, 39 Cal.4th 507, 46 Cal. Rptr.3d 742, 139 P.3d 119 (2006).

7 *Penn Central Transportation Company v. City of New York*, 438 U.S. 104, 98 S.Ct. 2646 (1978).

8 *Penn Central Transportation Company v. City of New York*.

9 *Tahoe-Sierra Preservation Council, Inc. et al. v. Tahoe Regional Planning Agency et al.* 535 U.S. 302 (2002).

10 Other significant takings cases include:
*Nectow v. Cambridge*, 277 U.S. 183 (1928).
*Kaiser Aetna v. United States*, 444 U.S. 164 (1979).
*Agins v. City of Tiburon*, 447 U.S. 255 (1980).
*San Diego Gas & Electric v. City of San Diego*, 450 U.S. 621 (1981).
*Williamson County Regional Planning Commission v. Hamilton Bank*, 473 U.S. 172 (1985).

*MacDonald, Sommer & Frates v. County of Yolo*, 477 U.S. 340 (1986).

*Keystone Bituminous Coal Association v. DeBenedictis* 480 U.S. 470 (1987).

*First English Evangelical Lutheran Church v. County of Los Angeles*, 482 U.S. 304 (1987).

*Concrete Pipe and Products v. Construction Laborers Pension Trust for Southern California*, 113 S.Ct. 2264 (1993).

*Dolan v. City of Tigard*, 114 S.Ct. 2309 (1994)

*Palazzolo v. Rhode Island*, 533 U.S. 606 (2001).

11 *Lucas v. South Carolina Coastal Council*, 112 S.Ct. 2886 (1992).

12 *Baker v. City of Milwaukie (Oregon)* 533 P.2d 772 (1975).

13 Richard F. Babcock, *The Zoning Game: Municipal Practices and Policies* (Cambridge, MA: Lincoln Institute of Land Policy, 1966), 3.

14 Jane Jacobs, *The Death and Life of Great American Cities* (New York: Random House, 1961), 150.

15 jhttp://canandaigua.govoffice.com/index.asp?Type=B_BASIC&SEC={476DBD96-4AF5-483B-9F7A-BAE9D3E81E30, (accessed May 29, 2009)

16 *State ex rel. Zupancic v. Schimenz*, 46 Wis.2d 22, 174 N.W.2d 533 (1970).

17 Quoted in Miller Canfield, "Miller Canfield and McKenna Associates Announce Contract Zoning Seminar," http://www.millercanfield.com/news-284.html (accessed May 29, 2009).

18 "Definition of a Form-Based Code," Form-Based Code Institute., http://www.formbasedcodes.org/definition.html (accessed March 7, 2010).

19 Edward M. Bassett, *Zoning: The Laws, Administration and Court Decisions the First Twenty-Five Years* (Manchester, NH: Ayer Company Publishers, 1936), 70.

20 *Church of Jesus Christ of Latter-Day Saints v. Jefferson County*, 741 F. Supp. 1522, 1534 (N.D.) Ala. 1990; and Roman P. Storzer and Anthony R. Picarello, Jr., "The Religious Land Use and Institutionalized Persons Act of 2000: A Constitutional Response to Unconstitutional Zoning Practices," http://www.becketfund.org/files/861488fc5325be844c5d284f1c341956.pdf 932 (accessed May 29, 2009).

21 Religious Land Use and Institutionalized Persons Act (RLUIPA), 42 U.S.C. §§2000cc, et seq.

22 Utah County Community Development, "Utah County Land Use Ordinance," (updated 5 April 2007), http://www.co.utah.ut.us/apps/WebLink/Dept/COMDEV/LandUseOrdinance_3.pdf (accessed May 29, 2009), 142-3.

23 Maine Coast Heritage Trust, "Property Taxes," http://www.mcht.org/land_protection/options/property_taxes/ (accessed May 29, 2009).

## 15. Subdivisions, Site Plans, and Site Plan Review

1 Advisory Committee on City Planning and Zoning of the U.S. Department of Commerce, *Standard City Planning Enabling Act 14* (Washington, D.C.: U.S. Department of Commerce, 1928), 27.

2 Rock Springs, Wyoming, Subdivision Ordinances Web page, http://www.rswy.net/egov/gallery/1531256763351703.jpg (accessed March 20, 2010).

## 16. Capital Improvements Program and Local Government Financing

1 Graphic based on CIP for Chapel Hill, Capital Program,, Town to Chapel Hill, http://townhall.townofchapelhill.org/agendas/2009/05/06/1/15_capital.pdf (accessed June 6, 2009).

2 Florida Legislative Committee on Intergovernmental Relations, "Florida Impact Fee Review Task Force: Final Report and Recommendations," February 1, 2006. www.floridalcir.gov/UserContent/docs/File/taskforce/011806draftreport.pdf (accessed September 22, 2009).

3 Phil Gordon, "Tax Incentives for Retailers No Magic Bullet," *The Arizona Republic*, August 2, 2004, http://mail.planetizen.com/node/13971 (accessed May 31, 2009).

4 The concept of site-value taxation was introduced in Henry George, *Progress and Poverty* (1897; New York: Cosimo Classics, 2006 reprint).

5 Arthur C. Nelson and Mitch Moody, Executive Summary of *Paying for Prosperity: Impact Fees and Job Growth* (Washington, DC: Brookings Institution, June 2003), http://www.brookings.edu/reports/2003/06metropolitanpolicy_nelson.aspx (accessed July 7, 2009).

6 Mayor Stephen Goldsmith, "New Hope for the Cities," *Civic Bulletin*, No. 5 (June 1996). http://www.manhattan-institute.org/html/cb_5.htm (accessed July 7, 2009).

7 Joel Garreau, *Edge City* (New York: Doubleday, 1991), 185.

# GLOSSARY

ADVOCACY (EQUITY) PLANNING: Participatory and redistributive policy as part of the planning process.

AERIAL PHOTOGRAPHS: Images of the earth's surface that depict land cover, produced by professional aerial survey companies.

AGGLOMERATION: Clustered land use activities that benefit from being located near each other.

AGGREGATE DATA: Information collected as a whole as opposed to provided in component parts.

ARTERIAL ROADS: Major thoroughfares designed for large quantities of traffic but not designated as highways or interstate roads.

BAROQUE PLANNING: Urban development pattern that accentuates grand architecture, large boulevards with significant axes, centralized open spaces and plazas, and other elements of classic design.

BLIGHT: Neglected, abandoned, or largely underutilized structures or neighborhoods.

BROWNFIELD: An environmentally contaminated site that requires remediation before new uses can occur.

BUILD-OUT ANALYSIS: A quantitative technique that provides an estimate of maximum allowable future growth in a community by land use type and therefore helps identify the potential need for services and infrastructure.

BUSINESS IMPROVEMENT DISTRICT (BID): Organization of commercial property owners in a delineated area that assess member fees to pay for additional services not normally provided by the government.

BUSINESS INCUBATOR: Building with individual offices or cubicles and shared services used by small start-up companies who receive administrative assistance during initial growth.

CAPITAL IMPROVEMENT PLAN/PROGRAM (CIP): Local government plan that indicates annual future budget allocations for major physical improvements.

CENSUS TRACT: A geographic area established by the U.S. Census Bureau to collect statistical data.

CENTRAL BUSINESS DISTRICT (CBD): Commonly the focal point of a community; the "downtown" that contains commercial and service uses.

CHARRETTE: Collaborative group activity used to develop a community design proposal.

CITY BEAUTIFUL: An urban design movement stimulated by the World Columbian Exposition of 1893 in Chicago that emphasized city planning focused on grand classical public architecture, open space and landscape design.

CITY EFFICIENT (CITY FUNCTIONAL): A movement that changed the emphasis of urban planning from design to engineering, infrastructure, economics, and land use law.

CLUSTER DEVELOPMENT: Division of a large parcel that sites buildings in close proximity, leaving sizeable open spaces where further construction is prohibited.

COHORT SURVIVAL FORECASTING: A statistical calculation used to project population based on fertility rates, death rates, and migration data.

COHOUSING: A community where individuals own a residence but share certain common facilities.

COMMERCIAL STRIP: Elongated areas of commercial use with convenient access and parking that develop adjacent to a main road.

COMMUNITY DEVELOPMENT BLOCK GRANT (CDBG): Federal funding given to communities for discretionary use.

COMPREHENSIVE PLAN OR MASTER PLAN: Document adopted by government officials to guide decisionmaking for future growth.

CONCURRENCY: Local requirements requiring installation of infrastructure before building permits are issued for new development.

CONDITIONAL USE ZONING: Zoning category requiring specified land use concerns be addressed before approval is granted for a development project; also called special use zoning.

CONDOMINIUMS: A type of legal land ownership that involves purchase of a specific part of a shared property surrounded by a "commons" area that is available for use by all members of an owners' association.

CONNECTOR ROAD: Subsidiary road that services arterial roads.

CONSOLIDATED METROPOLITAN GOVERNMENT: Several units of local government functioning under one regional government umbrella.

CONTRACT ZONING: A legal document that reduces government regulations for a development in return for a developer providing additional onsite public benefits; see incentive zoning.

COUNCIL OF GOVERNMENTS (COG): A group of counties and smaller governing bodies united under a single agency that serves as a regional planning organization and provides other public services to local members.

DEMOGRAPHICS: The analysis of population data.

DESIGN: Planning that includes a creative or aesthetic aspect.

DESTINATION BUSINESS: An economic activity that can entice people to travel to it for its individual attraction.

DOWNTOWN DEVELOPMENT AUTHORITY (DDA): A quasi-governmental body created to encourage rehabilitation or development projects in a prescribed geographic area—typically a downtown.

DUE PROCESS: A legal process ensuring a citizen's right to be heard before action is taken by a government body or a court of law.

EASEMENT: A document describing rights removed from private property through a voluntary donation to a government or non-profit organization, typically resulting in financial benefit to the property owner. Easements may also include the right of property use or access given by another property owner.

EDGE CITY: Urbanizing area that develops as an identifiable entity along major transportation intersections at the periphery of a larger city and which initially has no autonomous legal status or boundaries.

EGRESS: A constructed exit from a parking lot or building designed to provide safe movement out.

EMINENT DOMAIN: A provision of law that allows government to acquire private property for public benefit by giving the owner just compensation.

ENTERPRISE ZONE: A delineated area created to offer special incentives, usually tax advantages or a relaxation of regulations, to attract development and economic expansion.

ENVIRONMENTAL ASSESSMENT: A required government report that describes the status of the natural environment and the project's impact.

ENVIRONMENTAL IMPACT STATEMENT (EIS): A required federal or state report citing the impact on the environment of a significant development proposal.

EQUITY PLANNING: See advocacy planning.

EUCLIDEAN ZONING: A zoning hierarchy of major land uses where residential (the most restrictive zone) is at the apex of a pyramid but is allowed in commercial zones, and where residential and commercial uses are allowed in industrial zones (least restrictive zone); also called pyramidal zoning.

EXCLUSIVE AGRICULTURAL ZONING: Districts established in an ordinance that prohibit nonfarm-related development.

EXPRESS PERMITTING: Government offices located in proximity to each other to expedite development approvals.

FEDERAL MANDATES: Requirements established by the federal government that necessitate lower levels of government to enact policies, often without monetary appropriations, to avoid penalties.

FIFTH AMENDMENT: Part of the Constitution's Bill of Rights stating that private property cannot be taken for public use without just compensation to the owner.

FINAL SITE PLAN: Modifications to a preliminary site plan required during government review before construction can proceed.

FISCAL IMPACT ANALYSIS: Government cost/benefit assessment pertaining to new development and associated human needs.

FLOODPLAIN: Land adjacent to a river channel that contains hydric soils and is subject to periodic flooding.

FLOOR AREA: Total floor surface of all stories of a building measured from wall to wall.

FLOOR AREA RATIO (FAR): An established zoning standard that regulates the intensity of land use on a site by dividing the total floor area by the area of the property that it occupies, expressed as a decimal number.

FORM-BASED CODES: A type of land regulation that places more emphasis on physical design and surrounding compatibility and less on the category of land use.

FOURTEENTH AMENDMENT: Part of the Constitution that extends due process and equal protection to every citizen and ensures that all governmental actions pertaining to private property owners be reasonable and fair.

FREEDOM OF INFORMATION ACT (FOIA): A law that allows access to government information by providing a process for citizens to request government records.

GARDEN CITIES: New towns located on the periphery of major cities designed to combine the best of city and rural living.

GATED COMMUNITY: A walled residential district that restricts access to non-owners through security points of entry.

GENERAL FUND: Primary savings account for a governmental unit where tax revenue is deposited and used for authorized expenditures.

GENTRIFICATION: Revitalization of an urban neighborhood, often by the private sector, that significantly upgrades the quality of the district, but causes the displacement of existing residents because of higher property values.

GEOGRAPHIC INFORMATION SYSTEMS (GIS): Interactive computer software that allows the use of overlay map displays and data bases for analyses and interpretive graphics.

GOALS: Carefully worded general statements used to project a community's desire for its future.

GREENFIELD: Open space that has not been subject to development.

GROUND FLOOR COVERAGE (GFC): The area of a lot devoted to construction compared to the overall lot size; part of a zoning standard.

GROWTH MANAGEMENT: Governmental regulations that guide the location and intensity of development to prevent sprawl.

HISTORIC DISTRICTS: Geographic areas designated to protect historic resources by identifying and regulating changes to exteriors of historic structures.

HOMELESS: A largely unseen group of people living without housing who spend most nights in supervised facilities, abandoned buildings, or on the street.

HOMEOWNERS ASSOCIATION: A group of residents living in a

neighborhood that elects its governing body to oversee and enforce rules applying land use within the neighborhood.

IMPACT FEES: Charges assessed to a developer when building permits are issued to pay for off-site capital improvements attributed to the project.

INCENTIVE ZONING: See contract zoning.

INCLUSIONARY ZONING: Residential development projects that require a specified portion of the overall units be available for low- and moderate-income individuals or families.

INFRASTRUCTURE: The functional composition of a community, such as streets and water and sewer lines.

INGRESS: Entrance into a parking lot or building designed and constructed to provide safe movement.

INTERURBAN: A form of light rail mass transportation that connected communities, popular primarily from the 1900s to the 1930s.

LAND ASSEMBLY: The consolidation of many small land parcels into one large parcel under single ownership to facilitate large development projects.

LOCAL STREETS AND ROADS: Lowest level of the road hierarchy that carries local traffic to connector and arterial roads.

LONG LOTS: French settlement pattern where individual parcels fronted on waterways; historically divided into lengthy, narrow parcels that allowed each new landowner to retain waterway frontage.

MAIN STREET PROGRAM: A program under the auspices of the National Trust for Historic Preservation established to rehabilitate older commercial buildings and revitalize traditional downtown districts.

MANUFACTURED HOUSING: A house or part of a house built off-site in an industrial facility and moved to a final residential location.

MASTER PLAN (see Comprehensive plan)

METES AND BOUNDS: A survey system based on distances and angles from locally recognized natural reference points to other reference points.

MIL: One dollar for every thousand dollars of taxable property value.

MIXED-USE DEVELOPMENT: A blending of different types of land uses in a single development.

NEW URBANISM: New communities with plans based on the values and physical structure depicted by older cities; also called Neotraditional Urbanism.

NON-CONFORMING USE: A land use lawfully existing before new zoning regulations prohibited it; legally "grandfathered" (permitted).

OBJECTIVES: Action statements prepared to achieve planning "goals."

OVERLAY DISTRICT: An additional zoning requirement that is placed on a geographic area but does not change the underlying zoning.

PERFORMANCE GUARANTEE: Developer money or other financial assurances placed in an escrow account to be held by the government until the completion of the developer's site plan responsibilities.

PERFORMANCE ZONING: An ordinance that specifies flexible uses for a site based on their impact/intensity rather than a list of permitted uses found in traditional zoning.

PERMEABILITY: Rate of time for a liquid to pass through a soil profile.

PHASE 1 ENVIRONMENTAL ASSESSMENT: An initial review of environmental conditions at a site to determine if further environmental investigation is necessary.

PHASE 2 ENVIRONMENTAL ASSESSMENT: More intense investigation requested by the government/landowner if a Phase 1 study notes possible environmental concerns.

PHASE 3 ENVIRONMENTAL ASSESSMENT: A detailed remediation plan required when an environmental concern is identified during a Phase 2 study.

PLANNED UNIT DEVELOPMENT (PUD): A zoning category that provides flexibility and possible mixed land uses and may involve phased development.

PLANNING COMMISSION: A government body that oversees and assists a community's planning staff and makes recommendations to elected officials.

PRELIMINARY SITE PLAN: A formal, initial stage in the preparation of site plans for development required by zoning law.

PRIVATIZATION: The use of private sector contractors to fulfill the responsibilities of public sector employees.

PUBLIC HEARING: A meeting conducted by governmental officials or their designated private consultants to gain citizen input.

PURCHASE OF DEVELOPMENT RIGHTS (PDR): Acquisition from a property owner of the right to develop, overseen by a government or nonprofit organization.

PYRAMIDAL ZONING: See Euclidean zoning

QUARTER ZONING: An agricultural density standard for development that limits one dwelling unit in separate 40-acre parcels, or 1/16 of a 640-acre "section."

REGIONAL PLANNING: Group of local governments responsible for planning future growth beyond a single political jurisdiction.

REVENUE BONDS: Bonds sold to finance projects that will produce revenue for a community.

SEPTIC SYSTEM: An in-ground self-contained processing unit to treat human waste from structures where sewer infrastructure is unavailable.

SETBACK: A zoning regulation that states the minimum distance for placement of structures from front, side, and rear property lines.

SITE PLAN: Scaled drawing(s) and notations that depict the location and arrangement of construction and infrastructure of a development project.

SITE PLAN REVIEW: A detailed examination of elements of a site plan by planning staff to determine whether all elements of the plan comply with local legal requirements.

SITE VALUE TAXATION: A turn-of-the-twentieth century tax policy that places higher tax rates on unimproved land and lower tax rates on developments that improve the land, to discourage underutilization of land and speculation (also known as single tax, two-tiered taxation, and land value taxation).

SLIDING SCALE ZONING: A geometric increase in acreage requirements for permissible development (as opposed to a fixed number of units per acre in traditional zoning ordinance).

SMART GROWTH: Policies to avoid sprawl that often emphasize neotraditional urban values, compact land use, walkability, and public transportation.

SOIL SURVEY: Map of soil characteristics prepared by federal governmental soil scientists.

SPECIAL USE ZONING: See Conditional use zoning.

SPRAWL: Unplanned or poorly planned urban growth at a city's outer margin that extends infrastructure into low-density development or agricultural and open-space lands.

STATE HISTORIC PRESERVATION OFFICE (SHPO): State-level office that administers the responsibilities contained in the National Historic Preservation Act of 1966.

STRATEGY: A specific approach to attain an objective; see Goals and Objectives.

STRENGTHS, WEAKNESSES, OPPORTUNITIES & THREATS (SWOT): An analysis tool that allows a group to evaluate what is good and bad in a community based on internal and external factors.

SUBAREA PLAN: A document or report prepared to guide development in a portion of a community; may be a component of a comprehensive plan.

SUBDIVISION PLAT: A map that indicates how a single parcel of land is divided into smaller parcels or lots.

SUSTAINABILITY: An approach that focuses on how areas of land and water can be developed so its quality is preserved for future generations.

TACTICAL PLANNING: A planning approach that focuses on short-term needs and possibilities and identifies who, what, how, when, where, and cost of the planning solution; see also Traditional planning.

TAKING: Governmental regulation that deprives the owner of a private property without providing fair compensation.

TAX ABATEMENT: Government adjustment of property tax obligations for a fixed period of time intended to encourage new economic opportunities or expand existing ones.

TAX INCREMENT FINANCING (TIF): A widely used economic tool that increases property tax revenue in delineated geographic districts by using any property tax revenue increases to improve the designated area.

TEAR-DOWN HOME: Housing acquired with the intent to demolish and construct more expensive housing on the same lot.

TENEMENT LAWS: Nineteenth-century legislation creating minimum standards for the health, safety, and welfare of renters and other multi-occupancy users in crowded urban residential structures.

TIGER (TOPOLOGICALLY INTEGRATED GEOGRAPHIC ENCODING & REFERENCING): Digitized map data developed by the U.S. Census Bureau.

TOPOGRAPHIC MAPS: Large-scale maps produced by the U.S. Geological Survey indicating land surface morphology and cultural features.

TRADITIONAL/RATIONAL PLANNING: A planning approach based on objective research, analytical techniques, quantification, and science; see also *Tactical planning*.

TRANSFER OF DEVELOPMENT RIGHTS (TDR): Permission granted a property owner by local government code to sell his/her right to develop to a private developer who then is allowed to intensify development elsewhere beyond a required zoning density.

TRANSIT-ORIENTED DEVELOPMENT (TOD): Intensification of mixed-use development in zones around mass transportation terminals.

TRANSPORTATION MODEL: Data collection and analyses used to forecast future transportation needs.

TREND ANALYSIS: Extrapolation of future trends based on the past.

URBAN GROWTH BOUNDARY (UGB): A boundary established by intergovernmental agreement to limit infrastructure improvements and control the extent of future urban development around a city.

URBAN HOMESTEADING: A government program allowing individuals at little or no cost to acquire homes that have reverted to public ownership with the understanding that they will repair the structures and bring them into compliance with building codes.

URBAN RENEWAL: Part of the 1949 Housing Act that initiated removal of substandard buildings and assisted individuals trying to purchase better housing.

VARIANCE: A minor relaxation of provisions in a zoning ordinance to prevent unnecessary hardship.

VISIONING: A process where citizens work with planners at an early stage in the planning process to identify long-term physical, economic, and social community goals.

WALKABLE COMMUNITIES: Planned communities that emphasize compact, mixed-use development and alternatives to dependency on automobiles.

WATERSHED: The area drained by a river.

WETLAND: Land area that is underwater part of the year and results in hydric soils and vegetation highly tolerant to long periods of standing water.

ZONING: Governmental regulations for land use and related developmental requirements, intended to implement the comprehensive plan.

ZONING BOARD OF APPEALS/ADJUSTMENTS (ZBA): An appointed body in a community that acts as a judicial body for specified zoning issues.

ZONING ORDINANCE: A document with text and maps adopted by elected officials to regulate land use and development.

# ABBREVIATIONS AND ACRONYMS

A/EA/E A/E/C A/E/C Architecture Engineering and Contracting industry

AFT American Farmland Trust

AICP American Institute of Certified Planners

APA American Planning Association

ACSP Association of Collegiate Schools of Planning

BID Business Improvement District

BLM Bureau of Land Management

CAD Computer-Aided Design

CBD Central Business District

CIP Community Improvement Program

CDBG Community Development Block Grant

COG Council of Governments

CIP Capital Improvements Program

DDA Downtown Development Authority

DOT Department of Transportation

EA Environmental Assessment

EIS Environmental Impact Statement

EPA Environmental Protection Agency

FAR Floor Area Ratio

FEMA Federal Emergency Management Agency

FHA Federal Housing Administration

FOIA Freedom of Information Act

FONSI Finding of No Significant Impact

FTA Federal Transportation Administration

FTZ Foreign Trade Zones

GFC Ground Floor Coverage

GIS Geographic Information System (or Science)

HOP Housing Opportunities Program

HUD U.S. Department of Housing and Urban Development

IDA Intensely Developed Area

LDA Limited Development Area

LRV Light Rail Vehicles

MPO Metropolitan Planning Organization

NAICS North American Industry Classification System

NALS National Agricultural Land Study

NEPA National Environmental Policy Act of 1969

NOAA National Oceanic and Atmospheric Administration

NPS National Park Service

NWS National Weather Service

PAB Planning Accreditation Board

PDR Purchase of Development Rights

PFA Priority Funding Areas

PILOP Payment in Lieu of Parking

PILOT Payment in Lieu of Taxes

PUD Planned Urban Development

RCA Resource Conservation Area

RCRA Resource Conservation Recovery Act

RFP Request for Proposal

RFQ Request for Qualifications

RLUIPA Religious Land Use and Institutionalized Persons Act

R/UDAT ("roo-dat") Rural/Urban Design Assistance Team

SBA Small Business Administration

SCPEA Standard City Planning Enabling Act

SHPO State Historic Preservation Office

SWOT Strengths, Weaknesses, Opportunities, and Threats

TDR Transfer of Development Rights

THPO Tribal Historic Preservation Office

TIF Tax-Increment Financing

TIGER Topologically Integrated Geographic Encoding and Referencing

TOD Transit-oriented Developments

TMS Transportation Modeling System

UDAG Urban Development Action Grant

UGB Urban Growth Boundary

ZBA Zoning Board of Appeals (or Adjustments)

# LIST OF EXERCISES

Chapter 2. **Conceptual Approaches to Planning**
Exercise 1. Redevelopment of the Biltmore Farmstead Site 29

Chapter 3. **The Scope of Planning at the Federal, State, Regional, and Local Levels**
Exercise 2. Prepare a Survey of Downtown Shoppers for Rivertown 48

Chapter 4. **The Comprehensive Plan**
Exercise 3. Development of a Subarea Plan in Rivertown 67

Chapter 5. **Planners and the Design Process**
Exercise 4. New Town Design near Rivertown 83

Chapter 6. **Urban Planning and Downtown Revitalization**
Exercise 5. Rivertown Tomorrow 96
Exercise 6. Adult World Book Store in Rivertown 98

Chapter 7. **Housing**
Exercise 7. Locating a New Shelter for the Homeless in Rivertown 107

Chapter 8. **Historic Preservation and Planning**
Exercise 8. Delineate Historic District Boundaries in Rivertown 121

Chapter 9. **Local Economic Development**
Exercise 9. Developing a Preliminary Economic Development Plan in Rivertown 138

Chapter 10. **Transportation Planning**
Exercise 10. Transportation Study in Rivertown 148

Chapter 12. **Rural and Transitional Land Use Planning**
Exercise 11. Development for the Cartwright Farm in Rivertown 167
Exercise 12. Interpretation of Contours in Rivertown 171

Chapter 14. **Zoning and Other Land Use Regulations**
Exercise 13. Parking Requirements in Rivertown 191
Exercise 14. A Taking in Rivertown? 196

Chapter 15. **Subdivisions, Site Plans, and Site Plan Review**
Exercise 15. Jolly Burger Restaurant Proposal for Rivertown 207

Chapter 16. **Capital Improvements Program and Local Government Financing**
Exercise 16. Modify the Rivertown Capital Improvements Program 213
Exercise 17. Tax-Increment Financing Caulation for Riveretown 216

# SELECTED READINGS

*Suggested readings, listed by topic, with most recent first:*

## Planning Practice

*Local Planning: Contemporary Principles and Practice* (Washington, D.C.: International City/County Management Association, 2009)

John M. Levy, *Contemporary Urban Planning* (Englewood Cliffs, New Jersey: Prentice Hall, 2008)

J. Barry Cullingworth, *Planning in the USA: Policies, Issues, and Processes* (New York: Routledge, 2008)

Thomas L. Daniels, John H. Keller, Mark B. Lapping, and Katherine Daniels, *The Small Town Planning Handbook (Third edition)* (Chicago: Planners Press, American Planning Association, 2007)

Roger Waldon, *Planners and Politics: Helping Communities Make Decisions* (Chicago: Planners Press, American Planning Association, 2007)

Elisabeth M. Hamlin, Priscilla Geigis, and Linda Silka (editors), *Preserving and Enhancing Communities: A Guide for Citizens, Planners, and Policymakers* (Amherst, Massachusetts: University of Massachusetts Press, 2007)

Philip R. Berke and David R. Godschalk, *Urban Land Use Planning (Fifth Edition)* (Champaign, Illinois: University of Illinois Press, 2006)

Charles Hoch, Linda C. Dalton, and Frank S. So (editors), *The Practice of Local Government Planning* (Washington, D.C., International City/County Management Association, 2000)

Paul C. Zucker, *What Your Planning Professors Forgot to Tell You: 117 Lessons Every Planner Should Know* (Chicago: Planners Press, American Planning Association, 1999)

Albert Solnit, Charles Reed, Duncan, and Peggy Glassford, *The Job of the Practicing Planner* (Chicago: Planners Press, American Planning Association, 1988)

## Planning History

Richard T. LeGates and Frederic Stout, *The City Reader* (New York: Routledge, 2007)

Erik Larson, *The Devil in the White City: Murder, Magic, and Madness at the Fair that Changed America* (New York: Crown Publishers, 2004)

Andro Linklater, *Measuring America* (New York: Penguin Group, 2003)

Alexander Garvin, *The American City: What Works and What Doesn't* (New York City: McGraw-Hill Professional, 2002)

Peter Hall, *Cities of Tomorrow: An Intellectual History of Urban Planning and Design in the Twentieth Century* (Cambridge, Massachusetts: Blackwell Publishers Inc., 1996)

Jay M. Stein (editor), *Classic Readings in Urban Planning: An Introduction,* (New York City: McGraw-Hill, 1995)

Spiro Kostof, *The City Shaped: Urban Patterns and Meanings Through History* (Boston: Little, Brown and Company, 1991)

Robert A. Caro, *The Power Broker: Robert Moses and the Fall of New York* (New York City: Vintage Books, 1974)

Jane Jacobs, *The Death and Life of Great American Cities* (New York: Random House, 1961)

Lewis Mumford, *The City in History: Its Origins, Its Transformations, and Its Prospects* (New York City: Harcourt, Brace & World, 1961)

## Comprehensive Planning

Eric Damian Kelly and Barbara Becker, *Community Planning: An Introduction to the Comprehensive Plan* (Washington, D.C.: Island Press, 2000)

Daniel H. Burnham and Edward H. Bennett, *Plan of Chicago,* (reprint, New York: Da Capo Press, 1970)

## Urban Design

Frederick R. Steiner and Kent Butler, *Planning and Urban Design Standards* (Hoboken, New Jersey: John Wiley and Sons, 2007)

Urban Design Associates, *The Urban Design Handbook: Techniques and Working Methods* (New York City: W.W. Norton, 2003)

Peter Calthorpe, *The Next American Metropolis: Ecology, Community, and the American Dream* (New York City: Princeton Architectural Press, 1995)

Allan B. Jacobs, *Great Streets* (Cambridge, Massachusetts: The MIT Press, 1995)

Peter Katz, *The New Urbanism: Toward an Architecture of Community* (New York: McGraw-Hill Professional, 1993)

Kevin Lynch, *Good City Form* (Cambridge, Massachusetts: The MIT Press, 1981)

Christopher Alexander, Sara Ishikawa, and Murray Silverstein, *A Pattern Language: Towns, Buildings, Construction* (New York: Oxford University Press, 1977)

Edmund Bacon, *Design of Cities* (New York: The Viking Press, 1967)

Kevin Lynch, *The Image of the City* (Cambridge, Massachusetts: MIT Press, 1960)

## Downtown Revitalization

Charles C. Bohl, *Place Making* (Washington, D.C.: Urban Land Institute, 2002)

William H. Whyte, *City: Rediscovering the Center* (New York: Doubleday, 1988)

## Historic Preservation

Norman Tyler, Ted J. Ligibel, and Ilene R. Tyler, *Historic Preservation: An Introduction to Its History, Principles and Practices* (New York: W.W. Norton, 2009)

Donovan D. Rypkema, *The Economics of Historic Preservation: A Community Leader's Guide* (Washington, D.C.: National Trust for Historic Preservation, 2005)

## Economic Development

Edward J. Blakely and Ted K. Bradshaw, *Planning Local Economic Development: Analysis and Practice* (Thousand Oaks, California: Sage Publications, 2002)

Thomas S. Lyons and Roger E. Hamlin, *Creating an Economic Development Action Plan* (Westport, Connecticut: Praeger, 2001)

## Environmental Planning

John Randolph, *Environmental Land Use Planning and Management* (Washington, D.C.: Island Press, 2003)

Ian McHarg, *Design With Nature* (Hoboken, New Jersey: John Wiley and Sons, 1995)

Frederic O. Sargent, et al., *Rural Environmental Planning for Sustainable Communities* (Washington, D.C.: Island Press, 1991)

R. Gene Brooks, *Site Planning: Environment, Process, and Development* (Englewood Cliffs, New Jersey: Prentice Hall, 1988)

Harlow C. Landphair and John L. Motloch, *Site Reconnaissance and Engineering: An Introduction for Architects, Landscape Architects, and Planners* (New York: Elsevier, 1985)

## Rural and Transitional Land Use Planning

Kenneth T. Jackson, *Crabgrass Frontier: The Suburbanization of the United States* (New York: Oxford University Press, 2009)

Jonathan Barnett (Editor), *Smart Growth in a Changing World* (Chicago: Planners Press, American Planning Association, 2007)

Howard Frumkin, Lawrence Frank, and Richard Jackson, *Urban Sprawl and Public Health: Designing, Planning and Buildings for Healthy Communities* (Washington, D.C.: Island Press, 2004)

Andres Duany, Elizabeth Plater-Zyberk, and Jeff Speck, *Suburban Nation: The Rise of Sprawl and the Decline of the American Dream* (New York: North Point Press, MacMillan, 2001)

Randall Arendt, Elizabeth A. Brabec, Harry L. Dodson, and Christine Reid, *Rural by Design: Maintaining Small Town Character* (Chicago, Illinois: Planners Press, American Planning Association, 1994)

James Howard Kunstler, *The Geography of Nowhere: The Rise and Decline of America's Man-Made Landscape* (New York: Simon & Schuster, 1993)

Joel Garreau, *Edge City* (New York: Doubleday, 1991)

Mark P. Lapping, Thomas L. Daniels, and John W. Keller, *Rural Planning & Development in the United States* (New York: Guilford Publications, 1984)

## Zoning and Land Use Regulation

Donald L. Elliott, *A Better Way to Zone: Ten Principles to Create More Livable Cities* (Washington, D.C.: Island Press, 2008)

Jonathan Levine, *Zoned Out: Regulation, Markets and Choices in Transportation and Metropolitan Land Use* (Washington, D.C.: RFF Press, 2005)

Rutherford H. Platt, *Land Use and Society: Geography, Law, and Public Policy* (Washington, D.C.: Island Press, 2004)

Charles A. Lerable, *Preparing a Conventional Zoning Ordinance* (Chicago: American Planning Association, Planning Advisory Service, 1995)

# CREDITS

The authors thank the following people and organizations for their permission to use photographs and illustrations in this book. All images not credited below are by Norman Tyler.

**Introduction**
0.1 Randy Fox

**1. The Practice of Planning**
1.2 Alfonso Robinson for HatCityBLOG, www.hatcityblog.com

**2. Conceptual Approaches to Planning**
2.1 Marco Martinelli, www.marcomartinelli.it
2.2 Library of Congress
2.3 Robert Cameron, Cameron and Company
2.4 From *The Dream City: A Portfolio of Photographic Views of the World's Columbian Exposition* (St. Louis, Missouri: N. D. Thompson Publishing Co., 1893)
2.5 Emilio Mercado
2.6 Australia Department of Home and Territories
2.7 Ebenezer Howard, *Tomorrow: A Peaceful Path to Real Reform*
2.8 Copyright 2009 Artists Rights Society (ARS), New York/ ADAGP, Paris/FLC
2.9 Copyright 2009 Frank Lloyd Wright Foundation, Scottsdale, AZ/Artists Rights Society (ARS), NY
2.11 After a drawing by Alice Constance Austin

**3. The Scope of Planning at the Federal, State, Regional, and Local Levels**
3.1 Bureau of Land Management
3.2 Minnesota Metropolitan Council
3.3 TARCOG (Top of Alabama Regional Council of Governments)
3.4 Jassmit, Wikipedia Commons, http://commons.wikimedia. org/wiki/File:Downtown_indy_from_parking_garage_zoom. JPG
3.5 Sammamish, Washington, City Council
3.6 Sarah Rutter, photographer
3.8 James Schafer AICP
3.10 City of Reading, Pennsylvania
3.12 Richard Schwartz

**4. The Comprehensive Plan**
4.2 Based on data from the U.S. Census Bureau
4.3 Based on data from the U.S. Census Bureau
4.4 Based on data from the U.S. Census Bureau
4.5 Based on data from the U.S. Census Bureau
4.6 U.S. Department of Commerce, Economics and Statistics Administration
4.7 ESRI Corporation
4.10 Loudoun County, Virginia, government
4.11 Loudoun County, Virginia, government
4.14 Alan J. Sorensen AICP, President, Planit Main Street, Inc.

**5. Planners and the Design Process**
5.1 Riverside Historical Commission
5.2 Library of Congress
5.3 Daniel H. Burnham and Edward H. Bennett, *Plan of Chicago*
5.4 Duany Plater-Zyberk & Associates
5.5 Marissa Leoni, 2005
5.7 Regional Plan Association
5.9 Malcolm Wells
5.10 *Preservation Design Manual*, Preservation Urban Design Incorporated
5.15 Andrew Armbruster
5.16 Russ Stephenson, AIA, LEED AP, and the Walker Collaborative

**6. Urban Planning and Downtown Revitalization**
6.2 Edobric (Shutterstock Image No. 8923576)
6.3 GoogleEarth
6.5 Jack Gates
6.7 Minnesota Mall of America
6.8 Bill Ryan
6.10 Andrew Morgan, teacherontwowheels.com
6.11 United States Navy
6.12 San Francisco Redevelopment Agency and Lennar Urban IBI Group
6.13 City of Rome, Georgia, Downtown Development Authority
6.16 Portland Department of Planning and Sustainability

## 7. Housing

7.1 Missouri Builders
7.2 U.S. Census Bureau American Community Survey
7.4 U.S. Geological Survey
7.5 U.S. Federal Government
7.8 Glacier Circle, Andrea Bibby
7.9 Lucky Clover RV and Mobile Home Park, Melbourne, Florida
7.10 Jillian Morgan

## 8. Historic Preservation

8.1 Mount Vernon, Fairfax County, Virginia, Nomination for National Register of Historic Places
8.2 Joe Eddleman, www.CharlestonHistoricHomes.com
8.3 Leon Ritter (Shutterstock 525140)
8.5 Reinhard Jahn, Wikipedia Creative Commons, Attribution-Share Alike 2.0 Germany
8.6 Andrew Collins for gaytravel.about.com
8.8 Google Earth
8.9 National Park Service

## 9. Local Economic Development

9.3 James Steldl (Shutterstock #12114280)
9.4 Sante Fe Business Incubator
9.5 Shelly Evans, evansrvadventures.com
9.7 Arnett Muldrow & Associates
9.8 Hank Shiffman, http://www.shiffman.org/
9.10 Quinn|Evans Architects, Ann Arbor, Michigan
9.11 Minneapolis Department of Community Planning and Economic Development
9.12 City of El Paso, Texas

## 10. Transportation Planning

10.2 Los Angeles Metro Library and Archive
10.6 Massachusetts Turnpike Authority
10.10 Scott System, Inc., Denver, Colorado: Carolyn Braaksma, Project Artist
10.13 Ted Kildegaard, Zephyr Travel & Tours, zephyrtravel.us
10.14 Jeff Martin, http://www.netjeff.com
10.15 Roosevelt Island Operating Corporation
10.16 The Greenway Collaborative, Inc.
10.17 The Greenway Collaborative, Inc.
10.21 Harry Puncec, photographer
10.22 Calthorpe Associates

## 11. Environmental Planning at the Local Level

11.1 Courtesy of Columbia River Crossing Project
11.2 North Central Pennsylvania Regional Planning and Development Commission
11.3 U.S. Geological Survey
11.4 Iofoto (Shutterstock 6230944)
11.5 Eastern Shore Soil and Water Conservation District
11.7 DeWitt Braud, Coastal Studies Institute, Louisiana State University

11.8 NASA Archives; Reference Number: MSFC-75-SA-4105-2C
11.9 Chicago Department of Environment

## 12. Rural and Transitional Land Use Planning

12.2 Lynn Betts, USDA Natural Resources Conservation Service
12.3 Robert M. Ward
12.5 Jeff Vanuga, USDA Natural Resources Conservation Service
12.6 U.S. Geological Survey
12.7 U.S. Geological Survey
12.9 Washtenaw County, Michigan, Planning Department
12.10 U.S. Soil Conservation Service
12.11 ESRI
12.12 Courtesy of Mike Dueweke, Institute for Geospatial Research and Education, Eastern Michigan University
12.13 Courtesy of Mike Dueweke, Institute for Geospatial Research and Education, Eastern Michigan University
12.14 Courtesy of Mike Dueweke, Institute for Geospatial Research and Education, Eastern Michigan University

## 13. Evolution of Land Use Controls

13.2 After Plan of the Settlement of Green Bay, from the Report of J. Lee, Esq., 1821
13.3 U.S. Geological Survey
13.6 From "A Zoning Primer," U.S. Department of Commerce, 1926, Revised Edition

## 14. Zoning and Other Land Use Regulations

14.1 Chapel Hill Planning Department
14.3 Scenic America
14.4 Google Maps
14.5 Stephen Whatley, stephenwhatley@googlemail.com
14.5a Community Redevelopment Agency of the City of Los Angeles
14.8 Richard Crossed, Chairman, Conifer Development Corporation
14.9 Based on a drawing by Brad Strater

## 15. Subdivisions, Site Plans, and Site Plan review

15.1 City of Rock Springs, Wyoming
15.4 Wendy Hicks, Hicks Properties, Fairfield, Ohio

## 16. Capital Improvements Program and Local Government Financing

16.1 Based on a graphic by Town of Chapel Hill Department of Business Management
16.3 Google Maps

## Appendixes

AD.2 City of Ypsilanti, Michigan
AD.3 City of Chapel Hill, North Carolina
AD.4 U.S. Geological Service

# INDEX

Page numbers in *italic* refer to illustrations.

accreditation of educational institutions, 17–18
action-oriented planning, 32
aerial photography, 172–73
affordable housing, 110–11
    legal obligation to provide, 186
agriculture
    conservation easements for, 201
    economic benefits, 165
    fiscal impact analysis, 217
    land economics, 165
    soil surveys for, 174
    transfer of development rights to protect, 201–2
    trends, 165
    zoning for, 200, 234
    *see also* rural areas
Ahwahnee Principles, 125–27
Alabama, 39
Alaska, 149
Alexander, Christopher, 69, 73–74
Allensworth, Don T., 188
alleys, 77
Alonso, William, 86, 87
American Institute of Architects, 83
American Institute of Certified Planners, 16, 17
American Planning Association, 16, 17, 117
Americans with Disabilities Act, 36, 118
Andover, Massachusetts, 64–65
annexation process, 168
Appalachian Regional Commission, 37
approval through litigation, 209
ARC/INFO, 175
Arendt, Randall, 69
asset mapping, 54, 124
Association of Collegiate Schools of Planning, 17
Atlanta, Georgia, 45
Austin, Alice Constance, 30
Austin, Texas, 79–80
automobile
    advantages of, as transportation method, 142
    in decline of interurban transportation, 140–41
    evolution of American cities, 141
    infrastructure design, 144–47
    negative effects, 141–42
    parking, 146–47, 191, 235–36, 239–40
    road congestion, 142
    speed control, 144

Babcock, Richard, 185, 196
Bacon, Edmund, 23, 28
*Baker v. City of Milwaukee*, 196
Baltimore, Maryland, 92–93, 104
Bassett, Edward, 199
Berry, Brian J. L., 90
Bettman, Alfred, 185
Big Dig project (Boston), 143
bikeways, 150–51
blight, 90, 194
Blue, Robert, 194
Bluenergy, 130
bonds, 212
Boston, Massachusetts, 75, 92, 143
Boulder, Colorado, 78
BP oil rig disaster (2010), 162
Brandeis, Louis, 45
British settlements in North America, 182
Broadacre City, 27–28
brownfields, 158, 163
bubble diagram, 80
building design
    aesthetic regulation of, 199
    contextual considerations in, 77
    earthquake risk considerations in, 162
    economic value of, 77
    in form-based codes, 198–99
    height-to-width ratio, 77
    weather and climate considerations in, 77
    zoning regulation of, 190
build-out analysis, 174–75
Bureau of Land Management, 35

Burnham, Daniel, 19, 24, 32, 71–73
business improvement districts, 95

Calthorpe, Peter, 125, 153
Cambridge, Massachusetts, *150*, 151
Canada, 34–35, 37, 90
Canandaigua, New York, 197
Canberra, Australia, 25–26
capital improvements program
    budget schedule, *211*
    committee for, 210
    comprehensive plan and, 66, 212–13
    credit rating and, 211
    fiscal impact analysis, 217
    funding for projects under, 211–12, 214, 215, 219
    guidelines, 211
    planner's role in preparing, 43
    process, 211
    purpose, 210, 219
    scope of, 210–11
    sources of funding for, 211
Cary, North Carolina, 83
casinos, 133
census data, 56–58, 102, 124–25, 176
central business district
    cross-impact analysis, 127–28
    in evolution of cities, 86–87, 100
    sample zoning ordinance, 233
chambers of commerce, 135
Channahon, Illinois, 145
Chapel Hill, North Carolina, *189*, *243*
charettes, 83
Charleston, South Carolina, 114
Chesapeake Bay Critical Area Program, 160
Chicago, Illinois, 19, 24, *24*, 70–73, 75–76, 132–33, 149, 162–63
churches, 199–200
City Beautiful movement, 19, 20, 70–73
city council, 41
City Efficient movement, 19, 20
Civil Rights Acts, 104
Cleveland, Ohio, 31
climate change, 163
clustered housing, 77, 200
coastal and shoreline areas, 158–60
Code of Ethics and Professional Conduct, 16
cohort survival forecasting, 59
co-housing, 108–9
collaborative planning, 32
colleges and universities, 137–38
color coding, 62
Coltsville Historic District (Hartford), *120*, 121
Columbia, Maryland, 31, 76
Columbian Exposition (Chicago, 1893), 24, *24*, 71
Columbia River Crossing Improvement Project, 157
commercial establishments
    building abandonment, 90–91
    causes of blight, 90

central business district model of urban development, 86–87, 100
    downtown revitalization strategies, 91
    downtown zoning for, 96–98
    evolution of zoning controls on, 184–85
    growth in square footage of, 90
    industry trends, 90
    lack of distinctive building design among, 90
    market segment analysis, 128
    neighborhood design, 76
    participants in downtown revitalization efforts, 93–96
    in pyramidal zoning hierarchy, 185–86
    rational for downtown revitalization, 91–92
    role of downtown retail, 88–91
    sample zoning ordinance, 233
    sex-oriented, 97, 98
    tax abatement programs for, 216
    in transit-oriented development, 153
    *see also* industrial manufacturing
commons, as concern of planning practice, 14
Community Development Block Grants, 34, 36, 93, 106, 135
community planning. *see* planning; urban planning
Community Reinvestment Act, 94
Comprehensive Economic Development Strategies, 136–37
comprehensive plan
    adoption and acceptance, 53
    capital improvements program and, 66, 212–13
    color coding system, 62
    components, 61–63
    data collection for, 54–58, 68
    design elements, 62
    diagram of creation process, *54*
    economic development considerations, 62–63
    environmental protection in, 63
    federal urban renewal program and, 103–4
    forecasting in, 58–61, 68
    forms of, 53–54
    goals and objectives, 64–65
    historic preservation component, 62, 117, 123
    housing component, 62
    implementation, 66, 68
    land use component, 62
    legal status of, 53
    presentation and adoption, 65
    print resources, 258
    process conceptualization of, 53
    promoting real estate investment in, 129
    public participation in, 63–64, 68
    published form, 65
    purpose of, 53, 68
    regulations in floodplain areas, 161
    review and revision, 67
    Rivertown example, 226–29
    schedule, *54*
    scope of, 53
    significance of, 13
    strategies, 65
    subarea plans, 67–68

transportation component, 63
urban growth boundaries in, 98–99
use of statistical methods in, 61
zoning and, 66, 196
computer modeling
geographic information systems, 175–77
for transportation planning, 147–48
condemnation proceedings, 111, 194
conditional use zoning, 190, 192
sample ordinance provisions, 235
condominiums, 204
conservation easements, 201
consolidated metro governments, 40
constitutional law, 181, 187, 192–93, 195
contextual consideration in design, 77, 80
contract zoning, 197–98
Corbett, Michael, 125
Corbusier, Le, 27
cost-benefit analysis, 127
Council of Governments, 39
Country Club Plaza (Kansas City), 89
creative class, 91–92, 127
creative thinking skills, 15
Crook County, Oregon, 200
cross-impact analysis, 127–28
Crosswait, Rebecca, 133

Daley, Richard M., 162–63
Dallas, Texas, 89
Dallas County, Iowa, 166
Davis, California, 109
Deadwood, South Dakota, 133–34
Death and Life of Great American Cities, The (Jacobs), 30
Delaware, 36
demographic patterns and trends
creation of comprehensive plan, 54, 55–60
family size, 55
forecasting, 58–61
homeless population, 106–7
in housing, 101–2
life expectancy, 55
mobility data, 55–56
scope of data, 54, 55–60
Demonstration Cities and Metropolitan Development Act, 104
density
build-out analysis, 174–75
Le Corbusier's urban design, 27
incentive zoning, 197
rural zoning, 200
Wright's urban design, 27–28
Department of Housing and Urban Development, 19–20, 36, 104, 106
Department of the Interior, 119
Department of Transportation, 143–44
department stores, 88–89
design
in New Urbanist approach to community planning, 73–74

planning and, 69, 85
role of, 69
see also building design; urban design
Design of Cities (Bacon), 28
Design with Nature (McHarg), 175
Detroit, Michigan, 86
development associations as community government, 219
director of planning, 42
discrimination, zoning regulation and, 186, 188
downtown areas
abandoned commercial buildings in, 90–91
central business district model, 86–87, 100
community identity and, 91
evolution of retail sector in, 88–90
example of successful revitalization, 92–93
financing for revitalization efforts, 94, 95, 100
historical evolution, 86–87, 100
Main Street Program approach to revitalization, 96
overlay zone, 96–97
participants in revitalization of, 93–96, 100
residential life in, 91–92
revitalization rationale, 91–92, 100
revitalization resources, 259
revitalization strategies, 91
Rivertown, 222–24
zoning, 96–97
downtown development authorities, 95
Duany, Andres, 14, 73, 125
DuBois, Pennsylvania, 158
due process, 192–93, 195
Dundee Realty Co. v. City of Omaha, 186

earthquakes, 162
earth sheltered houses, 78
easements, 118, 201
Economic Development Administration, 136–37
economic development plan
Ahwahnee Principles for, 125–27
asset mapping for, 124
casino gambling as part of, 133
community participants, 128–29, 134–35
creative class as component of, 127
current challenges in local governance, 124
data collection for, 124–25, 134, 139
development process, 124–25
government assistance, 139
government assistance in preparation of, 135–38
interaction of elements in, 125
labor market evaluation for, 124
performance evaluation, 127–28
planner's role, 128–29, 138
promoting small businesses in, 130
public–private partnerships to promote, 130, 134–35
rationale for, 139
real estate investment incentives in, 129
Rivertown exercise, 138–39
role of higher education institutions in, 137–38

sports stadiums as part of, 134
tax base evaluation for, 124
tourism component of, 130–33
economic functioning
    affordable housing programs, 110–11
    agricultural economy, 165, 166–67
    benefits of good design, 77
    benefits of historic district designation, 116
    consideration of, in comprehensive plan, 62–63
    consideration of, in good planning, 14
    costs of parking facilities, 146–47
    financing of downtown revitalization, 94, 95, 96, 100
    fiscal impact analysis, 217
    historical evolution of American cities, 86–87
    historic preservation rationale, 117–18
    housing investment, 111–12
    importance of transportation in, 140
    local government financing, 214–19
    mortgage financing, 94, 103
    privatization of municipal services, 217–18
    promoting real estate investment, 129
    retail trends, 90
    role of downtown retail, 88–91
    transportation sector, 142
    urban homesteading rationale, 107–8
    *see also* capital improvements program; economic
            development plan
edge cities, 86–87
*Edge City* (Garreau), 219
education and training of planners, 15–16, 17–18, 19
Elephante, Carl, 122
eminent domain, 193–94, 202
enforcement, zoning, 191–92
    site plan performance guarantees, 208–9
enterprise funds, 211–12
enterprise zones, 135
environmental protection
    advantages of performance zoning for, 198
    advantages of rehabilitation *versus* new construction, 117–
            18, 122
    in Ahwahnee Principles for economic development, 126
    benefits of undeveloped land, 165
    comprehensive plan for, 63
    conservation easements for, 201
    in floodplain areas, 160–61
    in future of planning profession, 13
    government programs for, 155, 163–64
    planning considerations, 155, 157–58, 164
    print resources for planners, 259
    remediation options, 155–56
    in shoreline and coastal zones, 158–60
    site assessments and impact statements, 155–56, 164
    site plan provisions for, 207
    transportation system considerations, 141–42
    use of soil surveys for, 174
    in wetland areas, 161
Environmental Systems Research Institute, 175
equity planning, 31

ethics guidelines for planning professionals, 16
Euclidean zoning, 185–86
*Euclid v. Ambler Realty Company,* 185, 187
exclusionary zoning, 186
exercises
    capital improvements program management, 213
    delineating historic district boundaries, 121–22
    developing economic development plan, 138–39
    farm land development, 167–68
    farmstead site redevelopment, 29
    homeless shelter location, 107
    Main Street Program implementation, 96
    map reading, 171–72
    new town design, 83–85
    parking requirements in zoning, 191
    proposed adult bookstore, 98
    site plan review, 207–8
    subarea plan development, 67–68
    survey, 48–49
    takings claim, 196
    tax-increment financing calculation, 216
    transportation study, 148

Farmer, Paul, 15
Federal Emergency Management Agency, 155
federal government
    aid to homeless, 107
    Civil Rights Acts, 104
    economic development programs, 135–37
    environmental programs, 155, 163–64
    in evolution of planning profession, 19–20
    grant-in-aid programs, 35–36
    historic preservation activities, 114, 115, 118
    housing programs, 34, 103–6, 113
    influence of, in local planning, 34–35, 49
    land owned by, 35
    legislative mandates from, 36
    support for downtown revitalization efforts, 94, 95–96
    transportation planning, 34, 143–44, 149
    urban renewal program, 103–4
Federal Highway Administration, 146
Federal Housing Administration, 103
Federal Land Policy and Management Act, 35
Federal Transit Administration, 149
ferry boats, 149
fiscal impact analysis, 217
floodplains, 160–61
floor area ratio, 190
Florida, Richard, 92, 127
forecasting techniques, 58–61, 68
foreclosures, home, 112
foreign trade zones, 136
Forester, John, 32
form-based codes, 198–99
Freedom of Information Act, 46
French settlements in North America, 182
Friedmann, John, 13–14

garden cities, 26–27
Garreau, Joel, 87, 219
gated communities, 108
general obligation bonds, 212
gentrification, 108
geographic information systems, 15, 175–77
*Gesellschaft,* 86
*Golden v. Planning Board of the Town of Ramapo,* 186
Goldsmith, Stephen, 218
Gordon, Phil, 216
grandfathered properties, 192
Grand Rapids, Michigan, 142
graphics software, 82
Great Depression, 19
Great Lakes Basin Commission, 37
greenbelt communities, 19
Griffin, Walter Burley, 25–26
ground floor coverage, 190
guidelines, design, 78–79

Haar, Charles, 53
Habitat for Humanity, 106
*Hadacheck v. Sebastian,* 184
Hall, Peter, 71
Hartford, Connecticut, *120,* 121
Haussmann, Georges-Eugène, 23–24
height restrictions, 190
height-to-width ratio, 77
historic districts
    benefits of designation, 116
    commission responsibilities, 118–19
    earliest, 114
    legal framework for, 115–16, 118, 122–23
    number of, 116
    rehabilitation standards, 119
    size and scope of, 120–21
historic preservation
    comprehensive plan elements, 62, 117, 123
    easements, 118
    educational opportunities in, 116
    federal role in, 34
    financial incentives for, 117–18, 123
    historical evolution of movement for, 114–15, 122
    legal environment for, 115–16
    organizations involved in, 116
    print resources, 259
    rural heritage, 165
    sustainable design goals and, 122
    *see also* historic districts
homelessness, 106–7
Homestead Act (1862), 184, 187
homesteading programs, 107–8
housing
    code enforcement, 111
    co-housing arrangements, 108–9
    comprehensive plan section, 62

data collection for comprehensive plan, 54
demographic patterns and trends, 101–2
economics of, 111–12
financing services for, 94, 103
forecasting needs, 59
foreclosures, 112
gated communities, 108
gentrification of neighborhoods, 108
government role, 34, 102–6, 113
house values, 112
inclusionary, 110–11
manufactured, 110
mobile homes, 110
mortgage interest tax deduction, 103, 111–12
planning goals, 113
private sector investment in, 111–12
in pyramidal zoning hierarchy, 185–86
rural zoning, 200–201
significance of, in planning, 101
teardown phenomenon, 112–13
urban homesteading, 107–8
urban renewal program, 103–4
Housing Acts (1949; 1954), 103–4
Housing and Community Development Act, 105–6
Howard, Ebenezer, 26–27
Hunter, Floyd, 45
Hurricane Katrine, 161–62

identity, community
    Ahwahnee Principles for economic development, 127
    benefits of historic district designation, 116
    downtown revitalization and, 91
*Image of the City, The* (Lynch), 88
impact fees, 203, 214
incentive zoning, 197
inclusionary housing, 110–11
Indianapolis, Indiana, 40, 217–18
industrial manufacturing
    brownfields, 158, 163
    in cities, 86
    evolution of zoning restrictions on, 184–85
    in pyramidal zoning hierarchy, 185–86
inferential statistics, 61
infrastructure
    federal programs for development of, 137
    financing sources for building and maintaining, 214
    transportation system elements, 144–47
    *see also* capital improvements program
Inner Harbor (Baltimore), 92–93
Institute for a Competitive Workforce, 135
institutional district, 233–34
Intermodal Surface Transportation Efficiency Act, 40, 144
International Joint Commission, 37
international trade, 136
internships, planning, 18
ISTEA program, 40, 144

Jackson, Henry, 35
Jacobs, Jane, 30–31, 46
Jeanneret-Gris, Charles-Edouard. *see* Le Corbusier
Jenney, William LeBaron, 24, 70
Johnson administration, 104

Kansas City, Missouri, 89
Katz, Peter, 125
Kelo, Susette, 194
*Kelo v. City of New London*, 193–94
Key West, Florida, 149
Kotval, Zenia, 90
Krumholz, Norman, 31

labor market
    employment multipliers, 125
    evaluation for economic development plan, 124
    federal programs to improve, 136–37
    sources of new jobs, 130
    travel to work, 153–54
Lakewood, Colorado, 152
Land and Water Resources Planning Act, 35
land assembly programs, 137
land banks, 137
Land Ordinance (1785), 183–84, 187
landscaping, 207, 234–35
land use
    capital facilities needs for different categories of, 212–13
    categories, 62, 185, 188, 189–90
    constitutional provisions on, 181
    environmental planning, 155
    fiscal impact analysis, 217
    hierarchy of, 185–86
    historical evolution of regulation of, 183–84, 186–87
    historical patterns and trends, 181–84
    justification for government regulation, 181
    sample plan, *242*
    transportation infrastructure, 141
    *see also* comprehensive plan; planning; zoning
Lawson, Bryan, 80
leadership role of planners, 15
legal issues
    conceptual basis of land use regulation, 181
    contract zoning, 197–98
    eminent domain, 193–94, 202
    evolution of land use regulation in U.S., 183–84, 186–87
    evolution of zoning regulation, 185, 186
    in historic preservation, 115–16
    site plan approval through litigation, 209
    takings, 194–96
    *see also* zoning
L'Enfant, Pierre Charles, *22, 23*
light rail systems, 149
Link, Theodore C., 120
Linowes, R. Robert, 188

Llano del Rio, 30
local service district, 232–33
Locke, John, 181
long term planning
    Ahwahnee Principles for economic development, 126
    evolution of urban design approaches, 26–27
    political pressure as obstacle to, 44
    role of comprehensive plan, 13
    traditional approach, 31–32
    in urban design, 75
Los Angeles, California, 184, 194
Loudon County, Virginia, 60, 61
*Lucas v. South Carolina Coastal Council*, 196
Lugar, Richard, 40
Lynch, Kevin, 88

mail surveys, 47
Maine, 36
Main Street Program, 95–96
*Making of Urban America, The* (Reps), 183
Mall of America (Minneapolis), 89–90
manufactured housing, 110
mapping and surveying
    aerial photography, 172–73
    for build-out analysis, 174
    geographic information systems, 175–77
    site plan requirements, 206
    soil surveys, 173–74
    in subdividing land, 203, 209
    topographic, 170–72
    for western U.S. settlement, 183–84
Marcuse, Peter, 186
market segment analysis, 128
Markusen, Ann, 14
Maryland's Chesapeake Bay Critical Area Program, 160
mayors, 41
McHarg, Ian, 175
McKenna, Phillip, 198
McKinney-Vento Homeless Assistance Act, 107
Melbourne, Florida, *110*
Menino, Thomas, 143
metropolitan planning organizations, 39–40
Miami Beach, Florida, 116
Michigan, 36–37
millage, 211
Miller, J. Jefferson, 92
Milwaukee, Wisconsin, 92, 131–32
Minneapolis, Minnesota, 89–90, 104
Minnesota Metropolitan Council, 37–38
mixed-use development, 76, 77
mobile homes, 110
Montgomery County, Maryland, 152
Moses, Robert, 28, 30
Moule, Elizabeth, 125
Mount Vernon Ladies' Association, 114
Mt. Laurel Township, New Jersey, 186

Mullin, John R., 90
Mumford, Lewis, 142
municipal council, 41
Myrtle Beach, South Carolina, 90

Nashville, Tennessee, *131*
National Agricultural Lands Study, 166
National Alliance of Preservation Commissions, 116
National Association for the Advancement of Colored People, 186
National Association of Homebuilders, 110
National Environmental Policy Act, 155–56
National Historic Preservation Act, 115, 122
National Housing Act, 103
National Park Service, 34, 35, 114
National Planning Board, 19
National Register of Historic Places, 115, 122
National Trust for Historic Preservation, 114–15
Navy Pier (Chicago), 132–33
negotiated planning, 32
neighborhood design, 76
    good building design in, 77–78
New London, Connecticut, 193–94
New Orleans, Louisiana, 114, *115*, 161–62, 184
*New Theory of Urban Design, A* (Alexander), 69
New Urbanism, 73–74
New Village, Pennsylvania, 81–82
New York, New York, 18, 30
    Central Park, 24–25
    evolution of zoning in, 184, 195
    Moses's work in, 28
    tenement laws, 102
*Next Step: How to Plan for Beauty, Comfort, and Peace with Great Savings Effected by the Reduction of Waste* (Austin), 30
Nichols, Jesse C., 89
Nixon administration, 105
*Nollan v. California Coastal Commission*, 195
nonconforming use, 192
    sample zoning provisions, 235
North American Industry Classification System, 124–25, 128

obelisks of Rome, 21–23
Oklahoma, 36
Olmstead, Frederick Law, 24–25, 70
on-line surveys, 47, 48–49
open meetings law, 46
open space requirements, 234
overlay zone, 96–97
    historic district as, 118
Owens, Wilfred, 142

Pacific Railroad Act, 184
Paris, France, *23*, 23–24
parking facilities, 146–47, 191
    sample zoning provisions, 235–36, 239–40

*Penn Central Transportation Co. v. City of New York*, 195
*Pennsylvania Coal v. Mahon*, 194
performance zoning, 198
Perry, Clarence, 76
Petaluma, California, 99
Philadelphia, Pennsylvania, 28–29, 114
Photosynth, 82
PLACE zoning approach, 198
planned unit developments, 197
planning
    balancing of stakeholder interests in, 44
    community leadership role of, 15, 20
    constitutional basis of governance and, 34
    definition, 13–14
    department structure and responsibilities, 42
    design of public spaces before buildings, 69–70
    economic development and, 134
    evolution of conceptual approaches to, 21–29
    federal government influence on local, 34–36, 49
    goals for housing, 113
    good qualities of, 14–15
    importance of zoning in, 186, 188, 202
    limitations of, 68
    minimizing impact of home foreclosures, 112
    one-stop office for development and, 66
    policy modeling, 59–61
    political context of, 43–45, 50
    print resources for, 258
    problem formulation in, 138
    regional, 37–39, 49
    role of capital improvements program, 210
    in rural and transitional areas, 168–70
    scope of, 14
    site plan review, 206–7
    smart growth approach to, 98
    stakeholders in, 44
    structure and function of local government in, 40–43, 49–50
    subdivision rules, 203–4
    three Cs, 13
    traditional approach, 31–32
    *see also* profession of planning; urban planning
Planning Accreditation Board, 17
planning commission, 41–42
    site plan approval, 208
*Plan of Chicago*, 19
Plater-Zyberk, Elizabeth, 14, 73, 125
platting, 203, 209
Poletown, Michigan, 193
policy modeling, 59–61
politics
    equity planning perspective on, 31
    local influence makers, 45
    in local planning process, 43–45, 50
    obstacles to long-term planning, 44
    in planning commission role, 41–42
    principles of tactical planning, 32
    in Robert Moses's career, 28
Polyzoides, Stefanos, 125

porches, 77
Portland, Oregon, 78–79, 99–100, 149, 157
post offices, 34
PowerPoint, 15
preapplication meeting, 206
preliminary site plan, 206–7
*Preparing a Historic Preservation Plan*, 117
priority funding areas, 98
private sector
    business incubators, 130
    housing investment, 111–13
    planning consultants in, 16–17, 20, 42
    public–private cooperation for economic development,
            128–29, 130, 134–35
    *see also* commercial establishments
privatization
    of city services, 217–18
    of residential communities, 219
profession of planning
    advantages of, 13
    certification, 16
    compensation, 16
    continuing professional development in, 15–16
    demographic profile of, 16
    education and training for, 17–18, 20
    employment settings, 16
    ethical practice, 16
    future prospects, 13
    interdisciplinary nature of, 17, 20
    leadership role of, 15, 20
    mission of, 20
    networking, 18
    origins and historical development of, 18–20, 32–33
    primary characteristics of activities of, 14
    in private sector, 17–18, 20
    public interest obligation in, 16
    skills and personal qualities for, 15, 17, 32
    specialization patterns in, 16, 17
    tactical planning conceptualization of, 32
property rights
    conceptual basis of land use regulation and, 181
    due process provisions, 192–93
    eminent domain and, 193–94, 202
    takings law, 194–96
Pruitt-Igoe Project, 104–5
public housing, 103–5, 106
Public Housing Act, 104
Public Land Survey System, 183
public participation in planning process
    Ahwahnee Principles for economic development, 125–26
    announcement and conduct of public meetings, 45–46
    community activism, 46–47
    community planning, 82–83
    comprehensive plan creation, 63–64, 68
    digital technology for, 49
    diversity of participants, 64
    forms of participation, 64
    importance of, 45

methods for, 82–83
    planner skills for facilitating, 15
    planning profession's commitment to, 14
    principles of tactical planning, 32
    site plan review, 208
    survey techniques to promote, 47–49
public purpose, 193
public space
    in American cities, 88
    as concern of planning profession, 14
    exemplary designs, 75–76
    good design qualities, 75
    qualitative considerations in urban planning for, 87–88
public transit systems, 140–41, 148–50
public welfare
    advocacy planning for, 30–31
    in conceptual basis of zoning, 188
    design of Central Park for, 24–25
    eminent domain based on, 193–94
    in equity planning principles, 31
    evolution of zoning law to protect, 184–85
    responsibility of planners, 16
    strategies for identifying needs, 45
Public Works Administration, 103
purchase of development rights, 201
pyramidal zoning hierarchy, 185–86

quality of life and place
    as concern of planning practice, 14
    urban planning considerations, 87–88
Quillien, Jenny, 73–74

rapid growth areas, build-out analysis for, 174–75
rationalist planning, 31–32
Reagan administration, 19–20, 106
real estate investment, 129
    land assembly programs, 137
redevelopment agencies, 93–94
regional planning, 37–39, 49
Regional Planning Association, 37
religious institutions, 199–200
Religious Land Use and Institutionalized Persons Act, 199–200
Rensselaerville Institute, 81
Reps, John, 183
Request for Qualifications/Proposals, 17
Resource Conservation and Recovery Act, 158
revenue bonds, 212
*Rise of the Creative Class, The* (Florida), 127
Riverside, Illinois, 25, 70
Rivertown simulation
    capital improvements program, 213
    city history, 221
    classroom implementation, 221
    comprehensive plan, 226–29
    consumer survey, 48–49
    contour maps, 171–72

downtown, 222–24
economic development plan for, 138–39
environmental concerns, 225
farm land development, 167–68
historic district, 121–22
homeless shelter, 107
layout and buildings, 221–25
Main Street Program exercise, 96
map, *241*
new town design, 83–85
online resources, 221
parking requirements, 191
populace, 225–26
proposed adult bookstore, 98
purpose, 9–10, 221
redevelopment of farmstead site, 29
site plan review, 207–8
subarea plan exercise, 67–68
takings case exercise, 196
tax-increment financing district, 216
transportation study, 148
zoning ordinance, 230–40
Roelofs, Barbara, 46
Rome, Georgia, 95
Rome, Italy, 21–23
Roosevelt (F.D.) administration, 19
Rouse, James, 31, 93
rural areas
annexation by cities, 168
benefits of undeveloped land in, 165
build-out analysis, 174–75
conservation easements, 201
land area, 86, 177
mapping and surveying techniques, 170–74, 177
planning activities in, 168–70, 177
population movement patterns, 56
print resources for planners, 259
purchase of development rights, 201
soil surveys, 173–74
tax strategies to preserve natural areas, 202
threats to, 165–66
transfer of development rights, 201–2
zoning in, 200–202
*see also* agriculture
*Rural by Design: Maintaining Small Town Character* (Arendt), 69
Rural/Urban Design Assistance Team, 83

SAFETEA-LU program, 143–44
safety and security
appeal of gated communities, 108
routes to schools, 153
Sager, Tore, 32
Sammamish, Washington, 41
San Antonio, Texas, 152
San Bernadino County, California, 163
Sandburgh, Carl, 71
San Diego, California, 92, 149

Sandy Springs, Georgia, 218
San Francisco, California, 94, 149, 184
Sante Fe, New Mexico, 130
schools
community plans centered around, 31
in comprehensive plan, 63
transportation design, 153
Scottsdale, Arizona, 66, 79
Seaside, Florida, 73, *74*
Seattle, Washington, 116–17, 149, 151
Section 701 programs, 35–36
senior communities, 109
setbacks, 190
sex-oriented businesses, 97, 98
shopping centers and malls, 89–90, 152
Siena, Italy, 87
signage, 191
*Simon v. Town of Needham,* 186
site condominiums, 204
site plan
approval through litigation, 209
comprehensive plan implementation through regulation of, 66
elements, 205, 209
goals of review, 206
performance guarantees, 208–9
planning commission approval, 208
requirements for, 205–6
review procedure, 191, 206–8, 209
sample zoning provisions, 236–38
site-value taxation, 216–17
Sixtus V, Pope, 21–23
SketchUp, 82
small area forecasting, 59–61
Small Business Administration, 135–36
small businesses
federal programs for, 135–36
incubator facility for, 130
new job creation in, 130
Small Business Innovation Research, 136
Small Business Investment Corporation, 136
smart growth, 98
social functioning
consideration of, in good planning, 14
effects of federal urban renewal program, 104
evolution of planning considerations of, 29–31, 30–31, 33
homeless population, 106–7
local influence makers, 45
*see also* demographic patterns and trends
socialist principles, 30
soil surveys, 173–74
*Southern Burlington N.A.A.C.P. v. Mt. Laurel Township,* 186
Southfield, Michigan, 89
Spanish settlements in North America, 181–82
sports stadiums, 134
St. Louis, Missouri, 104–5, 120
St. Paul, Minnesota, *129*
stadiums, 134
Standard City Planning Enabling Act, 203

Standard State Zoning Enabling Act, 185
state government
    economic development programs, 137–38
    environmental regulations, 155
    evolution of land use regulations, 184
    planning role, 36–37
State Historic Preservation Offices, 115
statistical data
    for build-out analysis, 174
    for comprehensive plan, 61
Stein, Gertrude, 91
Stevens, Suzanne, 28–29
Stone, Clarence, 45
storm water control, 207
street design, 144–46
subarea plans, 67–68
subdivisions, 203–4, 209
suburbs
    costs of sprawl, 166
    early planning concepts for, 26–28
    evolution of zoning laws and, 185
    gated communities, 108
    threats to rural land, 165–66
Sullivan, Louis, 70
surveys of public opinion, 47–49
sustainable design
    Ahwahnee Principles for economic development, 125–27
    as concern of planning practice, 14
    definition, 122, 162
    elements of, 162
    historic preservation and, 122
    planning considerations, 163
SWOT, 65

tactical planning, 32, 33
Tahoe City, California, 43
Tahoe-Sierra Preservation Council, Inc. v. Tahoe Regional Planning
        Agency, 195
takings law, 194–96
Taney, Roger, 181
taxes
    abatement programs, 216
    asset mapping for economic development plan, 124
    benefits of conservation easements, 201
    considerations in public land assembly programs, 137
    costs of suburban sprawl, 166
    credits to promote historic preservation, 118
    funding for capital improvement projects, 211, 212, 219
    incentives in enterprise zones, 135
    mortgage deductions, 103, 111–12
    planning considerations, 214
    property, 211, 215
    purpose, 214
    site-value taxation, 216–17
    as source of local government financing, 214–17
    strategies to preserve natural areas, 202
    tax-base sharing plans, 37–38

tax-increment financing, 214–16
    urban homesteading program rationale, 108
telephone surveys, 47
Tennessee Valley Authority, 19
three-dimensional graphics software, 82
TIGER/Line files, 58
Tomorrow: A Peaceful Path to Real Reform (Howard), 28
Tönnies, Ferdinand, 86
topographic maps, 170–71
tourism
    benefits of historic district designation, 116
    economic development strategies, 130–33
    four-times rule, 131
townhouse developments, 77
traditional approach to planning, 31–32, 33
traffic-calming strategies, 144
trams, 150
transactive planning, 32, 39–40
transferable development rights, 201–2
transit-oriented development, 153
transportation
    bicycle, 150–51
    comprehensive plan for, 63
    computer modeling, 147–48
    connectivity routes, 144–45
    context-sensitive design, 146
    as determinant of urban area, 141
    economic significance, 142
    federal role in, 143–44
    historical development in U.S., 140–41, 154
    impacts of, 141–42, 154
    influence of national highway system on local planning, 34
    interurban trolley systems, 140–41
    neighborhood design considerations, 76, 77
    parking facilities, 146–47
    role of public transit, 148–50
    to schools, 153
    significance of, in U.S. growth, 140
    street design, 144–45
    transit-oriented development, 153
    walking, 151–52
    to and from work, 153–54
trend analysis, 58
Tugwell, Guy, 19
Tyler, Norman, 221

Unfunded Mandates Reform Act, 36
Unigov, 40
Union Station (St. Louis), 120
United Nations, 122, 162
urban design
    at city scale, 75–76
    contextual considerations, 80
    design guidelines for, 78–79, 85
    for downtown revitalization, 96
    to encourage walking, 75, 76, 77
    evolution of approaches to, 70–74, 85

exercise, 83–85
at individual project level, 77–78
key principles, 74–75, 85
long-term perspective, 75
at neighborhood scale, 76–77
planning and, 69
print resources, 258
process, 80–82, 85
public participation in, 82–83
public spaces in, 69–70, 75
transportation technology as factor in, 141
*see also* design; downtown areas; urban planning
Urban Development Action Grants, 93
urban planning
evolution of conceptual approaches to, 21–29
growth boundaries, 98–100
historical evolution of cities, 86
origins and historical development of, 18–20
population movement patterns, 56
qualitative considerations in, 87–88
role of, 87
smart growth approach to, 98
traffic management, 144
*see also* downtown areas; planning; urban design
urban renewal program, 103–5
Urban Transportation Modeling System, 147–48
U.S. Forest Service, 35
Utah County, Utah, 200

Van Buren Township, Michigan, 176–77
variances, 192, 193
Vaux, Calvert, 24
Vazquez, Leonardo, 20
Venice, Italy, 87–88
Veterans Administration, 103
visioning process, 82–83, 125–26

walking, urban design to encourage, 75, 76, 77, 151–52
routes to schools, 153
Wallace, David, 92
Washington, D. C., 22, 23, 96–97, 116, 149, 184
Washtenaw County, Michigan, 170–71, 172–73, 174, 244
Watt, James, 20
weather and climate, design considerations, 77
Webber, Melvin, 43
Wells, Malcolm, 78
wetlands, 161–62
Whyte, William, 75
Winnetka, Illinois, 112–13

women's issues, 30
Workforce Reinvestment and Adult Education Act, 136
Wright, Frank Lloyd, 27–28, 70

Ypsilanti, Michigan, *242*

zoning
accessory uses, 190
administration, 191–92
amendment process, 192
appeals of decisions, 192
build-out analysis, 174–75
coastal and shoreline areas, 159
comprehensive plan implementation in, 66, 196
conceptual basis of, 188
conditional uses, 190, 192
for downtown revitalization, 96–97
due process provisions relevant to, 192–93
earthquake risk considerations, 162
enforcement, 192
exclusionary, 186
form-based codes, 198–99
goals of, 188, 202
historical evolution of, 19, 184–86, 187
importance of, as planning tool, 186, 188, 202
inclusionary, 110–11
language of, 188–89
negotiated alternatives to, 196–98, 202
nonconforming use classification in, 192
objections to traditional application of, 196
parking regulations, 191
performance, 198
permitted uses, 189–90
print resources, 259
pyramidal conceptualization of, 185–86
regulation of religious institutions, 199–200
regulation of structures in, 190
in rural areas, 200–202
sample map, *243*
sample ordinance, 230–40
schedule of district regulations, 189–90
sex-oriented businesses, 97, 98
sign regulation, 191
site plan review, 191
supplemental regulations, 190
takings law and, 194–96
text of ordinance, 188–89
variances, 192, 193
*Zoning Game, The* (Babcock), 196